*Oracle Press*™

Oracle VM Implementation and Administration Guide

About the Author

Edward Whalen is the founder of Performance Tuning Corporation (www
.perftuning.com), a consulting company specializing in database performance,
administration, virtualization, and disaster recovery solutions. Prior to starting
Performance Tuning, he worked at Compaq Computer Corporation as an OS
developer, and then as a database performance engineer. He has extensive
experience in database system design and tuning for optimal performance. His
career has consisted of hardware, OS, and database development projects for many
different companies. Edward Whalen has written four other books on the Oracle
RDBMS and five books on MS SQL Server. He has also worked on numerous
benchmarks and performance tuning projects with both Oracle and MS SQL Server.
Edward Whalen is recognized as a leader in database performance tuning and
optimization.

About the Technical Editors

John Margaglione managed ISV partnerships and enablement at Oracle
Corporation, including the Oracle VM, VirtualBox, SGD, and VDI platforms. John
has worked with virtualization technologies for over eighteen years, starting with
CMS on IBM mainframes, and has worked with major technology vendors to find
innovative uses of virtualization technology from applications to disk. John has a
degree in statistics and applied mathematics from the University of Illinois at
Urbana-Champaign, and is a certified Oracle VM Implementation Specialist.

Gary Parker is a senior Oracle consultant with Performance Tuning Corporation.
Gary is Oracle certified and has extensive experience in consulting, database
administration, and system administration. His experience includes more than
fifteen years tuning and administering Oracle databases and implementing Oracle
RAC, Grid Control, Data Guard, and Oracle applications running on UNIX, Linux,
and Windows operating systems on both physical and virtual environments.

ORACLE®   *Oracle Press*™

Oracle VM Implementation and Administration Guide

Edward Whalen

McGraw Hill

New York   Chicago   San Francisco
Lisbon   London   Madrid   Mexico City   Milan
New Delhi   San Juan   Seoul   Singapore   Sydney   Toronto

The McGraw·Hill Companies

Cataloging-in-Publication Data is on file with the Library of Congress

McGraw-Hill books are available at special quantity discounts to use as premiums and sales promotions, or for use in corporate training programs. To contact a representative, please e-mail us at bulksales@mcgraw-hill.com.

Oracle VM Implementation and Administration Guide

1 2 3 4 5 6 7 8 9 0   QFR QFR   10 9 8 7 6 5 4 3 2 1

ISBN   978-0-07-163919-4
MHID   0-07-163919-5

Sponsoring Editor	Technical Editors	Composition
Wendy Rinaldi	John Margaglione, Gary Parker	Cenveo Publisher Services
Editorial Supervisor	**Copy Editor**	**Illustration**
Janet Walden	LeeAnn Pickrell	Cenveo Publisher Services
Project Editor	**Proofreader**	**Art Director, Cover**
Howie Severson, Fortuitous Publishing Services	Paul Tyler	Jeff Weeks
Acquisitions Coordinator	**Indexer**	**Cover Designer**
Stephanie Evans	Jack Lewis	Pattie Lee
	Production Supervisor	
	James Kussow	

Contents at a Glance

Contents

PART II
Installing and Configuring Oracle VM

PART IV

Installing and Configuring the Guest OS

PART V

Appendixes and Glossary

Acknowledgments

 would like to thank John Margaglione and Gary Parker for their hard work technical editing this book. They not only did a great job editing but offered suggestions along the way as well. Good technical editors can either make or break a book. Gary and John put in a lot of effort to make this book what it turned out to be. I would also like to thank web developer and designer Brandi Boyd for her work on Chapter 4.

Thanks also to Stephanie Evans, Wendy Rinaldi, and all of the staff at Oracle Press/McGraw-Hill Professional for their hard work and professionalism. This is my second book as an author with Oracle Press/McGraw-Hill Professional and both experiences were great. This publishing company is excellent to work with.

I'd like to thank my wife Felicia and the dogs for putting up with all the time I spent working on the book, and I also want to acknowledge the support and encouragement from my family. Finally I'd like to thank some of the people that have encouraged me professionally including Jeff Bertman, Michael New, Marci Garcia, and Steve DeLuca.

Introduction

 n a few short years virtualization has evolved from being an interesting way to build and use test machines to a standard way of doing business in the data center. Virtualization as we know it today was introduced in 1998, and since then, it has undergone many improvements and revisions. Oracle VM, which is based on the Xen Hypervisor, was introduced at the Oracle OpenWorld conference in 2007. After Oracle purchased Sun Microsystems in 2010, Oracle VM was rebranded as Oracle VM Server for x86, and the Sun Solaris virtualization technologies were renamed Oracle VM Server for SPARC. Oracle also recently released Oracle VM Virtual Box, a new type 2 hypervisor-based product.

Virtualization provides a number of benefits over the traditional hardware system. Most of the benefits are economic, in that server consolidation, performance improvements, and speed of provisioning all provide value. Some of the main reasons companies choose virtualization are

- **Server consolidation**   Many heterogeneous servers can be configured on the same virtual host, thus providing an economical server platform.

- **Provisioning**   In a virtual environment, servers can easily and quickly be deployed.

- **Functional separation**   Where multiple applications might have had to share the same operating system in the past, they can now be configured on separate operating systems.

- **Performance**   Some applications simply don't scale well with many CPUs and large amounts of memory. For better performance, a larger server can be used by breaking it down into smaller operating systems where the sum of the parts is greater than the whole.

- **Hosting** It is less expensive and easier to rent out a virtual machine than an entire server.

- **Training** Training environments can easily be replicated, used, and destroyed for a single class.

This book covers not only the benefits and advantages of virtualization, but also how to install, configure, size, and administer an optimal virtualized environment using Oracle VM.

How to Use This Book

This book will be useful for both the implementer and user of Oracle VM. Included are methods of designing a VM Server farm as well as how to configure it, along with the day-to-day operations involved in administering the VM Server farm. Also included are step-by-step instructions covering many of the standard tasks performed by the VM Manager. This book also covers multiple methods of managing Oracle VM via OEM Grid Control, the Oracle VM Manager, the Oracle VM CLI, and Xen commands. All of these tools work well, so choose the one that works best in your environment.

Being a technical book, many of the chapters are independent of one another. Once you have read through the book, it can be used as a reference by referring to the chapter that covers the topic that you are interested in at the time. A great deal of effort has gone into verifying the examples and making sure that they are correct.

This book consists of 20 chapters, a glossary, and two appendixes, as described next.

Part I: Introduction

Chapter 1: Introduction to Virtualization This chapter is the foundation for the entire book. Virtualization concepts are introduced, and the basics of the Oracle VM Server farm's different building blocks are covered.

Chapter 2: What Is Oracle VM? This chapter builds on the first chapter and provides more specifics on Oracle VM: what it is, how it works, and what it is made up of. The history of Oracle VM and Oracle's commitment to virtualization is provided here.

Chapter 3: Oracle VM Architecture Oracle VM is based on Xen technology. This chapter presents the different components of Xen, as well as the differences between the virtualization types: hardware, software, HVM, and paravirtualization.

Chapter 4: Oracle VM Lifecycle Management   The lifecycle of the virtual machine represents the different states that the virtual machine can exist in and how to get there. This chapter shows the various ways a virtual machine is managed from a theoretical standpoint.

Chapter 5: Planning and Sizing the Enterprise VM Server Farm   Capacity planning and sizing are an important part of designing the Enterprise VM farm. In this chapter, sizing guidelines are presented as well as tips on how to properly plan the Oracle VM Server farm.

Part II: Installing and Configuring Oracle VM

Chapter 6: Installing the Oracle VM Server   This chapter is a tutorial on how to install and configure the Oracle VM Server system. A walkthrough is shown on proper installation techniques.

Chapter 7: Installing and Configuring Oracle VM Manager   The Oracle VM Manager is a web-based application provided with Oracle VM that is used to manage it. This chapter is a tutorial on how to install and configure the Oracle VM Manager application and includes a walkthrough on proper installation techniques.

Chapter 8: Configuring the Oracle VM Management Pack   Another way to manage the Oracle VM Server farm is via Oracle Enterprise Manager (OEM) Grid Control. The capability is added to OEM Grid Control via the Oracle VM Management Pack. How to install and configure the Oracle VM Management Pack is provided in this chapter.

Chapter 9: Installing and Configuring the Oracle VM CLI   A command-line interface (CLI) to the Oracle VM Manager is available from Oracle. How to install this CLI utility is presented in this chapter.

Chapter 10: Configuring the VM Server Network   The VM Server Network is an important component of the Oracle VM Server system. How to configure the VM Server Network and how to add additional network hardware is described in this chapter.

Chapter 11: Configuring the VM Server Storage   In addition to networking, the storage used for virtual machines is very important. In fact, nothing can hurt performance of a VM Server more than a poorly configured I/O subsystem. How to configure the VM storage repository is discussed in this chapter.

Part III: Managing Oracle VM Servers and Guests

Chapter 12: Creating Server Pools and Servers   The server pool is the set of servers that runs virtual machines and is the cornerstone of the Oracle VM system. How to create server pools and servers is presented in this chapter.

Chapter 13: Configuring Server Resources   Server resources include shared disks, ISO image, and templates. Templates are a key feature of Oracle VM. How to manage the server resources is described in this chapter.

Chapter 14: Monitoring and Tuning the Virtual Machine Server   Performance is an important part of managing the Oracle VM system. How to monitor and tune the Oracle VM system is presented in this chapter. As you will see, there are many tools and ways to monitor the Oracle VM system.

Part IV: Installing and Configuring the Guest OS

Chapter 15: Creating Templates   Templates are one of the key features of Oracle VM. They are used to save "golden copies" of virtual machine images that can be quickly and easily deployed. Many different templates, with different pre-installed applications, can be saved. This chapter describes how to create templates using the Template Builder, and how to save an existing virtual machine as a template.

Chapter 16: Using Templates to Create Virtual Machines and Configuring Resources   This chapter covers the topic of creating virtual machines from templates that have been created.

Chapter 17: Creating Virtual Machines Manually   If templates are not used, virtual machines can be created manually. This chapter explains that process.

Chapter 18: Converting Other Virtual Images to Oracle VM   It is often useful to take virtual machine images from other virtualization platforms such as VMware and Hyper-V and convert them to Oracle VM images. That process is covered here. In addition, a physical machine can be converted into a virtual machine as well, as shown in this chapter.

Chapter 19: Managing the VM Environment and Virtual Machines   This chapter provides some useful information and tips on how to best manage the virtual machine environment and the virtual machines themselves.

Chapter 20: Virtualization Summary and Best Practices   The final chapter provides a summary of the book and virtualization itself, along with a collection of best practices and tips.

Part V: Appendixes and Glossary

Appendix A: Configuring Linux Support Functions   Appendix A provides instructions on staging software images as well as instructions on how to set up Linux as an NFS server. Also included is information on how to set up a Linux server as a PXE and tftpboot server.

Appendix B: Oracle VM Log Files   Appendix B provides a list and descriptions of the various log files that you might find useful for Oracle VM debugging and monitoring.

Glossary   The glossary provides a list of terms, including acronyms, and their definitions. It is intended to be a quick and easy reference point.

Because things tend to change over time, updates and new information will be provided at my blog. A link to that blog can be found at www.perftuning.com/blogs or at www.edwardwhalen.com.

PART I

Introduction

CHAPTER

1

Introduction to Virtualization

n recent years, virtualization has changed the way we look at computing. Instead of using many different computer systems for different tasks, with virtualization, we can use a single system to host many applications. Not only has virtualization increased in popularity, but it has also sparked new hardware CPU innovation, including Intel VT-x and AMD-V technologies. Over the next few years, virtualization will be a core technology in every data center. Oracle VM, although a relatively new entry in the virtualization market, is based on stable and proven technology.

This chapter provides an overview of virtualization technologies, including the various types of virtualization and its typical uses. The reasons that companies choose to use virtualization and how they use it are also discussed. Subsequent chapters discuss the mechanics of installing, configuring, and managing Oracle VM.

What Is Virtualization?

Virtualization is the abstraction of computer hardware resources. This definition is very general; however, the broad range of virtualization products, both hardware and software, makes a more specific definition difficult. There are hardware products that allow for virtualization, software products that create virtual systems, and hardware that assists with software virtualization. All of these products and options perform essentially the same function: they separate the operating system and applications from the underlying hardware.

A number of different types of virtualization are available, including the following:

- Hardware virtualization

- Full software virtualization

- Paravirtualization

- Hardware-assisted software virtualization

- Component or resource virtualization

As this book progresses, you will learn about these types of virtualization and their attributes. You will also obtain the information you need to decide which type of virtualization to use.

Although virtualization allows you to abstract resources away from the hardware layer, you'll still discover some limitations. With today's commercially available technology, virtualization—or at least the most popular types of virtualization—allows you to abstract only like architectures. For example, if you use software virtualization that runs on x86 or x86_64 architecture, you can run only virtual hosts with either an x86 or x86_64 operating system. In other words, you can't virtualize a SPARC system on an x86 or x86_64 architecture.

At this time, several major virtualization products are on the market:

■ VMware was one of the first companies to offer a fully virtualized hardware platform environment, including a range of products with fully virtualized environments. VMware was founded in 1988 and was acquired by EMC in 2003. In addition to hardware virtualization, VMware also offers some paravirtualized drivers.

■ Microsoft Hyper-V was recently released. Hyper-V provides both fully virtualized and guest-aware virtualization (if you are running a Windows guest).

■ Xen Hypervisor is an open-source standard for virtualization and runs on multiple platforms. The first public release of Xen was in 2003, and the company was acquired by Citrix in 2007. Xen currently supports both Hardware Virtual Machine (HVM) and Paravirtualized Machine (PV). Xen does not offer any paravirtualized drivers.

■ Oracle VM is a free, next-generation server virtualization and management solution from Oracle that makes enterprise applications easier to deploy, manage, and support. The Oracle VM hypervisor is an open-source Xen project with Oracle enhancements that make it easier, faster, and more efficient. In addition, Oracle VM is currently the only virtualization product supported for the Oracle Relational Database Management System (RDBMS) and other Oracle products. Oracle VM supports both HVM and PV and provides a set of paravirtualized drivers for both windows and Linux Paravirtualized Hardware Virtual Machines (PVHVM).

In addition, numerous proprietary hardware and software products allow you to virtualize specific vendors' hardware and operating systems. Many products are also available to virtualize networks, storage, and so on; although some of these will be discussed in this book, as appropriate, the focus is on Oracle VM.

Reasons for Virtualizing

There are many reasons for creating systems in a virtualized environment rather than using physical hardware. In general, if your applications allow for virtualization, a virtualized environment lets you allocate sufficient resources to your applications using less power and with fewer cooling and space requirements. If applicable, in a virtualized environment, many virtualized systems can run on one physical computer, consuming fewer resources. Here are the top reasons for virtualizing:

- Server consolidation
- Server provisioning
- Functional separation
- Performance improvement
- Backup/restore
- Hosting and cloud computing
- Training, testing, quality assurance, and practice

Server Consolidation

Server consolidation is probably the top reason for virtualizing your environment. To consolidate servers, you take multiple computer systems and collapse them into, or consolidate them into, one server. Server consolidation is often, though not necessarily, accomplished using virtualization. From an Oracle database perspective, you can consolidate servers in multiple ways. You can consolidate servers by taking databases from several servers and putting them on a single server, each with their own instance (database). You can take databases from several servers and put them on a single database server within the same Oracle instance, either with or without partitioning. Finally, you can consolidate multiple Oracle databases onto a single server by creating multiple individual virtual machines on a single server and then creating a single Oracle database instance on each virtual machine.

Single Server, Multiple Instances

This option allows you to migrate multiple databases to a single server. You then configure the memory and CPU resources for each instance, thus dividing resources among the various instances. With this option, you consolidate multiple instances onto the same database server and still have some control over how the resources are allocated. The downside, as with the next option, is that some system resources, such as open files and the number of processes, can be exceeded. In addition, a single instance can sometimes utilize a disproportionate amount of system resources.

Single Server, Single Instance

With this option, you run all of the data from all of the instances to be consolidated from the same Oracle instance. This way you can share resources more easily, but other problems, such as security issues, often arise. In addition, a single instance often utilizes a disproportionate amount of system resources. Performance issues can also occur, as all logical databases must share a single set of initialization parameter values for the Oracle database instance. This option is usually not the one to choose when consolidating Oracle databases.

Multiple VMs, Multiple Instances

This option allows you to configure and manage each database separately, as with the first option. However, because each Oracle instance runs on its own virtual server, this option has a few additional benefits. Because you can move a VM dynamically between underlying VM servers, you have more flexibility of resources. If a system needs more resources, you can move it or another VM sharing that server, thus lessening the load.

This option's downside is that the OS is duplicated, causing more overhead than with the first option. When consolidating an Oracle database, you'll find both this option and the first option are often good choices.

Server Provisioning

One of the primary advantages of using virtual machines is the ability to provision servers quickly and efficiently. A virtual environment allows you to keep templates of various types of servers—such as application servers and database servers—and deploy and put them into production easily in a matter of minutes or hours. The process of provisioning a server typically involves either copying a server or building a new server from a template. Once you have deployed this new server, you run scripts to rename the server, change its IP address, etc., getting it into production quickly.

By prestaging servers and templates, you can quickly, efficiently, and precisely deploy servers. By using a prestaged server, you also avoid mistakes, which makes the provisioning process faster and more exact. You can easily pick what type of server to deploy from your library of templates and prestaged servers. The Oracle VM architecture allows you to deploy the new server into any system in the server farm that you desire, creating a high performance, scalable server in a very short time.

Functional Separation

Various applications don't work well together in an operating system. The reason is primarily due to resource contention in certain subsystems in the OS, such as the memory subsystem, the I/O subsystem, or the OS scheduler. Often application servers do not scale (achieve higher performance) when additional resources such as CPUs or memory are added. In these cases, using several smaller servers (two CPUs, 2GB of RAM) is better than using a larger server with many CPUs and lots of RAM. This is especially true of Java, which doesn't scale very well with large amounts of memory and multiple CPUs.

Even when application servers don't scale well with large numbers of CPUs and lots of RAM, you can still take advantage of the cost effectiveness of these systems by virtualizing them. Scaling problems typically occur in the application itself; in the OS scheduler, where the system simply can't keep track of too many processes; or in Java. Java applications typically can't take advantage of more than 2–3GB of RAM. By virtualizing, you can assign each system a reasonable amount of resources that the application can handle. Because the process tables and application queues exist in the virtual server and not on the host, the virtual environment will continue to scale. Fortunately, the Oracle database server scales very well with CPU and memory resources.

In addition, you can use functional separation to split management responsibilities, provide additional security, and reduce contention. By virtualizing and splitting up applications by vendor or group, you can allocate a single application to a single server and still not waste hardware resources.

Performance Improvement

As mentioned in the previous section, application servers often perform better as several smaller servers rather than one large server. Therefore, virtualizing a large server into multiple smaller ones can often improve application server performance. By splitting up a large host system into multiple smaller VMs, you can often achieve not only higher performance but also a greater level of scalability.

In addition, the virtual environment provides a feature that you can't find in physical servers: the ability to move the VM to another host. This gives you the flexibility and ability to alter the physical characteristics of the underlying host while the virtual machine is still up and running, giving you the benefits of live load balancing and performance improvements without interrupting service to the VM user.

By moving VMs from one host to another while live, you use resources efficiently and you can reuse them when needed. If a host becomes too busy, you can add another to the server pool and move VMs to it as needed.

Backup/Restore

An often overlooked feature of virtual machines is the ability to back them up quickly and efficiently because the virtual machine looks essentially like several large files to the host OS. Most performance problems that occur during backups are due to the number of small files in a system. When backing up a small file, the backup software takes more time opening and closing the file and finding all of the parts of the file than it actually takes to read the contents and back them up. The amount of data backed up per second drops significantly for small files.

When backing up an operating system, the backup software traverses the entire directory structure and opens, copies, and then closes each file. With large files, the software spends more time copying data. With small files, the software takes more time opening and closing files. Because the virtual disks are actually a large file in the OS, backups are very fast.

Backups from the VM can be problematic if the VM is running because the state of the files is constantly in flux (a file might only be halfway written when the backup occurs). Memory may also be in flux. Considering that most systems use hard drive files for swap, the backup could become corrupted using this approach. Therefore, you must consider a backup of a virtual machine file a "crashed server." You should back up the virtual server image when the virtual OS is shut down.

If you're running backups from the VM itself in order to back up specific items or to back up the database directly using RMAN, then the advantages you achieve by backing up the entire VM image are not realized.

For the same reasons that backing up the entire virtual disk is much faster than backing up each individual file within the virtual disk, restoring is similarly optimized. Restoring one large virtual disk file is much faster than restoring each file individually within the virtual machine.

Hosting and Cloud Computing

One of the most common uses of virtualized machines is for hosting environments. Hosted environments and cloud computing use virtualized machines to provide on-demand computing to their clients. Depending on the underlying hardware, dozens of virtualized systems might be running on the same underlying host server(s). This model allows the hosting vendor to provide virtual systems to its clients on an as-needed basis. In addition, the hosting vendor can easily size the system to the desired number of CPUs and RAM instantly.

Many vendors now offer hosted solutions and cloud computing. *Cloud computing* defines a type of computer resource that is available over the Internet and is made up of resources that you know little about. These resources, usually in the form of a Linux or Windows cloud computer, are provided with a set number of CPUs, a set amount of memory and disk space, and are available to be used anywhere. Typically the end user doesn't really know anything about the underlying hardware or software. This resource is just a commodity.

NOTE
Two types of cloud computing are available: private and public. Private clouds are hosted using internal networks. Public clouds are available via the Internet to different users or customers.

Cloud computing has become more popular in recent years as many customers have decided to abandon expensive data centers and to acquire just the resources needed to run their business. Cloud computing is less expensive than traditional computer systems—up to a point. The higher-end cloud computers tend to be a little pricey.

Training, Testing, Quality Assurance, and Practice

Some of the most popular uses of virtualization are for training, testing, quality assurance (QA), and, of course, just plain practice. Virtual environments are absolutely ideal for testing environments, because they are easy to set up, use, and refresh. All of these types of activities benefit from those features.

Training

Training is by far one of the best uses of virtualization. Oracle employs a great deal of virtualization for training purposes. By using virtual machines, you can reset the VMs for the next week's classes by simply removing and replacing them with new copies. You can add, ahead of time, the correct software, class exercises, and configuration and then re-deploy whenever necessary. Oracle has an entire library of training classes, including ones on:

- Oracle 11*g*

- Oracle 10*g*

- Oracle RAC

- Oracle on Windows

- Oracle Application Server

By storing several classes, you can easily retask your training facility to handle any class you need. Since many classroom environments are not CPU intensive, you can create several virtual machines on the same underlying host.

Training systems are easy to set up as well as access. By using technology such as Virtual Network Computing (VNC), students can access the systems and run X-Windows programs such as the Oracle Universal Installer (OUI) and the Database Configuration Assistant (DBCA). Later in this book, I will cover VNC in more detail. You can also create a training system assigned to individual students, so they can experience managing an entire OS environment. When the class is finished, or if the student causes irreversible problems with the system, you simply remove and re-create it.

Testing

Testing is an important part of every system. Unfortunately, many companies do not have the resources to purchase test systems, leading to severe problems and risk to the production environment. I have actually been called in on occasion to assist with recovering from problems that resulted from performing an upgrade or patch without thoroughly testing it on a test server before putting it into production. The reason for not having a test server is always budgetary.

With a virtual environment, you can put a test system into place efficiently and economically. This way, your database administrators (DBAs) can test upgrades, patches, installations, new configurations, and even undertake performance testing. Without a proper test system, the DBA might miss some step or important detail of a patch or upgrade that he or she might not otherwise notice. By testing installations, configurations, and deployments, the DBA will be more comfortable with and better at doing these tasks. Test systems are one of the most important resources you can have. And once you've finished testing, with one click, you can move the test system into production.

By using Oracle VM, you can create multiple test environments and also save these environments at various stages, so you can deploy the next step over and over again, thus testing exactly what you need to test. You also can preconfigure virtual machines with different versions of the OS and various configurations, including Real Application Clusters (RAC).

QA
Having a set of virtual machines for QA has many advantages. You can keep multiple versions of operating systems, databases, and applications and test modifications multiple times using different variations. This way, you can perform multiple tests with very little setup time. You can also refresh and reset the QA system whenever a new code drop is released so you test it efficiently.

Practice
Having a system to practice and test new things on is always good. You can hone your skills and try new things such as backup methods, patching, and upgrades. By practicing and testing new things, you improve your skills, leading to professional advancement and self-confidence.

Overview of Virtualization Technologies
Virtualization has been around for quite a while now; however, its mass appeal has only been realized with the extensive improvements that have appeared in the last few years. In virtualization's early days, you had to purchase very expensive hardware; now, due to its commoditization, you can use commodity PC servers and download free virtualization software to get started.

A number of different virtualization technologies are available in the market today, including the following:

■ Full software virtualization

■ Hardware-assisted software virtualization or Hardware Virtual Machine (HVM)

■ Paravirtualization or Paravirtualized Machine (PV)

■ Hybrid virtualization technology (PVHVM)

■ Component or resource virtualization

Depending on your situation, you might be able to take advantage of one or more of these virtualization types. In this section, I'll explore each virtualization type, along with their pros and cons. Each type has its own attributes, which provide specific benefits. The type of virtualization that you choose depends on your needs. Oracle VM supports hardware-assisted software virtualization, paravirtualization, and the hybrid PVHVM.

Full Software Virtualization

In *full software virtualization,* all the hardware is simulated by a software program. Each device driver and process in the guest OS believes it is running on actual hardware, even though the underlying hardware is really a software program. Software virtualization even fools the OS into thinking that it is running on hardware.

One of the advantages of full software virtualization is that you can run any OS on it. It doesn't matter if the OS in question understands the underlying host hardware or not. Thus, older OSs and specialty OSs can run in this environment. The architecture is very flexible because you don't need a special understanding of the OS or hardware.

The OS hardware subsystem discovers the hardware in the normal fashion. It believes the hardware is really hardware. The hardware types and features that it discovers are usually fairly generic and might not be as full-featured as actual hardware devices, though the system is functional.

Another advantage of full software virtualization is that you don't need to purchase any additional hardware. With hardware-assisted software virtualization, you need to purchase hardware that supports advanced VM technology. Although this technology is included in most systems available today, some older hardware does not have this capability. To use this older hardware as a virtual host, you must use either full software virtualization or paravirtualization.

NOTE
Only hardware-assisted software virtualization requires advanced VM features; full software virtualization does not. VMware ESX works on older hardware that does not have any special CPU features. This type of virtualization is also known as emulation.

Unfortunately, full software virtualization adds a lot of overhead. This overhead translates into extra instructions and CPU time on the host, resulting in a slower system and higher CPU usage. With full software virtualization, the CPU instruction calls are trapped by the Virtual Machine Manager (VMM) and then emulated in a software program. Therefore, every hardware instruction that would normally be handled by the hardware itself is now handled by a program.

For example, when the disk device driver makes an I/O call to the "virtual disk," the software in the VM system intercepts it, then processes it, and finally makes an I/O to the real underlying disk. The number of instructions to perform an I/O is greatly increased. This process is diagrammed and explained in further detail in Chapter 3.

With networking, even more overhead is incurred since a network switch is simulated in the software. Depending on the amount of network activity, the overhead can be quite high. In fact, with severely overloaded host systems, you could possibly see network delays from the virtual switch itself. This is why sizing is so important.

Hardware-Assisted Software Virtualization

Hardware-assisted software virtualization is available with CPU chips with built-in virtualization support. Recently, with the introduction of the Intel VT and AMD-V technology, this virtualization type has become commoditized. This technology was first introduced on the IBM System/370 computer. It is similar to software virtualization, with the exception that some hardware functions are accelerated and assisted by hardware technology. Similar to software virtualization, the hardware instructions are trapped and processed, but this time using hardware in the virtualization components of the CPU chip.

By using hardware-assisted software virtualization, you get the benefits of software virtualization, such as the ability to use any OS without modifying it, and, at the same time, achieve better performance. Because of virtualization's importance, significant effort is going into providing more support for hardware-assisted software virtualization. Hardware-assisted virtualization also supports any operating system.

Using hardware-assisted software virtualization, Oracle VM lets you to install and run Linux and Solaris x86–based OSs as well as Microsoft Windows. With other virtualization techniques, Oracle VM only allows Linux OSs. This technique also makes migrating from VMware systems to Oracle VM easier, as described in Chapter 10.

As mentioned earlier, both Intel and AMD are committed to supporting hardware-assisted software virtualization. They both introduced virtualization technology around the mid-2005–2006 period, which is not that long ago, and their support has improved the functionality and performance of virtualization. Intel and AMD do not yet fully support paravirtualization; however, hardware-assisted software virtualization components are changing at a very fast pace, with new features and functionality being introduced continually.

NOTE
Hardware-assisted virtualization is really the long-term virtualization solution.

Intel

Intel supports virtualization via its VT-x technology. The Intel VT-x technology is now part of many Intel chipsets, including the Pentium, Xeon, and Core processors family. The VT-x extensions support an Input/Output Memory Management Unit (IOMMU) that allows virtualized systems to access I/O devices directly. Ethernet and graphics devices can now have their DMA and interrupts directly mapped via the hardware. In the latest versions of the Intel VT technology, extended page tables have been added to allow direct translation from guest virtual addresses to physical addresses.

AMD

AMD supports virtualization via the AMD-V technology. The AMD-V technology includes a rapid virtualization indexing technology to accelerate virtualization. This technology is designed to assist with the virtual-to-physical translation of pages in a virtualized environment. Because this operation is one of the most common, by optimizing this function, performance is greatly enhanced. AMD virtualization products are available on both the Opteron and Athlon processor families.

NOTE
The virtual machine that uses the hardware-assisted software virtualization model has become known as the Hardware Virtual Machine, or HVM. This terminology will be used throughout the rest of the book and refers to the fully software-virtualized model with hardware assist.

Paravirtualization

In *paravirtualization,* the guest OS is aware of and interfaces with the underlying host OS. A paravirtualized kernel in the guest understands the underlying host technology and takes advantage of that fact. Because the host OS is not faking the guest 100 percent, the amount of resources needed for virtualization is greatly reduced. In addition, paravirtualized device drivers for the guest can also interface with the host system, reducing overhead. The idea behind paravirtualization is to reduce both the complexity and overhead involved in virtualization. By paravirtualizing both the host and guest operating system, very expensive functions are offloaded from the guest to the host OS.

The guest essentially calls special system calls that then allow these functions to run within the host OS. When using a system such as Oracle VM, the host operating system acts in much the same way as a guest operating system. The hardware device drivers interface with a layer known as the hypervisor. The hypervisor, which is also known as the *Virtual Machine Manager (VMM),* was mentioned earlier in this chapter.

Hybrid Virtualization Technology (PVHVM)

Since Oracle Enterprise Linux (OEL5), Oracle has provided the ability to create a HVM that uses a few specific paravirtualized device drivers for network and I/O. This hybrid virtualization technology provides the benefits of a paravirtualized virtual machine with the additional hardware accelerations available within the HVM. This technology is still new but might be the future of virtualization. This type of virtual machine is known as a Paravirtualized Hardware Virtual Machine or PVHVM. This virtual machine type has the benefits of both the HVM system and the PV system.

Component or Resource Virtualization

Component or resource virtualization has come to mean many different things, depending on the context. Probably the most popular form of component or resource virtualization is in the area of storage. Network resources can also be virtualized but are not as common.

Storage virtualization is simply the abstracting of logical storage from physical storage. This process has been going on for many years and is very popular. Storage virtualization has tremendous advantages as well as a few drawbacks.

Benefits of Storage Virtualization

Storage virtualization has many benefits. It is easy to use and easy to expand. Storage virtualization lets you add drives to a virtual disk while the system is live and running. Management of the storage system can be done external to the database and system administrators. Storage virtualization also supports large numbers of disk drives and virtual disks.

Virtual disk systems have been around for a long time—especially if you consider Redundant Array of Inexpensive Disks (RAID) to be a virtual storage system. RAID meets the definition of the virtual storage system as an abstraction of logical storage from physical storage. RAID systems provide both performance (from multiple disk drives) and redundancy to protect the system from the loss of a component. As you can see, storage virtualization actually provides many benefits.

Drawbacks of Storage Virtualization

The drawback of storage virtualization is you lose control of I/O resources. The I/O subsystem is one of the most important subsystems for database performance. If the I/O subsystem is overloaded, it can lead to high latencies, which, in turn, lead to slow query performance. The I/O subsystem's performance depends on several factors, including the number of disk drives (or spindles) and how busy those drives are.

In a virtualized storage environment, the storage presented to the server is abstracted from the physical storage. Logical Unit Numbers (LUNs), or virtual disks, are made up of multiple disk drives, and multiple LUNs can span the same disks. Unfortunately, this means you might not know exactly where your storage is coming from and how many other systems are sharing the same drives with that storage, which can cause unpredictable performance.

Because I/O performance is so important to the Oracle database, Oracle Automatic Storage Management (ASM) disks should be made up of LUNs with dedicated drives (i.e., no other LUNs sharing the disk drives). In some virtualized storage environments, this is not possible, however. In fact, some storage systems automatically stripe all LUNs across all drives in the system.

Depending on the I/O subsystem's flexibility, different configuration options are available that might let you have more control over storage. In a theoretical environment, the abstraction of logical to physical shouldn't matter. Unfortunately, in the real world, the speed of the disk drives are finite and thus must be allocated properly.

Miscellaneous

Other forms of virtualization exist that haven't been mentioned in this chapter. These virtualization methods typically involve expensive proprietary hardware. Since this book is focused on Oracle VM, which doesn't use any proprietary hardware, those technologies have been excluded from this chapter. This book will, however, discuss technologies that are similar to and share some of the same ideas as Oracle VM, primarily VMware ESX Server and Xen. As you will learn in the next chapter, Oracle VM has its roots in Xen technology.

The Hypervisor

The hypervisor is what makes virtualization possible. The hypervisor is the component that translates the virtual machines into the underlying hardware. There are two types of hypervisors: The type 1 hypervisor runs directly on the host hardware; the type 2 or hosted hypervisor runs in software. In addition, some proprietary hardware has a hypervisor built into the hardware. The hypervisors that we are concerned with are the type 1 and type 2 hypervisors.

Type 1 Hypervisor

The *type 1* (or *embedded*) hypervisor is a layer that runs directly on the host hardware, interfacing with the CPU, memory, and devices. Oracle VM and VMware ESX Server both use the type 1 hypervisor. The hypervisor treats the host OS in much the same way as a guest OS. The host OS is referred to as Domain 0 or dom0 and guests are referred to as Domain U or domU, as shown in Figure 1-1. Here you can see that all virtual machines must go through the hypervisor to get to the hardware. The dom0 domain is a virtual system just like the domU virtual machines (but has more capabilities as discussed later). Currently, the type 1 hypervisor is considered the most efficient and is the most recommended hypervisor.

NOTE
*Even though Oracle VM and VMware both use a
type 1 hypervisor, these hypervisors are significantly
different. VMware handles device drivers directly
in the hypervisor; Xen handles them in dom0 or a
driver domain.*

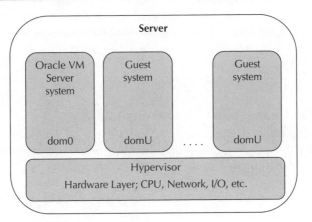

FIGURE 1-1. *The type 1 hypervisor represented graphically*

As you can see from Figure 1-1, the dom0 domain does not differ much from other domains in the virtual environment, except that you access it differently and it is always enabled by default. In addition, dom0 has unlimited rights to hardware, whereas domU only has access through a layer of indirection and only to what dom0 grants it. Because the type 1 hypervisor is essentially part of the OS, it must be installed on the hardware itself and support the devices installed on the system.

Type 2 Hypervisor

The *type 2* or *hosted* hypervisor runs as a program and is used for software virtualization. Because the type 2 hypervisor runs as a program, it has neither the same priority as the type 1 hypervisor nor the ability to access the hardware directly. Its main advantage is you can install it on a variety of host systems without modification. The type 2 hypervisor works with both full software virtualization and hardware-assisted software virtualization. VMware Server is an example of a type 2 hypervisor.

Recently Oracle has released a new product, Oracle VM VirtualBox, which is a type 2 hypervisor-based product.

Hardware Virtualization vs. Paravirtualization

Both hardware-assisted software virtualization and paravirtualization have benefits and drawbacks. With the recent changes in hardware, the software and the technology are changing at a rapid pace.

Currently there are three major types of virtualization: full software, hardware-assisted software, and paravirtualization. Full software virtualization and hardware-assisted software virtualization are very similar as no additional coding or configuration is required (except perhaps to enable virtualization in the BIOS). The main comparison, therefore, really falls between hardware-assisted software virtualization and paravirtualization.

Virtualization Changes Are Happening Rapidly

This section provides guidelines rather than recommendations. At the time of writing this chapter, things are probably much different than they will be when you are reading it. The technology is changing very quickly, and these recommendations might have changed. Do your own research and make your own decisions based on the existing technology.

Benefits of Hardware-Assisted Software Virtualization

The main benefit of software virtualization is its flexibility. You can run any OS on the guest that is compatible with the underlying hardware. That is, if your underlying hardware is Intel or AMD, then the guest must run on Intel or AMD hardware. A number of combinations of 32-bit and 64-bit OSs can run in this environment.

With a 64-bit host, you can run 32-bit or 64-bit guests. Either type of guest is supported, and you can combine both 32-bit and 64-bit guests. When running a 32-bit host, a 64-bit is only available with hardware assistance. If the host system is a 32-bit server without VM technology (hardware assist), the host only supports 32-bit guests. This is described in more detail in Chapter 3.

Drawbacks of Hardware-Assisted Software Virtualization

The main drawback of hardware-assisted software virtualization is I/O and network performance. Because hardware calls are being trapped and processed in software, there is a great deal of overhead. The use of hardware assistance accelerates these operations if they are in the supported system calls (mainly memory), but the technology is still very young and evolving at a rapid pace.

Benefits of Paravirtualization

The primary benefit of paravirtualization is performance. Because the guest OS understands that it is actually running in a VM environment, it can bypass some software interpretations of hardware calls and go directly to the underlying host or hypervisor. Both the guest and host must be running the VM (xen) kernel so they understand and can communicate with the underlying hypervisor.

Drawbacks of Paravirtualization

The main drawback of paravirtualization is the restriction on the supported OS. Because the host and guest must both be running a VM kernel, at this time, paravirtual drivers support only Linux, Solaris x86, and Windows.

Another drawback of paravirtualization is the lack of hardware support. Currently, paravirtualization does not take advantage of the new VM hooks that hardware vendors are adding to their CPU chips. In the future, this is likely to change. When paravirtualization is accelerated with hardware, performance will increase dramatically.

Because the VM kernel must be used, converting a VMware or other image to a paravirtualization virtual machine is difficult. This shortcoming can be resolved,

Hybrid Virtualization

As mentioned earlier, there is a new hybrid type of virtual machine known as the PVHVM. This type of virtual machine uses a combination of a HVM kernel that can take advantage of hardware acceleration and paravirtual I/O and network device drivers. The PVHVM is still very new and has not been used extensively. In the near future the use of PVHVM systems will become more common and more information will become available. Information on the latest in PVHVM technology can be found by visiting my website and blog (see the Introduction of this book for that information).

however, and is covered in Chapter 10, but you will find it is a little more difficult than converting a VMware image to a hardware-assisted software virtualization environment.

If you are running a Linux guest, paravirtualization is the recommended method of virtualization because of its performance benefits. Upcoming chapters provide information on creating both hardware-assisted software virtualization and paravirtualization guests.

Summary

This chapter has introduced you to virtualization and its different types. The information provided is intended to be fairly generic, since Oracle VM specifics will be provided throughout the book. Both software and paravirtualization were described, as well as the benefits and drawbacks of both technologies. Because hardware support for virtualization is changing so rapidly, some of the information in this chapter may be obsolete by the time you read this book; however, the general principles and methods will remain the same.

This chapter compared hardware-assisted software virtualization and paravirtualization. This comparison is based on the technology as it exists today. Soon hardware extensions for virtualization will improve as well as hardware support for paravirtualization. Virtualization is now at the forefront of CPU technology and is leading the new technological revolution.

CHAPTER
2

What Is Oracle VM?

racle is relatively new to the virtualization arena; however, Oracle's technology is based on established technology. Oracle introduced Oracle VM at the Oracle World conference in 2007 and made the product available for download shortly after that. Oracle touted this as being one of its largest software announcements in the history of the company. The Oracle VM product consists of two major components: the Oracle VM Server and the Oracle VM Manager.

Since Oracle's recent acquisition of Sun Microsystems, Oracle VM has been rebranded as Oracle VM Server for x86. At the same time, the virtualization products that are available for the Sun hardware product line have been rebranded as Oracle VM Server for SPARC. In addition, Oracle has added desktop virtualization to its product line with Oracle VM VirtualBox. In this book, Oracle VM Server for x86 will be referred to simply as Oracle VM. Any of the other products will be referred to by its full name.

In this chapter, you will learn about the history of Oracle VM and Xen, its underlying technology, as well as some of the competition. This chapter also covers some of the key features of Oracle VM and the Oracle VM template library.

History of Oracle VM

Oracle VM is a relative newcomer to the field, considering that its biggest competition, VMware, was introduced in 1998 and is majority owned by EMC. VMware introduced its first virtualization product for the desktop in 1999 and its first server product in 2001. Then, in 2003, VMware introduced the VMware Virtual Center, the vMotion, and Virtual SMP technology. These products made virtualization viable for server consolidation in the enterprise. Prior to that, VMware was primarily used only as a test or training platform. In 2004, VMware introduced 64-bit support. EMC also acquired VMware in 2004.

As with Oracle VM, VMware is supported on the Intel/AMD x86 platforms only. This, in part, has led to the race between Intel and AMD to focus their efforts on providing an extensive set of features that optimize virtualization on their platforms. With both Oracle VM and VMware, fully virtualized systems are now supported. In addition, Oracle VM supports paravirtualization, in which the underlying operating system realizes that it is running on a virtual system and makes intelligent choices based on that knowledge. Although VMware provides replacement drivers for video and I/O, it isn't the same as paravirtualization. However, both products also support any OS that will run on the x86 platform in a fully virtualized guest.

The third major player in the virtualization market is Microsoft with its Hyper-V product. The Microsoft Hyper-V virtualization solution is a hypervisor-based virtualization product that was introduced in 2008. This product appears to be targeted primarily to the MS Windows environment.

One final player in the virtualization market is Citrix. Citrix recently purchased XenSource, but the company isn't pushing it as a dominant virtualization platform, as Citrix tends to focus more on the desktop replacement rather than the virtualization environment.

These companies do not represent the entirety of the virtualization market and virtualization products, but they do represent Oracle VM's main competition. The focus of this book is Oracle VM; although there are many other virtualization products, including hardware virtualization, these will not be covered here.

Even though Oracle VM is a relative newcomer to virtualization, virtualization technology is not new to Oracle. Oracle VM is based on the Xen Hypervisor, which is a proven and stable technology. To understand the history of Oracle VM, you must first look at the history of the Xen Hypervisor.

History of Xen

The Xen virtualization product began around the same time as VMware. The product began at the University of Cambridge Computer Laboratory and its first version was released in 2003. The leader of the project then went on to found XenSource. Unlike both VMware and Hyper-V, Xen is maintained by the open-source community under the GNU General Public License. In 2007, XenSource was acquired by Citrix Systems.

Whereas VMware and Hyper-V only support the x86 architecture, Xen supports x86, x86_64, Itanium, and PowerPC architectures. As mentioned in Chapter 1, the Xen architecture is based on a hypervisor. This hypervisor originally allowed only Linux, NetBSD, and Solaris operating systems to operate in a paravirtualized environment. However, since the introduction of Xen 3.0 and hardware virtualization support in hardware, unmodified OSs can now operate in Xen.

Oracle VM 2.2 is based on the Xen 3.4 kernel. In order to fully appreciate where the Xen 3.4 kernel is, let's look at a brief history of the Xen Hypervisor. The following is a brief timeline of Xen history:

2002	Development begins on the Xen Hypervisor.
2003	The first releases of Xen are made available.
2004	The second release of Xen is made available, and the first Xen developers' summit is held.
2005	XenSource is founded and version 3.0 is released.
2006	XenEnterprise is released. Linux begins adding enhancements for virtualization. VMware and Microsoft adopt paravirtualization as well. In addition, this year marks the launch of the Amazon EC2 (Enterprise Cloud 2).
2007	Citrix acquires XenSource. Oracle announces Oracle VM, which is based on the Xen Hypervisor. The original version is Oracle VM 2.1.
2008	Xen begins showing up embedded in Flash memory.
2009	Oracle releases Oracle VM 2.2 based on Xen 3.4.

Let's look at a few of the major releases in more detail. Because Xen is the basis for Oracle VM, understanding where it is coming from and how the various releases have evolved is important.

Xen 1.*x*

Xen 1.0 was the first release of the Xen product and included all of the basic pieces needed to support virtualization. The original release supported only the Linux operating system, but at the time of its release, the Xen development team was already working to enable Microsoft Windows to run in a virtual environment. The original release of Xen was based on paravirtualization, in which the guest operating system is modified so it is aware that it is actually running in a virtualized environment. This awareness improved performance, but did not allow the full range of OSs to run unmodified in a virtualized environment. Xen 1.0 reached its goal of allowing any application that ran on the guest OS to be able to run in an unmodified manner, however.

Microsoft Windows was the first non-Linux operating system ported to Xen, but Microsoft pulled support shortly after announcing it was beginning work on its own virtualization technologies.

Xen 2.*x*

The Xen 2.0 release again targeted the x86 market and included a number of substantial new features. The most impressive of these new features gave users the ability to perform a "live migration" of a virtual guest from one host to another with no interruption in service. This feature is known as vMotion in VMware and is one of the truly outstanding features of virtualization. Using this feature, users could adjust and manage the load on the underlying hosts without interrupting service to the guest OS. In addition, XenSource improved the manner in which virtual I/O devices were used and configured, especially in the area of networking.

Xen 3.*x*

Even though Xen 2.0 and, in some respects, 1.0 had significant features, it wasn't until Xen 3.0 that Xen was truly ready for the enterprise. The features enabled in this version made Xen viable as an alternative to physical servers and increased its popularity. These features have created the explosion in the virtualization market. In the past few years, the popularity and variety of virtualization has grown tremendously.

In this section, I'll cover the history of Xen 3.*x* in more detail.

Xen 3.0 Xen 3.0 included many features that were required for enterprise computing. These features include

- **32P support** Added support for up to 32-way SMP guest operating systems. This support was important for larger applications such as databases.

- **64-bit** Provided 64-bit support for the x86_64 platform, including Intel and AMD processors.

- **PAE** Added support for the Intel Physical Addressing Extensions (PAE) to support 32-bit servers with more than 4GB physical memory. Although not as efficient as 64-bit, this support was better than nothing.

- **Fully virtualized** When using the Intel VT-x (and AMD's AMD-V), made it possible to run unmodified guest operating systems as Hardware Virtual Machines (HVMs). This feature is sometimes known as hardware-assisted virtualization. It allowed for OSs such as Microsoft Windows and earlier releases of Linux and UNIX to run as unmodified guests.

- **Miscellaneous enhancements** Added other enhancements including improved utilities, graphics, and Advanced Configuration and Power Interface (ACPI) support.

Without 64-bit support, many people found it difficult to migrate their applications to a virtualized environment. This is probably the most significant improvement in the Xen 3.x family.

Xen 3.1 The Xen 3.1 release, although not as significant as the 3.0 release, added many valuable new features:

- **XenAPI support** Added support for XenAPI 1.0. This API uses XML configuration files for virtual machines as well as VM lifecycle management operations.

- **Save/restore/migrate** Added the preliminary save/restore/migrate support for HVMs.

- **Dynamic memory** Introduced dynamic memory control for non-paravirtualized machines in this version.

- **32-bit on 64-bit** Added support for a 32-bit OS (including PAE) to run on a 64-bit host.

- **Raw partitions** Added support for virtual disks on raw partitions in this version.

Xen 3.2   As with 3.1, Xen 3.2 was not as significant as the 3.0 release, but added many valuable new features:

- **XSM**   Added Xen Security Modules (XSM) support in this release.

- **Suspend**   Added the ACPI S3 suspend-to-RAM support for the host system.

- **PCI pass-through**   Added the first preliminary release of the PCI pass-through support (assuming supported hardware).

- **Bootloader**   Added preliminary release for a wider range of bootloaders in fully virtualized (HVM) guests, using a full emulation of x86 "real mode."

- **Faster graphics**   Included faster standard (nonsuper) VGA modes for HVM guests.

- **Timers**   Added support for configurable timer modes for HVM guests.

Xen 3.3   As with 3.2, the Xen 3.3 release was not as significant as the 3.0 release, but probably had the most new features of any of the minor releases:

- **Power management**   Added power management for P & C states to the hypervisor. In CPU terms, P-states are operational states and C-states are idle states. See Appendix A for power state information.

- **PVGrub**   Added support for booting the PV (Paravirtualized) kernels using the actual grub inside the PV domain instead of the host grub.

- **PV performance**   Improved paravirtualized performance by removing the domain lock from the pagetable-update paths.

- **Shadow3**   Optimized the shadow pagetable algorithm, improving performance.

- **Hardware assist**   Added hardware-assisted paging enhancements, including 2MB page support to improve large memory performance.

- **PVSCSI drivers**   Allowed for SCSI access direct into the PV guests rather than through a translation layer through PVSCSI drivers.

- **Device passthrough**   Added miscellaneous driver enhancements to allow device passthrough rather than through a translation layer, including multiqueue support on NICs.

- **Full x86**   Added full x86 real-mode emulation for HVM guests on Intel VT, allowing for a wider range of legacy guest OSs.

Xen 3.4 Xen 3.4 is the current Xen release used by Oracle in Oracle VM 2.2. The Xen 3.4 release did not introduce any major new features but did improve many existing features:

- **Device passthrough** Adds more enhancements that were started in the Xen 3.3 release.

- **Offlining** Adds support for CPU and memory offlining where unused CPUs and memory can be "turned off" to save resources.

- **Power management** Enhances the power management features that were introduced in Xen 3.3, including scheduler and timers optimized for peak power savings.

- **Hyper-V** Adds support for the Viridian (Hyper-V) enlightenment interface.

This history of the Xen virtualization monitor shows the dynamic nature of virtualization technology and the care taken to provide the latest and greatest features possible. In addition to the features provided by Xen, Oracle has added a management console designed to assist with the use and management of Xen and Oracle VM. The next section describes the additional features provided by Oracle.

NOTE
Oracle VM does not immediately integrate new versions of Xen, as the value of Oracle VM over the base Xen distribution is rock-solid stability for enterprise use. Oracle fully tests every new Xen feature before using it in Oracle VM. New features can be manually enabled by modifying the vm.cfg file or by using the Xen APIs directly. Oracle does not support this.

Oracle VM Features

Oracle VM is based on the Xen Hypervisor, but there is more to Oracle VM than just the server software itself. Oracle has taken the Xen Hypervisor and added enhancements and fixes as well as improved the management of the virtualized environment. Oracle VM is made up of two components: the Oracle VM Server and the Oracle VM Manager.

Oracle VM Server

The Oracle VM Server, which is based on the Xen Hypervisor technology, has been enhanced to provide better manageability, scalability, and supportability. In addition to modifying the Xen Hypervisor for their own product, Oracle's engineering team contributes to the development of the mainstream Xen software.

Oracle VM Server Features

The Oracle VM Server is the application that actually manages and runs the virtual guests. The Oracle VM Server, which is installed on a bare system, consists of the Xen Hypervisor and a dom0 guest that is used for management and monitoring, and the OVS agent that runs within dom0. As you will see throughout this book, the Oracle VM Manager is what really makes much of Oracle VM work. Features of the Oracle VM Server include:

- **High availability**   You can configure resources to restart guests on another host if the underlying host fails.

- **Live migration**   You can relocate guests from one host to another with no loss of service. This feature is great for load balancing as well as system maintenance. Oracle VM is the only virtualization technology that performs live migration using an encrypted connection by default, providing an additional layer of security.

- **Load balancing**   If configured, Oracle VM automatically load balances upon guest startup, thus providing the best overall performance to the VM farm.

- **Performance**   Oracle VM is optimized for performance, and the Xen Hypervisor is among the fastest forms of virtualization.

- **Rapid provisioning**   Through the use of cloning and virtual machine templates, Oracle VM can quickly and efficiently create new guest systems.

- **VM templates**   Oracle provides a wide-range of preconfigured virtual machine templates that can take the guesswork out of configuration. These templates are available from www.oracle.com.

These features and more are covered in detail throughout the remainder of this book. In the next chapter, the Oracle VM/Xen architecture is covered in detail.

VM Guest Support

Oracle VM 2.2 supports a full range of guest operating systems, which are listed in the following table:

Guest OS	Paravirtualized 32-bit	Paravirtualized 64-bit	Hardware Virtualized 32-bit	Hardware Virtualized 64-bit
Oracle Enterprise Linux (OEL) 4.x & 5.x	•	•	•	•
Red Hat Enterprise Linux (RHEL) 4.x & 5.x	•	•	•	•
Red Hat Enterprise Linux 3.x			•	•
Microsoft Windows 2000			•	•
Microsoft Windows 2003	•	•	•	•
Microsoft Windows XP Pro	•	•	•	•
Microsoft Windows Vista	•	•	•	•
Microsoft Windows 2008 SP1	•	•	•	•

On 32-bit CPUs, only 32-bit guests are allowed.
No Microsoft operating systems are fully paravirtualized. PV drivers are available for Windows XP/2003/Vista/2008, but having a PV driver is different from having a paravirtualized operating system delivered from Microsoft.

Host Hardware Requirements

In order for Oracle VM to run optimally, there are some minimum requirements on the class of machine; however, most modern systems will work. Here are the requirements:

- **Host platforms**   Oracle VM currently supports Intel and AMD x86 and x86_64 platforms. The minimum CPU is the i686; however, to run HVM fully virtualized guests, you must use CPUs with virtualization acceleration. Intel CPUs indicate virtualization acceleration with the "vmx" flag and the AMD processors with the "svm" flag.

- **Memory**   The minimum memory required, according to the Oracle documentation, is 2GB, but since the number of VMs that can be supported depends on the amount of memory, 2GB is way too low. The amount of memory should be proportional to the size and number of VMs. Currently, Oracle VM Server supports a maximum of 1TB of RAM. Of this 1TB of RAM, you can allocate 510GB to a 64-bit guest and 63GB of RAM to a 32-bit guest.

- **CPUs**   As mentioned previously, having CPUs that support virtualization is advantageous. A minimum of one CPU is required, but this number is not suitable for more than one or two guests. A maximum of 64 CPUs is currently supported. The best practice is to reserve one core for dom0 and use the remaining cores/processors for domU's.

- **Disk support**   Oracle VM currently supports SCSI, SAS, IDE/SATA, NAS, iSCSI, FC, and FCoE storage.

Chapter 4 contains more detailed information on how to determine the number of CPUs and amount of memory needed for particular applications properly.

Oracle VM Manager

A major feature of Oracle VM is the management console, which is called the Oracle VM Manager. The Oracle VM Manager is a web-based application that you use to monitor and configure the entire VM farm. You install and configure the Oracle VM Manager on a Linux system. This Linux host can be a standalone server or a virtual machine; however, if you choose to install the Oracle VM Manager on an Oracle VM guest, you will have to manage that VM manually. That is, you cannot start the guest via the console because it is hosting the console.

You can download the standalone Oracle VM Manager from the same location as the Oracle VM Server (www.oracle.com). Since release 5, Oracle VM Manager has also been incorporated into Oracle Enterprise Manager (OEM) Grid Control with the Oracle VM Management Pack. OEM Grid Control with the VM Management Pack allows for centralized management and monitoring of hosts, databases, applications, and virtual machines. You can see an example of the standalone Oracle VM Manager in Figure 2-1. The VM Manager console is where you perform operations such as VM creation, live migration, starting, and stopping.

In addition to the Oracle VM Manager, command-line utilities are available. These command-line utilities let you script and easily modify and save operations. Later in this book, I cover the standalone Oracle VM Manager, the Grid Control add-in, and the command-line utilities in detail.

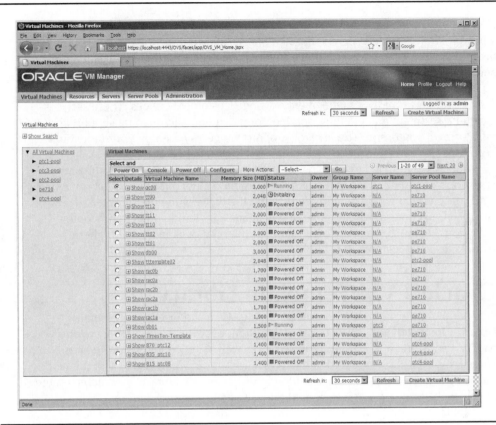

FIGURE 2-1. *Oracle VM Manager*

Oracle Support for VM

Currently Oracle VM is available free of charge. Oracle derives their revenue from selling support on Oracle VM as well as supporting their many other products on the Oracle VM platform. You'll find both advantages and disadvantages to going the "single vendor" route with software deployments. By deploying Oracle VM, Oracle Enterprise Linux (OEL), and Oracle applications and purchasing Oracle support, you only have one place to go in the event of a failure. The disadvantage is lack of selection.

On the other hand, Oracle support is still available if you use Red Hat Enterprise Linux. If you purchase Oracle support for Red Hat Enterprise Linux, your updates will come from Oracle's servers, not Red Hat's. After running the up2date utility on the Red Hat server, there will be no differences between the Red Hat installation and an OEL installation. Oracle keeps OEL in lock-step with Red Hat at all times.

As with all Oracle products, Oracle stands behind its software. In addition, to assist customers rapidly, Oracle offers Advance Customer Services. These services include assessment and planning services, deployment, and ongoing support and/or monitoring if you desire. The level of support you get is based on your individual needs.

Oracle is committed to ongoing virtualization support and to supporting the open-source community in this area. They simply cannot afford to be left out when it comes to virtualization, which seems to be the wave of the future. After all, with virtualization comes a whole range of advantages, including power and cooling reduction, centralized management, and optimized provisioning. All of these advantages are covered in this book.

Oracle's VM Template Library

One of the most exciting advantages of Oracle VM is the extensive Template Library. Oracle not only supplies the VM system, but also the operating system, database software, applications, and so on, as well as preconfigured templates. These templates allow you to deploy applications rapidly because part of the work has already been done for you. The Oracle VM Template Library is available on the Oracle website at www.oracle.com in the software download section.

Oracle's preconfigured templates are easy to deploy and configure. Each template is designed for a specific application stack and, as such, has been tested and validated. Thus, these templates make downloading, deploying, and running applications easy.

After you've downloaded the templates from the Oracle website, you can easily import them into the Oracle VM Manager. Once imported into the VM Manager, you can configure new guests from those templates. I'll cover how to create guest systems from templates in Chapter 8. Once you have created the virtual machine, it is just a matter of configuring and deploying the guest.

The Oracle Template Library is divided into 64-bit and 32-bit templates. You might find it a little surprising, but a lot of software still has not been ported to 64-bit Linux. This includes some Oracle products as well. This section provides a brief overview of the 32-bit and 64-bit templates that are currently available at the writing of this book.

Most of the VM templates provided by Oracle are Just enough OS (JeOS) installation, based on the Oracle standard of installing just the components needed to perform the task at hand. This not only provides for an efficient OS deployment but also helps to meet security standards as well.

Oracle 64-bit VM Templates

At the time of writing this chapter, the Oracle Template Library actually contains more 32-bit templates than 64-bit templates. This is unfortunate, seeing as the goal is to phase out 32-bit Linux as quickly as possible. The 64-bit Linux is preferable because it provides a superset of 32-bit (with more memory capabilities and less limitations.

The following 64-bit Oracle VM templates are available from http://edelivery .oracle.com/oraclevm.

Template	Description
Oracle Database 11.1.0.6 on OEL 5.2	This template provides an OEL 5.2 x86_64 platform with the Oracle Database 11.1.0.6 preinstalled. During the initial boot process, the host and OS are configured.
Oracle Database 10.2.0.4 on OEL 5.2	This template provides an OEL 5.2 x86_64 platform with the Oracle Database 10.2.0.4 preinstalled. During the initial boot process, the host and OS are configured.
Oracle Enterprise Linux 5.x (paravirtualized)	Oracle provides a number of different templates with a basic OEL 5.x configuration. It offers a selection of specific versions and provides two sizes: Small: 1 vCPUs, 1GB RAM, 4GB root partition Large: 2 vCPUs, 2GB RAM, 10GB root partition
Oracle Enterprise Linux 4.x (paravirtualized)	Oracle provides a number of different templates with a basic OEL 4.x configuration. It offers a selection of specific versions and provides two sizes: Small: 1 vCPUs, 1GB RAM, 4GB root partition Large: 2 vCPUs, 2GB RAM, 10GB root partition
WebLogic Server	This template includes a complete runtime installation of the WebLogic Server including: OEL JeOS (Just enough OS) Operating System Oracle JRockit JDK
VM Template Builder	This template includes the JeOS and the Oracle VM Template Builder. The VM Template Builder is an application designed to help create custom JeOS templates.

Template	Description
PeopleSoft templates	The PeopleSoft template family consists of several templates:
	■ PeopleSoft HCP Database Template, which includes the preconfigured database server
	■ PeopleSoft Application and Batch Server with Tuxedo and Verity
	■ PeopleSoft Pure Internet Architecture with Oracle WebLogic
JD Edwards templates	JD Edwards has a large number of templates. These templates consist of the following:
	■ Deployment Server
	■ Enterprise Server
	■ HTML Server
	■ Database Server
	■ Update System
	■ Server Manager Installer
Oracle E-Business Suite	As with most of the application templates, you have a couple to choose from, including:
	■ Vision Database Tier. This template includes the applications and database needed to run Oracle E-Business Suite.
	■ Application Tier. This template includes the application tier necessary to run Oracle E-Business Suite.

Many 64-bit templates are available currently and more are being added. It is interesting to note that third-party application vendors are now beginning to add templates to the library as well.

Oracle 32-bit VM Templates

As mentioned earlier, Oracle has more 32-bit templates than 64-bit templates, which is primarily due to the fact that many applications still have not been ported to 64-bit Linux.

The following 32-bit Oracle VM templates are available from http://edelivery .oracle.com/oraclevm.

Template	Description
Oracle Database 11.1 and 10.2 on OEL 5	This template provides an OEL 5.3 or 5.2 x86 platform with the Oracle Database 11.1.0.7 or 11.1.0.6 preinstalled. During the initial boot process, the host and OS are configured.
Oracle Database 10.2.0.4 on OEL 5	This template provides an OEL 5.3 or 5.2 x86 platform with the Oracle Database 10.2.0.4 preinstalled. During the initial boot process, the host and OS are configured.
Oracle Enterprise Linux 5.x (paravirtualized)	Oracle provides a number of different templates with a basic OEL 5.x configuration. It offers a selection of specific versions and provides two sizes: Small: 1 vCPUs, 1GB RAM, 4GB root partition Large: 2 vCPUs, 2GB RAM, 10GB root partition
Seibel	Both Mid-Tier and Database VM templates are available with the Siebel Industry Application. Several versions of the Siebel templates are available.
WebCenter	A standard template for Oracle Application Server WebCenter.
Oracle Fusion Middleware with SOA	This template is the Oracle Fusion Middleware Service Oriented Architecture on WebLogic Server.
Oracle Fusion Middleware on Oracle Containers for JEE	This is another Oracle Fusion Middleware template. This template is the Oracle Fusion Middleware Service Oriented Architecture on Oracle Containers for JEE.
Oracle VM Manager	This VM template has the Oracle VM Manager already configured.
Oracle WebLogic Server	This template has the Oracle WebLogic Server installed and configured.
Oracle Enterprise Manager (OEM) Grid Control	This is the Oracle Enterprise Manager Grid Control Server, including the OMS and database.
Oracle Enterprise Manager (OEM) Grid Control Agent	This template is essentially an OEL 5.x release with the Oracle Enterprise Manager (OEM) Grid Control Agent preinstalled.
Oracle Identity Management	This template includes the Oracle Identity Management (IDM) installed and configured.

Template	Description
OBIEE	The Oracle Business Intelligence Enterprise Edition (OBIEE) software is installed on this template.
Oracle E-Business Suite	Several E-Business Suite templates are available. They include:

- **Vision Database Tier**   This includes the applications and database needed to run Oracle E-Business Suite.
- **Application Tier**   This includes the application tier necessary to run Oracle E-Business Suite.

Oracle has provided an extensive set of preconfigured templates. These templates are built using the JeOS (Just Enough OS) Linux software and configuration scripts necessary to deploy the system and the application. Specifics on how to use many of these templates and how to use templates in general are provided in Chapter 8.

Summary

This chapter continued with the introduction to virtualization and Oracle VM. The chapter began by explaining more about what Oracle VM is. You cannot understand what Oracle VM is without also understanding what Xen and the Xen Hypervisor are. This chapter gave a brief introduction into those concepts and also briefly touched on Oracle's support for virtualization and the open-source manner in which Xen is developed and supported.

The chapter concluded with an overview of the Oracle Template Library. This template library provides a way to download and deploy a complete virtualization environment quickly and easily. These templates are built using the Oracle JeOS Linux distribution. In addition, most of the templates include preinstalled applications that are ready to be configured and deployed. Of course, these templates might need customizing, which will be covered in Chapter 15.

The next chapter explores the Oracle VM architecture, including not only the architecture of the VM Server and VM Manager but also the Xen Hypervisor architecture as well. By understanding how Xen and Oracle VM work, you will better understand how to configure and tune them.

CHAPTER
3

Oracle VM Architecture

iscussing the Oracle VM architecture is difficult without also including the Xen architecture, which is the underlying technology. In this chapter, you will learn about the different components of both. By understanding how the components work, you will administer, tune, and size the virtual environments within the Oracle VM system more effectively.

Oracle VM Architecture

Oracle VM is a virtualization system that consists of both industry standard open-source components (mainly the Xen Hypervisor) and Oracle enhancements. Oracle does not use the stock Xen Hypervisor; it has performed significant modifications and contributions to the open-source Xen Hypervisor development. In addition to Xen utilities, Oracle provides its own utilities and products to enhance and optimize Oracle VM.

As discussed previously, the Oracle VM system is made up of two components: the Oracle VM Manager and the Oracle VM Server, as shown in Figure 3-1. The basic

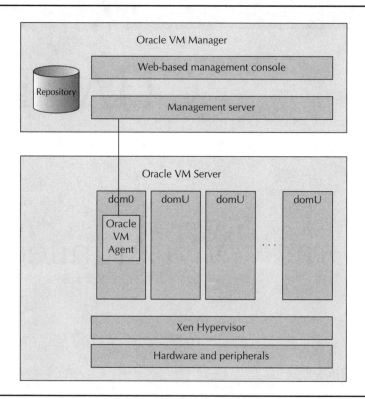

FIGURE 3-1.   *Oracle VM architecture*

architecture is comprised of the VM Manager, which you can install on either a standalone server or a VM (Red Hat Enterprise Linux or Oracle Enterprise Linux), and the VM Server, which can be a virtual machine server, a server pool master, or a utility server. You can also download and install the Oracle VM Manager from a preconfigured template that is available from Oracle. A hardware system can be any one of these types of servers or serve multiple roles.

Oracle VM combines a number of hardware systems to provide virtualization services beyond what a single server could provide. Oracle VM does this by creating a set of servers that work together in a server pool. A group of servers providing services that far exceed the capabilities of a single server is also known as a *server farm* or *data center*.

Servers and Server Pools

A server pool is made up of one server pool master and one or more virtual machine servers and utility servers. The server pool master controls the server pool; the utility server manages storage, templates, and so on; and the virtual machine server supports virtual machines. The server pool is a collection of systems that are designed to provide virtualization services that serve a specific purpose. It is defined by a single VM Manager and shares some common resources, such as storage. By sharing storage, the load of running virtual servers can be easily shared among the hosts that are members of the server pool. A server pool requires a server pool master, utility server, and virtual machine server. Without a shared disk, a server pool can exist on only one server, which must be created with all three roles. With a shared disk a server pool must have a server pool master, one or more utility servers, and one or more virtual machine servers.

Server Pool Shared Storage

You can create a virtualization environment made up of multiple host servers as a single server pool or as multiple server pools. How you configure them is determined by several factors. As mentioned earlier, a shared disk subsystem is required. This shared disk system must have some type of hardware that can share disk storage safely—typically either SAN or NAS storage. When using SAN storage, the disks are configured with the OCFS2 filesystem. Because OCFS2 (Oracle Cluster File System 2) is a clustered filesystem, sharing among VM Servers functions properly.

When using NAS storage for VM guest storage, you have a couple of different options. NAS storage can be configured as either NFS or iSCSI. If the NAS presents NFS storage, the VM Server can use that storage directly since NFS is inherently shared. If the storage is presented as iSCSI, then you must format it as OCFS2, just like SAN storage. A clustered filesystem is required because of the shared nature of the VM server pool. When using NFS as a repository source, Oracle VM will use the distributed lock manager (DLM) from OCFS2 to handle file locking. This locking service is called *dm-nfs*.

If you use a single host for the VM Server, you can use local storage. In a single server environment, there is no need to share the VM guest storage. However, in a single host environment, neither load balancing nor high availability is possible. In a nonshared environment, you can use an ext3 filesystem for the VM storage as well; however, this is not recommended. By default, the Oracle VM Server installation uses the remainder of the hard drive to create a single large OCFS2 partition for /OVS where the virtual machines are stored. Although supported, reformatting the storage as ext3 offers no benefits and has several performance drawbacks in the Oracle VM environment.

Server Pool Requirements

In addition to shared storage, you must create the server pool on hardware that has the same architecture and supports the same hardware virtualization features. You cannot create a server pool between a 64-bit and a 32-bit system. In addition, you cannot place a 64-bit system with hardware virtualization into a server pool with a 64-bit system that does not support hardware virtualization features.

NOTE
The Oracle VM Manager does not specifically prohibit the creation of a mixed environment. It is possible to create a server pool with mixed architectures. But when the time comes to restart a virtual machine, or to live migrate a virtual machine to a new host, Oracle VM will perform a runtime check and disallow restarting or moving to a different architecture, which is why a mixed environment is not recommended.

Although not required, it is a good idea to create a server pool of the same speed and number of processors per system. This setup allows for better load balancing. Mixing various performance levels of VM servers can skew load balancing. Therefore, creating a server pool of similarly configured systems is a good idea.

Always consider the requirements of the largest VM. In order for High Availability (HA) to work (or for live migration), you need another server with sufficient resources. If a virtual machine has been granted 32 vCPUs, and only one server in the pool has that many vCPUs, then the virtual machine cannot be restarted or moved. This is not an argument for using larger servers in the pool as much as it is an argument for using horizontal scaling. Databases can use Real Application Clusters (RAC) and middleware can use its own clustering to keep vCPU and RAM requirements per VM reasonable.

Configuring the Server Pool

You can create server pools based on both the available hardware and the type of business use. If there is no shared storage available, create individual server pools. If the hardware is diverse, then create individual server pools. You can also create server pools based on how the hardware and the VM guests will be used. The recommended approach, however, is to create one or more VM Server farms that can support the entire environment.

If the VM Server farm needs to support VMs for many different departments, you might find it beneficial to create a separate server pool for each group of virtual machines. This setup creates both a physical and logical separation of systems. In other cases, where each group only has a few virtual machines, sharing all of the virtual machines in one server pool might be beneficial. Planning and architecting a VM environment will be covered in more detail in the next chapter.

The primary factor when designing server pools is normalizing the loads on the pool. For example, you should mix virtual machines with high CPU use but low disk I/O with virtual machines that need high disk I/O but low CPU. You can also design a server pool to handle one type of load, for example, a compute cluster. In this case, servers are provisioned with a lot of CPU and memory but with inexpensive NAS storage instead of expensive SAN resources.

The VM server pool is made up of one or more virtual machine servers, one or more utility servers, and a single server pool master. Let's look at these server roles in more detail.

Oracle VM Server   The virtual machine server is the core of the Oracle VM server pool. The virtual machine server is the Oracle VM component that hosts the virtual machines. The VM Server is responsible for running one or more virtual machines and is installed on bare metal, leaving only a very small layer of software between the hardware and the virtual machines. This is known as the hypervisor. Included with the Oracle VM Server is a small Linux OS, which is used to assist with managing the hypervisor and virtual machines. This special Linux system is called domain 0 or dom0.

The terms *domain, guest, VM guest,* and *virtual machine* are sometimes used interchangeably, but there are slight differences in meaning. The *domain* is the set of resources on which the virtual machine runs. These resources were defined when the domain was created and include CPU, memory, disk, etc. The term *guest* or *VM guest* defines the virtual machine that is running inside the domain. A guest can be Linux, Solaris, or Windows and can be fully virtualized or paravirtualized. A *virtual machine* is the OS and application software that runs within the guest. Visit the Oracle virtualization website at www.oracle.com/us/technologies/virtualization/024974.htm for the most up-to-date support information.

Dom0 is a small Linux distribution that contains the Oracle VM Agent. In addition, dom0 is visible to the underlying shared storage that is used for the VMs.

Dom0 is also used to manage the network connections and all of the virtual machine and server configuration files. Because it serves a special purpose, you should not modify or use it for purposes other than managing the virtual machines.

In addition to the dom0 virtual machine, the VM Server also supports one or more virtual machines or domains. These are known as domU or *user domains*. The different domains and how they run are covered in more detail later in this chapter in "Xen Architecture." The Oracle VM domains are illustrated in Figure 3-2.

The VM Server's main responsibility is to host virtual machines. Many of the management responsibilities and support functions are handled by the Oracle VM Agent.

Oracle VM Agent The Oracle VM Agent is used to manage the VM Servers that are part of the Oracle VM system. The Oracle VM Agent communicates with the Oracle VM Manager and manages the virtual machines that run on the VM Server. The VM Agent consists of three components: the server pool master, the utility server, and the virtual machine server. These three components exist in the Oracle VM Agent but don't necessarily run on all VM servers.

Server Pool Master The server that currently has the server pool master role is responsible for coordinating the actions of the server pool. The server pool master receives requests from the Oracle VM Manager and performs actions such as starting VMs and performing load balancing. The VM Manager communicates with

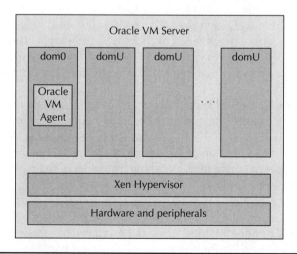

FIGURE 3-2. *Oracle VM domains*

the server pool manager and the server pool manager then communicates with the virtual machine servers via the VM Agents. As mentioned earlier, you can only have one server pool master in a server pool.

Utility Server   The utility server is responsible for performing I/O-intensive operations such as copying, moving, and renaming files in operations like cloning. The utility server creates new virtual servers, removes virtual servers, and clones, among other operations.

Virtual Machine Server   The virtual machine server is responsible for controlling the VM Server virtual machines. It performs operations such as starting and stopping the virtual machines. It also collects performance information from the virtual machines and the underlying host operating systems. The virtual machine server controls the virtual machines. Because the virtual machines are actually part of the Oracle-enhanced Xen Hypervisor, this will be covered later in "Xen Architecture."

Oracle VM Manager

The Oracle VM Manager is an enhancement that provides a web-based graphical user interface (GUI) where you can configure and manage Oracle VM Servers and virtual machines. The Oracle VM Manager is a standalone application that you can install on a Linux system. In addition, Oracle provides another way to manage virtual machines via an add-on to Oracle Enterprise Manager (OEM) Grid Control. Both options are covered in this book.

The Oracle VM Manager allows you to perform all aspects of managing, creating, and deploying virtual machines with Oracle VM. In addition, the Oracle VM Manager provides the ability to monitor a large number of virtual machines and easily determine the status of those machines. This monitoring is limited to the status of the virtual machines.

When using OEM Grid Control, you have the additional advantage of using the enterprise-wide system monitoring capabilities of this application as well. Within OEM Grid Control, not only are you able to manage virtual machines through the VM Manager screens, but also you can add each virtual machine as a host target, as well as any applications that it might be running. In addition, OEM management packs can provide more extensive monitoring and alerting functions.

The VM Manager can perform a number of tasks, among which is virtual machine lifecycle management. Lifecycle management refers to the lifecycle of the virtual machine as it changes states. The most simple of these states are creation | power on | power off | deletion. Many other states and actions can occur within a virtual machine. The full range of lifecycle management states are covered in Chapter 4. The VM Manager is shown in Figure 3-3.

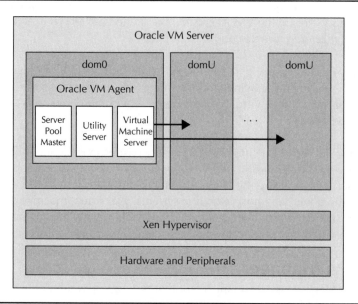

FIGURE 3-3. *The VM Manager*

Users and Roles

A user account is required to access and use the Oracle VM Manager. These users can be assigned different roles. Here are the roles, each of which has a different level of privilege:

- **User** The user role is granted permission to create and manage virtual machines. In addition, the user role has permission to import resources.

- **Manager** The manager role has all of the privileges of the user role. In addition, the manager role has permission to manage server pools, servers, and resources.

- **Administrator** The administrator role has all of the privileges of the manager role. In addition, the administrator role is responsible for managing user accounts, importing resources, and approving imported resources.

Management Methods

You have several options for managing Oracle VM Manager, including the Oracle VM Manager GUI tool and the OEM Grid Control add-in for Oracle VM. You can also use an Oracle VM command-line tool that is available for download from Oracle. Finally, you can use the Xen tools built in to the Oracle VM Server. Which tool is right for you varies based on what you are trying to do.

For monitoring the Oracle VM system, a graphical tool is often the most efficient and easiest to use. You can quickly see the state of the system and determine if there are problems. You can sort and group the virtual machines by their server pool and determine the current resource consumption on the underlying hardware easily. In addition, performing tasks such as creating virtual machines is very straightforward with the assistance of wizards.

Xen Architecture

The core of the Oracle VM system is the software that runs the virtual machines. This software is the Xen virtualization system. The Xen virtualization system consists of the Xen Hypervisor and support software. Xen is a virtual machine monitor for x86, x86_64, Intel Itanium, and PowerPC architectures (Oracle only supports the x86 and x86_64 architectures). At the core of the Xen virtualization system is the Xen Hypervisor.

The Xen Hypervisor is the operating system that runs on the bare metal server. The guest OSs are on top of the Xen Hypervisor. The Xen Hypervisor, after booting, immediately loads one virtual machine: dom0. Dom0 is nothing more than a standard virtual machine but with privileges to access and control the physical hardware. Each guest runs its own operating system, independent of the Xen Hypervisor. This OS is not a further layer of a single operating system, but a distinct operating system being executed by the Xen Hypervisor. The guest OSs consist of a single dom0 guest and zero or more domU guests. In Xen terminology, a guest operating system is called a *domain*.

dom0

The first domain to be started is Domain 0 or dom0. This domain has special privileges and abilities including:

- Boots first and automatically with the hypervisor

- Has special management privileges

- Has direct access to the hardware

- Can see and manage the storage where the virtual machine images are stored

- Contains network and I/O drivers used by the domU systems

The Oracle VM dom0 is a Just enough OS (JeOS) Oracle Enterprise Linux (OEL) operating system with the utilities and applications necessary to manage the Oracle VM environment. The Oracle VM Server installation media installs the dom0, which is a 32-bit OEL system including the Oracle VM Agent. The 32-bit system is installed even on 64-bit hardware.

In the small Linux OS (an OS without a lot of extra features and packages installed), dom0 contains two special drivers, known as *backend drivers*: the backend network driver and the backend I/O or block driver. You can see both in Figure 3-4. Oracle calls these the "*netback* and *netfront*" and "*blkback* and *blkfront*" drivers, respectively.

The network backend driver (netback) communicates directly with the hardware and takes requests from the domU guests and processes them via one of the network bridges that have been created. The block backend driver (blkback) communicates with the local storage and takes I/Os from the domU systems and processes them. For this reason, dom0 must be up and running before the guest virtual machines can start.

domU

All of the other guest virtual machines are known as domU or *user domain guests*. If they are paravirtualized guests, they are known as *domU PV guests*. Hardware virtualized guests are known as *domU HVM guests*. Access to the I/O and network is handled slightly differently depending on whether the guest is a paravirtualized or a hardware virtualized system.

PV Network and I/O

The paravirtualized guest has a network and a block PV driver that communicates with the network and block drivers on the dom0 system via shared memory that resides in the hypervisor. The PV driver on the domU system shares this memory

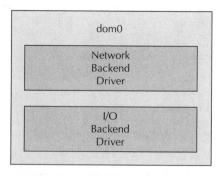

FIGURE 3-4. *Backend drivers*

with the PV driver on the dom0 system. The dom0 system then receives a request from domU via an event channel that exists between the two domains. Here are a few examples for a PV read and write.

domU Read Operation   A domU read operation uses the event channel to signal the PV block driver on dom0, which fulfills the I/O operation. Here are the basic steps to perform a read:

1. An I/O request is made to the PV block driver on the domU system.

2. The guest PV block driver issues an interrupt through the event channel to the dom0 PV block driver, requesting the data.

3. The dom0 PV block driver receives the request and reads the data from disk.

4. The dom0 PV block driver places the data in memory in the hypervisor that is shared between the dom0 and the domU guest.

5. The dom0 PV block driver then issues an interrupt to the domU PV block driver via the event channel.

6. The domU PV block driver retrieves the data from the memory shared with the dom0 PV block driver.

7. The domU PV block driver then returns the data to the calling process within the guest.

This process is illustrated in Figure 3-5.

Even though this process seems sophisticated, it is an efficient way to perform I/Os in a paravirtualized environment. Until the newer hardware virtualization enhancements were introduced, paravirtualization provided the most performance possible in a virtualized environment.

domU Write Operation   The domU PV write operation is similar to the PV read operation. A domU write operation uses the event channel to signal the PV block driver on dom0, which then fulfills the I/O operation. Here are the basic steps to perform a write operation:

1. A write request is made to the PV block driver on the domU system.

2. The domU PV block driver places the data in memory in the hypervisor that is shared between the domU guest and dom0.

3. The guest PV block driver issues an interrupt through the event channel to the dom0 PV block driver, requesting the data be written out.

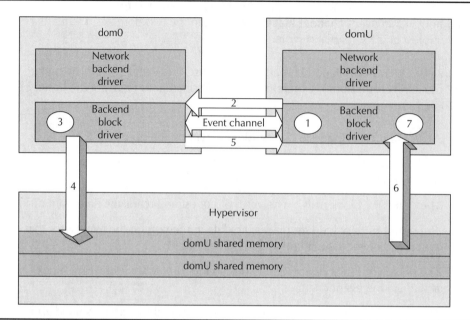

FIGURE 3-5.   *A domU read operation*

4. The dom0 PV block driver retrieves the data from the memory that is shared with the domU PV block driver.

5. The dom0 PV block driver receives the request and writes the data to disk.

6. The dom0 PV block driver then issues an interrupt to the domU PV block driver via the event channel.

7. The domU PV block driver then returns the success code to the calling process.

This process is illustrated in Figure 3-6.

As with the PV read operation, although somewhat complex, this operation is efficient.

HVM Network and I/O

The HVM guest does not have the network and block PV drivers. Instead, a process (daemon) is started on the dom0 system for each domU guest. This daemon intercepts the network and I/O requests and performs them on behalf of the domU guest.

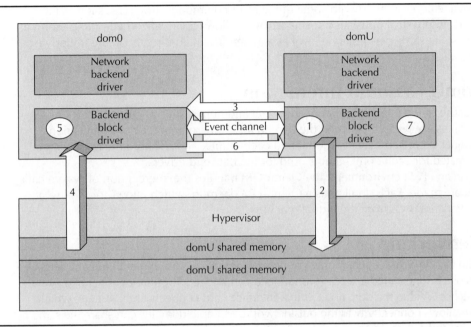

FIGURE 3-6. *A domU write operation*

This daemon is the Qemu-DM daemon. This daemon looks for calls to the disk or network and intercepts them. These calls are then processed in dom0 and eventually returned to the domU system that issued the request.

With hardware acceleration, the ability to access hardware at near native speed has been enabled. This is accomplished by taking the software interface that had been used to intercept I/O and network operations and processing it via hardware acceleration. Although an evolving technology, it has recently performed operations at nearly the speed of direct OS to hardware interaction.

Hypervisor Operations

The Xen Hypervisor handles other operations that the OS normally performs, such as memory and CPU operations. When an operation such as a memory access is performed in the virtual guest, the hypervisor intercepts it and processes it there. The guest has a pagetable that maps the virtual to physical memory, believing that it owns the memory; however, this is retranslated to point to the actual physical memory via the hypervisor.

Here is where the introduction of new hardware has really made today's virtualization possible. With the Intel VT and AMD-V architectures, the CPUs have added features to assist with some of the most common instructions, such as the virtual to physical translations. This advance allows a virtualized guest to perform at almost the same performance level as a system installed directly on the underlying hardware.

domU to dom0 Interaction

Because of the interaction between domU and dom0, several communication channels are created between the two. In a PV environment, a communication channel is created between dom0 and each domU, and a shared memory channel is created for each domU that is used for the backend drivers.

In an HVM environment, the Qemu-DM handles the interception of system calls that are made. Each domU has a Qemu-DM daemon, which allows for the use of network and I/Os from the virtual machine.

Networking

With Oracle VM/Xen, each physical network interface card in the underlying server has one bridge called a *xenbr* (pronounced xen bridge). These bridges act like virtual switches. Within the domain, a virtual interface card connects to the bridge, which then allows connectivity to the outside world. Multiple domains can share the same xenbr, and a domain can be connected to multiple bridges. The default is to map one xenbr to each physical interface, but through trunking/bonding, you can and should (it is recommended) take multiple physical NICs and present them as a single xenbr.

The bridges and Ethernet cards are visible to the dom0 system and can be modified there if needed. When the guest domain is created, a Xen bridge is selected. You can modify this later and/or add additional bridges to the guest domain. These additional bridges will appear as additional network devices, as shown in Figure 3-7.

Hardware Virtual Machine (HVM) vs. Paravirtualized Virtual Machine (PV)

In this chapter and in others throughout the book, you will learn about the differences between fully virtualized and paravirtualized systems. Much debate remains over which is better to use. The fully virtualized system currently has the advantage in that you do not need to modify the OS to use this form of virtualization. In addition, both Intel and AMD have put great effort into optimizing for this type of virtualization.

Prior to the introduction of virtualization acceleration, using paravirtualization was much more efficient. Because the kernel and device drivers were aware that they were part of a virtualized environment, they were able to perform their functions more efficiently by not duplicating operations that would have to be redone at the dom0 layer. Paravirtualization, therefore, has always been seen as more efficient.

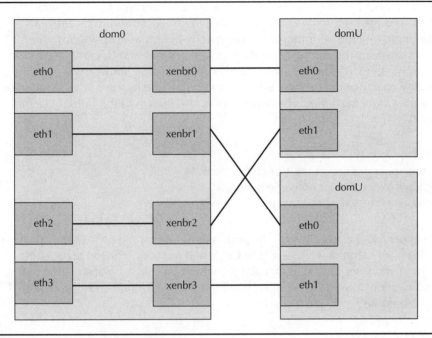

FIGURE 3-7. *Xen networking*

With the introduction of the hardware assist technology, however, fully virtualized systems now have an advantage. Many of the traps that required software emulation are now done by the hardware, thus making it more efficient and perhaps more optimal than paravirtualization. Now work is being done to provide hardware assist technology to paravirtualization as well. The next generation of hardware and software might possibly create a fully hardware-assisted paravirtualized environment that is the most optimal.

At the current stage of technology, both paravirtualization and Hardware Virtual Machine (HVM) are high performing and efficient. Choosing which to use most likely depends on your environment and your preferences. I recommend and run both paravirtualized and HVM (and now PVHVM) guests. Both choices are good ones.

Xen Hypervisor or Virtual Machine Monitor (VMM)

The Xen Hypervisor is the lowest, most innermost layer of the Xen virtualization system. The hypervisor layer communicates with the hardware and performs various functions necessary to create and maintain the virtual machines; the most basic and important of these functions is the scheduling and allocation of CPU and memory resources. This area is also where the most activity has occurred in recent years in terms of improving the performance and capacity of virtual host systems. The hypervisor abstracts the hardware for the virtual machines, thus tricking the virtual machines into thinking that they are actually controlling the hardware, when they are actually operating on a software layer. In addition, the hypervisor schedules and controls the virtual machines. The hypervisor is also known as the *Virtual Machine Monitor (VMM)*.

NOTE
In some documentation the Virtual Machine Monitor is known as the Virtual Machine Manager. For the purposes of this book, the two terms are synonyms.

The hypervisor has two layers. The bottommost layer is the hardware or physical layer. This layer communicates with the CPUs and memory. The top layer is the VMM. The hypervisor is used to manage the virtual machines by abstracting the CPU and memory resources, but other hardware resources, such as network and I/O, actually use dom0.

Type 1 Hypervisors

There are two types of hypervisors. The type 1 hypervisor is installed on, and runs directly on, the hardware. This hypervisor is also known as a *bare-metal hypervisor*. Many of the hypervisors that are on the market today (including Oracle VM) are type 1 hypervisors. This also includes products such as VMware, Microsoft Hyper-V, and others. The Oracle Sun Logical Domains (now known as Oracle VM Manager for SPARC) is also considered a type 1 hypervisor.

Type 2 Hypervisors

The type 2 hypervisor is known as a *hosted hypervisor*. A hosted hypervisor runs on top of an operating system and allows you to create virtual machines within its private environment. To the virtual environment, the virtual machine looks like any other virtual machine, but it is far removed from the hardware and is purely a software product. Type 2 hypervisors include VMware Server and VMware Workstation. The Oracle VM Solaris 10 container is considered a type 2 hypervisor as well.

Hypervisor Functionality

In a fully virtualized environment, the Xen Hypervisor (or VMM) uses a number of traps to intercept specific instructions that would normally be used to execute instructions on the hardware. The hypervisor traps and translates these instructions into virtualized instructions. The hypervisor looks for these instructions to be executed, and when it discovers them, it emulates the instruction in software. This happens at a very high rate and can cause significant overhead.

In a paravirtualized environment, the Xen-aware guest kernel knows it is virtualized and makes modified system calls to the hypervisor directly. This requires many kernel modifications, but provides a more efficient way to perform the necessary OS functions. The paravirtualized environment is efficient and high-performing.

The primary example of this is in memory management. The HVM environment believes that it is a normal OS, thus it has its own pagetable and virtual-to-physical translation. In this case, the virtual-to-physical translation refers to virtual memory, not virtualization. The virtualized OS believes it has its own memory and addresses it as such. For example, the virtualized environment might think it has 2GB of physical memory.

The pagetable contains the references between the virtualized system's virtual memory and its (virtualized) physical memory; however, the hypervisor really translates its (virtualized) physical memory into the actual physical memory. Thus, the virtual-to-physical translation call is trapped (intercepted) and run in software by the hypervisor, which translates the memory call into the actual (hardware) memory address. This is probably the most-used system operation.

This is also where the hardware assist provides the biggest boost in performance. Now, instead of the operation being trapped by the hypervisor, this operation is trapped by the hardware. Thus, the most commonly used instructions that the hypervisor typically traps are not trapped and run in the hardware, which allows for almost native performance.

Hardware Virtualization Support

Both Intel and AMD have been providing virtualization support for several years. AMD has created the AMD-V extensions to the x86_64 line, which include virtualization technology known as *Rapid Virtualization Indexing* that allows for hardware translation of guest virtual memory. In addition an *Input/Output Memory Management Unit* (IOMMU) allows guests to use peripheral devices directly. This is accomplished through DMA and interrupt remapping.

Intel VT-x processors also include many virtualization features, including Extended Page Tables (EPT) that allow for hardware translation of guest virtual memory. Intel also includes I/O accelerations know as Virtualization Technology for Directed I/O (VT-d).

Both Intel and AMD continue to add additional support for virtualization for both performance and functionality improvements.

Features of Oracle VM

Oracle VM is a full-featured product. It is a fully functional virtualization environment that comes with an easy-to-use management console as well as a command-line interface. Some of the features of Oracle VM include the following:

- **Guest support** Oracle VM supports many guests. The number of guests that you can support on a single server is limited only by the memory and CPU resources available on that server.

- **Live migration** Oracle VM supports the ability to perform live migrations between different hosts in a server pool. This allows for both high availability and load balancing.

- **Pause/resume** The pause/resume function provides the ability to manage resources in the server pool by quickly stopping and restarting virtual machines as needed.

- **Templates** The ability to obtain and utilize templates allows administrators to prepackage virtual systems that meet specific needs. The ability to download preinstalled templates from Oracle gives administrators an easy path to provide prepackaged applications.

These features make Oracle VM an optimal platform for virtualization.

Hardware Support for Oracle VM

Although the Xen architecture supports several platforms, Oracle has chosen to focus on the Intel/AMD x86 architecture. Since the Oracle acquisition of Sun Microsystems, Oracle has rebranded some of the virtualization technologies that are built into the Sun hardware and Solaris operating system as Oracle VM. The Sun virtualization technology is not covered in this book. For the purposes of this book, Oracle VM refers only to the x86 virtualization technology.

As with most software products, the Oracle VM documentation provides a minimum hardware requirement. This minimum is usually very low and does not allow for even basic usage of the product. Therefore, the hardware requirements that are provided in Table 3-1 include both the Oracle minimum requirements and additional minimum requirements provided by me.

The choice of hardware depends mostly on the type of virtual machines you intend to run as well as the number of machines. This is covered in much more detail in Chapter 5.

Requirement	Oracle Recommendation	Author Recommendation
Minimum CPUs/cores	1/1	2/4
Maximum CPUs/cores	64 cores	64 cores
CPU type for paravirtualization	Intel AMD	Hardware with virtualization support, Intel VT-x, or AMD SVM
CPU type for hardware virtualized guests	Intel VT-x AMD SVM	Intel VT-x AMD SVM
Minimum/recommended memory	1GB/2GB	4GB/based on guests
Maximum memory	x86 (32-bit) 63GB x86_64 (64-bit) 510GB	x86 (32-bit) not recommended x86_64 (64-bit) 510GB
Supported disk type for VM files	SCSI, SAS, IDE/SATA, NAS, iSCSI, FC, FCoE	SCSI, SAS, NAS, iSCSI, FC, FCoE

TABLE 3-1. *Oracle VM Actual Minimum Requirements*

Summary

This chapter provided some insight into the Oracle VM architecture. By understanding the architecture, you will find it is easier to understand the factors that influence performance and functionality. The beginning part of the chapter covered the components of the Oracle VM system—the Oracle VM Server and the Oracle VM Manager as well as the Agent, which is a key component of the system.

Because of Oracle VM's use of the Xen Hypervisor, this chapter also covered the architecture of the Xen virtualization environment and the Xen Hypervisor. The Xen virtualization system is an open-source project, which is heavily influenced by Oracle since Oracle relies on it. This chapter provided an overview of the Xen system and Xen Hypervisor, as well as detailed some of the hardware requirements necessary to run Oracle VM and Xen. Although Xen runs on a number of different platforms, Oracle VM only supports the x86 and x86_64 environments at this time. Oracle VM will work on 32-bit hardware, but I recommend running Oracle VM on 64-bit if at all possible.

With the acquisition of Sun Microsystems, the Oracle VM family now provides support for hardware virtualization as well as software virtualization (Xen). This book is about the Oracle VM products based on Xen technology and does not cover the hardware virtualization products available with the Oracle/Sun line of products.

The next chapter covers virtual machine lifecycle management. Lifecycle management is the progression of the various states that the virtual machine can exist in—from creation to destruction. Within lifecycle management, you will also study the various states of the lifecycle of virtual machines.

CHAPTER
4

Oracle VM Lifecycle
Management

ifecycle management pretty much explains itself. Oracle VM *lifecycle management* describes the change in state of the virtual machine from creation to destruction and every state in between. For example, the lifecycle of a virtual machine starts with the machine being built, then goes on to its being started, paused, restored, halted, and eventually deleted. This is the virtual machine lifecycle. Of course, you can transition between a number of states, and this chapter describes those states.

Within the lifecycle of a virtual machine are five major states: nonexistent, halted, running, paused, and suspended. Various tasks can take place within these states. The transitions you can make vary according to which state the machine is in. Each of these five states allows for specific actions or transitions to other states.

Almost as interesting as the five major states of existence are the many ways in which transitions occur both to and from each state of existence. All of this comprises the virtual machine lifecycle, which is described in this chapter.

The Oracle VM Virtual Machine Lifecycle

A virtual machine built with Oracle VM has a number of states that it can exist in. For the purpose of this chapter, I will add an additional state: nonexistent. This state will be used as the starting point and ending point of the lifecycle and describes a state of nothingness, from which the virtual machine is created and where it is returned to after its removal from the system and release of the system resources it utilizes.

From nonexistence, the virtual machine is created, or born, and enters the lifecycle. It may enter many states within the lifecycle before returning to a state of nothingness. This entire process is known as the lifecycle. Managing the lifecycle refers to how users transition between these various states.

The various states that a virtual machine can exist in consist of the following:

- **Nonexistent** This is the starting and ending point, where there is nothing. The virtual machine has no definition or state and uses no system resources. This is the state before the virtual machine is created and after the virtual machine has been removed from the VM Server. From the nonexistent state, you create the virtual machine.

- **Halted** The virtual machine is defined in this state. Both a configuration file and data files exist. In the halted state, the virtual machine consumes disk space but does not consume memory or CPU resources. From the halted state, you can start, save, clone, edit, or delete the virtual machine.

- **Running**   This is the operational state of the virtual machine from which tasks and processes are performed. When in the running state, the virtual machine consumes not only disk space but also memory and CPU resources. From the running state, you can stop, reboot, pause or suspend, and migrate or edit the virtual machine.

- **Paused**   This state preserves the machine's current settings and application states without releasing system resources, allowing the machine to resume this state with a short load period. In this state, the virtual machine consumes memory and disk resources but very little CPU resources. When in the paused state, you can unpause the virtual machine.

- **Suspended**   In this state, the machine's current settings and application states are preserved by saving them to respective files and essentially turning off the virtual machine, releasing system resources and allowing the machine to resume the same settings, applications, and processes upon leaving the state. In this state, the virtual machine only consumes disk resources. From the suspended state, you can resume the virtual machine.

These states are illustrated in Figure 4-1. This figure shows all of the states that are possible in Oracle VM and the transitions that are available.

Creation and Deletion

The virtual machine is "born" when you create it. The virtual machine "dies" when you delete it. Everything that happens between creation and deletion is the virtual machine's lifecycle. The lifecycle is not complete until you delete the machine: its lifecycle does not end upon entering shutdown or suspended states.

When you create or clone a virtual machine, it initially enters the halted state. In this state, you can modify the virtual machine's configuration before starting it. A virtual machine is typically in the halted state when you remove it from the system, thus allowing for proper resource cleanup.

When in the halted state, you can add resources to the virtual machine, such as memory, vCPUs, network resources, and more disk space. You can modify a few resources while the virtual machine is running, but in order for them to become visible to the virtual machine, a reboot is often required.

Starting and Stopping

In Xen terminology, starting a virtual machine is referred to as "creating the domain," and stopping or shutting down the virtual machine is known as "destroying the virtual machine." From the halted state (shutdown) the virtual machine can move to the running state. You do this by starting the guest VM.

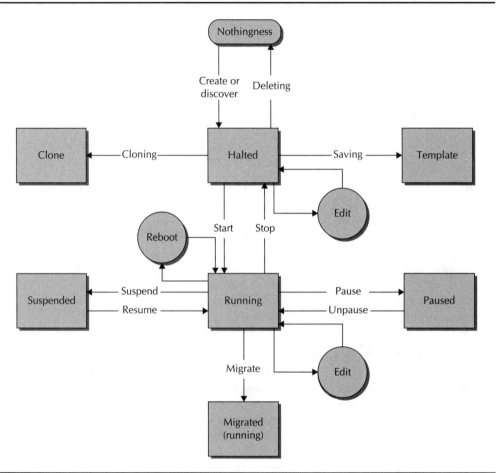

FIGURE 4-1. *The Oracle VM lifecycle*

From the running state, you can stop the virtual machine. Depending on the command you used, this stop might be a hard stop (similar to pulling the power cord) via the **xm destroy** command or a graceful shutdown using the **xm shutdown** command. Whenever possible, shutting down the system gracefully rather than performing a hard shutdown is better. If you perform a hard stop, you might find it takes much longer to restart the virtual machine. For example, halting a system might cause the database application running on that system to take much longer to restart since it has to perform data recovery.

Paused and Suspended

Both the paused and suspended states offer the ability to stop the virtual machine in its exact current operating state and to return the machine to that state upon resuming. The difference between the two states is the manner in which the machine's settings are preserved and how the resources that the virtual machine uses are affected.

Putting a virtual machine into the *paused* state simply stops the execution of further commands momentarily, much like a Windows desktop enters Sleep mode. In the paused state, the machine's applications and settings are left in the state that they were in when the paused state was entered—simply stopped. The settings and application states are not saved to files that are then used upon resuming; they are simply stopped as they are. This allows for a fairly short load period upon resuming, but the virtual machine also continues to utilize (some of) the machine's resources.

If the desire is to simply halt execution of the virtual machine for a short period of time and to restart it quickly, then you should choose to pause. This option provides a fast restart but will hold system resources. If the VM Server were to fail, the paused system will be lost and require recovery if applicable.

Suspending a virtual machine essentially turns the machine off while preserving its current settings. Application states, data, and other settings are copied to their respective files and any resources used by the virtual machine are released. Upon resuming a suspended virtual machine, after an initial load period, during which the machine retrieves its settings and application states from these saved files and resumes use of the server resources, all applications resume the same state they were in.

Suspending a system is a good option if you want to stop the system at a particular point in time and keep it in that state for an extended period of time. However, if you want to not use the system for a while, simply shutting it down might be a better option.

Cloning, Creating a Template, and Migration

Cloning a virtual machine involves creating a new virtual machine from a template or duplicating an existing virtual machine. A cloned virtual machine is an exact copy, or duplicate, of the machine or template it is cloned from. This option is great for creating a copy of a virtual machine. By copying a virtual machine that is already configured for the desired application, you save significant time by avoiding time-consuming tasks like adding packages and installing and configuring applications.

Templates allow you to create virtual machines rapidly using preconfigured settings. Templates are not virtual machines themselves; rather they are profiles that determine what resources the machine will use. The Template Library is one of Oracle VM's most significant features. Templates allow you to save a preconfigured system and reuse it over and over again to provision additional virtual machines quickly and efficiently. With a few configuration changes, you can quickly put the new virtual machine into production, allowing you to add more capacity in an efficient manner.

Migrating a virtual machine involves moving the execution of an existing machine from one VM Server where it's currently running to another VM Server, without duplicating the virtual machine. Migration helps you balance resources as well as achieve high availability. With Oracle VM, you can migrate a virtual machine while remaining in a running state. This way you can also balance resources while the virtual machine is live. If you need additional CPU resources and/or memory and they are not available on the VM Server the virtual machine is currently running on, you can move it live to a VM Server that has sufficient resources. Once the migration is completed, you can add resources. In addition, if maintenance is required, you can abandon a VM Server while the maintenance is completed and then return to it when the maintenance has been completed.

State Management and Transitions

The major states of the virtual machines were introduced earlier in this chapter. The transitions from various states vary based on what state the virtual machine is in. This section describes these transitions and states. From each state, specific state transitions can be accomplished. Of course, all states can move to the halted state if the virtual machine server fails and all states can move to the nonexistent state if the storage repository fails, but in this chapter, we are really only concerned with orderly and normal transitions.

Halted

In the halted state, the virtual machine exists but is only consuming storage resources. The virtual machine is not running and is nonfunctional. From the halted state, you have several options. They include the following:

- **Starting** From the shutdown state, you can start the virtual machine. This activates the system, taking it to the running state. Once the virtual machine has started, a Power-On Self Test (POST) process runs and then the OS boots. At an early stage of the starting process, the virtual machine console becomes available.

- **Cloning**   Cloning allows you to copy a halted virtual machine to either the same or a different server pool. A cloned system is identical to the original. During this process, the virtual machine is not available.

- **Save as a template**   In order to create a template of a virtual machine, it must be in the halted state. A running virtual machine that you copy will most likely result in a corrupted image. The template process saves the virtual machine images as well as the virtual machine configuration file. The virtual machine configuration file is modified to reflect the template path.

- **Deleting**   You can remove a virtual machine from the halted state. You can probably delete the image files of a running virtual machine but doing so might leave the VM Server in an unknown state. Of course, deleting a running virtual machine causes it to crash.

- **Editing**   In order to edit a virtual machine, it should be in the halted state. Modifications include adding disks, network adapters, and so on. In this state, you can add disks and/or modify the ones that you have. You can modify a few options with the system running, but the underlying OS might not recognize those changes.

Halted systems are currently not running, and therefore are in the ideal state for the operations mentioned here.

Running

In the running state, the virtual machine is available for users and can be accessed. In this state, no changes can be made to the virtual machine configuration. A state transition is required before the virtual machine can be modified. The following state transitions are available from the running state:

- **Shutdown**   Shutting down the virtual machine moves it from the running state to the halted state. You can do this either via an orderly shutdown or by halting it (similar to powering it off). An orderly shutdown is preferable, if at all possible. By halting the system, you might have to perform recovery operations, resulting in performance problems on startup.

- **Reboot**   The reboot state is identical to a system reboot in Linux. The system is shut down and then restarted.

- **Live Migration**   You can migrate the virtual machine to another VM Server without ceasing operation via live migration from the running state. There are many reasons for migrating the virtual machine, such as load balancing, maintenance, and so on.

- **Edit** You can edit a few things while the system is in the running state, including memory (up to Max Memory Size). Regardless of whether Oracle VM allows the edit to occur while the virtual machine is running, it depends on the virtual machine itself to recognize the changes. Not all operating systems recognize dynamic configuration changes.

- **Pause** Entering the pause state preserves the machine's current settings and processes in memory without releasing system resources, allowing for quick resumption of the virtual machine's state. The pause state can return to the running state via an unpause transition.

- **Suspend** The suspend state preserves the virtual machine's current state, settings, and processes and releases the system resources used by the machine until the suspend state is abandoned. The suspend state can return to the running state via the resume transition.

The running state is where most of the work gets done. This is the most useful state.

Pause

Entering the pause state preserves the machine's current settings and processes in memory without releasing system resources, allowing for quick resumption of the virtual machine's state. From the paused state, the virtual machine can enter the running state or the shutdown state and the following transitions are possible:

- **Resume** Via the resume transition the virtual machine returns to its previous state and processes at the point where the paused state was entered after a short load period. Resuming results in the virtual machine entering the running state.

- **Shutdown** In the shutdown mode, the virtual machine is powered off and moves to the halted state.

This state is only useful for short periods of time. In the event of a virtual machine server failure, the paused state is lost.

Suspend

From the suspend state, the virtual machine can transition to the running and the shutdown states. Suspending a virtual machine retains the current state of the machine by saving data to their respective files and releasing system resources and allows the virtual machine to resume the same state when the machine is unsuspended. The following transitions are possible from the suspend state:

■ **Unsuspend**   The unsuspend transition causes the virtual machine to resume operations, settings, and processes that were operating at the time the paused state was entered after a short load period. The result of the unsuspend transition is the running state.

■ **Shutdown**   In the shutdown state, the virtual machine has "died" and does not exist.

This state is similar to the paused state, but the virtual machine can stay in this state for a long time because it is not taking up significant system resources.

Summary
The virtual machine lifecycle is defined by the various states in which it exists and operates during the machine's operation. Five basic states exist within the lifecycle, each state allowing for different tasks and configurations. The beginning of the lifecycle is the creation of the virtual machine. The end of the lifecycle is the deletion of the virtual machine. The states in between are known as the lifecycle of the virtual machine.

One of the most important steps in configuring the Oracle Enterprise VM farm is planning and sizing. Underestimating needed resources can cause significant problems down the road. In the next chapter, you will learn how to plan and size the Oracle Enterprise VM farm.

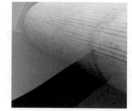

CHAPTER
5

Planning and Sizing the Enterprise VM Server Farm

ne of the most important steps in configuring the Oracle Enterprise VM Server farm is planning and sizing. *Planning* involves all aspects of both sizing and configuration. *Sizing* is the art and science of determining the amount of hardware required for a system that you are configuring. A mistake or underestimation of needed resources could cause significant problems later on when performance is an issue. In this chapter, you will learn how to plan and size the Oracle Enterprise VM Server farm.

Planning the VM Server Farm

You have several choices to make when planning the VM Server farm, including the number of servers, their configuration (server pool masters, utility servers, VM Servers), and their sizing. Before getting started, let's look at the definition of a VM Server farm.

A *server farm* is another word for a data center. The server farm is a collection of systems that are used to serve an enterprise when the use of one system will not provide the sufficient capacity needed to support the enterprise. Thus, the Oracle Enterprise VM Server farm is the collection of systems used to support the virtualization needs of the Oracle Enterprise. The Enterprise VM Server farm can be made up of one or more VM Server pools, which are made up of one or more VM Servers.

One Pool or Multiple Pools

From a high level, it might appear that putting all of the Oracle VM systems into the same server pool would be most efficient. This is certainly an efficient way to manage all of your resources with the least effort since all of the VMs can now run on all of the underlying hosts. However, a few other concerns might make this impossible.

First, all of the systems in the VM Server pool should be running on the same hardware platform because a 64-bit virtual machine cannot migrate to a 32-bit host. The Oracle VM Manager will not prohibit mixed server pools; it really just isn't a good idea because of the problems you might run into. If all of the VMs are 32-bit, a mixed (64-bit and 32-bit) server pool would work, although live migration features might not work. Some features, such as the HA Auto-Restart feature, will work as long as all of the virtual machines are 32-bit. And all of the systems in the server pool must have the same basic hardware architectures.

Second, all of the systems in the VM Server pool should support the same level of hardware virtualization. Many systems remain in production that are 64-bit, but that do not support hardware virtualization. As with 32-bit and 64-bit support, it is not recommended that the two processor types be configured in the same pool. If only paravirtualized guests are being used, mixing both systems with hardware virtualization support and hardware without hardware virtualization support is feasible. In addition, features such as HA Auto-Restart, live migration, HVM, and so on, will dictate whether a mixed environment can be used.

Sometimes determining what type of processor you have and what support is available for virtualization is not easy. In the case of the Intel chipset, there is an easy-to-use web page that will help you: http://ark.intel.com. From here, you can determine the support available for your system. Here's an example.

From /proc/cpuinfo, I retrieved the following information:

```
Intel(R) Xeon(R) CPU              E5520  @ 2.27GHz
```

I then entered the model number E5520 on the Intel website and, among other information, obtained the following:

```
Intel® Virtualization Technology
```

This information tells you that the processor on this system is capable of supporting hardware-assist virtualization. You can find similar information on the AMD website.

Once you've resolved hardware compatibility issues, then you need to decide whether to create one large server pool or several server pools.

Single Server Pool

The primary reason for creating a single server pool is simplicity. This simplicity means easier configuration and administration. Because everything is in a single server pool, you have a single set of templates and images as well as a single storage system. Moving any virtual machine to another system in the server pool is easy and failover is straightforward. A single server pool means less work to manage, seeing as you have one master, one or more utility servers, and one or more VM Servers all grouped together. The only real planning challenge is in the sizing of the server(s).

Multiple Server Pools

Multiple server pools make sense for a lot of installations for several reasons. Some of the reasons are technical, but others are purely a matter of politics and/or policy considerations. Multiple server pools mean multiple sets of storage and multiple sets of servers; however, you can still manage them with the same VM Manager. You can also create multiple VM Managers if desired.

One of the primary reasons for separate server pools is separation of data. Many enterprise security policies require data from different departments or sometimes even different projects to be stored separately. This is especially true in the government where data secrecy might demand separation of data. This separation of data is accomplished by configuring separate server pools.

Another reason for separate server pools is Quality of Service (QoS). Dividing components into separate server pools based on different levels of performance, uptime, monitoring, and management is quite common. The higher the QoS, the more you would typically pay for that service. It makes sense to pay only for the service level that you require. Getting less service for testing, development, and training environments than for the production environment is okay.

To create separate service levels, split the virtual machines into different server pools. The various server pools might have different numbers and types of servers, different storage, and more networking equipment based on the level of service required. A server that guarantees a higher level of service might allocate fewer virtual machines per CPU than one with a lower guaranteed performance level. This is true of storage as well.

Another reason for separate server pools is to separate environments based on access and function. Thus production, testing, and development can be allocated in separate server pools, which guarantees that there is no unintended access or overlap. This allows you to create a barrier between environments. This architecture provides security as well as isolates performance issues into their own environments.

Regardless of your reasons, if you decide to create multiple server pools or a single server pool, you must plan. Planning must include sizing and determining the number of systems for the server pool master, utility servers, and VM Servers.

Planning the Server Pool

You have multiple ways to set up the server pool. The server pool is composed of one server pool master, one or more utility servers, and one or more virtual machine servers. Even though the systems are configured as different server types, the software installed is identical; in fact, the server is not designated a server type until you've configured it. Therefore, each server starts out identical and is configured as a specific server type. The three server types are server pool master, utility server, and VM (virtual machine) Server. A VM Server can be designated to perform a single server role, two roles, or all three roles.

Server Pool Master

One server is designated as the *server pool master*. If you'll recall, the server pool master is simply a specific component of the VM Agent. The server pool master is the communication conduit between the VM Manager and the Agent as well as the interface to other Agents on other VM Servers. The server pool master manages load balancing, among other functions. When the administrator requests that a virtual machine start, the server pool master determines which VM Server is the least loaded and dispatches the request to start the virtual machine. Typically, the server pool master is also a utility server or a virtual machine server as well, unless it is a server pool master for a large and very busy pool.

Utility Servers

The *utility server* is the server that does most of the I/O-related work. This work consists of operations such as copying and moving files. The utility server is responsible for creating new virtual machines as well as deleting virtual machines. Unlike the server pool master, you can have several utility servers in the server pool. If more than one utility server is in the pool, the server pool master determines which utility server is least loaded and will dispatch the request there.

The number of utility servers that are needed in a server pool depends on the amount of activity that is typically handled by the utility server. If the server pool mostly runs virtual machines and does not create new virtual machines very often, then fewer utility servers are required. The number and type required is purely load related.

TIP
It's best to have more utility servers when the farm is initially launched, as the number of VMs being created and deleted will be very high, causing high utility server loads. Once the farm is stable, the need for utility servers will decrease, and the number of utility servers can be reduced.

VM Servers

The VM Server is really what Oracle VM is all about. This is the server that supports the hypervisor and runs virtual machines. There are one or more VM Servers in a server pool. The number and type of VM Servers is determined by the number and type of virtual machines that need to be supported. When an administrator requests that a virtual machine start, the server pool master determines which VM Server has the most resources available and starts the virtual machine there. If a VM Server is not found with sufficient resources, an error is returned to the VM Manager.

Server Pool Configurations

You can set up server pools in several ways: All-in-One configuration, Two-in-One configuration, and individual configuration. Which configuration you decide to use depends on the size of your configuration.

All-in-One Configuration

The All-in-One configuration is the most straightforward configuration. This configuration is made up of the server pool master, utility server, and VM Server all residing on the same VM Server. This configuration functions well for either the VM Server farm where there is only a single or a few servers or the configuration where many virtual machines are managed, but there are very few changes.

Large Servers and Oracle VM

Several hardware vendors have released new hardware with many multiple core processors and large amounts of RAM. These systems are now able to support 128 cores and up to 1TB of RAM. These servers are well suited for Oracle VM, and with a system this large and expandable, the All-in-One configuration is often the configuration of choice. Just make sure you have two of everything for redundancies sake in case you experience a problem.

The All-in-One configuration can consist of a single server, as shown in Figure 5-1, or as a single server that supports the server pool master, utility server, and VM Server, and one or more additional VM Servers, as also shown in Figure 5-1.

The advantage of the All-in-One configuration is that configuring and managing it is easy. This configuration does have the disadvantage in that there is a single point of failure if the single VM Server were to fail (if there is only one). This configuration is becoming more common as hardware is released that is capable of supporting enormous numbers of virtual machines.

Because you can easily add additional VM Servers to a server pool (assuming the storage used is capable of being shared), you can always start with an All-in-One configuration and add to it as needed.

VM Manager

Server pool master
Utility server
VM Server

FIGURE 5-1. *All-in-One configuration plus VM Manager*

Two-in-One Configuration

The Two-in-One configuration involves setting up the server pool master and utility server on the same server. The Two-in-One server configuration is for larger configurations where separating the VM Server from the server pool master and utility server is necessary; however, it is not necessary to have more than one utility server. The Two-in-One configuration is shown in Figure 5-2.

The Two-in-One configuration makes sense where the VM Server farm is moderately sized and you need to separate administrative functions from virtual machine functions. If the separation is for preference, rather than load, you can configure the server pool master and utility server system as a smaller server than the VM Servers.

Individual Configuration

The individual configuration is where the server pool master, the utility server(s), and the VM Server(s) are on separate systems. This configuration is typically reserved for very large VM Server farms where you have many VM Servers (or very

FIGURE 5-2. *The Two-in-One configuration*

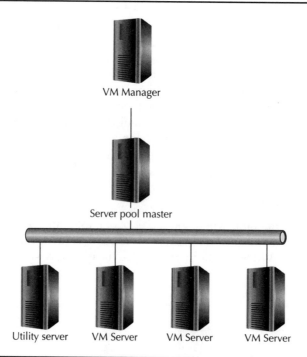

FIGURE 5-3. *The individual configuration*

large ones), and you require lots of performance available for tasks such as starting
and stopping virtual machines, copying and creating virtual machines, and so on.
This configuration provides the highest amount of performance of the three
configurations because all of the functions are separate; however, sizing is still an
important matter. The individual configuration is shown in Figure 5-3.

The type of configuration you choose is partially based on the capacity that you
need for the VM Server farm and partially based on anticipated growth of the farm.
Fortunately, if you decide to change things later, this is one area where modifications
are easy.

Sizing and Capacity Planning

Perhaps more important than the configuration of the VM Server farm is sizing and
capacity planning for the farm. If the VM Server farm is undersized, performance
and capacity will suffer and your system will not run at the desired level of service
or capacity.

Computer Sizing

Sizing is the act of determining the amount of hardware needed for an anticipated workload.

Capacity planning is the act of determining the amount of additional hardware necessary to add to an existing system in order to meet future workloads.

Both sizing and capacity planning are as much an art form as a science. There is mathematics involved, monitoring and analyzing of existing workloads, and a lot of extrapolation. Probably more so than most activities—the better the data input into the exercise, the better the end result.

In addition to the traditional variables used for sizing and capacity planning, such as number of servers, number of CPUs, RAM, and so on, CPU virtualization acceleration features must now be taken into consideration as well. These new virtualization acceleration technologies allow for more virtual machines to be run more efficiently than ever before on the same hardware. In addition, server features such as NUMA technology affect performance.

Sizing and capacity planning are among the most challenging tasks that you must undertake in planning the VM Server farm. As such, they are two of the most important as well. As mentioned earlier, an undersized system will cause performance problems later. In the next sections, both sizing and capacity planning are covered.

Sizing

Sizing is the act of determining the amount and type of hardware needed for a new installation of an application. Sizing differs from capacity planning in that the

NUMA Systems

Non-Uniform Memory Architecture (NUMA) systems use multiple memory controllers that are each assigned to a CPU or set of CPUs. This is different from a *Symmetric Multiprocessor (SMP)* system, where all CPUs share the same memory controller. NUMA allows you to add more CPUs to the system with better performance. Because a memory controller is a finite component, in an SMP environment, the number of CPUs supported is limited by the memory controller.

hardware will be supporting a new application or a new installation of hardware, rather than upgrading or adding to the hardware that already exists for a system. For example, if a computer system will be replaced by another system that has more resources or is faster, sizing is involved. If that same system will have more CPUs or more memory added to it, capacity planning is involved.

This section makes the assumption that the sizing exercise is geared toward taking nonvirtualized systems and virtualizing them—in other words, taking standalone systems and sizing a virtualized environment to accommodate new virtual machines to run the applications formerly running on the standalone servers. The section on capacity planning is geared toward managing the capacity of an already virtualized environment.

The steps involved in sizing a new system are data collection, analysis, and design. The better the data collection, the better the design will be. Keep in mind that there will still be a lot of work to do in the analysis stage where you analyze and decompose the data.

Data Collection

Sizing the new system starts with collecting as much data as you can about the application and the expected workload. If the new system is a replacement for an existing system, much of this data is readily available. You can collect data by monitoring the existing system. If possible, create specific tests or conditions where a single virtual machine is running, so you can analyze a specific workload.

A few different types of data are collected. Data collection is used to collect information about the workload that will be run. In addition, data is collected about the number and type of virtual machines that will be deployed. Collect this data in a workbook that you can then use to determine the number and size of systems to include in the design.

Workload Data Collection Collecting data about the required workload is typically done using any tools that are available in the OS that is being deployed with whatever systems are available. If this is a completely new system and there are no available reference systems, sizing is more difficult. As mentioned before, the better the data, the better the result.

If you're modeling Linux systems, use tools such as sar, top, iostat, and vmstat. These utilities provide information about the system's current CPU utilization as well as memory utilization and I/O utilization. Collect data over a fairly long period of time, so you can gather both averages and peaks. Collect a minimum of one month of data, though longer is recommended.

If you're modeling Windows systems, use Performance Monitor (perfmon). Perfmon provides data on CPU, memory, and I/O utilization. You can use this data to help size the new system. Windows perfmon not only is capable of collecting a large variety of data, but also is capable of saving it as well. Its major downside is its inability to export that data in text form.

Requirements Collection   Requirements collection involves interviewing management to determine the number of virtual machines that are needed and what they will be used for. Certain requirements, such as the number of systems, should be fairly easy to obtain. Other requirements, such as the needed amount of RAM, might be readily available due to specific requirements such as database size or you might need to ascertain it from the workload data collection.

RAM is one of the most important requirements since Oracle VM does not over-commit memory. Thus, you must size the host with sufficient RAM to support the sum of the RAM of the individual virtual machines. This differs from some other virtualization products such as VMware, which allow for over-committing of memory. The designers of Oracle VM and the Xen Hypervisor felt that over-committing of memory could lead to potential performance problems and that memory is inexpensive enough to make over-commit unnecessary.

In addition to memory, gather CPU requirements. The number of CPUs required for virtual machines might be determined by business rules or workload analysis. Typically, some business rules might require a minimum of two CPUs. If no business requirements are available, then you determine the number of CPUs by determining the workload that must be supported.

The amount of required disk space is usually determined by the group deploying the application(s). In addition to the amount of space, consider the performance capacity of the I/O subsystem. An underpowered I/O subsystem can result in performance problems from both the OS and the application standpoint.

Once you've gathered both performance data and physical requirements, you can then move on to the analysis stage. At this stage, the requirements and data that you've collected is translated into physical requirements for each virtual machine. Once you've completed the analysis, you can design the sized system.

Analysis

The analysis stage of the sizing process involves taking the data collected in the previous step and using it to calculate the amount of resources needed to meet the requirements determined during the collection stage. You can split the analysis phase into several phases. The first phase is to take the requirements from both the

Memory Over-Commit

Over-committing of memory is when more memory is allocated to virtual machines than is available in the VM Server. If more memory than was actually available were used, that memory would be paged out as is done in a normal virtual memory system. With Oracle VM, physical memory is allocated for each virtual machine when the virtual machine is created.

CPU Metrics Collection

The CPU metrics that you collect should be the average CPU utilized during normal work hours. Why is this important? If you use the overall average CPU utilization, the value would be skewed lower in most cases due to the lack of off-hours activity. For example, let's say a system runs at 50 percent utilization between 6:00 AM and 6:00 PM and is idle overnight. This is a daily average of 25 percent. If 25 percent were used to size a system, the system would be dramatically undersized during normal work hours. In addition, not only should the system be sized based on a normal work-hours load, but also it should be sized based on peak load. Configure the system to handle a peak steady-state load with relative ease. *Peak load* is the highest load seen during the measurement period. The peak load is slightly different than a spike because the peak load is somewhat sustained, whereas a spike is a one-time event.

collected requirements and, if available, the workload collection process. Enter that information in a spreadsheet and adjust it (i.e., translate it to a single reference platform) if you used different systems for data collection.

In the second phase, this data is summed over all of the systems identified in the requirements. This provides you with the data necessary to identify the total resources required for the host(s). Remember, hardware improvements allow the load on several slower CPUs to be replaced with fewer faster CPUs. Once you've collected the data and calculated the totals, it is time to start thinking about the potential solutions.

Translated Performance

The reason to adjust or translate the performance information is to give you a standard metric to use. For example, adding 50 percent of a 1-GHz processor and 50 percent of a 2-GHz processor together is difficult. By adjusting the 50 percent of a 1-GHz processor to be 25 percent of a 2-GHz processor, you can compare the two. The danger is that the adjustment is somewhat arbitrary, especially if you are comparing unlike CPUs, such as Sun SPARC and Intel/AMD. In the following examples, I have chosen to adjust the performance to meet that of the fastest CPUs available or that might be used for the new system. The assumptions and conversion should be documented.

In the following examples, the process and some ideas are presented to illustrate how to put together an analysis spreadsheet.

Example 1   In the example shown in Table 5-1, data has been collected for several older 1-GHz systems and some newer 2-GHz systems.

NOTE
The CPUs are adjusted to 1 = 100% of a 2-GHz x86_64 CPU = 1.0. Whether the CPU is 32-bit or 64-bit is immaterial; performance is equivalent. Therefore, two CPUs running at 75 percent is equivalent to 150 percent, but adjusted to the reference CPU, this translates back to .75.

Using this spreadsheet, you can then begin the design stage.

Example 2   In the example shown in Table 5-2, data has been collected for a half-dozen very busy systems. This information will be used to analyze how much equipment is needed for the new installation. In this case, there are some holes in the data for new systems that don't have an equivalent running system to collect data from.

NOTE
The CPUs are adjusted to 1 = 100% of a 2.2-GHz x86_64 CPU = 1.0. Therefore, two CPUs running at 75 percent is equivalent to 150 percent, or 1.5.

Using this spreadsheet, you can then begin the design stage.

VM	# of CPUs	Type	% Utilization	Adjusted CPU	Memory	Disk
1	1	x86 1 GHz	50%	0.25	1GB	8GB
2	2	x86 1 GHz	75%	0.75	3GB	20GB
3	2	x86_64 2 GHz	30%	0.6	8GB	40GB
Total				1.6	12GB	68GB

TABLE 5-1.   *Sizing Information*

VM	# of CPUs	Type	% Utilization	Adjusted CPU	Memory	Disk
1	2	x86_64 2.2 GHz	80%	1.6	4GB	20GB
2	2	x86_64 2.2 GHz	75%	1.5	8GB	20GB
3	2	x86_64 2.2 GHz	60%	1.2	8GB	40GB
4	2 requested		NA		16GB requested	200GB
5	2 requested		NA		8GB requested	100GB
6	2 requested		NA		4GB requested	100GB
Total				4.3 + ?	46GB	480GB

TABLE 5-2. *Sizing Information*

Design

The design stage is where you choose the hardware for the VM Server system(s) and create a configuration. Sizing systems involves three components: the amount of memory, the number of CPUs, and the amount of disk space and performance required.

Sizing Memory   Because Oracle VM does not over-allocate memory, sizing memory is probably the easiest part of this exercise. Simply sum the memory required for each of the virtual machines to be supported and add an additional gigabyte for dom0. In the case of the two examples provided earlier in this chapter, the required memory is pretty self-explanatory.

Sizing CPUs   Sizing CPUs is a little bit more challenging than sizing memory. This is mainly because CPUs are a shared resource and are always over-allocated. *Over-allocating* means it is common that more CPUs are allocated to the virtual machines than actually exist on the VM Server system. Fully allocating CPUs to virtual machines is not feasible because they will not be fully utilized.

It is possible and very probable that virtual machines will utilize all of their allocated CPUs at one time or another, but it is very unlikely that they will run at that load for an extended period of time. This is why over-allocating CPU resources is possible. Because CPU resources are limited, by using a 1-1 allocation of CPUs to virtual machines, the number of VM Server CPUs would be much higher than really needed. The idea is to have as many as you need, but not to buy more than is necessary.

Sizing Disk   Disk or I/O sizing has become much more difficult since most storage is virtualized now. That is, a disk or array is no longer allocated for a single purpose. Instead, pieces of the same array are allocated to many different purposes and potentially to different organizations and applications. Storage sizing is broken into two main components: sizing for capacity and sizing for performance.

Sizing for capacity is easy. In the first example shown in Table 5-1, 68GB of storage is required. In the second example in Table 5-2, 480GB of storage is required. That's the easy part. The more difficult part is identifying the performance characteristics that are needed and sizing properly for that. If the I/O subsystem is undersized, the entire environment might suffer.

Unfortunately, sizing for performance involves extensive monitoring and data collection, which often is very difficult to do. In addition, various storage subsystems provide additional features, such as caching and acceleration, that enhance performance. Each storage subsystem works differently and it requires specific knowledge to be able to ascertain which features will benefit Oracle VM.

Capacity Planning

Capacity planning is the process of planning the capacity of the system in order to meet changing requirements. Capacity planning is different from sizing in that instead of dealing with a new system and a somewhat unknown workload, it directly involves the system currently being used, thus more information is available. Capacity planning results in either adding additional hardware (upgrading) or replacing the existing hardware with new hardware. Whether upgrading or replacing the hardware, the capacity planning exercise requires the same steps as with sizing: data collection, analysis, and design.

Unlike traditional servers, Oracle VM provides a straightforward, almost seamless, upgrade path. If the VM Server farm needs additional capacity, add a new VM Server to the server pool. With the addition of the new VM Server, you can migrate virtual machines to the new VM Server seamlessly, thus spreading out the load to a new server. If a specific virtual machine needs additional capacity, you can easily add CPUs and memory (as long as they are available on the VM Server).

In addition, the Oracle VM Server farm requires capacity planning not only for the VM Servers, but also for the virtual machines themselves. Capacity planning for the Oracle VM Server farm involves monitoring both the VM Server itself and the individual virtual machines. As mentioned earlier in this section, the basic steps involved in capacity planning are similar to those involved in sizing: data collection, analysis, and design.

VM 2.2.1 Limitations

Oracle VM 2.2.1 supports VM Servers with up to 64 CPUs, but a single virtual machine can have a maximum of 32 virtual CPUs assigned to it. With the updated package xen-3.4.0-0.1.21 or later, Oracle VM Server 2.2.1 can support up to 128 physical CPUs. The memory limit for Oracle VM 2.2 varies based on the type of virtual machine:

- 32-bit paravirtualized guest: 63GB
- 64-bit paravirtualized guest: 510GB
- 32-bit HVM guest: 63GB

Some of these limitations are likely to change in future releases. The limit for a 32-bit system will always be 64GB due to 32-bit limitations.

Data Collection

In the section on sizing, the focus was geared toward collecting data from individual servers with the goal of sizing a virtualized environment to host them. This section is geared toward collecting data from an already virtualized environment.

Data collection from a capacity planning standpoint is a little different from a sizing exercise. Here, you already have existing systems that hopefully have long-term monitoring enabled on them. Oracle Enterprise Manager (OEM) Grid Control is an excellent product for monitoring virtualized environments for capacity planning purposes because of the ability to save years' worth of data that you can then analyze.

In addition, tools such as the Xen Top command (**xm top**) will display resource utilization in an existing environment. An example of **xm top** is shown in Figure 5-4.

If only the memory and number of virtual CPUs for the various domains are desired, you can acquire this with the command **xm list**, as shown in Figure 5-5.

These statistics provide enough information to give you a good idea of how the individual virtual machines are performing and an idea of how things are currently running. Unfortunately, the xm top utility does not provide data in a tabular form that can be saved, unlike other OS utilities, such as sar.

Analysis

In the capacity planning analysis phase, you have to do more than in the analysis phase of the sizing exercise. When sizing, you design the system for the workload you have analyzed. When doing capacity planning, you analyze trends and determine future workloads. This involves extrapolation of existing data. Oracle Enterprise Manager (OEM) Grid Control is an excellent tool for gathering long-term trend data for analysis.

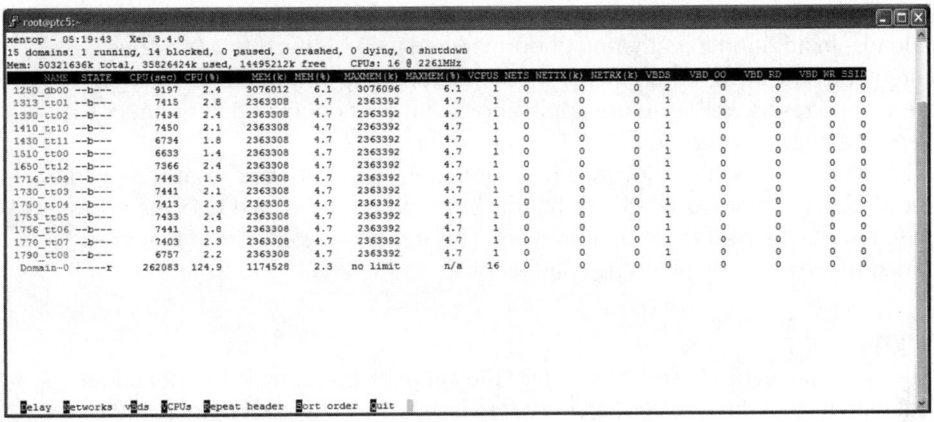

```
root@ptc5:~
xentop - 05:19:43   Xen 3.4.0
15 domains: 1 running, 14 blocked, 0 paused, 0 crashed, 0 dying, 0 shutdown
Mem: 50321636k total, 35826424k used, 14495212k free    CPUs: 16 @ 2261MHz
      NAME  STATE   CPU(sec) CPU(%)     MEM(k) MEM(%)  MAXMEM(k) MAXMEM(%) VCPUS NETS NETTX(k) NETRX(k) VBDS   VBD_OO   VBD_RD   VBD_WR SSID
 1250_db00 --b---       9197    2.4    3076012    6.1    3076096       6.1     1    0        0        0    2        0        0        0    0
 1313_tt01 --b---       7415    2.8    2363308    4.7    2363392       4.7     1    0        0        0    1        0        0        0    0
 1330_tt02 --b---       7434    2.4    2363308    4.7    2363392       4.7     1    0        0        0    1        0        0        0    0
 1410_tt10 --b---       7450    2.1    2363308    4.7    2363392       4.7     1    0        0        0    1        0        0        0    0
 1430_tt11 --b---       6734    1.8    2363308    4.7    2363392       4.7     1    0        0        0    1        0        0        0    0
 1510_tt00 --b---       6633    1.4    2363308    4.7    2363392       4.7     1    0        0        0    1        0        0        0    0
 1650_tt12 --b---       7366    2.4    2363308    4.7    2363392       4.7     1    0        0        0    1        0        0        0    0
 1716_tt09 --b---       7443    1.5    2363308    4.7    2363392       4.7     1    0        0        0    1        0        0        0    0
 1730_tt03 --b---       7441    2.1    2363308    4.7    2363392       4.7     1    0        0        0    1        0        0        0    0
 1750_tt04 --b---       7413    2.3    2363308    4.7    2363392       4.7     1    0        0        0    1        0        0        0    0
 1753_tt05 --b---       7433    2.4    2363308    4.7    2363392       4.7     1    0        0        0    1        0        0        0    0
 1756_tt06 --b---       7441    1.8    2363308    4.7    2363392       4.7     1    0        0        0    1        0        0        0    0
 1770_tt07 --b---       7403    2.3    2363308    4.7    2363392       4.7     1    0        0        0    1        0        0        0    0
 1790_tt08 --b---       6757    2.2    2363308    4.7    2363392       4.7     1    0        0        0    1        0        0        0    0
  Domain-0 -----r     262083  124.9    1174528    2.3   no limit       n/a    16    0        0        0    0        0        0        0    0

Delay  Networks  vBds  VCPUs  Repeat header  Sort order  Quit
```

FIGURE 5-4. *xm top*

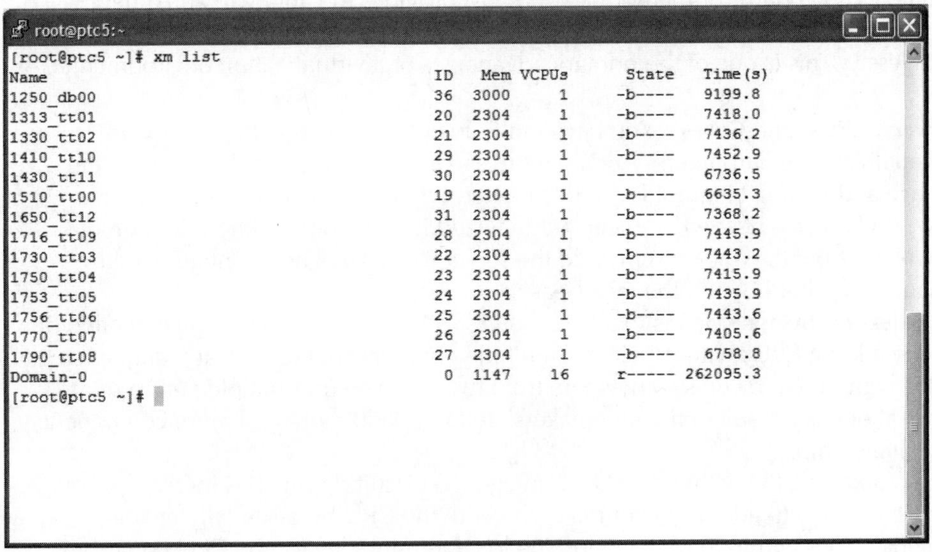

```
root@ptc5:~
[root@ptc5 ~]# xm list
Name                                        ID   Mem VCPUs      State   Time(s)
1250_db00                                   36  3000     1     -b----    9199.8
1313_tt01                                   20  2304     1     -b----    7418.0
1330_tt02                                   21  2304     1     -b----    7436.2
1410_tt10                                   29  2304     1     -b----    7452.9
1430_tt11                                   30  2304     1     ------    6736.5
1510_tt00                                   19  2304     1     -b----    6635.3
1650_tt12                                   31  2304     1     -b----    7368.2
1716_tt09                                   28  2304     1     -b----    7445.9
1730_tt03                                   22  2304     1     -b----    7443.2
1750_tt04                                   23  2304     1     -b----    7415.9
1753_tt05                                   24  2304     1     -b----    7435.9
1756_tt06                                   25  2304     1     -b----    7443.6
1770_tt07                                   26  2304     1     -b----    7405.6
1790_tt08                                   27  2304     1     -b----    6758.8
Domain-0                                     0  1147    16     r----- 262095.3
[root@ptc5 ~]#
```

FIGURE 5-5. *xm list*

Because capacity planning involves trend analysis and extrapolation, gathering long-term data is absolutely critical. Plot this data and extrapolate it for future workloads. In addition to gathering performance data, you need to gather business requirements. Business requirements should include any information related to future workloads as well as future applications and user counts, such as new call centers opening, addition of personnel, and so on.

The final area of analysis involves how far into the future to look. Some companies prefer to plan hardware upgrades to handle workloads for the next two years; others want to handle the next three or four years. This is a business decision that must be included in the capacity planning calculations.

Design

The design stage varies based on whether the capacity planning is for individual virtual machines or for the VM Server. If the design is for a virtual machine, the modifications could be as simple as adding CPUs and/or adding more memory from the VM Manager. If the capacity planning activity is for the VM Server itself, then you may be adding hardware, but, probably more likely, more VM Servers.

Virtualization provides much more flexibility than traditional servers. Rather than having to move applications to new servers and/or shutting down the server to add new CPU boards or memory, Oracle VM provides the ability to add a new VM Server to the server pool and then migrate virtual machines to that new server seamlessly. This is one of the primary advantages of a virtualization environment.

Servers, CPUs, and Cores   You have multiple options when adding hardware to a virtualization environment. Adding more servers to a server pool by sharing the storage and joining the pool is an easy matter. Once you have determined that a new VM Server is needed, you can actually add it to the pool without incurring downtime from the pool. Simply add the server to the pool and configure load balancing and/or HA and the rest is easy.

A less costly approach is to add resources to an existing server. You can often do this by adding CPUs with or without multiple cores. There are now an abundance of CPUs with multiple cores—anywhere from two up to eight. Multiple core systems came about as a result of the chipmakers' ability to add more and more components to a single chip.

A *core* is a CPU within a CPU. As integrated circuit density has increased, you have the ability to add more compute power to the CPU by essentially creating multiple CPUs within the CPU chip. The local terminology for the CPU chip is a *socket,* whereas the individual compute engines within the chip are referred to as the *cores*.

The multiple-core CPU is an evolution of CPU technology. In the early days of the PC, the Intel/AMD architecture had a single core and appeared to the OS as a single CPU. PC vendors eventually developed multiprocessor systems that enabled more capacity within the same server. Later technology was known as *hyperthreading* or

> ### A Little Bit of Computer History
> The author of this book started out his OS/database career at a major computer manufacturer. Here, I personally experienced the introduction of the 80386 processor and 32-bit memory addressing. At that time, we used to joke that nobody would ever be able to afford 4GB of RAM. Since that time, the capacity of computer systems has dramatically increased while the price has dramatically decreased.

hyperthreaded CPU. This appeared to the PC as an additional CPU, but, in reality, hyperthreading was a method of taking advantage of CPU instruction cycles that might otherwise be wasted. Even though the OS thought that the hyperthreaded CPU was an additional CPU, it really only provided an additional 30 to 50 percent more performance.

The multiple-core CPU is actually an additional CPU built into the die of the chip. So the chip itself has multiple "CPUs" built in. These CPU chips also include the multiprocessor technology needed to maintain multiple CPUs and manage memory access between the chip and the RAM. Some designs even include a memory controller on the chip.

In addition to the multicore features, hardware acceleration for virtualization has been introduced that allows virtual machines to run at near native CPU speed. This has helped make virtualization very economical.

Regardless of whether additional CPUs/cores or entire VM Servers are added to increase the VM Server farm capacity, planning ahead is important. Planning for additional hardware when the system is out of capacity is too late. At that point, users will already be complaining.

Storage   Storage is fairly easy to plan for from a capacity standpoint but often difficult to plan for from a performance standpoint. This is because storage administration is often not done by the same personnel who manage the servers and the virtual environment. In addition, there are many factors to consider, such as I/O subsystem cache, storage channels (such as fiber channel switches), and storage virtualization itself.

> ### NUMA Technology
> Some newer CPU chips use NUMA technology. With NUMA technology, you have multiple memory controllers that service a specific set of CPUs or cores. This differs from a Symmetric Multiprocessor (SMP) system that employs only one memory controller. Each CPU sees the same memory, thus it is symmetric.

Storage-size capacity planning is best accomplished by keeping long-term monitoring data about the size and usage of your storage system. It is impossible to perform capacity planning tasks by looking at a single data point. To project future growth, you have to have data regarding past performance. Tools such as OEM Grid Control can assist with this, monitoring both the space usage of the individual virtual machines and the VM Server itself. Since Oracle VM storage uses OCFS2, obtaining space information is not difficult. If no tools are available, it is easy to create a crontab script to collect space information on a regular basis. This will provide valuable information for future capacity planning.

Monitoring and Capacity Planning

Monitoring is extremely important to capacity planning. The better the data, the better the outcome of the capacity planning exercise. The key to monitoring for capacity planning is to develop metrics. These metrics should be relevant, informative, and useful. A key initiative in many organizations is to develop enterprise metrics collection. The term *enterprise metrics* refers to metrics from all aspects of the business. These metrics might include business metrics as well as technical metrics. By gathering business metrics, you can anticipate future growth needs from the growth of the company itself.

Systems should be monitored on a regular basis and statistics kept for as long as possible. This data should be stored in a database so you can view various reports in different ways. This allows metrics to be combined to produce relevant data. Without long-term monitoring and good data, future capacity planning will suffer.

In many ways, capacity planning is more challenging than sizing because it involves projection into the future. But if you've collected good data, the job will be much easier. In addition, good performance data will assist with performance tuning as well as capacity planning.

Summary

A lack of proper planning can often lead to a poorly performing system. By performing a proper sizing, the right hardware can be allocated for the right job. This chapter provided information on how to perform sizing and capacity planning for the Oracle VM Server farm, along with information on how to monitor the performance of the VM Server Farm. (Performance monitoring is covered throughout this book as well.)

In the next chapter you will learn how to install the Oracle VM Server. Later chapters discuss how to install and configure the Oracle VM Manager and OEM Grid Control Plugin for Oracle VM.

PART II

Installing and Configuring Oracle VM

CHAPTER
6

Installing the
Oracle VM Server

nstalling the VM Server is a very straightforward process. Mostly this is because Oracle VM Server for x86 only supports the bare metal installation method, which means that Oracle VM is installed directly onto the hardware as you would with Linux or Windows. The idea is to install the VM Server system without very many options or customizations and then configure it later. In this chapter, you will walk through the process of installing the Oracle VM Server.

Hardware Prerequisites for Oracle VM Server

The hardware requirements for Oracle are very minimalistic. Oracle recommends that you have at least one dual-core CPU and at least 2GB of RAM. In addition, 2GB of swap space and 4GB of disk space is required. As with most software vendors, the minimum requirements don't allow for any functionality, such as installing actual virtual machines.

Since sizing was covered in the last chapter it won't be repeated, except to remind you that it is important to perform a sizing exercise. The CPUs, RAM, and disk space must provide enough resources to support the virtual environment that you want to create. As such, you need a lot of disk space to support virtual machines. Table 6-1 lists a few examples of virtual machine sizes.

Multiple disks are not necessary. The Oracle VM installer will slice up the disk for you during the installation. All that you need is sufficient space to perform the installation. Adding resources later is not difficult and that process will be covered later in this book.

The requirements shown in Table 6-1 are for a single virtual machine. A typical Oracle VM Server will support many virtual machines. To determine the total amount of disk space needed, multiply the requirements listed by the number of

Virtual Machine	Estimated Disk Space
Basic Linux OS	4GB
Oracle Database on Linux	20GB + database size
Application Server on Linux	12GB
Windows 2008	32GB

TABLE 6-1. *Virtual Machine Disk Space Requirements*

virtual machines of that type. You might create a worksheet similar to the one shown here:

Virtual Machine Disk Space Requirements: Virtual Machine Type	Size	Number	Total Size
Basic Linux Server	4GB	10	40GB
Oracle Database on Linux	20GB + database	4	80GB
Application Server (Linux)	12GB	5	60GB
Windows Server	32GB	10	320GB
Total			500GB

Installing the VM Server

You have several installation methods to choose from. The Oracle VM Server can be installed from a CD-ROM, the hard drive, or the network. The network installation consists of installing from NFS, FTP, or HTTP. The CD-ROM installation is the most common and perhaps easiest to perform because no additional configuration steps are required.

Installing from CD-ROM

To install from CD-ROM, place the CD-ROM into the drive and then power on the server. After POST (Power-On Self Test), the Oracle VM Server installer will appear. As mentioned before, the VM Server installation will install the hypervisor and dom0. Later, when you configure the VM Server, you'll decide whether it is a server pool master, utility server, or VM Server.

NOTE
Because of the large number of screens involved in installing the VM Server, only screenshots where actions are required will be shown. Other screens will be described but not shown.

The POST screen is controlled by the hardware and performs operations such as testing memory and discovering and enabling devices at the hardware level. POST is an important part of the system boot process. The POST process performs operations that are crucial to the configuration and setup of devices. In addition, depending on the hardware installed, POST provides options to configure devices by pressing a specific CTRL key series during the initialization of that device. For example, during POST, the Fibre Channel Host Bus Adapter (HBA) card might launch a configuration program when you press CTRL-Z or some other key

The VM Server Boot Process

The installation process boot is similar in terms of looks to the Oracle VM startup; however, the VM Server startup continues to do more work. With the Oracle VM Server, the boot program starts the Xen Hypervisor and the dom0 boot screen. Once the Xen Hypervisor has created dom0, it has exclusive access to the console. Dom0 will then take over the start process. So although the startup processes look the same, they are quite different.

combination. If necessary, configure any devices that require configuration at this stage. It is better to configure the hardware devices before any software is installed.

Once POST has completed, the OS installation process begins by booting the Oracle VM installer. During the startup of the Oracle VM installer, you will see additional device configuration steps. This process ends with the Oracle VM boot screen.

Once POST has completed, the Oracle VM installation process begins. The following are the steps to install a typical Oracle VM Server:

1. The first installation screen looks like a Linux boot screen, as shown here. The installer runs a minimal installation program based on the installer for Oracle Enterprise Linux. It is different from the Oracle VM Server boot process that starts the hypervisor and then dom0.

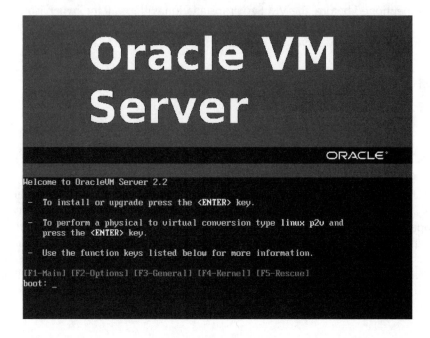

At this boot screen, you're presented with the option to perform a new installation/upgrade or to convert a physical system to a virtual system. For the example presented here, press ENTER to start the installation process.

2.   Once the OS has booted, you will specify if the CD-ROM should be checked. If the CD-ROM is questionable or uncertain, select OK to check the media. Otherwise press TAB to skip and proceed to the next screen. Unless you have had previous problems with the installation medium or the devices have been problematic, it is usually fine to skip this step.

3.   The next screen prompts for the keyboard type. Select the keyboard type for the Oracle VM Server. This screen is self-explanatory. Select the keyboard you'll use by scrolling through the options until the desired keyboard is found and then TAB to the OK button and press ENTER.

4.   If this is a new system or a newly created disk or disk array, the Warning screen will appear. This screen states that there are no partitions on this disk. Select Yes to proceed. This causes the disk to be formatted or reformatted as applicable.

5.   The next screen provides several options for partitioning the disk for Oracle VM, as shown here. The first option is to remove all of the partitions and create the default layout. This is the most common option chosen. The second option is to remove only Linux partitions and create the default layout. This option is useful if the OS or hardware vendor has created a utility partition on the disk. The third option is to use free space. The fourth is to create a minimal layout, which works well for USB installations. The final choice is to create a custom layout.

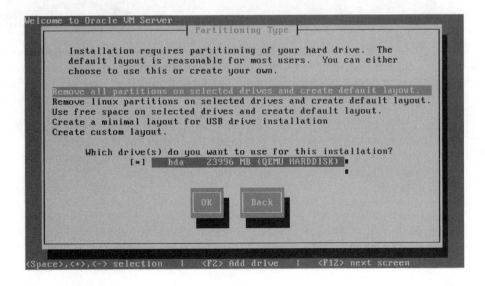

6. The next screen (Warning screen) is just a confirmation of the previous disk layout selections. Be sure that you want to overwrite this disk before proceeding. If you are unsure, click No; otherwise, click Yes and proceed.

7. On the Review Partition Layout screen, you are prompted if you want to review the partition layout before proceeding. Reviewing the disk configuration is always a good idea. If you want to review the partitions, select Yes and proceed.

8. The Partitioning screen allows you to review the disk partitioning layout, as shown next. Here, you can change the configuration as applicable. Make sure the /OVS partition has sufficient space for virtual machines.

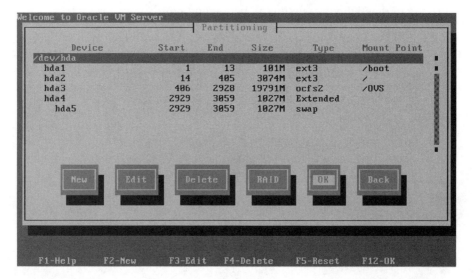

9. Next you'll see the Boot Loader Configuration screen. Select where the boot loader should go. Typically the boot loader is located with the Master Boot Record (MBR). Put the boot loader on the MBR or the first sector of the boot partition. Click OK when you are finished.

10. Next is the Oracle VM Management Interface screen. This screen is where you select the network interface to use for Oracle VM management. If there is more than one network interface, select the one you will use for communication between the Agent and the VM Manager. Click OK to proceed.

11. Now you have a little work to do. Hopefully an IP address has already been allocated for the Oracle VM Server. In the IPv4 Configuration for ethx screen, you assign the IP address to each network adapter. You can do this

either via DHCP or a static address. A static address is used in the example shown here.

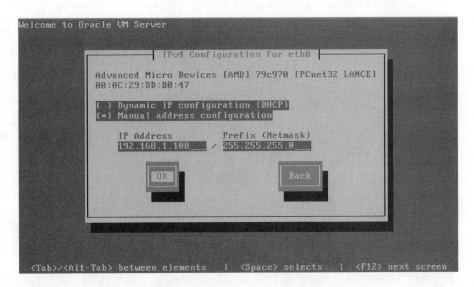

12. Once all of the network adapters have been configured, you'll be prompted for more general network information, as shown next. The Miscellaneous Network Settings screen is used to set the gateway and primary and secondary DNS servers.

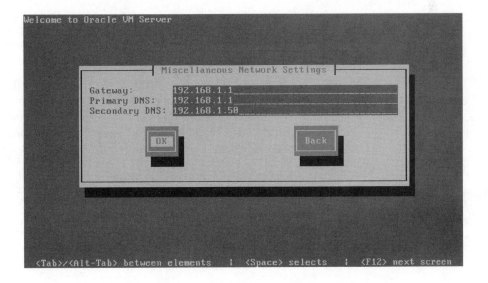

13. In the Hostname Configuration screen, shown in the next image, you choose either automatic DHCP or manual configuration for the host name. If you select the manual option, type in the host name where indicated.

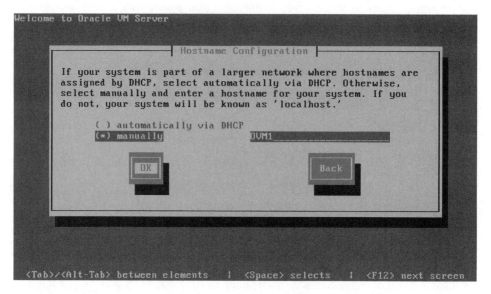

14. Next select the time zone for the VM Server on the Time Zone Selection screen. There are many time zones to choose from. Scroll through the list until you find the time zone for your location. Once you've selected that time zone, click OK.

15. On the Oracle VM Agent Password screen, you are prompted for the Agent password. This password will be used for the VM Manager to communicate with the VM Agent. You must type in the password twice for validation.

16. Next is the Root Password screen. This is where you set the root password for the dom0 domain. Set and confirm the root password. No rigorous checking of passwords is performed, so it is up to you to create a sufficiently complex password to protect your system. Remember security is important! Once you have completed this, click OK to continue.

NOTE
The root password should be different than the VM Agent password. Using the same password could cause issues if different administrators administer the OS within the virtual machines and the VM Servers.

17. Now the installation begins. It starts by checking the dependencies as shown in the Dependency Check screen. This should run fairly quickly. Once this screen has finished, it will automatically exit, leaving you at the Verification screen.

18. Before the installation begins a final verification appears. A message states that the installation log will be stored in /root/install and prompts you to continue the installation. Once you have noted this, click OK to continue the installation.

19. Those of you who are familiar with Linux installations will recognize the Package Installation screen. Since the Oracle VM Server is a small distribution of Linux, it shouldn't take too long to install. The Package Installation screen shows you the packages as they are being installed. When the installation process has completed, this screen will automatically proceed to the next screen.

20. The Completed screen will appear when all of the packages have been installed and the system is ready for reboot. After removing the media from the CD-ROM drive, select Reboot and the system will reboot.

21. Once the system has rebooted, the End User License Agreement screen will be displayed. You must agree with the license to enable the VM Server. If you disagree with the license, the system shuts down. If you agree with the terms of the licensing agreement, click the Agree button. The configuration steps now begin.

22. Once the license agreement has been acknowledged, the normal Linux login screen is displayed. At this point, the VM Server is ready to use. You will choose whether this VM Server is a server pool master, utility server, or virtual machine server during the configuration stage. You can now log into the dom0 server with the password that you provided earlier in the installation process.

This completes the Oracle VM Server installation using a CD-ROM. Other options include installing from the hard drive, NFS, FTP, and HTTP, and they will be described next.

Installing from Sources Other than CD-ROM

In order to install from other sources such as the hard disk or network, you still need to boot the Oracle VM Server installation from the CD-ROM.

At the boot selection screen, instead of pressing ENTER as is done with the CD-ROM installation (refer to the illustration in step 1 of the previous section), type the following command at the boot prompt and then press ENTER.

```
linux askmethod
```

After the keyboard selection screen, the Installation Method screen will be displayed as shown here:

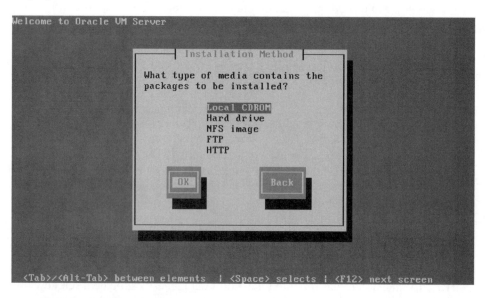

From this point, the installation varies based on the installation method you've selected.

Installing from Hard Disk

For the hard disk installation method, select Hard Drive. This will begin the installation from the hard disk.

The Select Partition screen is used to select the partition that contains the installation images and to select the directory within that partition where those images reside. It is a good idea to write this information down before starting the installation so you don't have to figure this out while the prompt is on the screen. The Select Partition screen is shown here:

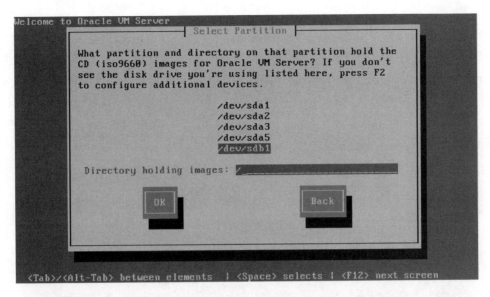

This method is great for reinstalling Oracle VM since the installation media is already preinstalled on one of the disk partitions. Keep in mind that this can also be media installed on a USB drive. The drive itself must be either Fat32 or VFAT format, which happens to be the format of most USB drives you will find today. This method can also be used with disk cloning (i.e., copying the entire disk and modifying it) if available. You can place the image on the disk and then move the disk onto a new server.

The remainder of the installation is identical to installing from CD-ROM. Please refer to that section for installation information. You must have images of the Linux distribution on your disk before starting this installation.

Installing from NFS

If a number of Oracle VM Servers are being configured, installing from the network can be quite convenient. Often using the network can be much faster than using a CD-ROM. In addition, you can configure multiple VM Servers at the same time without having to duplicate CD-ROMs.

Installing from NFS is done in much the same way as the installation from hard drive method, except the installation will be performed from an ISO image that is on an NFS mounted disk. Once you've selected the NFS method, you need to set up the network for the VM Server system before you can use it connect to the NFS server. The VM Server can be configured either using DHCP or by manually setting the IP in the Configure TCP/IP screen.

If you've chosen manual IP address configuration, the Manual TCP/IP Configuration screen will appear, as shown next. Specify the IP address, netmask, gateway, and name server.

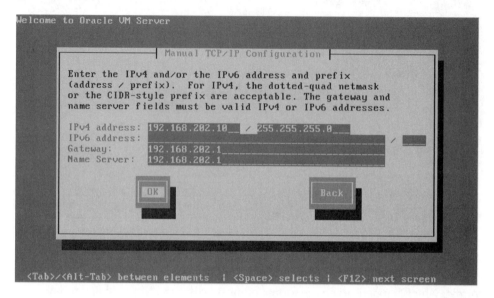

Once you've entered the IP address of the VM Server, the next screen appears, asking for the name or IP address of the NFS server that holds the Oracle VM Server image:

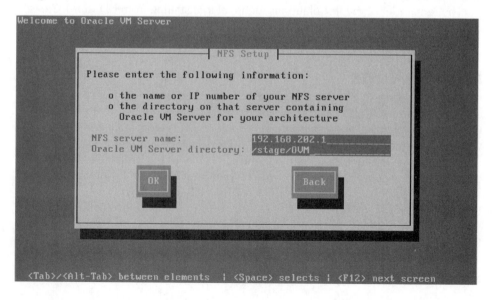

In addition, you must specify the directory where the Oracle VM Server image is stored.

Once the IP address has been set and the NFS directory specified, the installation will proceed with the same steps as the CD-ROM installation.

Installing from FTP

Installing from an FTP server provides the same benefits as installing from an NFS server. This option is useful when NFS is not configured and FTP is configurated. Installing from an FTP server begins with the same Manual TCP/IP Configuration screen shown previously.

Once you've configured the network, the FTP Setup screen appears, as shown next. You must specify the FTP site name and Oracle VM Server directory.

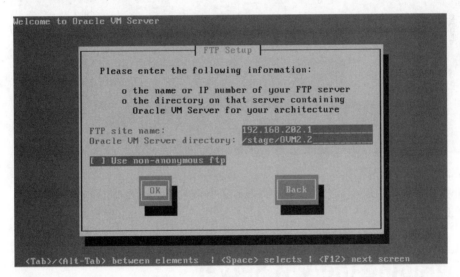

If the Use Non-anonymous FTP option is checked, the Further FTP Setup screen is displayed. Here you must input the username and password for non-anonymous FTP. This must be a valid user account and password on the FTP server.

Once the IP address has been set and the FTP directory specified, the installation proceeds with the same steps as the CD-ROM installation.

Installing from HTTP

Installing from an HTTP server starts out with the same Manual TCP/IP Configuration screen shown previously. Once you've set up the IP address, the HTTP Setup screen appears. Here, you specify the website name and Oracle VM Server directory.

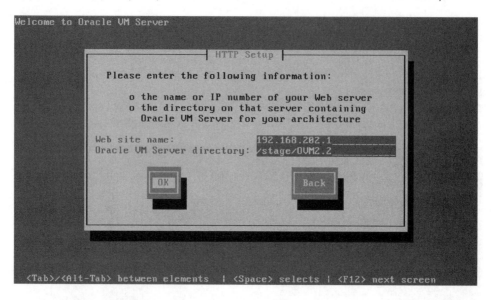

Once the IP address has been set and the HTTP Server and directory specified, the installation proceeds with the same steps as the CD-ROM installation. The three network options are fairly similar. Choose the method that meets your specific needs.

Upgrading the VM Server

From time to time a new version of Oracle VM is released. Depending on the nature of the release and the state of your Oracle Enterprise VM Server farm, upgrading to the latest release might be advantageous. To upgrade an Oracle VM Server to the latest release, start by booting the latest CD-ROM. The first screen is the boot screen, which was shown previously, followed by the option to check the CD, followed by the Select Keyboard screen.

NOTE
New releases come with upgrade instructions. Newer versions will most likely have improved upgrade procedures and instructions, so be sure to check the documentation. Also be sure to back up any customizations you've made before upgrading.

Once the preliminaries have been accomplished, the System to Upgrade screen is displayed. This screen allows you to choose between reinstalling a new system or upgrading to the latest release. In the example shown next, the Oracle VM 2.1.5 partition will be upgraded.

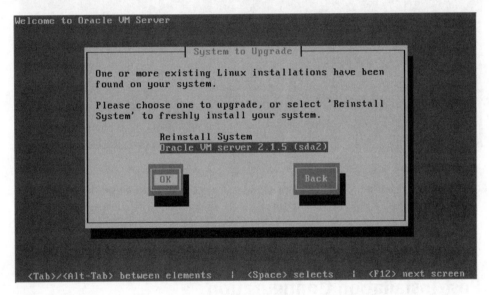

Next is the Upgrade Boot Loader Configuration screen. On this screen, the options are to update the boot loader, skip making changes, or create a new boot loader. The option to Update Boot Loader Configuration is usually the best choice.

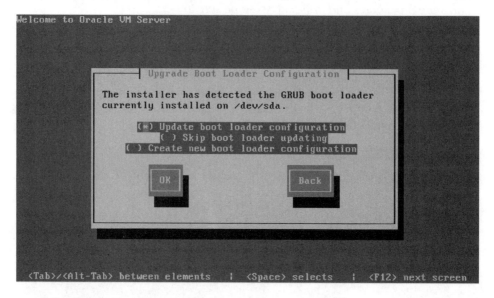

At this point, the dependencies are checked and the package list created. You have one final chance to back up and change things before the upgrade begins. When you are ready, click OK to continue.

At this point, the upgrade process starts. It will take several minutes depending on the speed of your hardware. Once the upgrade has completed, you will see the Completed screen. Pressing ENTER at this point completes the upgrade.

Post-Installation Configuration

In most cases the installation is finished at this point; however, in some cases additional configuration steps are necessary. The Oracle VM release notes for version 2.2.1 recommend that the memory for the dom0 system not be changed and be automatically set using the formula $502 + 0.205 \times$ physical memory in MB. In a recent installation for a system with 256GB of RAM, the default configuration was set to a dom0 memory configuration of 543MB. This is much less than the 5875 calculated using Oracle's formula.

In order to configure the dom0 memory correctly, edit the file /boot/grub/grub
.conf and change the setting of dom0_mem to the proper value using the formula
shown above. This change should only be done if the installation process configured
the dom0_mem setting incorrectly. Other modifications to the dom0 system are
described in the chapters on network and memory (see Chapters 10 and 11).

Summary

This chapter provided instructions on how to install the Oracle VM Server. There really
isn't much work to installing the VM Server. This process, although you have several
ways to do it, simply formats the disks and adds the software, including the VM Agent.
Once the VM Server has been installed, you need to configure it as a server pool
master, utility server, virtual machine server, or all of the above. Configuring the VM
Server is where the real work begins. That process will be discussed in the next few
chapters.

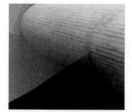

CHAPTER
7

Installing and Configuring
Oracle VM Manager

nstalling the VM Manager can be done either by installing the VM Manager on a Linux system (physical or virtual) or by installing a VM Template that already has the VM Manager preinstalled. This chapter will first describe how to install the VM Manager using the installation media and then how to install the VM Manager from a template.

Hardware and Software Prerequisites for VM Manager

To install the VM Manager, you first need to allocate a host system and install and configure the OS. The VM Manager runs on either a 64-bit or 32-bit version of Linux—either Oracle Enterprise Linux (OEL) or Red Hat Enterprise Linux (RHEL) version 4.5 or higher. The VM Manager does not use a full Oracle database for its repository; therefore, not as many OS packages are required to support its installation.

The VM Manager installation installs the following components:

- **Oracle Database 10g Express Edition (Oracle XE) database as the repository**   Optionally, if an Oracle XE database already exists, that one can be used. You may also use Oracle 10g or 11g—either Standard Edition, Enterprise Edition, or RAC.

- **Oracle Instant Client**   The Instant Client is installed if the use of another database is requested.

- **Oracle Containers for J2EE (OC4J)**   This layer is installed to support the VM Manager application.

- **Apache XML-RPC 3.0**   This library is installed to support the application.

Hardware Requirements for the VM Manager

The hardware requirements for the Oracle VM Manager are fairly straightforward. The system requirements are listed in Table 7-1.

The Oracle VM Manager system can be either a physical server or a virtual machine. A virtual machine is very capable of handling the workload of the VM Manager. In a fully virtualized environment, it seems like somewhat of a waste to dedicate a server to just running the VM Manager.

The contrary argument to using a virtual machine as the VM Manager is the philosophy that one should never monitor a critical system from within that system. This philosophy applies not only to the VM Manager, but also, potentially, to Oracle Enterprise Manager (OEM) Grid Control as well. If an OEM Grid Control system is

Component	Minimum Required Value	Notes
CPU	1 × 1.8 GHz	Two CPUs are recommended if there are more than four VM Servers.
Memory	2GB	If the VM Manager is sharing the system with other applications, such as DHCP Server and NTP Server, increase memory accordingly.
Hard disk space	4GB	8GB is recommended to be safe. Storage is cheap.
Swap space	2GB	This is required by the Oracle XE installer. If 2GB is not available, the installation will fail. During normal operations if swapping occurs, add memory.

TABLE 7-1. *Hardware Requirements for the Oracle VM Manager*

Virtual vs. Physical Host for the VM Manager

The VM Manager can very easily be hosted as a virtual machine. The hardware and software requirements are well within the parameters of what a virtual machine can provide. From a purely technical standpoint, running the VM Manager on a virtual machine makes a lot of sense. This argument holds true for OEM Grid Control as well. The most efficient way to host the Grid Control server is via a virtual machine.

The problem with hosting the VM Manager or Grid Control on a virtual machine within the environment that it is hosting is that, in the event of a hardware issue, both the VM Manager and the systems it is monitoring and managing are all unavailable. Even in a highly available environment, a power failure that disrupts power to the data center will most likely affect both systems.

Alternatives are to host the VM Manager and/or Grid Control on a physical system, preferably in another part of the data center. Another option is to host the VM Manager for one server pool in another server pool (hopefully in a different part of the data center). The final option is to host the VM Manager in a different building from the VM Servers. This option provides the most protection.

If absolute uptime is required for the Oracle VM Manager, install it on physical hardware running Oracle Clusterware. This will allow for failover to occur in the event of a system failure, and by not running in a virtual environment, the loss of that environment will not affect the VM Manager.

used to manage the virtual environment, installing OEM Grid Control on a separate host system might make sense.

Oracle recommends that production environments should never run the Oracle VM Manager as a guest operating system from within the Oracle VM environment that it is managing. For maximum uptime, install the Oracle VM Manager on two separate physical systems, each running Oracle Clusterware. This will allow for maximum uptime and reliability.

Testing and development environments can safely run the Oracle VM Manager using the template with minimal issues due to their lesser uptime requirements than production environments.

Documentation is available on the Oracle website on how to create a highly available Oracle VM Manager configuration using Oracle Clusterware. Because this information tends to be updated on a frequent basis, please check the Oracle website for the latest information.

Regardless of the type of hardware—physical or virtual—the software requirements are identical.

Software Requirements for the VM Manager

The software requirements for installing the VM Manager are very straightforward and direct. For any of you who have installed the Oracle Database Server or OEM Grid Control, you are already familiar with all of the requirements necessary to install those products. Compared to those installations, this process is very straightforward because the Oracle VM Manager uses the Oracle Database 10g Express Edition (Oracle XE). Oracle XE installation requirements are very simple.

The software prerequisites for installing the Oracle VM Manager are detailed in Table 7-2.

Modifying the Firewall (If Necessary)

If a firewall is enabled on the host system, you must allow the VM Manager ports to be accessed. If you don't, then browsers will not be able to access the VM Manager, nor will the VM Manager be able to access the Agents on the VM Server systems.

Modifying the firewall is accomplished by using the system-config-securitylevel tool. If you are unfamiliar with Linux, many of the configuration tools begin with "system-". This tool will run either as a graphical tool (as shown in Figure 7-1) or as a character-based tool (as shown in Figure 7-2). This tool runs as an X-Windows application.

Component	Notes
Oracle Enterprise Linux 4.5 or Red Hat Linux 4.5 64-bit or 32-bit	Either 64-bit or 32-bit Linux can be used; however, the application is a 32-bit application. The JeOS (Just Enough OS) installation (default only) is suggested. If this system will be used for other purposes, such as a DNS or DHCP server, please check the documentation for required packages.
libaio	The libaio package is required and should be installed from the installation medium that was used to install the OS.
Verify ports 8888 and 8889	Before installing, make sure these ports are available. This can be done via the **netstat** command. The following commands will tell you if the required ports are in use: **netstat –na | grep 8888** **netstat –na | grep 8889** If you don't get a response, then the ports are available.
Enable ports 8888 and 8889 through the firewall	If a firewall is enabled, allow ports 8888 and 8889 to be accessed through the firewall. How to do this is detailed later in this section.
Optionally enable SSL port	If the use of SSL is required, port 4443 must be enabled as well. How to do this is detailed later in this section.

TABLE 7-2. *Software Requirements for the Oracle VM Manager*

Follow these steps to enable access through the firewall for ports 8888 and 8889 and optionally 4443:

1. Select Enabled for the security level.

2. Click Customize in the Other Ports fields.

3. Enter this text: **8888:tcp,8889:tcp** or optionally **8888:tcp,8889:tcp,4443:tcp** as shown in Figure 7-3.

4. Save the configuration.

Once you've met the prerequisites, you are ready to install the Oracle VM Manager.

FIGURE 7-1. *The system-config-securitylevel tool (graphical)*

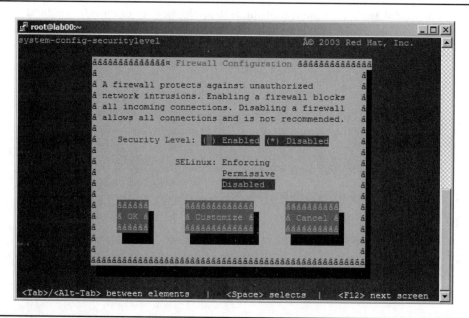

FIGURE 7-2. *The system-config-securitylevel tool (character-based)*

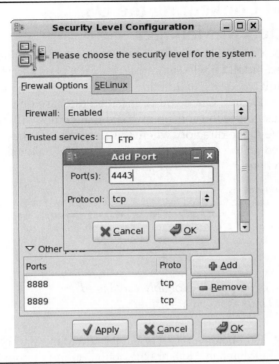

FIGURE 7-3. *The system-config-securitylevel tool*

TightVNC Installation

You must also install TightVNC on the Oracle VM Manager system to allow for access via the VM Console. You can download TightVNC from http://oss.oracle .com/oraclevm/manager/RPMS. Once you've downloaded the TightVNC rpm from Oracle, you install it using the **rpm** command, for example, **run rpm –ivh <TightVNC>.rpm**. Once TightVNC is installed, Windows clients can invoke VM Console mode.

Installing VM Manager

Installing the VM Manager is not a difficult process. Once the system has been properly configured for the installation, the installation itself is fairly straightforward. Only when you get to the stage where you are configuring Oracle VM does the complexity begin.

Installing and Configuring the OS for the Oracle VM Manager

Oracle recommends a minimal (default) Linux installation be used to install the Oracle VM Manager. Install Oracle Enterprise Linux (OEL) or Red Hat Enterprise Linux with the default packages. In addition, allocate hardware resources as shown earlier in this chapter. Once you've installed the base OS, you need to install libaio. It is best to use the version of libaio that comes with the Linux distribution. Navigate to the directory where this package is found (which CD it is on may vary, based on the version). Once there, install libaio using the **rpm** command as shown here:

```
# rpm -ivh libaio-0.3.106-3.2.i386.rpm
warning: libaio-0.3.106-3.2.i386.rpm: Header V3 DSA signature: NOKEY, key ID 1e5e0159
Preparing...                ######################################### [100%]
        package libaio-0.3.106-3.2.i386 is already installed
```

NOTE
The exact version of libaio will probably vary based on the version of Linux that you are using.

Once you've installed libaio, you can install the VM Manager. The VM Manager is delivered as a CD-ROM image. Here are the options to install from this image:

- **Create a CD-ROM**   Once you have a CD-ROM, it can be mounted on the system and then used as the installation source.

- **Mount the image as a virtual CD-ROM (virtual machine only)**   This allows the image to be accessed as if it were a CD-ROM.

- **Mount the image using the loop device**   An ISO image can be mounted directly on the system using this syntax: **mount –o loop <image> <mount point>**. This method is used for the example:

  ```
  # mount -o loop /tmp/OracleVM-Manager-2.2.0.iso /media/image
  ```

Once the ISO image has been mounted, change the directory to the mount point. You will run the installation from here.

Installing the VM Manager

From the mount point where the image has been mounted, you can run the runInstaller.sh script. Because the script isn't created with execute permissions, use the **sh** command to run it as shown here:

```
[root@test0 image]# cd /media/image
[root@test0 image]# ls
EULA  LICENSE  readme.txt  runInstaller.sh  scripts  source  TRANS.TBL
[root@test0 image]# sh runInstaller.sh
hostname: Unknown host
Welcome to Oracle VM Manager 2.2

Please enter the choice: [1|2|3]
1. Install Oracle VM Manager
2. Uninstall Oracle VM Manager
3. Upgrade Oracle VM Manager
```

Select Install Oracle VM Manager from the prompt by entering **1**.

```
1

Starting Oracle VM Manager 2.2 installation ...

Do you want to install a new database or use an existing one? [1|2]
1. Install a new Oracle XE database on localhost
2. Use an existing Oracle database in my network
```

In most cases, select option 1 to create a new Oracle XE database on the local system. Once you've selected option 1 again, the following feedback should be displayed. Choosing the default configuration for the management and listener ports is okay. The output should look something like this:

```
1

Prepare to install the Oracle XE database ...
Checking the supported platforms ... Done

Checking the prerequisite packages are installed ... Done

Checking the available disk space ... Done

Installing the oracle-xe-univ package (rpm) now ... Done

Oracle Database 10g Express Edition Configuration
-------------------------------------------------
This will configure on-boot properties of Oracle Database 10g Express
Edition.  The following questions will determine whether the database should
be starting upon system boot, the ports it will use, and the passwords that
will be used for database accounts.  Press <Enter> to accept the defaults.
Ctrl-C will abort.
```

```
Specify the HTTP port that will be used for Oracle Application Express [8080]:

Specify a port that will be used for the database listener [1521]:

Specify a password to be used for database accounts.  Note that the same
password will be used for SYS and SYSTEM.  Oracle recommends the use of
different passwords for each database account.  This can be done after
initial configuration:
Confirm the password:

Do you want Oracle Database 10g Express Edition to be started on boot (y/n) [y]:

Starting Oracle Net Listener ... Done
Configuring Database ... Done
Starting Oracle Database 10g Express Edition Instance ... Done
Installation Completed Successfully.
To access the Database Home Page go to "http://127.0.0.1:8080/apex"

Checking the availability of the database ...

Set default database schema to 'OVS'.
Please enter the password for account 'OVS':
Confirm the password:

Creating the Oracle VM Manager database schema ... Done

Installing the ovs-manager package (rpm) ... Done

Installing the oc4j package (rpm) ... Done

Please enter the password for account 'oc4jadmin':
Confirm the password:

Starting OC4J ... Done.
To access the OC4J Home Page and change the password go to http://127.0.0.1:8888/em
Deploying Oracle VM Manager application to OC4J container.
Creating connection pool ... Done
Creating data source ... Done
Deploying application help ... Done
Deploying application ... Done

Please enter the keystore password for the Web Service:
Confirm the password:

Setting keystore password for Web Service ... Done
Do you want to use HTTPS access for Oracle VM Manager (Y|n)?y

Configuring OC4J to use HTTPS ... Done
Stopping OC4J ... Done
Starting OC4J ... Done

Please enter the password for the default account 'admin':
Confirm the password:
Configuring SMTP server ...
Please enter the outgoing SMTP mail server(e.g. - mail.abc.com, mail.abc.com:25):
mail.ptc.com
```

```
Mail server checking, may need some time, please wait ...
Mail server 'mail.ptc.com' check failed, enter Y to change the name and retry or
N to keep hostname and continue(Y|n)?n
Setting the SMTP server to mail.ptc.com ... Done

Please enter an e-mail address for account 'admin': admin@ptc.com
Confirm the e-mail address: admin@ptc.com
Unable to send an email to 'admin@ptc.com', would you like to change the email
address(Y|n)?n
Updating e-mail address for account 'admin' to 'admin@ptc.com' ... Done

The console feature is not enabled by default.
For detailed setup, refer to Oracle VM Manager User's Guide

Installation of Oracle VM Manager completed successfully.

To access the Oracle VM Manager 2.2 home page go to:
    https://127.0.0.1:4443/OVS

To access the Oracle VM Manager web services WSDL page go to:
    https://127.0.0.1:4443/OVSWS/LifecycleService.wsdl
    https://127.0.0.1:4443/OVSWS/ResourceService.wsdl
    https://127.0.0.1:4443/OVSWS/PluginService.wsdl
    https://127.0.0.1:4443/OVSWS/ServerPoolService.wsdl
    https://127.0.0.1:4443/OVSWS/VirtualMachineService.wsdl
    https://127.0.0.1:4443/OVSWS/AdminService.wsdl

To access the Oracle VM Manager help page go to:
    https://127.0.0.1:4443/help/help
```

NOTE
You will be asked to input a number of passwords along the way. You can either use the same password for all of the components or choose to create individual passwords for each component. If you are using individual passwords, it's a good idea to write them down as you go.

As the installation progresses, you can watch the log files, which are stored in /var/log/ovm-manager. There are several log files, including the following:

- **ovm-manager.log**   This log is the VM Manager installation log.

- **db.log**   This log contains the database portion of the installation and is very useful for debugging any problems that might have occurred during the database portion of the installation.

- **oc4j.log**   This log contains the OC4J installation logs.

You can follow along as these logs are being written by using the **tail –f** command. With **tail –f**, you can see what the installation process is writing to the logs.

If you want to use an existing database, you can do this with Oracle XE, Oracle Database 10*g*, or Oracle Database 11*g* (Standard Edition, Enterprise Edition, or RAC). If you select to use an existing database, you will be prompted for the host name, listener port, SID, and SYS password. These answers will be used to define the connection to the repository database. In addition, you will be prompted for the schema where you want to install the VM Manager repository and for the OVS password. Once you've defined these, the installation proceeds as shown in this section.

Upgrading the VM Manager

Upgrading the VM Manager is a very straightforward process. From the initial installation screen, select option 3: Upgrade Oracle VM Manager. You will be prompted for several passwords and whether you want to back up the repository database or not. Once you've selected these options, the VM Manager will be upgraded without additional input.

Installing the VM Manager Template

In addition to the manual installation process, the Oracle VM Manager can be installed by downloading and installing a template from Oracle. Even though the Oracle VM Manager can be installed on either a 64-bit or 32-bit version of Linux, the Oracle VM Manager Template is a 32-bit Linux system.

Oracle has a number of virtual machine templates that you can download from their site. The Oracle VM Manager Template can be found in the 32-bit section of Oracle VM Templates. Download the template to the /OVS/seed_pool directory and unzip the files using the **unzip** command. Approximately 4GB of space is needed. After running unzip, the following files should exist in the /OVS/running_pool directory:

- Deploy_Manager_Template.sh

- OVM_EL5U3_X86_OVM_MANAGER_PVM.tgz

Normally, you would use the VM Manager to import the template and to create the virtual machine, but since that is not possible, you are required to manually create a virtual machine.

A number of prerequisites must be met before the VM Manager Template is installed. These prerequisites include:

- A new installation of a VM Server 2.2.0 system that has not been managed by any other VM Manager. This is usually the VM Server that the VM Manager Template is being installed on.

- The latest OVS Agent. You can download this from http://oss.oracle.com/oraclevm/server/2.2/RPMS/.

- A working VM Server 2.2.0 that you can install the VM Manager virtual machine on.

- At least 15GB of space in the /OVS/running_pool directory.

- At least 2GB of free memory on the VM Server system.

- A static IP address for the VM Manager.

- A VNC viewer.

- A shared disk system such as OCFS2 or NFS (if you're going to use HA).

Once you've met the prerequisites, you can use the VM Manager Template to create a virtual machine with the VM Manager.

Follow these steps to create the virtual machine:

1. Change the directory to the directory where the zip file was unzipped.

2. Run the Deploy_Manager_Template.sh script.

3. During the installation, you will need to answer the following questions:

   - The password for the VM Agent

   - Permission to build the VM Manager without HA (if no HA disk is found)

   - The static IP address of the VM Manager system

   - The netmask of the VM Manager system

   - The default gateway of the VM Manager system

   - The DNS Server for the VM Manager system

   - The hostname of the VM Manager system

   - The passwords for the following accounts:

- Database sys user

- OVS

- oc4jadmin

- Keystore password for the Web Service

4. At the prompt, select whether to use HTTPS or HTTP for VM Manager access. HTTPS provides a higher level of security than HTTP.

5. At the prompt, enter the admin password for the VM Manager.

6. At the next prompt, enter the SMTP system hostname.

7. At the prompt, enter the name of the server pool.

8. At the next prompt, enter the name and password of the account on the VM Server. This can be root with root's password.

9. Confirm all of the parameter values specified.

10. Complete the guest virtual machine configuration:

```
[root@ptc7 VMManager]# sh Deploy_Manager_Template.sh
Starting prerequisite checking ...

Checking the Oracle VM Server ... Done
Checking the xend status ... running
Done
Checking the Oracle VM Agent version ... Done
Checking the Oracle VM Agent status ... Done
Checking the Oracle VM Server free memory: 2122 MB
Done
Checking the available disk space ...
[ * ] c8be195f-d82f-4c43-8958-acd11b5fddc7 => /dev/sda3
**/dev/sda3 mounted, set as cluster root.
[ R ] c8be195f-d82f-4c43-8958-acd11b5fddc7 => /dev/sda3
You have 44 GB in /var/ovs/mount/C8BE195FD82F4438958ACD11B5FDDC7
Checking the running pool directory .../var/ovs/mount/C8BE195FD82F4-
C438958ACD11B5FDDC7/running_pool
Done
Checking the HA cluster prerequisite ...
Please enter the password for Oracle VM Agent: cluster_precheck...2.3
ptc
You can't enable HA for Oracle VM Manager now for the possible reasons:
1. The /var/ovs/mount/C8BE195FD82F4C438958ACD11B5FDDC7 is not a clustered
OCFS2 or NFS file system
2. There are one or more local repositories which are not clustered OCFS2 or
NFS file system

Do you want to continue deploying the Oracle VM Manager with disabled HA(Y|n,
default: y
[root@ptc7 VMManager]# sh Deploy_Manager_Template.sh
Starting prerequisite checking ...
```

```
Checking the Oracle VM Server ... Done
Checking the xend status ...running
Done
Checking the Oracle VM Agent version ... Done
Checking the Oracle VM Agent status ... Done
Checking the Oracle VM Server free memory: 2122 MB
Done
Checking the available disk space ...
[ * ] c8be195f-d82f-4c43-8958-acd11b5fddc7 => /dev/sda3
**/dev/sda3 mounted, set as cluster root.
[ R ] c8be195f-d82f-4c43-8958-acd11b5fddc7 => /dev/sda3
You have 44 GB in /var/ovs/mount/C8BE195FD82F4C438958ACD11B5FDDC7
Checking the running pool directory .../var/ovs/mount/C8BE195FD82F4-
C438958ACD11B5FDDC7/running_pool
Done
Checking the HA cluster prerequisite ...
Please enter the password for Oracle VM Agent: cluster_precheck...2.3

You can't enable HA for Oracle VM Manager now for the possible reasons:
1. The /var/ovs/mount/C8BE195FD82F4C438958ACD11B5FDDC7 is not a clustered
OCFS2 or NFS file system
2. There are one or more local repositories which are not clustered OCFS2 or
NFS file system

Do you want to continue deploying the Oracle VM Manager with disabled HA(Y|n,
default: yes)? y
continue...
Checking whether Oracle VM Agent DB is clean ... Done

Setting up the network for Oracle VM Manager ...
Oracle VM Manager needs to be configured using a static IP address. Follow
the prompts to provide your network settings for Oracle VM Manager.

Press any key to continue...
Enter static IP address: 192.168.1.10
Enter netmask: [255.255.255.0]
Enter gateway: 192.168.1.1
Enter DNS server: 192.168.1.1

Enter hostname (e.g, host.domain.com): vmcontrol.ptc.com
Generating parameter file ...


Note following password setting will be used for SYS and SYSTEM. Oracle
                recommends the use of different passwords for each database
account.
                This can be done after initial configuration.

Specify a password to be used for database accounts:
Confirm the password:

Please enter the password for account 'OVS':
Confirm the password:

Please enter the password for account 'oc4jadmin':
Confirm the password:
```

```
Please enter the keystore password for Web Service:
Confirm the password:

Do you want to use HTTPS access for Oracle VM Manager (Y|n)? n

Please enter the password for the default account 'admin':
Confirm the password:

Please enter the outgoing mail server (SMTP) hostname: mail.yahoo.com

Please enter an e-mail address for account 'admin': admin@yahoo.com
Confirm the e-mail address: admin@yahoo.com

Set Oracle VM Server Information:
Enter the Server Pool Name: vmpool

Enter the Oracle VM Server login user name: root
Enter the Oracle VM Server login password:
Please confirm the following information:
             Server Pool name                  : vmpool
             Oracle VM Server name              : ptc7
             Oracle VM Server login user name   : root
             Enable HA                          : false

Is the Oracle VM Server information correct(Y|n)? y
Untar the Oracle VM Manager template tarball ...
Untar the Oracle VM Manager template tarball ... Done
Move the parameter file to Manager.img
Done
Create Oracle VM Manager virtual machine ... Done
The Oracle VM Manager virtual machine is booting. To finish the Oracle VM
Manager configuration, connect to the virtual machine console using any
VNC Viewer from a desktop machine via the command:
vncviewer ptc7:5900

After Oracle VM Manager has been successfully deployed, access the Oracle
VM Manager home page at:
http://192.168.1.10:8888/OVS
```

This example of the Oracle VM Manager Template setup might vary with later versions or with any customizations or choices that you might make. However, it should be fairly similar.

TIP
There are two OS user accounts that are created by default:
user: root password: ovsroot
user: oracle password: oracle
The user 'oracle' belongs to the 'oinstall' and 'dba' groups. Also, the default vnc console password is 'oracle'. Please change these passwords as soon as possible.

Once you've configured the virtual machine, it is ready for you to use as the VM Manager server. The VM Manager has been preinstalled and configured as part of the template configuration steps.

Managing the VM Manager Host System

There is not a lot of management to do on the VM Manager system. The regular, required maintenance is really not different from the regular maintenance required for any Linux system and includes backups, log maintenance, and performance monitoring. There are a few slight differences between managing a physical machine and managing a virtual machine. These will be covered in the next sections.

Managing the VM Manager Physical Machine

Managing a physical VM Manager system is the same as managing any physical Linux server. Make regular backups of the system and especially of files that regularly change, including the VM Manager database repository. As with any physical system, normal maintenance routines, such as performance monitoring and error log monitoring, should be performed. There really isn't much required maintenance.

Managing the VM Manager Virtual Machine

Managing the VM Manager virtual machine is slightly different from managing a normal Linux virtual machine because the typical virtual machine is managed via the VM Manager. If a maintenance task requires shutting down the VM Manager guest, use command-line tools rather than the VM Manager; otherwise, it might leave the VM Manager in an inconsistent state.

If the VM Manager virtual machine is shut down, you cannot start it using the VM Manager. This is solved via the XM commands. You can easily start the virtual machine using the **xm create** command, as shown here:

```
# xm create /OVS/running_pool/<virtual system name>/vm.cfg
```

Similarly, you can shut down the VM Manager virtual machine using the **xm shutdown** command. This command will shut down the guest OS and power off the guest system. This command is shown here:

```
# xm shutdown <virtual system name>
```

As with the physical machine, there are a few regular maintenance tasks to perform such as backups and log management. By using a Just enough OS (JeOS) system, you do not have a lot of extraneous services and processes to worry about.

In general, neither the physical nor virtual VM Manager system requires a great deal of care. Treat them as a standard Linux system and perform standard maintenance operations.

Managing the VM Manager

The VM Manager is made up of the Oracle XE database and the OC4J applications. If necessary, you can start and stop the VM Manager with the **/sbin/service oc4j** command. The following commands are valid:

- **/sbin/service oc4j stop**   Stops the oc4j service.

- **/sbin/service oc4j start**   Starts the oc4j service.

- **/sbin/service oc4j status**   Returns the status of the oc4j service.

Using these commands, you can stop, start, or restart the oc4j service (and VM Manager) if necessary. Because they are part of the Linux services, they are started and stopped automatically with the system.

Summary

This chapter covered the tasks necessary to configure a Linux system to be ready to install the Oracle VM Manager. This method is often the preferred one for installing the VM Manager. Optionally, you can download the VM Manager virtual machine template from Oracle and install the VM Manager in the virtual machine environment.

Additionally this chapter covered the tasks necessary to perform regular maintenance on the virtual or physical machine that hosts the VM Manager. The bulk of the work in setting up the VM Manager environment is in the configuration of the VM Manager itself. This will be covered in later chapters.

CHAPTER
8

Configuring the Oracle
VM Management Pack

he last chapter covered the first of several ways to manage the Oracle VM system, through the Oracle VM Manager. The second way to manage the Oracle VM system is via the Oracle VM Management Pack for Oracle Enterprise Manager (OEM) Grid Control. This management pack allows you to manage virtual machines alongside other components of your enterprise that you are managing, such as databases, application servers, and so on.

This chapter introduces the OEM Grid Control Manager and shows you how to install and use the Oracle VM Management Pack, which you can then use within Grid Control. For those of you who might not be familiar with OEM Grid Control, the chapter begins with a brief overview of Grid Control and how to utilize it.

Oracle Enterprise Manager Grid Control

Oracle Enterprise Manager (known as OEM) is an Oracle premier tool to monitor and manage the enterprise grid and the applications that reside on it. OEM is a scalable, high-performance application that resides throughout the enterprise, providing information to a central repository that monitors these systems, sending alerts and initiating corrective action as necessary. OEM is now in its second generation with the newly released OEM 11*g*.

OEM provides graphical monitoring, dashboards, and root-cause analysis. Using the add-on packs, OEM can analyze all layers of an application, offering complete monitoring of the application stack. This gives you quick problem resolution and diagnostics. In addition, OEM sends alerts and takes corrective action.

OEM is a complete solution; however, you can integrate it with other packages and systems as desired. In addition, add-on monitoring packs have been developed by both Oracle and third-party vendors for purposes of extensibility and so you can customize each environment. Finally, you can also configure custom metrics and reports, allowing for very specific application monitoring and reporting.

OEM is composed of four major components: the database repository, the Oracle Management Server (OMS), the management console, and the Intelligent Agent.

Database Repository

The database repository holds performance, state, and configuration information. The repository can be held in an Oracle 10*g* or 11*g* database. The size of the database is determined by how many targets are monitored, the type of target, and how long the data should be saved. Once the data has been saved in the database, you can retrieve it later without having to access the target being monitored. This provides for maximum efficiency and performance.

The database repository is a standard Oracle database. The database repository has its own Oracle Home where the Oracle binaries are stored as well as a database.

This database can be created as part of the OEM installation, or you can use an existing database.

Oracle Management Service

The OMS is the Grid Control component that consists of the programs used to process the connections from the Agents and the scheduled tasks and to provide web services for the management console. The OMS is made up of a number of configuration files and a fairly large number of programs. The OMS is installed into its own Oracle Home separate from the database's Oracle Home.

Management Console

The management console is the interface in which the users view and run OEM Grid Control. The management console is a web application that provides many tabs providing different views of hosts, databases, applications, etc. In addition, the management console allows you to manage and monitor as many targets as you desire, thus giving you an enterprises-wide view of the state of operations.

Intelligent Agent

The Intelligent Agent is the heart of the OEM system. The Agent resides on each system that is being monitored and managed. The Agent collects and uploads data to the OMS server, which, in turn, inserts that data into the database repository. The Agent is also responsible for running scheduled tasks as well as performing corrective action that might be required.

There is usually only one Agent per server. This Agent monitors and manages all of the targets that are present on that server. Although one Agent per server is recommended, there are some cases where multiple Agents are installed on a server. This setup usually occurs where both a primary and standby OEM system are monitoring the same server. In this case, multiple Agents are required.

OEM Plug-ins and Connectors

In addition to the standard OEM Grid Control components, both Oracle and third-party vendors offer a number of plug-ins and connectors to extend Grid Control's capabilities.

A *plug-in* is an additional component that allows you to monitor both Oracle and third-party applications, such as storage. A number of plug-ins are available from the Oracle website and include the following (among others):

- **IBM DB2 Database**   Monitors and manages the IBM DB2 RDBMS.

- **Microsoft SQL Server**   Monitors and manages Microsoft SQL Server RDBMS.

- **Sybase Adaptive Server**   Monitors Sybase ASE Servers.

- **TimesTen In-Memory DB**   Monitors the Oracle TimesTen In-Memory Database.

- **Exadata Storage Server**   Monitors the Exadata Storage Server.

- **NetApp Filer**   Monitors the network appliance filers.

- **EMC Celerra**   Monitors the Celerra Servers.

- **EMC Symmetrix**   Monitors and provides performance information on EMC DMX storage.

- **EMC Clariion**   Monitors and provides performance information on the EMC Clariion storage system.

- **Application servers**   Monitors application servers such as JBoss, Apache Tomcat, IBM WebSphere, Microsoft Active Directory, Microsoft IIS, etc.

- **Virtualization servers**   Provides plug-ins for Oracle VM as well as VMware ESX server.

In addition to the Oracle-provided plug-ins, a number of plug-ins are provided by Oracle partners. These are also available on the Oracle website.

A *connector* is an add-in component that extends OEM Grid Control by allowing it to integrate with other monitoring products. Basically, a connector is a conduit to share OEM monitoring data with these other products. Some of the OEM connectors include:

- **BMC Remedy Service Desk**   Integrates with BMC's Remedy product to provide seamless connectivity to its workflow and incident management system.

- **PeopleSoft Enterprise HelpDesk**   Seamlessly integrates with the PeopleSoft HelpDesk to provide management and resolution.

- **Siebel HelpDesk**   Integrates with the Siebel HelpDesk.

- **HP ServiceCenter**   Integrates with HP's ServiceCenter help desk product.

- **Microsoft Operations Manager**   Provides a bidirectional exchange of alerts between Microsoft MOM and OEM.

- **HP OpenView**   Enables bidirectional exchange of alerts between HP OVO and OEM.

- **IBM Tivoli**   Enables bidirectional exchange of alerts between IBM Tivoli and OEM.

- **Microsoft products**   Provides connectors for both Microsoft System Center Operations Manager (SCOM) and Ops Center.

In addition, new connectors and plug-ins are introduced on a regular basis.

The Oracle VM Manager was developed after OEM was originally released and so was not included in the product, which is why a plug-in was developed. This plug-in easily integrates VM management with the Grid Control environment. The next section details how to install the VM Management Pack into OEM Grid Control.

Installing the Oracle VM Management Pack

Installing the VM Management Pack is similar to installing Oracle Database and Application Server patches: You verify the prerequisites and make any changes, if needed, and then apply the patch. For this particular patch, you need to follow several steps, which will be covered in the following sections. The OEM plug-in for Virtualization is delivered as an Oracle patch.

NOTE
At the time of writing this book, the virtualization patch for OEM Grid Control 10.2.0.5 is identified in Document ID 781879. This may have changed by the time you are reading this book, so please check support.oracle.com for the latest patch.

The first step in installing the Oracle VM plug-in for OEM is to download the patch and to read the README file. This file contains important information about the installation of this patch.

Prerequisites

You must meet several prerequisites before installing the patch, including verifying certain components and the Oracle inventory. The OEM Grid Control installation is made up of several Oracle Homes, and since you need to switch between them occasionally, it is convenient to use the **oraenv** command. In order for **oraenv** to reset the ORACLE_HOME environment variable, the ORACLE_SID environment variable, and the path, you must configure the /etc/oratab configuration file properly. These are example entries for OEM in /etc/oratab:

```
oms10g:/u01/oracle/OracleHomes/oms10g:N
emrep:/u01/oracle/OracleHomes/db10g:N
agent10g:/u01/oracle/OracleHomes/agent10g:N
```

Once you've set up these entries, you can set the environment using **oraenv**. In order to source (execute) the environment variables into the current environment, instead of spawning a subshell, use the **.** (dot or period), as shown here:

```
[oracle@gc01 ~]$ . oraenv
ORACLE_SID = [oracle] ? oms10g
[oracle@gc01 ~]$ echo $ORACLE_HOME
/u01/oracle/OracleHomes/oms10g
```

The oraenv program is a convenient way to set the correct environment, and because it is an Oracle-provided method, it will always work, regardless of the release or environment.

NOTE
The oraenv utility works with sh, ksh, and bash. An equivalent program coraenv is provided for C shell users.

Once the environment is set, you need to check the prerequisites.

Check Perl Version

Check the Perl version via the **perl –v** command, as shown here. Remember to use the OMS ORACLE_HOME for this test. This example uses the oraenv utility to set the correct Oracle environment for the OMS.

```
[oracle@gc01 ~]$ . oraenv
ORACLE_SID = [emrep] ? oms10g
[oracle@gc01 ~]$ perl -v

This is perl, v5.8.5 built for i386-linux-thread-multi
```

Check the OUI Inventory

To install the patch successfully, the inventory must be available and valid. Check this by using the **opatch lsinventory** command. Because this requires the path and environment variables to be properly configured, use **oraenv** to configure the environment, as shown here:

```
[oracle@gc01 ~]$ . oraenv
ORACLE_SID = [oms10g] ?
[oracle@gc01 ~]$ opatch lsinventory
Invoking OPatch 11.1.0.6.6
```

```
Oracle Interim Patch Installer version 11.1.0.6.6
Copyright (c) 2009, Oracle Corporation.  All rights reserved.


Oracle Home          : /u01/oracle/OracleHomes/oms10g
Central Inventory  : /u01/oracle/oraInventory
   from               : /etc/oraInst.loc
OPatch version     : 11.1.0.6.6
OUI version        : 10.2.0.5.0
OUI location       : /u01/oracle/OracleHomes/oms10g/oui
Log file location  : /u01/oracle/OracleHomes/oms10g/cfgtoollogs/opatch/
opatch2010-05-13_19-20-41PM.log
```

Notice the line where the Oracle inventory location is displayed. The inventory location should not change based on the value of the Oracle instance that you put into oraenv since there should be a single master inventory on the server.

OPatch

Oracle always recommends using the latest version of OPatch. OPatch can be found on support.oracle.com as note 224346.1. This support note points to the placeholder for the latest OPatch. From that location, download and install OPatch on the server you are going to patch. The opatch zip file contains the entire OPatch directory. Simply move the original OPatch directory out of the way and unzip the new one to the $ORACLE_HOME/OPatch directory. Once you've done this, the new OPatch should be available. Check by running **opatch version** as shown here:

```
[oracle@gc01 db10g]$ opatch version
Invoking OPatch 11.2.0.1.2

OPatch Version: 11.2.0.1.2

OPatch succeeded.
```

Check PAR File

Now that you've updated OPatch and set the proper path and environment variables, you need to check the PAR (Provisioning Archive) file. You check the PAR file by running the ParDeploy utility with the **–check** option, as shown here:

```
[oracle@gc01 db10g]$ /u01/oracle/OracleHomes/oms10g/bin/PARDeploy -check


ERROR !
Software Library has not been setup !
Please configure Software Library and try again.
```

If you see the preceding text, the library is not set up and must be configured. If you see a message informing you that the library is set up, you can proceed.

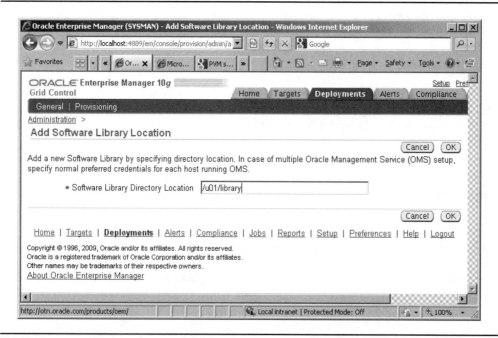

FIGURE 8-1. *OEM Grid Control Add Software Library Location screen*

You set up the library from the Grid Control provisioning page. From the OEM Grid Control console, navigate to Deployments | Provisioning | Administration, and under the Software Library Configuration section, click Add. The Add Software Library Location screen will appear as shown here in Figure 8-1.

Once this has completed, check the PAR file again. You should see the following response:

```
[oracle@gc01 db10g]$ /u01/oracle/OracleHomes/oms10g/bin/PARDeploy -check
Software Library is setup
```

Once you've verified and met these prerequisites, you can begin the actual installation.

Patching

To begin the patching process, shut down the OMS first. As mentioned before, utilize oraenv to assist with setting the correct environment variables and path. On each

OMS server, you can stop OMS using the **emctl** command from the oms10g environment.

```
[oracle@gc01 stage]$ . oraenv
ORACLE_SID = [oms10g] ?
[oracle@gc01 stage]$ emctl stop oms
Oracle Enterprise Manager 10g Release 5 Grid Control
Copyright (c) 1996, 2009 Oracle Corporation.  All rights reserved.
Oracle Management Server is Down.
```

Once the OMS is shut down, you need to connect to the Enterprise Manager repository. If the OMS and repository are on the same machine, use the repository network directory; otherwise, use the OMS network directory. You can do this by changing the TNS_ADMIN variable to point to the $ORACLE_HOME/network/admin location of the database or OMS Home network admin directory, as shown here:

```
OMS & repository on the same system        <emrep home>/network/admin
OMS & repository on different systems       <oms home>/network/admin
```

The goal is to create a tnsnames entry that points to the EM repository for each OMS server. Using sqlplus, test this by connecting into the EM repository as the sysman user:

```
[oracle@gc01 stage]$ export TNS_ADMIN=/u01/oracle/OracleHomes/db10g/network/admin
[oracle@gc01 stage]$ sqlplus sysman@emrep

SQL*Plus: Release 10.1.0.5.0 - Production on Thu May 13 21:28:46 2010

Copyright (c) 1982, 2005, Oracle.  All rights reserved.

Enter password:

Connected to:
Oracle Database 10g Enterprise Edition Release 10.1.0.5.0 - Production
With the Partitioning, OLAP and Data Mining options
```

Next, change directories to the patch directory. In this case, the patch directory is named 9380307. Once there, run OPatch. Those of you who are DBAs are very familiar with OPatch.

```
[oracle@gc01 /]$ cd /u01/stage/9380307
[oracle@gc01 9380307]$ opatch apply
Invoking OPatch 11.2.0.1.2
Oracle Interim Patch Installer version 11.2.0.1.2
Copyright (c) 2010, Oracle Corporation.  All rights reserved.
Oracle Home        : /u01/oracle/OracleHomes/oms10g
Central Inventory : /u01/oracle/oraInventory
from             : /etc/oraInst.loc
 OPatch version    : 11.2.0.1.2
 OUI version       : 10.2.0.5.0
 OUI location      : /u01/oracle/OracleHomes/oms10g/oui
```

```
Log file location : /u01/oracle/OracleHomes/oms10g/cfgtoollogs/opatch/
opatch2010-05-13_21-31-57PM..log
Patch history file: /u01/oracle/OracleHomes/oms10g/cfgtoollogs/opatch/opatch_his-
tory.txt
ApplySession applying interim patch '9380307' to OH '/u01/oracle/OracleHomes/oms10g'
Interim patch 9380307 is a superset of the patch(es) [ 8244731 ] in the Oracle Home
OPatch will rollback the subset patches and apply the given patch.

Running prerequisite checks...
Provide your email address to be informed of security issues, install and
initiate Oracle Configuration Manager. Easier for you if you use your My
Oracle Support Email address/User Name.
Visit http://www.oracle.com/support/policies.html for details.
Email address/User Name: admin@ptc.com
Password (optional):
OPatch detected non-cluster Oracle Home from the inventory and will patch the local
system only.
Please shutdown Oracle instances running out of this ORACLE_HOME on the local sys-
tem.
(Oracle Home = '/u01/oracle/OracleHomes/oms10g')
Is the local system ready for patching? [y|n] y
```

At this point, you'll see many lines of logging, which are not shown here. You might see several error messages. In the case of this example, you see a few warnings because the EM repository is an 11g database. In general, the final lines of logging should look something like this:

```
Return Code = 0

The local system has been patched and can be restarted.

--------------------------------------------------------------------------------
The following warnings have occurred during OPatch execution:
1) OUI-67620:Interim patch 9380307 is a superset of the patch(es) [ 8244731 ] in
the Oracle Home
--------------------------------------------------------------------------------
OPatch Session completed with warnings.

OPatch completed with warnings.
```

Repeat this step on all of the OMS servers. Once you've run OPatch on all OMS servers, run the post-installation script from only one server. This script is run from within SQLPlus. When prompted for the value of em_sql_root, enter **<oms home>/ sysman/admin/emdrep/sql,** spelling out the *<oms home>* directory completely.

```
[oracle@gc01 9380307]$ sqlplus sysman@emrep

SQL*Plus: Release 10.1.0.5.0 - Production on Thu May 13 21:41:53 2010

Copyright (c) 1982, 2005, Oracle.  All rights reserved.

Enter password:
```

```
Connected to:
Oracle Database 10g Enterprise Edition Release 10.1.0.5.0 - Production
With the Partitioning, OLAP and Data Mining options

SQL> @post_install_script.sql




Repository Owner: SYSMAN
job_queue_processes value before running post_install_script
---------------- ---------------
SID              Job Queue value
---------------- ---------------
emrep            1

PL/SQL procedure successfully completed.




Package body created.

No errors.
Enter value for em_sql_root: /u01/oracle/OracleHomes/oms10g/sysman/admin/emdrep/sql
```

The last few lines should look something like this:

```
job_queue_processes value after running post_install_script
---------------- ---------------
SID              Job Queue value
---------------- ---------------
emrep            1

PL/SQL procedure successfully completed.

SQL>
```

Once the SQL patching is complete, restart the OMS servers using **emctl start oms**:

```
[oracle@gc01 9380307]$ emctl start oms
Oracle Enterprise Manager 10g Release 5 Grid Control
Copyright (c) 1996, 2009 Oracle Corporation.  All rights reserved.
opmnctl: opmn is already running
Starting HTTP Server ...
Starting Oracle Management Server ...
Checking Oracle Management Server Status ...
Oracle Management Server is Up.
```

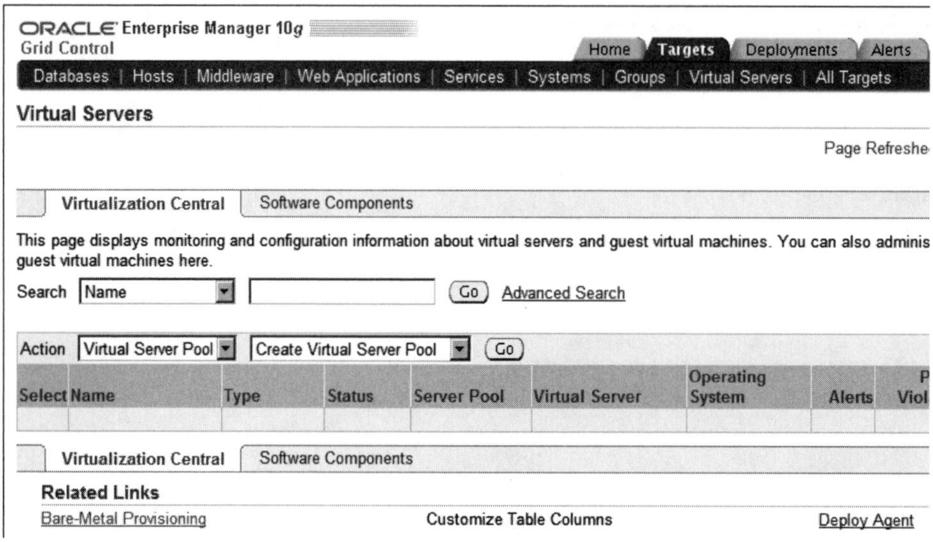

FIGURE 8-2. *Viewing the Virtual Servers Targets tab in OEM Grid Control*

Upon restarting the OEM Grid Control Console, the Virtual Servers item is now visible under the Targets tab, as shown in Figure 8-2.

When the Virtual Machines tab is visible, you've completely installed the Oracle VM Management Pack for OEM Grid Control. A few more steps are necessary to configure the Management Pack to manage virtual machines. This is covered in the next section.

Configuring the Oracle VM Management Pack

Now that you've completed the basic steps for installing the Oracle VM Management Pack for OEM Grid Control, you have some additional steps to perform in order to configure it. These steps include setting up VNC and configuring the Agents and server pools.

Configuring VNC

One of the features of Oracle VM is the ability to view and use the system console. Rather than develop a proprietary method, Oracle VM uses the industry standard Virtual Network Computing (VNC) protocol. With VNC, you can capture and display the system console for each virtual machine. In addition, VNC can be started on the virtual machines themselves, but that does not provide console access. As soon as the virtual machine begins booting, you can use VNC to watch the POST and startup steps.

VNC comes enabled with the VM Manager, but some additional steps are necessary to enable VNC with OEM Grid Control. First, you need to enable the TightVNC Java Viewer on the Grid Control OMS server.

NOTE
The TightVNC Java Viewer can be downloaded from http://oss.oracle.com/oraclevm/emplugin/tightvnc/ VncViewer.jar. Please check to make sure this is the current URL, as it might have changed since the publication of this book.

Download and copy the TightVNC Java Viewer into the *<OMS home>*/j2ee/ OC4J_em/applications/em/em directory. Once you've copied the VncViewer.jar file into this folder, restart the OMS.

Validating VM Agent and VM Server

The OEM Grid Control plug-in is only compatible with Oracle VM 2.1 and higher. Although it is unlikely that an earlier version is running, it is possible. Within Oracle VM 2.1.*x* and VM 2.2, specific versions of the Oracle VM Agent are required:

■ Oracle VM 2.1.2 or 2.1.5 requires ovs-agent 2.2-86 or higher.

■ Oracle VM 2.2 requires ovs-agent 2.2-31 or higher.

■ Oracle VM 2.2.1 requires ovs-agent 2.2-38 or higher.

You can determine the version of the Oracle VM Agent on the dom0 system by running **rpm –qa** as shown here:

```
[root@ptc7 ~]# rpm -qa | grep ovs-agent*
ovs-agent-2.3-31
```

If the version of the VM Agent is not sufficient, download the latest Agent from the Oracle Unbreakable Linux Network (ULN; http://linux.oracle.com), or download it from the Oracle technology network. You can also download it from the Oracle public yum repository at http://public-yum.oracle.com/repo/OracleVM/ OVM2/2.2.1/base/i386/ovs-agent-2.3-38.noarch.rpm.

Upgrading the VM Agent Using ULN

Upgrading the VM Agent using ULN is very easy. You only need to perform a couple of steps. The first step is to shut down the Oracle VM Agent using the **service ovs-agent** command, as shown here:

```
[root@ptc7 ~]# service ovs-agent stop
OVSAgentServer shutdown...
OVSAgentServer stopped.
```

Then upgrade the agent by entering **up2date -u**, as shown here:

```
[root@ptc7 ~]# up2date -u ovs-agent
```

Once you've upgraded the Agent, check it once again with the **rpm –qa** command to verify it has been correctly updated. Once that is done, you can restart the Agent. Start the Agent using the **service** command, as shown here:

```
[root@ptc7 ~]# service ovs-agent start
OVSAgentServer is now starting...
OVSAgentServer started.
```

In addition to the ULN, the ovs-agent package can be downloaded from the Oracle website as shown in the next section.

Upgrading the VM Agent Using RPMS

To upgrade the VM Agent using RPMS, first download the Agent RPM and then upgrade using the **rpm** command. The VM Agent can be found downloaded from these sites:

- http://oss.oracle.com/oraclevm/server/2.1

- http://oss.oracle.com/oraclevm/server/2.2

Find the latest Agent and download it. Once you've done that, stop, upgrade, and then restart the Agent. Stop the Agent using the following command:

```
[root@ptc7 ~]# service ovs-agent stop
OVSAgentServer shutdown...
OVSAgentServer stopped.
```

Upgrade the Agent using the **rpm –Uvh** command, as shown here:

```
[root@ptc7 ~]# rpm -Uvh ovs-agent-2.3-38.noarch.rpm
```

Once the Agent has been upgraded, check it once again with the **rpm –qa** command to verify that the Agent has been correctly updated. Then you can restart the Agent, using the **service** command, as shown here:

```
[root@ptc7 ~]# service ovs-agent start
OVSAgentServer is now starting...
OVSAgentServer started.
```

Once you've updated the agent and applied the patches, you still have a few more configuration steps needed for managing Oracle VM from OEM Grid Control.

Managing the Virtual Environment with OEM Grid Control

Once you have upgraded OEM Grid Control to support Oracle VM Management, you need to perform a few additional steps to configure the VM Server. The first step involves registering the server pool and the servers into Grid Control. Once you've completed this step, you can create new virtual machines in this environment.

The first step in setting up a VM Server for administration by OEM Grid Control is to add the server pool and server to the Grid Control Manager. Once the Virtual Server Management has been added to OEM Grid Control, you can find it by navigating to Targets and then selecting the Virtual Servers screen, which was shown in Figure 8-2. Initially, you will not see any servers or server pools.

Creating Server Pool

The first step is to add the server pool. This server pool must include at least one server, which acts as the server pool master. The server must not be managed by any other management server such as the VM Manager.

Clear the Agent Configuration

In order to remove an already managed server from VM Manager, follow these steps:

1. Stop the VM Agent by entering the command **service ovs-agent stop**.

2. Remove the configuration files. The files to be removed reside in /etc/ovs-agent/db. Remove these files with the command **rm –rf /etc/ovs-agent/db/***.

3. Start the VM Agent with the command **service ovs-agent start**.

Once the VM Server Agent has been cleared and is ready to be managed, bring it under control of the OEM Grid Control system.

Create the Server Pool and Server Configuration

From the Action drop-down list, select Action Virtual Server Pool and Create Server Pool and then click Go. The Create Virtual Server Pool screen will be displayed. Fill this screen in as shown in Figure 8-3.

NOTE
If the requiretty parameter is set in the /etc/sudoers file on the virtual server dom0 system, the Create Virtual Server Pool process will fail. Check the /etc/sudoers file for the following line:

```
Defaults     requiretty
```

If this line exists, comment it out as shown here:

```
#Defaults     requiretty
```

This will allow the process to succeed.

The following information must be provided to complete the Create Virtual Server Pool process:

- **Server Pool Name**   The name of the server pool that is being created.

- **Virtual Server Host**   The name of the VM Server.

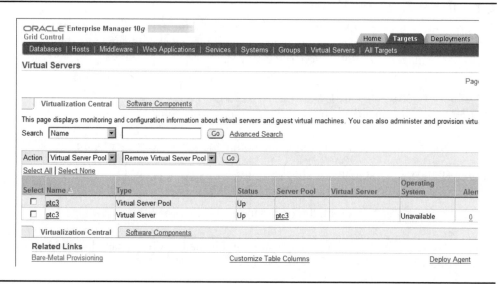

FIGURE 8-3.   *The Create Virtual Server Pool screen*

- **Monitoring Server Agent**   This is an active OEM Grid Control Agent and can be any existing Agent. In this example, it is the Agent that is on the Grid Control OMS Server itself. It must be a 10.2.0.5 Agent or newer.

- **Monitoring Server User**   Username of the Grid Control Agent owner.

- **Monitoring Server Password**   The previous user's password.

- **SSH Username**   The username on the virtual server that you are adding to the server pool.

- **SSH Password**   The previous user's password.

- **Oracle VM Agent Password**   The password of the OVS Agent on the virtual server you are adding.

- **OVS Proxy Location**   An existing staging directory on the virtual server.

Once you've filled in the fields on the screen and clicked the OK button, an OEM Grid Control job will run to create the virtual server pool. After the job has completed, the newly added virtual server pool will be visible, as shown in Figure 8-4.

Not all information will be immediately available. Items such as the Operating System might take a little while to be discovered and propagated. At this point, all that is left is to import any virtual machines that might already exist on that virtual server.

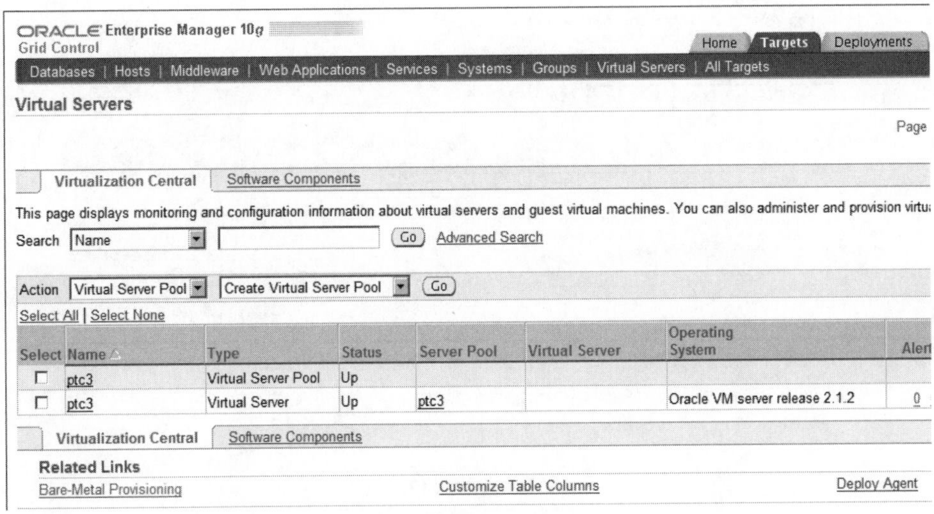

FIGURE 8-4.   *The Virtual Servers screen*

Importing Virtual Machines

Once the options have been selected and the virtual server pool(s) and virtual server(s) are visible, the final step in installing and configuring them with OEM Grid Control is to import any currently existing virtual machines into this environment. If this is a new installation, there will be no virtual machines, but if you're migrating this environment from the VM Manager, the virtual machines should be imported. To import existing virtual machines, select the virtual server pool to be scanned and then select Virtual Server Pool from the Action drop-down and then Discover Guest VM, as shown in Figure 8-5.

If there are Guest VMs already in this environment, they will appear in the Discover Guest VM screen, as shown in Figure 8-6. On this screen, you will configure the Guest VM Username and Password as well as the VNC Console Password. Since these are existing machines, use the already existing usernames and passwords in this current example.

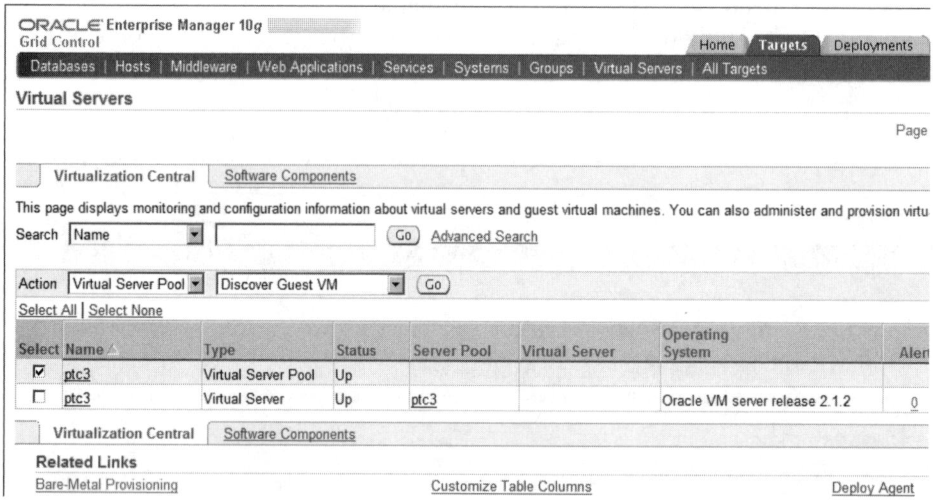

FIGURE 8-5. *Discover Guest VM*

Results

Select All | Select None

Select	Guest VM Name	Operating System	Guest VM Username	Guest VM Password	VNC Console Password
☐	370_ptc03	Oracle Enterprise Linux 4 ▼			
☐	780_ptc09	Oracle Enterprise Linux 4 ▼			
☐	790_ptc07	Oracle Enterprise Linux 4 ▼			
☐	875_ptc11	Oracle Enterprise Linux 4 ▼			

☑ TIP If you register a Running VM, the VNC password specified here will apply only after you reboot the VM.

FIGURE 8-6. *The Discover Guest VM screen*

The information may or may not have been picked up correctly, depending on the virtual machine's OS. If necessary, correct the operating system values. After filling in all of the required values and selecting all of the desired Guest VMs as shown in Figure 8-7, click Register VM to begin the VM registration process.

The Job Confirmation screen will appear, which you have probably seen before. If there are no issues, the Virtual Server screen will return first with a VM status of Discovering and eventually with a status of Running, as shown in Figure 8-8.

At this point, OEM Grid Control is now managing the Oracle VM environment. Throughout the remainder of this book, OEM Grid Control will be used for managing Oracle virtual machines.

Results

Select All | Select None

Select	Guest VM Name	Operating System	Guest VM Username	Guest VM Password	VNC Console Password
☑	370_ptc03	Oracle Enterprise Linux 5 ▼	root	••••••••	••••••
☑	780_ptc09	Oracle Enterprise Linux 5 ▼	root	••••••••	••••••
☑	790_ptc07	Oracle Enterprise Linux 5 ▼	root	••••••••	••••••
☑	875_ptc11	Oracle Enterprise Linux 5 ▼	root	••••••••	••••••

☑ TIP If you register a Running VM, the VNC password specified here will apply only after you reboot the VM.

FIGURE 8-7. *The completed Discover Guest VM screen*

FIGURE 8-8. *The Virtual Servers screen with virtual machines*

Summary

This chapter covered the process for installing and configuring OEM Grid Control to manage the Oracle VM environment. You now have several ways to create and manage Oracle VM virtual machines and servers. The methods include

- **Oracle VM Manager** The Oracle VM Manager provides a web-based utility to manage the entire VM environment.

- **OEM Grid Control VM plug-in** With this plug-in, the virtualized environment can be managed in the same manner as with the VM Manager. In addition, other components in the environment, such as applications on the VM Guests, can be monitored and managed as well.

- **Oracle VM CLI** The command-line interface provides a method for scripting many of the activities that are needed in the virtual environment.

- **Xen Tools** The Xen XM commands can be used to manage an individual VM Server.

Which tool is the right tool for a specific job or environment will be determined by that environment. In many cases, you might need and use a variety of tools concurrently.

CHAPTER
9

Installing and Configuring the Oracle VM CLI

ne might ask why anybody would be interested in a command-line interface (CLI) in this day and age, when we have several great graphical tools to configure and manage Oracle VM. The simple answer is this: scripting. By using the OVM CLI, you can easily generate and reuse scripts to perform many of the day-to-day tasks that you generally repeat with slight variations. In addition, you can automate tasks that involve many steps using the CLI.

Introduction to Oracle VM CLI

The Oracle VM CLI or command-line interface is a command-line method of performing many of the functions of the VM Manager. By using the command line, you do not need to use a browser or graphical user interface (GUI). However, the most advantageous feature of the Oracle VM CLI is the ability to take repetitious tasks and script them so you can then modify and run them over and over again without having to go through all of the normal keystrokes necessary in the GUI tools.

The OVM CLI is a front-end interface to the Oracle VM Manager. The VM Manager, rather than the Oracle VM Management Pack, must be configured as the management device for the VM Servers. The OVM CLI does not work with the Management Pack plug-in for OEM Grid Control. With that out of the way, let's look at how to configure and install the Oracle VM CLI.

You have several ways to install the Oracle VM CLI: either via the Unbreakable Linux Network (ULN), via the Oracle public yum servers, or via download and RPM. The first two choices are definitely the easiest to implement and the recommended methods. This chapter focuses on those methods of installing the Oracle VM CLI.

Installing OVM CLI with the ULN

In order to install the Oracle VM CLI either using the Unbreakable Linux Network (ULN) or using the Oracle public yum servers, you need to configure them for access. Because these processes are different, they will be covered separately in the next few sections.

Configuring ULN

To configure the ULN, you need to connect into the ULN website and register.

1. First connect to http://linux.oracle.com using a web browser. The first screen you will see is the welcome screen, as shown next:

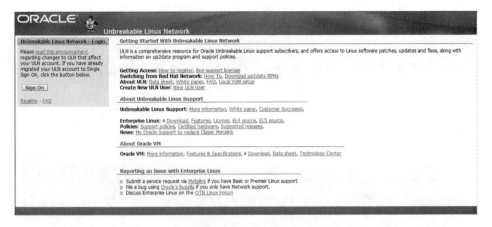

2. Once the connection has been established, the Oracle Single Sign-On screen appears. Sign on using the same login that you use to connect to the Oracle Support website or the Oracle Technology Network website. This screen is not shown for obvious reasons.

3. At the next screen, enter a valid Oracle CSI number that contains support for the Unbreakable Linux Network. Again, for security reasons, this screen is not shown. When you have entered this, the Home screen is shown, along with a list of subscribed channels:

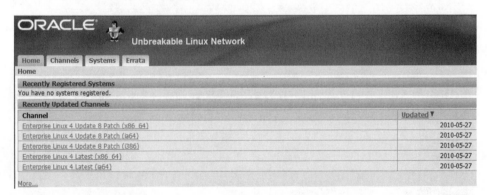

4. At this point, the ULN is configured, but the Linux system that you will install the Oracle VM CLI on is not configured with the ULN. You do this by registering the system with ULN using the **up2date** command. From a graphical console (or VNC), invoke the ULN registration by running the following command:

```
$ up2date -register
```

5. A window then pops up, requesting to install the GPG key:

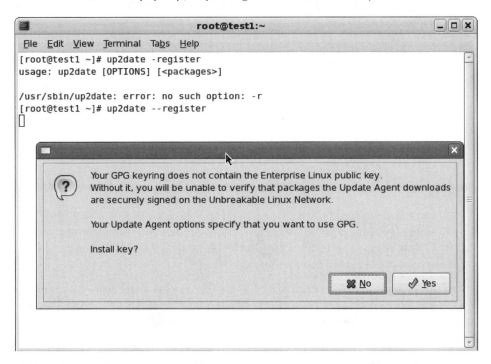

Click Yes. The Unbreakable Linux Network Update Agent screen appears next, as shown here. Click Forward to continue.

6. When the Unbreakable Linux Network Login screen appears, enter the login, password, and CSI you used previously to log in and register the system with the ULN. Click the Forward button.

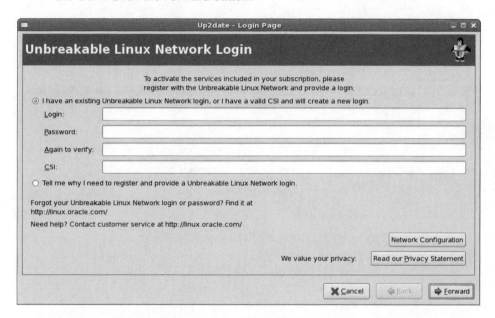

7. The Activate screen then appears, as shown in the following illustration. Here, you select options such as machine name and whether to send hardware information and a package list.

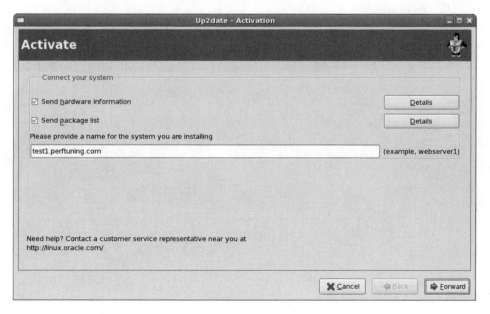

8. The Channels screen, shown next, then shows what channels this system has actively subscribed to, as well as the current channels that are configured on the Linux server.

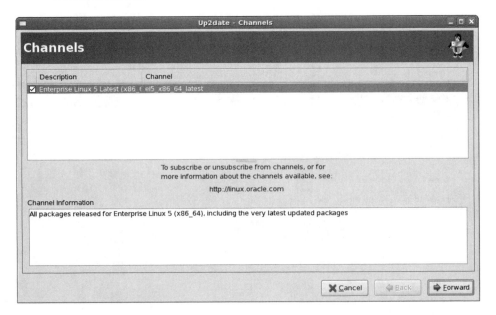

To view more information and/or add channels, click Forward and return to the browser that is connected to http://linux.oracle.com, as shown next. Notice that a system is now present. This is the system we just added.

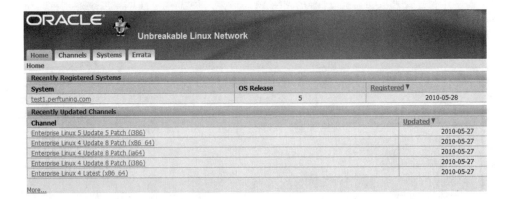

9. At this point, the system and ULN are set up and almost ready to install the ovmcli package. From the Home tab, click the system you want to configure. This changes the browser display so the Systems tab is active, as shown here:

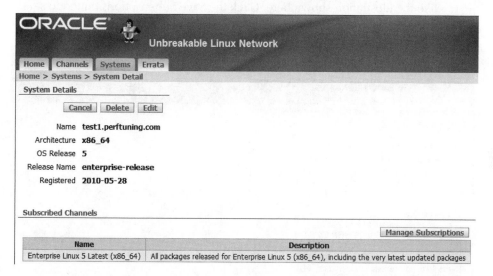

10. The system you want to install should be shown here. To configure this system so you can install the ovmcli package, you need to add two more channels. Click the Manage Subscriptions button to invoke the Manage Subscriptions screen:

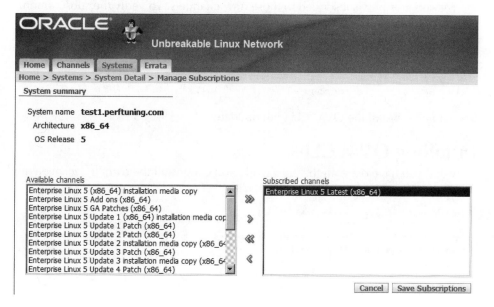

11. From this screen, select the Enterprise Linux 5 Add ons (x86_64) channel and click the > button between the Available Channels and Subscribed Channels boxes. Then select the Oracle Software addons for Enterprise Linux 5 (x86_64) and click the > button. The resulting screen should look like the illustration shown here. Click the Save Subscriptions button to save the configuration.

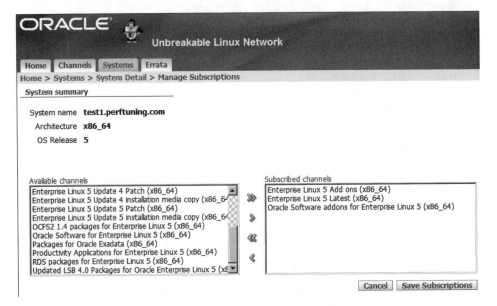

The server is now subscribed to those new channels. To verify the subscription, run the following command on the server:

```
[root@test1 ~]# up2date --show-channels
 el5_x86_64_addons
 el5_x86_64_latest
 el5_x86_64_oracle_addons
```

You can now install the OVM CLI with up2date.

Installing OVM CLI

Now that you have done all the hard work, you can install the ovmcli package with up2date using the following command:

```
[root@test1 ~]# up2date --install ovmcli

Fetching Obsoletes list for channel: el5_x86_64_addons...
########################################
```

```
Fetching Obsoletes list for channel: el5_x86_64_latest...

Fetching Obsoletes list for channel: el5_x86_64_oracle_addons...

Fetching rpm headers...
######################################

Name                              Version      Rel
-----------------------------------------------------------
ovmcli                            2.2          9.el5              noarch


Testing package set / solving RPM inter-dependencies...
######################################
ovmcli-2.2-9.el5.noarch.rpm ######################### Done.
python-ZSI-2.1-a1.el5.noarc ######################### Done.
Preparing                   ########################################### [100%]

Installing...
   1:python-ZSI               ########################################### [100%]
   2:ovmcli                   ########################################### [100%]
The following packages were added to your selection to satisfy dependencies:

Name                              Version      Release
-----------------------------------------------------------
python-ZSI                        2.1          a1.el5
```

As with many things, meeting the prerequisites and performing the setup comprises most of the work. Installing the OVM CLI itself is quite simple once everything is set up. The OVM CLI installation process has installed the ovm program. To verify that the installation has completed successfully, run the **ovm** command, as shown here:

```
[root@test1 ovmcli]# ovm
Usage: ovm [options] subcommand [suboptions]

Oracle VM Manager Command Line Interface

Subcommands:

group           ---     Group management
img             ---     Virtual machine image management
iso             ---     ISO image management
sd              ---     Shared virtual disk management
svr             ---     Server management
svrp            ---     Server pool management
tmpl            ---     Virtual machine template management
user            ---     User management
val             ---     System parameter management
vm              ---     Virtual machine management
config          ---     CLI configuration
```

```
connect          ---   Connect to Oracle VM Manager from CLI shell
exit             ---   Exit
help             ---   Show help
shell            ---   Launch an interactive shell
use              ---   Specify a server pool to use
vncviewer        ---   Start a VNC console
```

The OVM CLI has been installed and is working. Configuring the OVM CLI is the same regardless of the installation method; therefore, it will be covered after the section on installing the OVM CLI from the Oracle public yum server.

Installing OVM CLI from the Oracle Public yum Repository

In addition to installing the OVM CLI from the ULN, you can also install it without a subscription by using the Oracle public yum repository. Oracle has provided the public yum repository so the public can download additional packages and updates for OEL without having to subscribe to the ULN, even though a subscription to the ULN is very reasonably priced.

The Yellowdog Updater Modified (yum) system is a set of programs for providing package updates and additions. yum is an RPM-based package manager that can perform a number of functions related to package management both automatically and interactively. yum has an advantage over installing packages by hand using the Red Hat Package Manager (RPM) directly, in that it automatically determines dependencies and installs them as well as the requested package. If your computer is connected to the Internet, then you can use the Oracle public yum server directly with very little effort, as shown in the next few sections. If the system is on a secure network with no Internet access available, you can create an internal yum server, which is often done in secure environments.

This book will not cover the tasks necessary to configure a yum server, but it will cover configuring and using yum to install the ovmcli package. With the ULN and the public Oracle yum server, you'll discover that you don't need to use other methods to update and install packages. In the next section, you learn how to configure the yum client and then how to use the yum client to install OVM CLI.

Configuring the Oracle Public yum Repository

To access the Oracle public yum servers, you need to configure them so your system knows where they are. You do this via the /etc/yum.conf file. You add the location of the Oracle public yum servers to that configuration file so yum knows where to find the packages. As with the ULN, the packages are organized into channels. To install OVM CLI, you configure three channels:

- **Base Linux** This includes the base programs that are delivered on the installation medium.

- **EL5 Addons** This is needed due to the dependency of OVM CLI on python-ZSI, which is found in the EL5 Addons channel.

- **EL5 Oracle Addons** This contains the actual OVM CLI itself along with a few other Oracle-specific packages.

In order to configure those channels for yum usage, add the following lines to the /etc/yum.conf file:

```
[EL5]
name=EL5
baseurl=http://public-yum.oracle.com/repo/EnterpriseLinux/EL5/3/base/x86_64/
gpgcheck=0

[EL5_addons]
name=EL5 Addons
baseurl=http://public-yum.oracle.com/repo/EnterpriseLinux/EL5/addons/x86_64/
gpgcheck=0

[EL5_oracle_addons]
name=EL5 Oracle Addons
baseurl=http://public-yum.oracle.com/repo/EnterpriseLinux/EL5/oracle_addons/x86_64/
gpgcheck=0
```

Optionally, a better way to set up the yum repository is to download the latest repository setup from the Oracle public yum server itself by following these steps:

1. # cd /etc/yum.repos.d.

2. # wget http://public-yum.oracle.com/public-yum-el5.repo.

3. Edit the file /etc/yum.repos.d/public-yum-el5.repo and change the enable option to 1 for any repositories that are desired.

Once you've configured the yum repository, regardless of the method used, you can now validate, update, or download packages as needed. Below is confirmation that you have configured the respository.

```
[root@test2 ~]# yum list ovmcli
Loaded plugins: security
Available Packages
ovmcli.noarch                    2.2-9.el5                    EL5_oracle_addons
```

In order to get more information about the ovmcli package, run the **yum info** command. This command also verifies that yum is configured properly and that it can find the ovmcli package.

```
[root@test2 ~]# yum info ovmcli
Loaded plugins: security
Available Packages
Name        : ovmcli
Arch        : noarch
Version     : 2.2
Release     : 9.el5
Size        : 244 k
Repo        : EL5_oracle_addons
Summary     : Oracle VM CLI for linux
License     : Berkeley DB
Description: Oracle VM CLI, the command line interface for Oracle VM Manager.
            : Please see /usr/share/doc/ovmcli-2.0/README for setup information.
```

Once you have configured and verified the yum repository, you can install the ovmcli package, as shown in the next section.

Installing OVM CLI

Once you've configured the yum server, installing the ovmcli package is a fairly easy matter. If desired, you can easily display information about the package dependencies via the **yum deplist** command, as shown here:

```
[root@test2 ~]# yum deplist ovmcli
Loaded plugins: security
Finding dependencies:
package: ovmcli.noarch 1.0-1.el5
  dependency: python(abi) = 2.4
   provider: python.x86_64 2.4.3-27.el5
  dependency: /usr/bin/python
   provider: python.x86_64 2.4.3-27.el5
  dependency: /bin/sh
   provider: bash.x86_64 3.2-24.el5
  dependency: python >= 2.4
   provider: python.x86_64 2.4.3-27.el5
  dependency: python-ZSI >= 2.1
   provider: python-ZSI.noarch 2.1-a1.el5
   provider: python-ZSI.noarch 2.1-a1.el5
package: ovmcli.noarch 2.2-9.el5
  dependency: python(abi) = 2.4
   provider: python.x86_64 2.4.3-27.el5
  dependency: /usr/bin/python
   provider: python.x86_64 2.4.3-27.el5
  dependency: /bin/sh
   provider: bash.x86_64 3.2-24.el5
  dependency: python >= 2.4
```

```
 provider: python.x86_64 2.4.3-27.el5
dependency: python-ZSI >= 2.1
 provider: python-ZSI.noarch 2.1-a1.el5
 provider: python-ZSI.noarch 2.1-a1.el5
```

Notice that the python-ZSI package is a dependency. In this case, the EL5 Addons channel had to be added because of that dependency. If that channel were not defined, yum would issue an Unsatisfied Dependency error and would be unable to install the package.

Once all of the prerequisites have been satisfied, you can install the ovmcli package with the **yum install** command, as shown next. This command installs the package and all of its dependencies. The dependencies are checked first, and if everything looks good, you are prompted to install the package. Type **Y** and press ENTER and the package is installed.

```
[root@test2 ~]# yum install ovmcli
Loaded plugins: security
Setting up Install Process
Resolving Dependencies
--> Running transaction check
---> Package ovmcli.noarch 0:2.2-9.el5 set to be updated
--> Processing Dependency: python-ZSI >= 2.1 for package: ovmcli
--> Running transaction check
---> Package python-ZSI.noarch 0:2.1-a1.el5 set to be updated
--> Finished Dependency Resolution

Dependencies Resolved

================================================================================
 Package          Arch         Version          Repository             Size
================================================================================
Installing:
 ovmcli           noarch       2.2-9.el5        EL5_oracle_addons      244 k
Installing for dependencies:
 python-ZSI       noarch       2.1-a1.el5       EL5_addons             1.0 M

Transaction Summary
================================================================================
Install       2 Package(s)
Upgrade       0 Package(s)

Total download size: 1.3 M
Is this ok [y/N]: y
Downloading Packages:
(1/2): ovmcli-2.2-9.el5.noarch.rpm                      | 244 kB     00:00
(2/2): python-ZSI-2.1-a1.el5.noarch.rpm                 | 1.0 MB     00:00
--------------------------------------------------------------------------------
Total                                     2.8 MB/s | 1.3 MB     00:00
Running rpm_check_debug
Running Transaction Test
Finished Transaction Test
Transaction Test Succeeded
```

```
Running Transaction
  Installing     : python-ZSI                              1/2
  Installing     : ovmcli                                  2/2

Installed:
  ovmcli.noarch 0:2.2-9.el5

Dependency Installed:
  python-ZSI.noarch 0:2.1-a1.el5

Complete!
```

As with the previous method of installing the ovmcli package, running ovm verifies that the installation was successful.

Configuring the OVMCLI

Regardless of the installation method, you now need to configure the ovmcli utility so it can connect to the Oracle VM Server system. During the configuration process, you need the port number of the Oracle VM Server. To review, the port that is used to connect to the Oracle VM Manager varies based on whether you chose Secure Sockets Layer (SSL) during the Oracle VM Manager installation process. The following are the ports used by the Oracle VM Manager:

Interface	Port	URL
Standard Interface	8888	http://<VM Manager System>:8888/OVS http://control:8888/OVS
Secure Interface	4443	https://<VM Manager System>:4443/OVS https://control:4443/OVS

Using SSH Port Tunneling

In several of the examples, you may have noticed that the interface used for both the Oracle VM Manager and OEM Grid Control uses localhost as the system name. Obviously, there isn't a server called localhost using that name. The servers being used for the examples are in a private network in the author's remote lab. A single SSH port is allowed through the firewall. With this SSH connection and the Linux server it is connected to, the author uses port tunneling. SSH is set up to forward connections on specific ports through the firewall and through the SSH connection on the Linux server, forwarding them to the specified system. This allows for access to those systems directly from the author's desktop. Multiple tunnels can be set up at the same time. The author typically sets up tunnels for VNC, OEM, and Oracle VM Manager simultaneously.

Once the OVM CLI has been installed and the Oracle VM Manager host and port have been identified, it is time to configure the CLI. You do this using the **ovm** command with the **config** qualifier, as shown here:

```
[root@test2 ~]# ovm config
This is a wizard for configuring the Oracle VM Manager Command Line Interface.
CTRL-C to exit.

Oracle VM Manager hostname: ptccontrol
Oracle VM Manager port number: 4443
Deploy path (leave blank for default):
Location of vncviewer (leave blank to skip):
Enable HTTPS support? (Y/n): Y

Configuration complete.
Please rerun the Oracle VM Manager Command Line Interface.
```

If the vncviewer application has been installed, the directory where it's been installed should be specified. HTTPS support specifies that secure communication is used between the OVM CLI and VM Manager.

To verify the OVM CLI has been installed and is configured, try running a simple command such as **ovm svr ls**. This command lists the VM Server systems. Whenever a command is issued, a prompt is displayed for the username and password. To avoid this, you can enter them on the input line as well, by using the –u *<username>* and –p *<password>* parameters. These parameters are helpful for scripting, when interactive password processing can be difficult. The output of the **ovm svr ls** command is shown here:

```
[root@test2 ~]# ovm svr ls
Login: admin
Password:
Server_Host/IP Server_Name Status Server_Pool
ptc1           ptc1        Active ptc1-pool
ptc2           ptc2        Active ptc2-pool
ptc5           ptc5        Active pe710
You have new mail in /var/spool/mail/root
```

The result displays the three servers that are currently configured and under the control of this Oracle VM Manager. This output verifies that the OVM CLI is configured and properly communicating with the VM Manager.

Using OVM CLI

OVM CLI will be covered throughout this book, thus only a brief overview of how to use it is provided in this chapter. As mentioned earlier, the OVM CLI is invoked via the **ovm** command. The **ovm** command takes a number of qualifiers that either run specific commands or invoke an interactive shell. This interactive shell allows you to run multiple commands without having to log in repeatedly using a VM Manager username and password.

To get a listing of the qualifiers available for the OVM CLI, simply run **ovm** without any qualifiers. By not providing any qualifiers, the **ovm** command lists all available qualifiers, as shown here:

```
[root@test2 ~]# ovm
Usage: ovm [options] subcommand [suboptions]

Oracle VM Manager Command Line Interface

Subcommands:

    group         ---    Group management
    img           ---    Virtual machine image management
    iso           ---    ISO image management
    sd            ---    Shared virtual disk management
    svr           ---    Server management
    svrp          ---    Server pool management
    tmpl          ---    Virtual machine template management
    user          ---    User management
    val           ---    System parameter management
    vm            ---    Virtual machine management
    config        ---    CLI configuration
    connect       ---    Connect to Oracle VM Manager from CLI shell
    exit          ---    Exit
    help          ---    Show help
    shell         ---    Launch an interactive shell
    use           ---    Specify a server pool to use
    vncviewer     ---    Start a VNC console
```

The OVM CLI is a convenient way of running repeated commands without having to continually go through multiple VM Manager screens. You can also create multiple virtual machines quickly and easily, whereas using the GUI to create virtual machines can be somewhat time consuming.

Using the OVM Shell

As mentioned earlier, invoking the **ovm** command requires entering a username and password. If multiple commands are going to be issued interactively, the OVM shell is a convenient way to log into the OVM CLI to run multiple commands. The OVM shell is invoked with the **ovm shell** command, as shown in this example:

```
[root@test2 ~]# ovm shell
Login: admin
Password:
Type "help" for a list of commands.
ovm> help
Usage: subcommand [suboptions]
```

```
Oracle VM Manager Command Line Interface

Subcommands:

    group           ---     Group management
    img             ---     Virtual machine image management
    iso             ---     ISO image management
    sd              ---     Shared virtual disk management
    svr             ---     Server management
    svrp            ---     Server pool management
    tmpl            ---     Virtual machine template management
    user            ---     User management
    val             ---     System parameter management
    vm              ---     Virtual machine management
    config          ---     CLI configuration
    connect         ---     Connect to Oracle VM Manager from CLI shell
    exit            ---     Exit
    help            ---     Show help
    shell           ---     Launch an interactive shell
    use             ---     Specify a server pool to use
    vncviewer       ---     Start a VNC console

    "help <subcommand>" displays help message for that subcommand.
    "help all" displays complete list of subcommands.

    ovm>
```

Leaving the OVM shell is done via the **exit** command as with most Linux shells. The OVM shell is useful for interactive commands, but the real benefit of using OVM CLI is the ability to perform scripting. Scripting is described in the next section.

Scripting with OVM CLI

As with any task, if you have to do it more than a few times, creating a script is usually more convenient. Scripting has several benefits. First, a script can easily be modified and run repeatedly. It can even be parameterized so you can reuse it without having to rewrite the script. Second, a script is by its nature self-documenting. Using a script creates a record of how a particular task has been done. Third, a script can be set to be self logging. By creating a script to log its actions, you can save more useful documentation.

Scripting with the OVM CLI is done just as with any other Linux shell script. Invoke the OVM CLI with the username and password or the script can prompt for the information. An example of an OVM CLI script is shown here using the bash shell.

Example 1: Script to power off four VMs

```
#!/bin/bash

#
#  Script to power on lab01 - lab04
#

ovm -u admin -p ptc123 vm poweroff -n lab01 -s pe710
ovm -u admin -p ptc123 vm poweroff -n lab02 -s pe710
ovm -u admin -p ptc123 vm poweroff -n lab03 -s pe710
ovm -u admin -p ptc123 vm poweroff -n lab04 -s pe710
#!/bin/bash
```

Example 2: Script to power on four VMs

```
#
#  Script to power on lab01 - lab04
#

ovm -u admin -p ptc123 vm poweron -n lab01 -s pe710
ovm -u admin -p ptc123 vm poweron -n lab02 -s pe710
ovm -u admin -p ptc123 vm poweron -n lab03 -s pe710
ovm -u admin -p ptc123 vm poweron -n lab04 -s pe710
```

The real power of the OVM CLI is this ability to script various functions. This will be illustrated further throughout this book.

Summary

The OVM CLI is a useful command-line tool for quickly and efficiently issuing and scripting Oracle VM Manager commands without having to use the GUI interface. Its scripting feature is very convenient and allows you to set up repetitious tasks to run in the background without requiring extensive interactive action by the administrator. The downside of the OVM CLI is that it requires the Oracle VM Manager, thus it cannot be used on servers that are managed via OEM Grid Control. The method you select really depends on each individual configuration and its needs.

Chapter 10 discusses how to configure the network on the VM Server system itself. The network is an important component of the virtual machine and will need to be configured once the VM Server has been installed.

CHAPTER
10

Configuring the
VM Server Network

he two most important components of the VM Server that are the most likely to be modified on a regular basis are network and storage. The network configuration tends to change as the requirements for network bandwidth and subnets change. The storage requirements change more often because, with most environments, the need for storage always grows and never shrinks. Network requirements typically change at the virtual machine level, but the VM Server network does not often need to change. The configuration and functionality of the network is important. By making sure that network capacity has not been exceeded, you can optimize the performance of the virtual machines. Performance monitoring is covered in Chapter 14.

This chapter covers the VM Server network—how it is configured and how it is managed. Once it is configured and working properly, making significant changes is often unnecessary. The VM Server network configuration requirements are a bit complicated in the current release of Oracle VM. Future releases of Oracle VM will provide graphical tools to assist with the configuration of network devices.

NOTE
The most common addition to a VM Server network are VLANs. VLANs are used at the hardware switch layer, however, and do not normally affect the configuration of the VM Server.

Configuring and Managing the VM Server Network

The VM Server network allows virtual machines to share or use the networks that have been created for the host VM Server; thus, for multiple networks to be used with virtual machines, virtual networks must be created for the VM Server. For the virtual guest to communicate with other systems on the network outside of the VM Server, the virtual machine network adapter has to be configured on the same network as a Xen bridge.

Consider the Xen bridge to be a switch between the virtual machine world and the outside world. If the virtual machine is configured on the correct subnet, then the switch allows traffic to flow outside of the VM Server; if a different subnet is used, traffic can only communicate within the Xen bridge. In this manner, several subnets can use this switch. However, the bridge is not a router; therefore, it does not translate from one subnet to another.

You configure the Xen bridge manually by configuring the network device that is set up for the dom0 domain. To set up networking, perform the following steps:

1. Configure the network on the dom0 domain.

2. Configure the Xen bridge type.

Configuring the Xen network is not extremely complicated, and, in some cases, everything is done during the installation process, which makes much of this chapter informational only. However, to understand how networking works in an Oracle VM environment, you need to understand Xen networking and Xen bridges.

Xen Networking

The networks used by the virtual machines are run through the Xen bridges. The Xen bridge is the interface between the virtual world (virtual machines) and the physical world (your company network). You can configure the Xen bridges in a number of different ways, including bridged, NAT, and routed. Although all of these network types can be configured and will work, only the bridged network is supported by Oracle. Routed and NAT networks are usually found in smaller, home network environments. The bridged network is most commonly found in server environments. Since Oracle VM is designed for the data center, bridged networking is typically the network of choice.

The network type is usually based on the environment that the Oracle VM Server is running in. The most common and default configuration for Oracle VM is bridged networking. The other two—NAT and routed—can also be configured. Each type serves a different purpose and is configured separately.

- **Bridged networking**   Bridged networks allow the virtual machine network to reside on the same network as the Xen bridge. In order to be seen by other systems on the network, you must configure the virtual machine network adapter so it's on the same subnet as the dom0 xenbr adapter. Bridged networks allow you to easily add new virtual machines to the virtual machine farm that are accessible from other systems on the network.

- **NAT networking**   Network Address Translation (NAT) networks take the IP address of the VM Server. NAT allows multiple virtual machines to appear to themselves and to other virtual machines as if they have their own IP address, but to the outside world, it appears as if there is only the VM Server's IP address. This is similar to how your home router works. With NAT networks, connecting outside systems to the NAT system is difficult.

- **Routed networking**   The final type of networking is routed networking. With routed networking, traffic is routed through the dom0 (VM Server) system to a private subnet that is accessible by one or more virtual machines. Routed networks must be set up manually and are more difficult to maintain, but they provide functionality that might be useful in some cases.

You configure each of these networks somewhat differently.

NOTE
As mentioned earlier, Oracle VM is designed as a server virtualization product. Bridged networks, the default network type, are, therefore, the only supported network types in Oracle VM. Other networking types such as NAT and routed are really intended more for the home or personal network. Although NAT and bridged networks can be configured and work in Oracle VM, they are not recommended or supported and will not be covered in this book except for the brief description just given.

Configuring the Network Adapters

The first step in setting up Xen networking is to set up the adapters and Xen bridges on the dom0 system. This is similar to setting up the network on a standard Linux system. Once you have set up the network adapters, you'll create the xenbr devices from the Xen configuration files, as shown in the next sections.

The primary network adapter is configured during the installation process. The IP address and type of address assignment are determined during the initial installation setup. Static networking is recommended, rather than DHCP-assigned IP addresses. Even though it is an option, IPV6 can be safely disabled.

You configure the network adapters in the same way you configure a network adapter in Linux, by setting up the ifcfg files in the /etc/sysconfig/network-scripts directory. Each network adapter has a configuration file named /etc/sysconfig/network-scripts/ifcfg-eth0 .. ifcfg-eth*n*. These network adapter configuration files include network configuration information and information on how the adapter is configured, the IP address, the netmask, the gateway, and so on.

Static Configuration vs. DHCP

Although DHCP networking is possible, it is not recommended for Oracle VM Server systems. For small, home networks, you can use DHCP, but for server systems meant for multiple users, DHCP networking can be difficult to manage. If the Oracle VM Server uses DHCP for networking, the virtual machines should use DHCP as well.

Once the network has been configured and the system rebooted, the xenbr devices will be enabled and will show up when you run ifconfig. An example is shown here:

```
eth0      Link encap:Ethernet  HWaddr 00:0C:29:D4:B7:EE
          UP BROADCAST RUNNING MULTICAST  MTU:1500  Metric:1
          RX packets:129 errors:0 dropped:0 overruns:0 frame:0
          TX packets:91 errors:0 dropped:0 overruns:0 carrier:0
          collisions:0 txqueuelen:1000
          RX bytes:23913 (23.3 KiB)  TX bytes:12876 (12.5 KiB)

eth1      Link encap:Ethernet  HWaddr 00:0C:29:D4:B7:F8
          UP BROADCAST RUNNING MULTICAST  MTU:1500  Metric:1
          RX packets:158 errors:0 dropped:0 overruns:0 frame:0
          TX packets:32 errors:0 dropped:0 overruns:0 carrier:0
          collisions:0 txqueuelen:1000
          RX bytes:28525 (27.8 KiB)  TX bytes:6382 (6.2 KiB)

lo        Link encap:Local Loopback
          inet addr:127.0.0.1  Mask:255.0.0.0
          UP LOOPBACK RUNNING  MTU:16436  Metric:1
          RX packets:138 errors:0 dropped:0 overruns:0 frame:0
          TX packets:138 errors:0 dropped:0 overruns:0 carrier:0
          collisions:0 txqueuelen:0
          RX bytes:18467 (18.0 KiB)  TX bytes:18467 (18.0 KiB)

vif2.0    Link encap:Ethernet  HWaddr FE:FF:FF:FF:FF:FF
          UP BROADCAST RUNNING MULTICAST  MTU:1500  Metric:1
          RX packets:0 errors:0 dropped:0 overruns:0 frame:0
          TX packets:0 errors:0 dropped:52 overruns:0 carrier:0
          collisions:0 txqueuelen:32
          RX bytes:0 (0.0 b)  TX bytes:0 (0.0 b)

xenbr0    Link encap:Ethernet  HWaddr 00:0C:29:D4:B7:EE
          inet addr:192.168.10.9  Bcast:0.0.0.0  Mask:255.255.255.0
          UP BROADCAST RUNNING MULTICAST  MTU:1500  Metric:1
          RX packets:38 errors:0 dropped:0 overruns:0 frame:0
          TX packets:70 errors:0 dropped:0 overruns:0 carrier:0
          collisions:0 txqueuelen:0
          RX bytes:10253 (10.0 KiB)  TX bytes:12190 (11.9 KiB)

xenbr1    Link encap:Ethernet  HWaddr 00:0C:29:D4:B7:F8
          inet addr:192.168.11.9  Bcast:0.0.0.0  Mask:255.255.255.0
          UP BROADCAST RUNNING MULTICAST  MTU:1500  Metric:1
          RX packets:36 errors:0 dropped:0 overruns:0 frame:0
          TX packets:12 errors:0 dropped:0 overruns:0 carrier:0
          collisions:0 txqueuelen:0
          RX bytes:9675 (9.4 KiB)  TX bytes:3386 (3.3 KiB)
```

By default, the bridged network is created. You do not need to perform any additional configuration steps to use bridged networking; however, the steps to change to bridged networking are provided later in this section.

CAUTION
Mixing Xen network types is not recommended. You should decide whether to used bridged, NAT, or routed networks before creating virtual machines.

Configuring a Bridged Network

Configuring the bridged network is done by editing the /etc/xen/xend-config.sxp file. In order to enable bridged networking, make sure the following line is uncommented:

```
(network-script network-bridge)
(vif-script vif-bridge)
```

That's all that is necessary to enable bridged networking. Once the configuration file has been modified, reboot the VM Server to enable the bridged network. To validate the configuration, run ifconfig on the VM Server.

NOTE
You'll notice the vif virtual adapter has been created for each virtual machine that is running on the VM Server. This virtual network is configured as a bridged device. If you don't see the xenbr0 device, then the bridged network is not set up correctly. Check the configuration file and make any changes that might be necessary.

With bridged connections, the IP address that was assigned to eth0 should be the IP address on the xenbr0 adapter. This should be assigned automatically if the Xen adapters are properly configured.

NOTE
In some cases it is necessary to manage the networks manually. This is done by setting (network-script /bin/true) and creating the xen bridge interface manually in /etc/sysconfig/network-scripts. Consult Oracle documentation on the proper way to configure this with the version of Oracle VM that you are running.

Network Bonding

A degree of redundancy at the network level is often desirable. With redundancy, the VM Server system continues to operate even in the event of a single network failure. Common practice is to use network teaming or bonding to provide this extra bit of protection. *Network teaming* and *network bonding* are just different terms for the same thing: network redundancy. For the sake of this chapter, the term *network bonding* is used to describe this function.

Is Network Bonding Necessary?

Depending on your particular point of view, network bonding may or may not be necessary. If reliable hardware (both server and network) is used and redundant components are not available, then network bonding will result in extra effort without benefit. For example, using multiple network cards in the server system that are both plugged into the same network switch provides some degree of redundancy, but doing this does not eliminate all single points of failure, since the loss of the entire switch would still cause a complete network loss.

If you use active switching, you can use Network Address Controller (NIC) bonding to increase the throughput of a VM network. In some cases, for instance, if you have many virtual machines, a single 1 GbE network connection will not provide enough throughput. By increasing the number of NICs in the bond, you increase the throughput.

NIC bonding is done at the VM Server level and only involves a few steps. These steps consist of:

1. Disable Xen networking.

2. Update Xen configuration files.

3. Create the bonding interface.

4. Re-enable Xen networking.

These steps will now be covered in some detail:

1. Stop the Xen network by running **/etc/xen/scripts/network-bridges stop**. This command stops the Xen bridges. Run an **ifconfig** command to confirm that the xenbr devices are down.

2. Create the file /etc/xen/scripts/network-bridge-ovs with the following contents:

    ```
    #!/bin/sh
    /bin/true
    ```

3. Change the mode of /etc/xen/scripts/network-bridge-ovs to 755 using the **chown** command: **chown 755 /etc/xen/scripts/network-bridge-ovs**.

4. Edit /etc/xen/xend-config.sxp and replace (network-script network-bridges) with **(network-script network-bridge-ovs)**.

5. Enable NIC bonding at the Linux level by adding the following lines to /etc/modprobe.conf. Note the exact syntax varies based on the type of network device.

```
alias eth0 <driver> # where driver is tg3, e1000, etc.
alias bond0 bonding
options bonding mode=1 miimon=100 downdelay=200 updelay=200
```

6. Modify the network devices by first creating the Xen bridge bond device. Create the file /etc/sysconfig/network-scripts/ifcfg-xenbr0 with the following contents:

For Static Network	For DHCP
DEVICE=xenbr0	DEVICE=xenbr0
ONBOOT=yes	ONBOOT=yes
TYPE=Bridge	TYPE=Bridge
DELAY=0	DELAY=0
STP=off	STP=off
BOOTPROTO=none	BOOTPROTO=dhcp
IPADDR=10.0.0.1	
NETMASK=255.255.255.0	

7. Create the bond0 device configuration file. This file is /etc/sysconfig/network-scripts/ifcfg-bond0 and contains the following contents:

DEVICE=bond0
ONBOOT=yes
BRIDGE=xenbr0

8. Modify the eth*n* device files. You should already have an /etc/sysconfig/network-scripts/ifcfg-eth0 and /etc/sysconfig/network-scripts/ifcfg-eth1 device file. Modify these files as follows:

/etc/sysconfig/network-scripts/ifcfg-eth0	**/etc/sysconfig/network-scripts/ifcfg-eth1**
# Intel Corporation 82545EM Gigabit Ethernet Controller (Copper)	# Intel Corporation 82545EM Gigabit Ethernet Controller (Copper)
DEVICE=eth0	DEVICE=eth1
BOOTPROTO=none	BOOTPROTO=none
ONBOOT=yes	ONBOOT=yes
MASTER=bond0	MASTER=bond0
SLAVE=yes	SLAVE=yes
USERCTL=no	USERCTL=no
HWADDR=00:0C:29:D4:B7:EE	HWADDR=00:0c:29:d4:b7:f8

Note that HWADDR is replaced with the actual MAC address.

Network Bonding Hardware Support

In order for some types of bonding to work (i.e., load balancing and trunking), the network hardware must all support the same IEEE specifications or else they will not work reliably. Support must be end-to-end. Certain NAS vendors will not support your network unless this condition is met.

9. Restart the network with the **service network restart** command.

10. Restart the Xen daemon with the **service xend restart** command. The output should indicate that xend is running:

```
[root@ptc7 ~]# service xend restart
restarting xend...
xend daemon running (pid 3931)
```

11. Finally, verify the bridges are connected using the **brctl show** command:

```
[root@ptc7 ~]# brctl show
bridge name      bridge id              STP enabled      interfaces
xenbr0           8000.000c29d4b7ee      no               bond0
```

Once you've completed these steps, the Xen bridge device is now running using two Network Interface Cards (NICs). If one card were to fail, the other will take over, thus providing continuous availability depending on the error. As mentioned earlier, this only helps in a limited number of circumstances where the network cable or switch port has failed. In some cases, bonding won't help, as is the case with an entire switch failure.

Managing the VM Server Network

Typically there is not much to manage in the VM Server network. Most of the administration tasks involving the network are focused more on the virtual machines rather than the server network. Once you've completed the initial configuration of the network, typically no additional configuration is necessary.

When installing the VM Server system, you have an option to configure only one network controller. You can configure this network controller as either address allocated by using DHCP or static addressing. This first network controller is configured during the initial installation of the VM Server. Any additional network controllers are configured after completing the initial configuration. You have to perform only a few simple steps to complete this task.

Adding Network Resources

Adding additional network resources is very straightforward. Two different cases can make it necessary to configure network devices: when a new device is added or an initial configuration has recently been completed. Regardless of the reason for network configuration, the steps are the same.

The Linux Kudzu utility automatically discovers and performs the initial configuration of network devices. This configuration is done as a DHCP configuration. Once the network device has been created, a new configuration file will be created in the /etc/sysconfig/network-devices directory.

Modifying Network Resources

The configuration and modification of network devices can be performed manually or via GUI utilities that are available in the Linux system. Since the Oracle VM server is a JeOS (Just enough OS) operating system, the command-line tools are installed. The most straightforward and easiest way to configure the network is simply to modify the network configuration files. These files are /etc/sysconfig/network-scripts/ ifcfg-eth*n*. Each network adapter that is identified in the system will have one configuration file.

Each file represents a configuration for a network adapter. Some of the options have been shown earlier in this chapter. They include the boot protocol, IP address, netmask, gateway, and so on. A summary of the options, which are used when configuring the /etc/sysconfig/network-scripts/ifcfg-eth*n* file, are provided here:

- **DEVICE**   This specifies the device name, i.e., eth0.

- **BOOTPROTO**   This parameter determines how the IP address gets assigned to the network adapter. Options include DHCP, static, and none.

- **ONBOOT**   This specifies whether to start the device upon system boot. Can be yes or no.

- **IPADDR**   For static network configuration, this is the IP address that the adapter will use.

- **NETWORK**   For static network configuration, this is the subnet of the network.

- **NETMASK**   For static network configuration, this is the netmask the adapter will use.

- **BROADCAST**   This is the broadcast address used by the adapter.

- **GATEWAY**   Optionally, you can specify a default gateway for each adapter. If only one gateway is defined, you can specify it in the /etc/sysconfig/network file.

- **USERCTL**   This parameter specifies whether or not user control is allowed by non-root users. Can be yes or no.

- **DNS[1,2]**   This specifies the DNS server to use for that adapter if PEERDNS is set to true. This specifies a name server (i.e., DNS1=192.168.1.1).

- **PEERDNS**   This specifies whether to modify /etc/resolv.conf. Can be yes or no.

- **SRCADDR**   This specifies the source IP address of outgoing packets.

Once the Ethernet device has been modified, no other configuration is necessary, other than the steps detailed earlier in this chapter. When an Ethernet device is modified, the VM Server should be rebooted if possible to ensure a clean restart of the Ethernet and Xen devices.

To view the current network status and for debugging purposes, several tools are available in the Oracle VM Server. They include ifconfig, ethtool, and mii-tool. ifconfig has been discussed previously in this chapter and won't be repeated here, except to say that running ifconfig is the first step in finding what adapters are available.

ethtool displays detailed information about an Ethernet adapter. Run ethtool with the adapter name in order to view this information, as shown here:

```
[root@ptc5 ~]# ethtool eth0
Settings for eth0:
        Supported ports: [ TP ]
        Supported link modes:   10baseT/Half 10baseT/Full
                                100baseT/Half 100baseT/Full
                                1000baseT/Full
        Supports auto-negotiation: Yes
        Advertised link modes:  10baseT/Half 10baseT/Full
                                100baseT/Half 100baseT/Full
                                1000baseT/Full
        Advertised auto-negotiation: Yes
        Speed: 1000Mb/s
        Duplex: Full
        Port: Twisted Pair
        PHYAD: 1
        Transceiver: internal
        Auto-negotiation: on
        Supports Wake-on: g
        Wake-on: d
        Link detected: yes
```

Another useful tool for quickly determining the state of an Ethernet adapter is mii-tool. This tool does not provide extensive information but is useful for discovering the state of the adapter:

```
[root@ptc5 ~]# mii-tool eth0
eth0: negotiated 100baseTx-FD, link ok
```

The configuration of the VM Server network consists of two distinct operations: configuring the Ethernet adapter and configuring the Xen networking components. Each was shown previously in this chapter.

Monitoring the Network

Monitoring network performance and utilization is an important part of performance management. A number of tools are available to monitor network performance, as well as the configuration functionality. Since performance monitoring is covered in Chapter 14, those tools will not be covered in this chapter.

The **ifconfig** command, shown earlier in this chapter, provides information on virtual networks as well as physical network devices. In addition to the physical devices (eth0, eth1, eth2, etc.) and the Xen bridges (xenbr0, xenbr1, xenbr2, etc.), a device is shown for each virtual machine's network. As shown here, this appears in the form of a vif device. Because two network devices are defined on this virtual machine, two vif devices are shown.

```
vif5.0      Link encap:Ethernet   HWaddr FE:FF:FF:FF:FF:FF
            UP BROADCAST RUNNING MULTICAST  MTU:1500  Metric:1
            RX packets:0 errors:0 dropped:0 overruns:0 frame:0
            TX packets:0 errors:0 dropped:100 overruns:0 carrier:0
            collisions:0 txqueuelen:32
            RX bytes:0 (0.0 b)  TX bytes:0 (0.0 b)

vif5.1      Link encap:Ethernet   HWaddr FE:FF:FF:FF:FF:FF
            UP BROADCAST RUNNING MULTICAST  MTU:1500  Metric:1
            RX packets:0 errors:0 dropped:0 overruns:0 frame:0
            TX packets:0 errors:0 dropped:127 overruns:0 carrier:0
            collisions:0 txqueuelen:32
            RX bytes:0 (0.0 b)  TX bytes:0 (0.0 b)
```

The vif device is a virtual interface and appears as another network device in the dom0 domain. Because this is a virtual device, the MAC address shows up as unidentified, even though it is available to the network for DHCP and so on. Since this virtual machine has two virtual interfaces, they show up as vif5.0 and vif5.1. This virtual machine was assigned vif5. Other virtual machines will be assigned other vif devices.

To find more information about a virtual machine's network devices, use the **xm network-list <virtual machine>** command. For example, to find the network information for the virtual machine 50_test1, enter the following command:

```
[root@ovm1 ~]# xm network-list 50_test1
Idx BE    MAC Addr.     handle state evt-ch tx-/rx-ring-ref BE-path
0   0   00:16:3E:54:E7:1E    0     4      9    1280 /1281 /local/domain/0/backend/vif/5/0
1   0   00:16:3E:2D:98:48    1     4     10    1283 /1287 /local/domain/0/backend/vif/5/1
```

Here you can see the actual MAC address that has been assigned to the virtual network interfaces on the virtual machines. You can obtain additional information with the **xm network-list –l** command.

To monitor network performance, use the standard Linux command **sar**. Because all network activity eventually goes through the Xen bridges and physical devices, the performance of those devices can provide useful information. The **xm top** command can also be helpful. Both of these commands are covered in Chapter 14.

Summary

This chapter covered the configuration of the VM Server network, starting with Xen networking and ending with configuration of additional network adapters. You do not need to do a lot of work with the network, from a general administration standpoint. As mentioned in this chapter, you configure only the first network adapter as part of the initial installation and then configure other adapters after the VM Server is running. During the normal course of operations, changes do not typically need to be made—only if new adapters are added or networks changed due to business requirements.

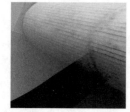

CHAPTER
11

Configuring the
VM Server Storage

t some point, the hardware resources that have been configured for a system might run out. Most often this occurs with disk resources. When this time comes, adding more resources is necessary. This chapter explains how to add and replace the VM Server storage.

When you need more storage for virtual machines, you can add it using the procedures described in this chapter. When you install an Oracle VM Server, you configure it using non-shared storage by creating an OCFS2 repository using local storage. This storage is quite sufficient for a standalone or all-in-one system. However, if you plan on enabling High Availability (HA) by creating a VM Cluster and a shared storage system is not configured, you need to actually replace the non-shared disk with the shared disk.

In addition to HA, shared storage using a Storage Area Network (SAN) or Network Attached Storage (NAS) offers additional benefits such as Enterprise Storage Management, the ability to add more storage easily, redundancy, and backup/restore features as well as other enterprise storage features. When planning the storage for the Enterprise VM farm, carefully consider the additional features available with SAN and NAS storage.

Shared Storage vs. Non-Shared Storage

Shared storage refers to storage that can be equally accessed by all VM Server systems in the server pool. This means that all of the servers can both read from and write to this storage. Several types of storage can be shared, including SAN and NAS systems.

SAN storage uses a network that is designed specifically for storage and does not allow normal network traffic. SAN systems typically include extensive redundancy and performance features. Because of that, SAN systems are usually fairly expensive. In the author's opinion, SAN systems are usually worth the cost. For SAN storage to be shared, you must configure it such that all of the nodes in the server pool can access the storage and you must configure it with a shared filesystem. Fortunately, Oracle VM comes with Oracle Cluster File System (OCFS2) built-in. OCFS2 is a high-performance cluster filesystem that was originally developed for Oracle Real Application Clusters (RAC).

NAS storage can also include many of the same redundancy and performance features as SAN storage, but because it uses off-the-shelf network hardware, it usually comes at a lower price. Both SAN and NAS storage are suitable for Oracle VM and, depending on the brand and model, both offer a high level of performance. NAS storage comes in two different varieties: iSCSI and NFS. The iSCSI protocol provides network storage for the Oracle VM Server that looks like a disk drive and must be configured with OCFS2 in order to be clustered. A Network File System (NFS) is inherently shared because the storage is presented to the Oracle VM system with the filesystem being managed at the storage system, not the host.

If a shared server pool (cluster) is desired, all storage used for virtual machines must be shared. Without shared storage, a cluster cannot pass the virtual machines between the different nodes. This is crucial for both HA and live migrations. In addition, the VM Servers must be configured as a server pool with shared storage. Later in this chapter, creating a cluster is covered.

Storage Repositories

Disk storage for the virtual environment is referred to as the *storage repository*. The storage repository is the home for the virtual machines, the ISO images, virtual machine templates, shared virtual disks, and so on. The top-level directory for the storage repository is /OVS. The directories below /OVS are used to store the important files used by Oracle VM. These directories are

- **running_pool** The running_pool directory contains all of the virtual machine images and configuration files. Each directory is created when the virtual machine is created.

- **seed_pool** The seed_pool directory is where the virtual machine templates are stored. As you will see later in this book, the templates are one of the most useful features of the Oracle VM system and are the most efficient way to create virtual machines.

- **iso_pool** This iso_pool directory is where the ISO images are stored. Each set of ISO images are stored in a subdirectory typically named for the OS release, i.e., OEL-5.5-x86_64, etc.

The Clustered Server Pool

A server pool does not need to use shared storage; in fact, the default installation is for the server pool to be created without shared storage. However, if shared storage is not used, some of the HA and load-balancing tools will not be available to the server pool. The clustered server pool is defined as a set of VM Servers that use the same shared storage. The shared storage is required for HA and is used for both HA and load balancing. You might define a clustered server pool as a server pool that has more than one server defined using shared storage. The clustered server pool uses a quorum to keep track of the cluster's state. This chapter covers both clustered and non-clustered storage. Unless otherwise mentioned, the term *server pool* refers to both the clustered and non-clustered server pool.

- **publish_pool**   The publish pool directory contains virtual machines that have been deployed as public.

- **SharedDisk**   The SharedDisk directory contains the shared disks that have been created for creating virtual clusters.

The /OVS directory is known as the *cluster root* and is actually a symbolic link that points to the /var/ovs/mount/*<uuid>* directory. In a non-clustered system, the /OVS filesystem is created using the OCFS2 filesystem. This is true even if the underlying storage is not shared. In the case of a shared disk, you can add more servers to the existing shared disk. In the case of a non-shared disk, you must replace the cluster root with a shared disk before you can create a cluster. This process is covered in this chapter.

If multiple disks are added to the Oracle VM system, multiple repositories are created. These additional repositories are mounted in /var/ovs/mount/<uuid>, where *uuid* is the Universally Unique Identifier (see Figure 11-1). The directory /OVS is a symbolic link to the top level of the root repository. You navigate to all other repositories directly.

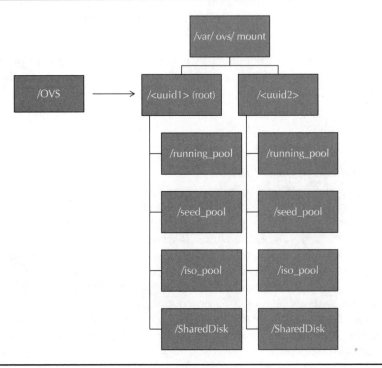

FIGURE 11-1.   *Multiple storage repositories*

Once multiple repositories have been created, Oracle VM determines how to use the storage. It attempts to even out the new virtual machines among the different repositories as best it can. The administrator cannot control which repository is used at this time, but it is still a great way of adding more storage easily. Adding repositories is usually more convenient than removing the existing storage, resizing it, and then remounting it.

Whether a single repository or multiple repositories are used, the rule is that if a VM Cluster is going to be used, all storage must be shared. In an all-in-one (non-clustered) configuration, either shared or non-shared storage can be used, but in a cluster, all storage must be clustered. This clustered storage can be either NFS or OCFS.

Before adding the storage to the Oracle VM system, you have to configure it. The next few sections cover the various methods for configuring storage.

Configuring the Hardware for Storage

Before you can configure the storage in Oracle VM, you must first configure it properly on the VM Server system itself. That is, the storage must be visible and working at the dom0 layer before you can add it to the VM Server and/or Cluster. The method employed to configure and verify the storage system depends on the type of storage and the amount and type of redundancy used by that storage. This process can be fairly simple, as with NFS storage, or fairly complicated, as with multipath storage.

The next few sections cover connecting to storage based on the type of storage and the amount of redundancy required. To review, several types of storage are supported by Oracle VM: directly attached disks, SAN storage, and NAS storage

Redundant Storage

Redundant storage is designed to be highly available because it is able to avoid a single point of failure. It accomplishes this by having at least two of each component. This way, even if a single component fails, access to storage is retained. Redundancy is accomplished in a number of different ways—through multiple paths to storage, Redundant Array of Inexpensive Disks (RAID) disk storage, and multiple power supplies.

Most of these components are transparent to the installer; however, creating redundant paths to storage requires intervention by the VM administrator. Multipath storage requires both hardware and software configuration on the VM Server system itself. You configure the hardware and software on the dom0 system.

with either iSCSI or NFS support. When using local storage, SAN, or NAS with iSCSI, you configure the storage using the OCFS2 filesystem. Local storage can also be created using the ext3 filesystem. When using a NAS with NFS, the filesystem used is determined by the backend storage. To the Oracle VM system, backend storage is considered NFS storage.

How the storage is configured at the hardware level does not vary based on whether it is used in a cluster. It does vary, however, at the VM Server configuration layer based on whether it is a cluster. The next sections cover hardware connectivity using multipath storage.

Connecting and Configuring the Storage

How you connect the storage varies based on the type of storage you're using. With SAN storage, setup typically involves adding and configuring one or more Host Bus Adapters (HBAs). These HBAs are typically designed for SAN storage and support either copper or fiber-optic connections and a device-specific driver must be added to the system as well. If so, use the instructions provided by the hardware vendor for installing the driver.

NAS storage can involve either the built-in Ethernet connections or the addition of an iSCSI HBA. If an iSCSI HBA is used, a device driver might be required. If a recent version of Oracle VM was installed, the device driver might be up to date, though often a new driver is recommended. Again, follow the hardware vendor's instructions for installing and updating the device driver.

NOTE
In order to support High Availability and live migration, the storage must be visible by all of the VM Servers in the cluster, which involves both hardware and software configuration, which is detailed in these next sections.

Depending on the type of storage, the configuration differs slightly. The various configurations are covered in the next sections.

Configuring SAN Storage

How you configure SAN storage varies based on the brand and type of SAN storage. In general, SAN storage uses an HBA that comes with a specific device driver; however, many of the most popular HBA drivers are now built into the Linux distribution. If multipath storage is available and desired, configure it using the instructions provided by the hardware vendor. Once you've added the storage, verify that it is visible to the

OS by viewing the contents of the /proc/partitions pseudo file. You should see output similar to what is shown here:

```
[root@ptc7 ~]# cat /proc/partitions
major minor   #blocks   name

    8    0   52428800 sda
    8    1     104391 sda1
    8    2    3148740 sda2
    8    3   48122707 sda3
    8    4          1 sda4
    8    5    1052226 sda5
    8   16   20971520 sdb
```

The storage that was originally configured during installation is sda3 and is configured as OCFS2 on non-shared storage. In order to configure this system as a cluster, the storage must be replaced with shared storage.

As mentioned earlier, the storage must be configured with OCFS2 and shared in order to use it in a cluster. The new disk must be formatted with the OCFS2 file system and added to the cluster. To configure it, you first need to partition the disk, using the **fdisk** command. Typically, a disk for this type of storage is partitioned as one single partition that covers the entire disk, as shown here:

```
[root@ptc7 ~]# fdisk /dev/sdb
Device contains neither a valid DOS partition table, nor Sun, SGI or OSF disklabel
Building a new DOS disklabel. Changes will remain in memory only,
until you decide to write them. After that, of course, the previous
content won't be recoverable.


The number of cylinders for this disk is set to 2610.
There is nothing wrong with that, but this is larger than 1024,
and could in certain setups cause problems with:
1) software that runs at boot time (e.g., old versions of LILO)
2) booting and partitioning software from other OSs
   (e.g., DOS FDISK, OS/2 FDISK)
Warning: invalid flag 0x0000 of partition table 4 will be corrected by w(rite)

Command (m for help): n
Command action
   e   extended
   p   primary partition (1-4)
p
Partition number (1-4): 1
First cylinder (1-2610, default 1):
Using default value 1
Last cylinder or +size or +sizeM or +sizeK (1-2610, default 2610):
Using default value 2610

Command (m for help): w
The partition table has been altered!

Calling ioctl() to re-read partition table.
Syncing disks.
```

Once the disk has been partitioned, another look at /proc/partitions should reveal the new partition, as shown here:

```
[root@ptc7 ~]# cat /proc/partitions
major minor  #blocks  name

   8     0   52428800 sda
   8     1     104391 sda1
   8     2    3148740 sda2
   8     3   48122707 sda3
   8     4          1 sda4
   8     5    1052226 sda5
   8    16   20971520 sdb
   8    17   20964793 sdb1
```

In the case of a multipath device, several copies of the same disk will most likely be visible in /proc/partitions. In the case of EMC PowerPath, the multipath device uses the format /dev/emcpowera*1*, etc. Take care to identify the correct device.

Once the device has been identified and partitioned, you can create the OCFS2 filesystem on that partition. You do this with the **mkfs.ocfs2** command. For Oracle VM, using a large cluster size and allocating at least eight slots (or more if more than eight nodes are in the cluster). Other options you might need include:

- **–b** *block-size*   Allows for larger block sizes if needed. Typically, the default of 4K is sufficient for Oracle VM.

- **–C** *cluster-size*   Allows for the cluster size to be increased. The **–T** command does this automatically.

- **–L** *label*   Allows the label name to be specified. This is not required for Oracle VM.

- **–N** *node-slots*   Sets the number of slots. Oracle VM requires a minimum of eight. You can increase this if more than eight cluster nodes are going to be defined.

- **–T** *filesystem-type*   Specifies the filesystem type for Oracle VM, which should be datafiles. With this option set, the cluster size is created based on the size of the filesystem. This parameter is important and should always be used.

These do not represent all of the options available to mkfs.ocfs2, but they do represent the ones needed for Oracle VM. The minimum parameters required are **–Tdatafiles** and **–N8**. The following is an example of creating the OCFS2 filesystem for Oracle VM:

```
root@ptc7 ~]# mkfs.ocfs2 -Tdatafiles -N8 /dev/sdb1
mkfs.ocfs2 1.4.3
Cluster stack: classic o2cb
```

```
Filesystem Type of datafiles
Filesystem label=
Block size=4096 (bits=12)
Cluster size=131072 (bits=17)
Volume size=21467889664 (163787 clusters) (5241184 blocks)
6 cluster groups (tail covers 2507 clusters, rest cover 32256 clusters)
Journal size=33554432
Initial number of node slots: 8
Creating bitmaps: done
Initializing superblock: done
Writing system files: done
Writing superblock: done
Writing backup superblock: 3 block(s)
Formatting Journals: done
Formatting slot map: done
Writing lost+found: done
mkfs.ocfs2 successful
```

Once you've created the OCFS2 filesystem, you can add it to Oracle VM and/or an Oracle VM Cluster. How to do this is covered after the sections on configuring the other storage types.

Configuring iSCSI Storage

Configuring iSCSI storage requires a few more manual steps. First, you configure the iSCSI disk storage at the storage server itself. How you do this varies based on the brand and type of iSCSI storage being used. In the case of iSCSI storage using an iSCSI HBA, you often configure it similarly to configuring SAN storage. This section covers iSCSI storage that is configured using the built-in iSCSI features of Oracle VM and Linux.

The first step is to set up and configure the iSCSI storage subsystem. Make note of the storage system IP address and make sure there are no issues with routing or firewalls. Once you have set up the subsystem, then you can configure iSCSI at the VM Server system.

The next step in configuring iSCSI storage is to enable the iSCSI subsystem. This is done within dom0 by executing **service iscsi start** as shown here:

```
root@ptc7 ~]# service iscsi start
iscsid (pid 2146 2145) is running...
Setting up iSCSI targets: iscsiadm: No records found!
                                                    [ OK ]
```

In this example, no initial iscsi targets have been found—that is, it hasn't been configured yet.

```
[root@ptc7 ~]# iscsiadm -m discovery -t sendtargets -p 192.168.10.1
192.168.10.1:3260,1 iqn.2005-02.com.ricecake.iscsi:00
```

Now that the disk is visible, you can configure and use it. If you have more than one disk that you don't desire, you can delete it from the configuration using the following command:

```
[root@ptc7 ~]# iscsiadm -m node -p 192.168.10.1:3260,1 -T iqn.2005-02.com.
ricecake.iscsi:00 -o delete
```

The goal is to have only the desired disks visible to the system. You verify this with the **iscsiadm –m node** command, as shown here:

```
[root@ptc7 ~]# iscsiadm -m node
192.168.10.1:3260,1 iqn.2005-02.com.ricecake.iscsi:00
```

Once verified, check for the storage in the /proc/partitions file. The /proc/partitions pseudo file lists all of the visible partitions. An example is shown here:

```
[root@ptc7 ~]# cat /proc/partitions
major minor  #blocks  name

   8     0   52428800 sda
   8     1     104391 sda1
   8     2    3148740 sda2
   8     3   48122707 sda3
   8     4          1 sda4
   8     5    1052226 sda5
   8    16   20971520 sdb
   8    17   20964793 sdb1
   8    32  624975648 sdc
```

If the new disk is not visible, restart the iscsi service with the following command:

```
[root@ptc7 ~]# service iscsi restart
Logging out of session [sid: 1, target: iqn.2005-02.com.ricecake.
iscsi:00, portal: 192.168.10.1,3260]
Logout of [sid: 1, target: iqn.2005-02.com.ricecake.iscsi:00, portal:
192.168.10.1,3260]: successful
Stopping iSCSI daemon:
iscsid dead but pid file exists                              [ OK ]
Turning off network shutdown. Starting iSCSI daemon:         [ OK ]
                                                             [ OK ]
Setting up iSCSI targets: Logging in to [iface: default, target:
iqn.2005-02.com.ricecake.iscsi:00, portal: 192.168.10.1,3260]
Login to [iface: default, target: iqn.2005-02.com.ricecake.iscsi:00,
portal: 192.168.10.1,3260]: successful
                                                             [ OK ]
```

Once you've completed this step and the partition is visible, follow the steps shown in the previous section to partition the disk with fdisk and format the disk with mkfs.ocfs2. At this point, you are now ready to configure the disk in Oracle VM.

Configuring NFS Storage

NFS storage is fairly easy to configure for Oracle VM. Once you have configured the storage, you should test it. Mount the storage on a mount point on the dom0 system. This mount point is something like /media/nfs or /media/nas. Mount the storage using the following command:

```
[root@ptc7 ~]# mount -t nfs ptcnas1:/OVS /media/nas
```

Verify the storage has mounted correctly by using the **df** command. The NFS drive that was just mounted should be visible. An example of the **df** command is shown here:

```
[root@ptc7 ~]# df -h
Filesystem            Size  Used Avail Use% Mounted on
/dev/sda2             7.8G  859M  6.6G  12% /
/dev/sdb1             137G  129G  8.1G  95% /OVS
/dev/sda1              99M   36M   58M  39% /boot
tmpfs                 330M     0  330M   0% /dev/shm
/dev/sda5              56G   27G   27G  51% /u01
/dev/sdc1             137G  1.1G  136G   1% /OVS/73FDA33DF6EB41349D8E7E3D56203F2F
ptcnas1:/OVS          921G  543M  920G   1% /media/nas
```

If the NFS mounted drive is visible and can be accessed, then unmount it. The pre-steps for the NFS configuration just involve validating the drive. No further steps are necessary. Unmount the drive using the **umount /media/nas** command.

The NFS drive is not partitioned and formatted. The partitioning and formatting have already been done at the NFS server system. The NFS drive only needs to be mounted to be able to use it.

NOTE
When using NFS storage, performance can be potentially enhanced by manually creating xen bridges, and not creating a xen bridge on the interface hosting storage. This assumes that the network adapter used for NAS storage does not host virtual machine networks.

Configuring SCSI Storage

The SCSI drive configuration is very straightforward. Unlike NAS or iSCSI, the drive needs to be connected only to the system. Depending on the SCSI controller and driver, adding the storage dynamically might be possible. Usually this requires a system reboot. Regardless of whether a reboot is necessary, when the device is available, it should be visible in /proc/partitions. You can verify this as shown in the example here. Once the drive is visible, you can partition and format it the same way as the SAN and iSCSI drive. Once you have completed this, add the storage to Oracle VM.

```
[root@ptc7 ~]# cat /proc/partitions
major minor  #blocks  name

    8     0   52428800 sda
    8     1     104391 sda1
    8     2    3148740 sda2
    8     3   48122707 sda3
    8     4          1 sda4
    8     5    1052226 sda5
    8    16   20971520 sdb
    8    32   20971520 sdc
```

The new visible SCSI disks are /dev/sdb and /dev/sdc. The storage shown is in 1K blocks; thus each disk is 20GB in size.

Adding the Additional Storage to Oracle VM

Once you have added the storage to the system at the hardware and Linux layer, you must add it to Oracle VM. You do this using the repos.py python program. This program has multiple options, including the following:

- **repos.py –n <repo>**   Add a new repository. This repository is specified by the descriptor, which is either a device or an NFS descriptor.

- **repos.py –d <uuid>**   Delete a repository. This removes a repository from Oracle VM.

- **repos.py –r <uuid>**   Set the root. For a cluster, this sets the cluster root to the repository specified by the <uuid>.

- **repos.py –l**   List the repositories.

- **repos.py –i**   Initialize all repositories. Do this with extreme caution because it will initialize all of the repositories.

- **repos.py –h**   Get help. Print the help information.

Either add /opt/ovs-agent-2.3/utils to your path or prepend the path onto the **repos.py** command. Adding storage to an existing Oracle VM system is done using this command. If you're creating a cluster, you must perform the additional step of setting the cluster root.

Configuring the Additional Storage in Oracle VM

Storage is added to Oracle VM using the repos.py python program as mentioned earlier. To add new storage with this command, use the **–n** option on **repos.py**, as shown here, based on the type of storage.

For NAS storage, use the following:

```
# /opt/ovs-agent-2.3/utils/repos.py -n ptcnas1:/OVS
```

An example of adding NAS storage is shown here. The first and last steps to list the storage both before and after adding it to Oracle VM are optional.

```
[root@ptc7 ~]# /opt/ovs-agent-2.3/utils/repos.py -l
[ * ] 667abae8-c8e8-445b-8a8a-055a28118797 => /dev/sdb2
[root@ptc7 ~]# /opt/ovs-agent-2.3/utils/repos.py -n ptcnas1:/OVS
[ NEW ] 1fb3622f-c6c3-4c8f-b61f-8752e1b980de => ptcnas1:/OVS
[root@ptc7 ~]# /opt/ovs-agent-2.3/utils/repos.py -l
[    ] 1fb3622f-c6c3-4c8f-b61f-8752e1b980de => ptcnas1:/OVS
[ * ] 667abae8-c8e8-445b-8a8a-055a28118797 => /dev/sdb2
```

For SAN, iSCSI, or SCSI storage, use the following:

```
# /opt/ovs-agent-2.3/utils/repos.py -n /dev/sdb1
```

It is like most things—most of the work is in the preparation. Once the storage is configured and ready, the actual task of adding it to Oracle VM is very straightforward and not extremely complicated.

Once the storage has been added, you can view it with the repository list command by running **repos.py –l**. This command lists the storage that is configured for Oracle VM. The storage you added will be used along with the existing storage that was already configured in the system. Oracle VM determines how to best distribute virtual machines across the storage.

NOTE
If this storage will be used for High Availability in an Oracle VM Cluster, all storage must be shared. Existing storage that is not shared can easily be retasked for local storage, such as backups.

The final step, if applicable, is to configure the Oracle VM Cluster.

Creating an Oracle VM Cluster

The final step in setting up storage for an Oracle VM Cluster is to create the cluster root. The *cluster root* is the top level of the directory structure. In an Oracle VM Cluster, the cluster root must be on shared storage.

If additional storage is replacing existing storage, such as replacing non-shared storage with shared storage, first, you have to remove the original storage. Do this with the **repos.py –d <uuid>** command. This command will delete the repository specified by the UUID.

Once the storage has been added, you can convert the desired storage to the cluster root and propagate it to all of the servers in the server pool. First list the storage using **repos.py –l**, as shown here:

```
[root@ptc7 ~]# /opt/ovs-agent-2.3/utils/repos.py -l
[    ] 1fb3622f-c6c3-4c8f-b61f-8752e1b980de => ptcnas1:/OVS
[ * ] 667abae8-c8e8-445b-8a8a-055a28118797 => /dev/sdb2
```

Once you have identified the drive to use as the cluster root, set it using the **repos.py** command with the **–r** option followed by the UUID of the desired storage. Setting the cluster root is shown here:

```
[root@ptc7 ~]# /opt/ovs-agent-2.3/utils/repos.py -r 1fb3622f-c6c3-4-
c8f-b61f-8752e1b980de
[ R ] 1fb3622f-c6c3-4c8f-b61f-8752e1b980de => ptcnas1:/OVS
[root@ptc7 ~]# /opt/ovs-agent-2.3/utils/repos.py -l
[ R ] 1fb3622f-c6c3-4c8f-b61f-8752e1b980de => ptcnas1:/OVS
[ * ] 667abae8-c8e8-445b-8a8a-055a28118797 => /dev/sdb2
```

Once you've set the cluster root and added servers to the server pool, the storage configuration will be propagated to those systems. As before, there aren't many options or much complexity involved in this.

If already existing non-shared storage is present in the system, you can remove it with the **repos.py** command with the **–d** option followed by the UUID, as shown here:

```
[root@ptc7 ~]# /opt/ovs-agent-2.3/utils/repos.py -l
[ R ] 1fb3622f-c6c3-4c8f-b61f-8752e1b980de => ptcnas1:/OVS
[ * ] 667abae8-c8e8-445b-8a8a-055a28118797 => /dev/sdb2
[root@ptc7 ~]# /opt/ovs-agent-2.3/utils/repos.py -d 667abae8-c8e8-
445b-8a8a-055a28118797
[ DEL ] 667abae8-c8e8-445b-8a8a-055a28118797 => /dev/sdb2
```

An optional step is to initialize the storage to make it available for use:

```
[root@ptc3 /]# /opt/ovs-agent-2.3/utils/repos.py -i
*** Storage repositories initialized.
```

Once the storage has been initialized, you can create the storage pool.

NOTE
*The storage is initialized when you add the first
server to the server pool. The **initialize** command
has been included here for completeness. It will not
hurt to initialize the storage, but it is not necessary.*

Before the storage pool has been created, the directories will not be visible
yet; however, you should mount the storage. You can verify it with the **mount**
command, as shown here:

```
[root@ptc7 ~]# mount
. . .
ptcnas1:/OVS on /var/ovs/mount/1FB3622FC6C34C8FB61F8752E1B980DE type
nfs (rw,addr=192.168.50.3)
```

Once the server pool has been created, the directories on /OVS will be created
and will be visible. Once this has occurred, the system is ready to start creating
virtual machines.

In a non-clustered environment, removing existing storage is typically unnecessary.
However, if you want to change the cluster root, you do this using the same **repos.py**
commands. In fact, there really isn't much difference between a clustered and
non-clustered system from the storage standpoint, with the exception that the storage
is shared and High Availability can be enabled on a clustered system.

Summary

This chapter covered storage management in an Oracle VM environment. Storage
configuration is a very straightforward process without much complexity. The real
complexity comes with configuring the hardware. Some storage vendors require
additional device drivers and multipathing software. These should be configured
according to the storage vendor's instructions.

Once you have configured the storage at the Oracle VM Server level, not many
options are available to configure. This part of the process is done when the virtual
machines are created or modified and will be covered in later chapters in this book.

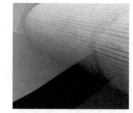

PART
III

Managing Oracle VM
Servers and Guests

CHAPTER
12

Creating Server
Pools and Servers

he VM Server pool is an integral part of the Oracle VM Server farm. The server pool is the collection of servers that is used to store virtual machines. Within the server pool, virtual machines can be migrated or failed over. A server pool consists of one or more servers configured together to execute the virtual machines.

The members of the server pool can assume the role of server pool master, utility server, or Virtual Machine server. The code for each role is in every Oracle VM Agent (ovs-agent). The utility server and VM Server roles can be dynamically assigned to any member of the server pool; however, the server pool master role can only be given to one server in the server pool, and it is not user-assignable.

Chapter 6 dealt with installing the VM Server. Once the VM Server has been configured and the VM Manager is operational, now you can configure the server pools. As a reminder, the VM Server consists of the underlying hardware, the Xen Hypervisor, and the Oracle VM Server Agent (ovs-agent). You use the VM Agent to configure the VM Server as the server pool master, the utility server, and the VM Server. The software installed during the installation process is identical, regardless of the role; it's how the software is configured that distinguishes the server type.

The VM Server system, which is shown in Figure 12-1, is made up of the underlying hardware, the Xen Hypervisor, and the dom0 domain, which includes the VM Agent.

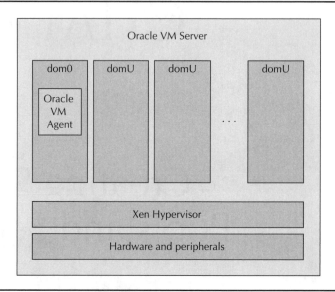

FIGURE 12-1. *The VM Server system*

As mentioned previously, what distinguishes the type of server is how it is configured. With the exception of the server pool master, the roles are configured from the Oracle VM Manager, OEM Grid Control, or the Oracle VM CLI. Each method is acceptable and supported, so you can decide based on your own preference. This chapter, along with several upcoming chapters, will walk through each method for creating, configuring, and managing the Oracle VM Server pool.

Configuring Server Pools

Configuring the server pool is a fairly straightforward process that involves configuring the VM Agent. First you create the server pool and then add additional servers. Once you have created the first server in the server pool, the additional servers can be added either with or without the High Availability option. The High Availability option requires that a shared disk be configured. With High Availability configured, you can perform both failover and live migration.

Before creating the server pool, you should do some planning. You should decide how many servers to create in the server pool and what function to assign to each server. The different types of server roles were described in detail in Chapter 3, but a brief review is provided here:

- **Server pool master**   The server pool master is the contact point from the server pool to the outside world as well as the dispatcher of work to the other servers in the server pool. The server pool master is responsible for load balancing by selecting the virtual machine server with the most available resources. Only one server pool master is in the server pool at any one time, but in the event of a failure, the role of server pool master will be assigned to another server in the pool.

- **Utility server**   The utility server is the server responsible for providing I/O operations such as creating virtual machines. Unlike the server pool master, several utility servers can be configured in the server pool.

- **VM Server**   The virtual machine (VM) server is the server role that does the real work—running the virtual machines. Its main purpose is to act as the hypervisor to the virtual machines. The pool must have at least one VM Server, though there can be many. Because the server pool is a load-balanced environment, the server pool master chooses the VM Server with the most available resources to start the next virtual machine.

The server pool, with its one server pool master, one or more utility servers, and one or more VM Servers, acts as an entity to provide virtual machine services. Because they support failover and load balancing, shared storage is required. The number and type of servers depends on the required workload and is specific to each environment's requirements. Because a VM Server requires a certain amount of resources, more virtual machines will require more hardware. These next sections first cover how to create the server pool and then how to configure and manage it as needed.

Using the Oracle VM Manager to Create and Manage Server Pools and Servers

The Oracle VM Manager is probably the most popular tool for managing Oracle VM for small and medium installations. The Oracle VM Manager is easy to install and to use. It is versatile and can do everything needed to manage and maintain an Oracle VM Server farm. This section discusses how to use the VM Manager to create and manage server pools and servers.

Creating Server Pools with the Oracle VM Manager

Creating a server pool with the Oracle VM Manager is a straightforward process that is presented here in a step-by-step fashion.

1. From the Server Pools screen, shown here, click Create Pool to invoke the Create Server Pool screen.

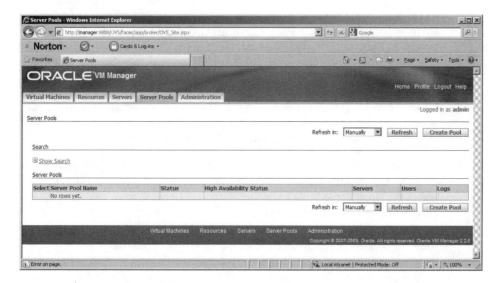

2. From the Create Server Pool screen, fill in the pertinent information about the server pool. The information required for creating a server pool is as follows:

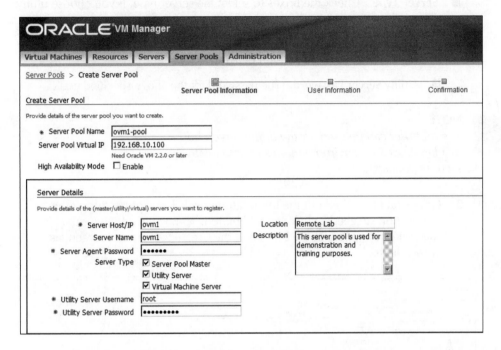

- ■ **Server Pool Name**   The name that will be used for the server pool in the VM Manager, OEM Grid Control, and so on. This name should be fairly descriptive—or at least descriptive enough so it is recognizable.

- ■ **Server Pool Virtual IP**   The IP address that will be used to access the server pool master. This IP address is different from the server's IP address and might move between servers.

- ■ **High Availability Mode**   Checking this box enables High Availability.

- ■ **Server Details**   The details for each individual server. Add the details one server at a time. You can add multiple servers in this process.

You must fill out the Server Details for at least one server before the server pool can be created. The following is the information needed to configure a server:

- ■ **Server Host/IP**   The IP address or name (if in a host file) of the server that will be added to the pool.

- ■ **Server Name**   The name that identifies the server in the pool.

- **Server Agent Password** The password used for the agent when the VM Server was installed.

- **Server Type** Check the boxes to select the server type. If you choose utility server, the following is also required:

  - **Utility Server Username** A privileged OS user account. Can be root or another user who can perform Oracle VM operations.

  - **Utility Server Password** The password for the above-specified user.

NOTE
The root user can be used for the utility server, but in a large, secured environment this might violate security policies.

3. Once you have filled out the information, click Test Connection. If the connection succeeds, click the Add button. The newly added virtual machine will appear at the bottom of the Create Server Pool screen, as shown here.

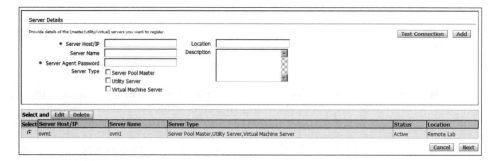

4. Once you have added one or more servers, click the Next button to
invoke the Administrative User screen. This allows users, other than the
administrative user, to administer this server pool. You do not need to add
users at this time, but you can if desired. The User Information screen is
shown here. Click Next to continue.

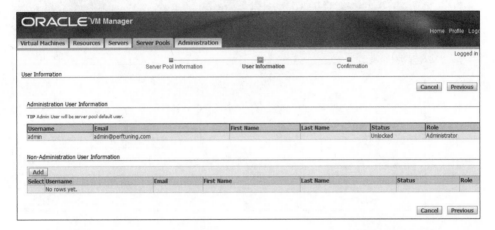

5. The final screen, shown next, is the Create Server Pool confirmation screen,
where you have a last chance to verify the information added in the
previous screens. When completed, click Confirm to create the server pool.

6. The Server Pools screen reappears. The status changes when the server pool is created. Once you've created the server pool, the status will appear as Active, as shown here.

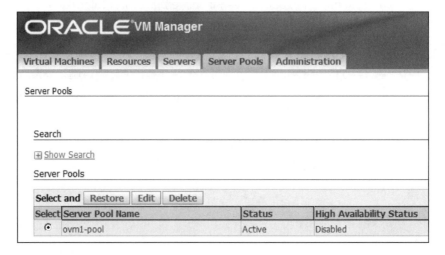

At this point, the server pool is ready to use. You can modify the server pool via the Server Pools tab in the VM Manager. Select the server pool you want to modify and click the Edit button. This will invoke the Edit Server Pool screen where you can enable High Availability and modify the Server Pool Virtual IP address. You perform other modifications via the Servers tab.

Managing Servers with the Oracle VM Manager

Managing the various servers that are configured within a server pool is done via the Servers screen, as shown in Figure 12-2. At the top of the screen on the

FIGURE 12-2. *The Oracle VM Servers screen*

right-hand side, you'll see the Add Server button. In addition, there are buttons to Reboot, Power Off, Edit, Delete, and Set Maintenance, which sets a server into maintenance mode.

Click one of the buttons to add or modify servers.

Add a Server to the Server Pool

Clicking the Add Server button invokes the Add Server screen. From this screen, you can add another server to the server pool. The Add Server screen requires the same information as the Create Server Pool screen: Server Host/IP, Server Name, Server Agent Password, Server Type (utility server and/or virtual machine server), along with one addition—the Server Pool Name. You can add a server to the pool here.

Modify Server Properties

The other buttons on the Servers screen (Figure 12-2) allow you to perform operations on the servers or to edit the server's properties:

- **Reboot**   Click this button to reboot the server. First, you will see a verification screen. If you are rebooting the server pool master, some functions might be temporarily unavailable.

- **Power Off**   Click this to power off the server after confirming your choice on the verification screen.

- **Edit**   Click to edit the server. You can modify properties such as IP address and server type. This option is covered in more detail following this list.

- **Delete**   Click this button to delete the server from the server pool.

- **Set Maintenance**   Putting the server into maintenance mode disables that server from running a new virtual machine. You will receive a prompt before any existing virtual machines are powered off. The server's resources are not available to the server pool while it is running in maintenance mode.

To modify an existing server, select the Server using the radio button and then click the Edit button. This invokes the Edit Server screen, which is shown in Figure 12-3. From this screen, you can change the server name and server role. If this is a utility server, you can change the username and password as well. In addition, you can modify the location and description comments.

In addition to the Edit Server tab, there are two additional tabs: Change Oracle VM Agent Password and Change Utility Server Password. These tabs allow you to change the Agent and user password remotely from the VM Server. The existing password is required, along with confirming the new password.

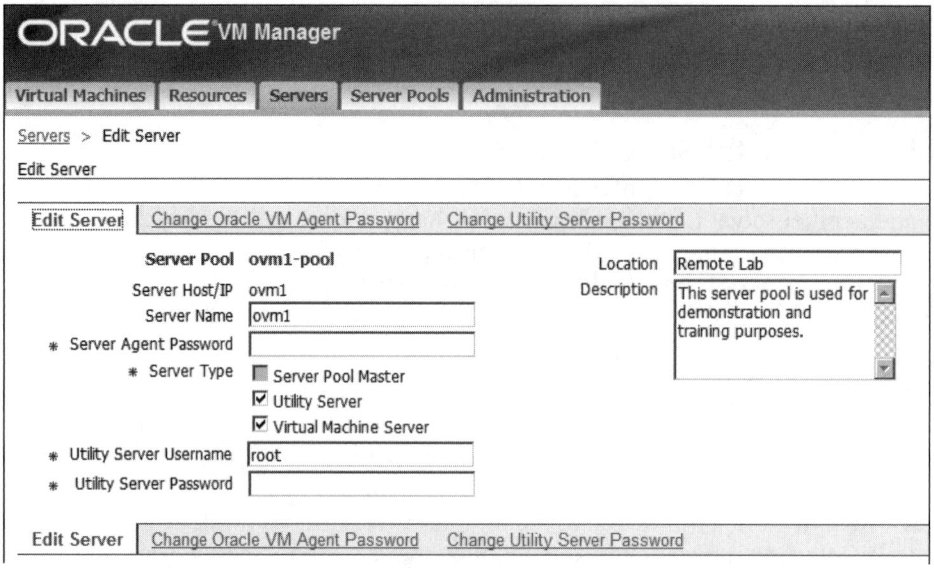

FIGURE 12-3. *The Edit Server screen*

As you can see, there really isn't a significant amount of work needed to create and maintain the server pool and servers. Most of the work to be done in maintaining the Oracle VM environment is related to creating and maintaining virtual machines. In the next section, the same configuration operations are covered using OEM Grid Control.

Using the OEM Grid Control to Create and Manage Server Pools and Servers

OEM Grid Control is typically used to manage the Oracle VM system in environments where OEM is already installed and configured and in larger VM Server farms. Since OEM Grid Control must be set up prior to configuring it for Oracle VM, additional work is needed. However, this work is well worth it because you can use OEM Grid Control not only to configure and manage the Oracle VM environment but also to manage and monitor the virtual machine's databases and applications.

Creating Server Pools with OEM Grid Control

Within OEM Grid Control, a virtual server pool is created from within the Virtual Servers subtab in the Targets tab. This tab shows the currently configured server pools and offers several options in the two drop-down menus. From the first menu, select Virtual Server Pool, Virtual Server, or Guest VM. From the second menu, if you selected Virtual Server Pool from the first menu, the following options are available:

- **Create Virtual Server Pool** Select this option to create a new server pool.

- **Remove Virtual Server Pool** Select this option to remove a server pool.

- **Manage Virtual Server Pool** Select this option to modify and manage a virtual server pool configuration.

- **Create Guest VM** Select this option to create a new guest VM within the server pool.

- **Discover Guest VM** Select this option to discover a guest VM within the server pool. Select this when you copy a VM from another server pool or restore it from a backup.

- **Clear Operator Error** Select to clear errors from the console.

The Virtual Servers subtab of the Targets tab is shown in Figure 12-4, where the Virtual Server Pool and Create Virtual Server Pool options have been selected.

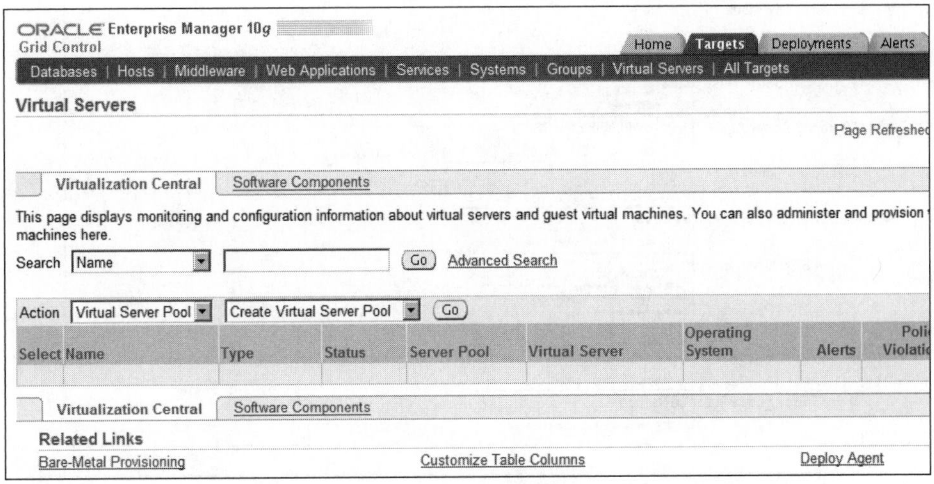

FIGURE 12-4. *The Virtual Servers subtab in OEM Grid Control*

Once you've selected the proper options, click the Go button to invoke the Create Virtual Server Pool screen. This screen, which is shown in Figure 12-5, contains multiple options that you must fill out to create the server pool properly. These options are

- **Virtual Server Pool Name**   Identifies the server pool.

- **High Availability Mode**   Designates whether HA will be enabled.

And in the Master Virtual Server Details section, these options are required:

- **Virtual Server Host**   Identifies the host name of the master server in the server pool.

- **Monitoring Server Agent**   Identifies the Grid Control Agent that will monitor the server pool. You select the Agent from a list of Grid Control Agents, and it can be the Agent on the Grid Control server itself if desired.

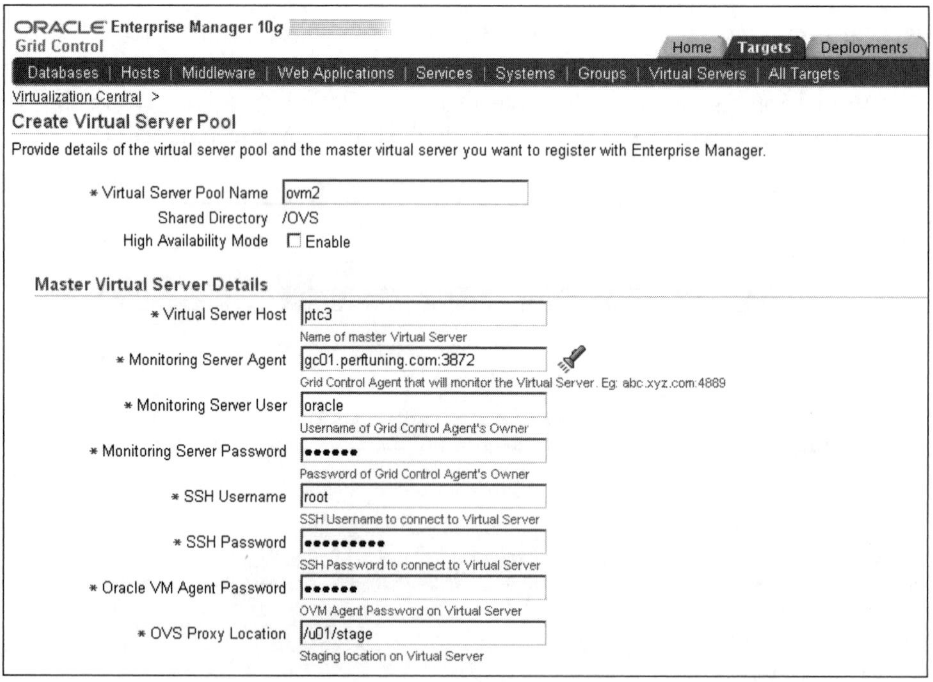

FIGURE 12-5.   *The Create Virtual Server Pool screen*

- **Monitoring Server User**   Identifies the username of the OS owner of the Grid Control Agent. In many cases, this will be the Oracle user, but it can be any user who can access the Agent.

- **Monitoring Server Password**   Identifies the password of the above-mentioned user.

- **SSH Username**   Identifies the username of the user with privileges on the server pool master.

- **SSH Password**   Identifies the password of the previous user.

- **Oracle VM Agent Password**   Identifies the password of the Oracle VM Agent on the server pool master being created.

- **OVS Proxy Location**   Identifies a directory for temporarily storing scripts for creating the server pool.

Once you have completed these options, as shown in Figure 12-5, click the OK button to continue. A confirmation screen will appear with the Job ID for the Grid Control job that was submitted to create the server pool.

The confirmation screen is just informational. Click OK to continue. After clicking OK, control is returned to the Virtual Servers screen, where you can monitor the progress of the server pool and server creation in the Status column. The Status column will eventually change to Up for both the Virtual Server Pool and the Virtual Server, as shown in Figure 12-6. Once both show a status of Up, the creation process has finished and the server pool is ready to use.

Once the server pool and virtual servers have been created, you can modify them from the Virtual Servers screen. This is detailed in the next section.

Managing Servers with OEM Grid Control

You can manage virtual server pools and virtual servers from the Virtual Servers screen within OEM Grid Control. As mentioned in the previous section, the Virtual Servers screen contains two drop-down menus. After selecting Virtual Server Pool from the first drop-down menu, you will be presented with more selections that allow for various operations: Create Virtual Server Pool, Remove Virtual Server Pool, Manage Virtual Server Pool, Create Guest VM, Discover Guest VM, and Clear Operator Error.

Remove the server pool by simply selecting the radio button next to the server pool to be removed; then select Virtual Server Pool and Remove Virtual Server Pool from the drop-down menus and click Go. A validation and confirmation screen will be displayed. Validate that everything is correct, select whether to remove files and force remove and then click Yes. This removes the server pool from the VM Server

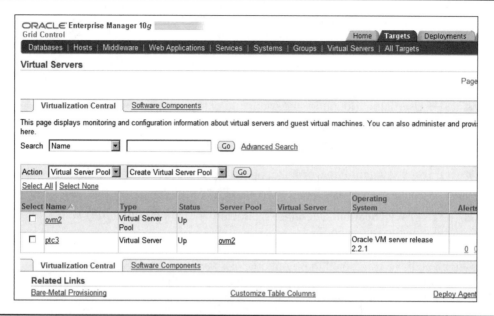

FIGURE 12-6. *The Virtual Servers screen with a new virtual server pool*

system; however, the system and Agent remain active and can be added to another server pool or used to create a new server pool.

The Manage Virtual Server pool option allows for several functions. On the Home tab of the Server Pool management screen, you can change the High Availability mode. This is shown in Figure 12-7.

The Resources tab is where you import resources into or allow them to be discovered by the server pool. Imported resources are those resources that are being brought into the server pool from another source, such as the Internet. The resources that can be imported include Shared Disks, Oracle VM Templates, and ISO Images. The Resources tab is shown in Figure 12-8.

Resources can be imported from an external source such as FTP or HTTP, from the server itself, or from a Linux Physical to Virtual (P2V) conversion. Selecting Import will send the browser to the Import GVM Template screen. Here, additional information is required.

Server resources and how to manage them will be covered in more detail in Chapter 13. Other operations that are available from the Virtual Servers configuration screen include Create a Guest VM and Discover a Guest VM, which are covered later in Chapters 16–18.

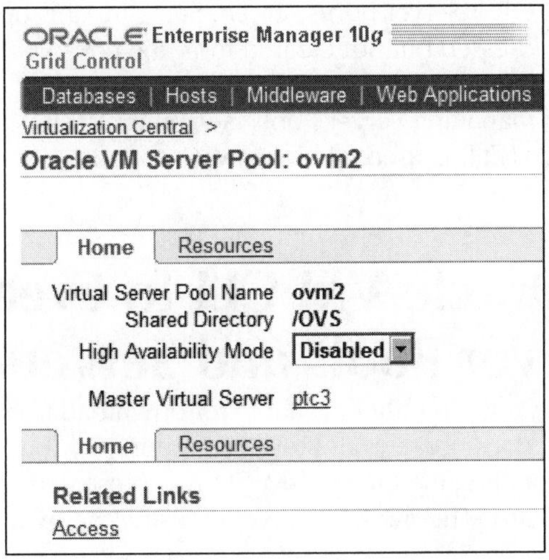

FIGURE 12-7. *The Server Pool Home screen*

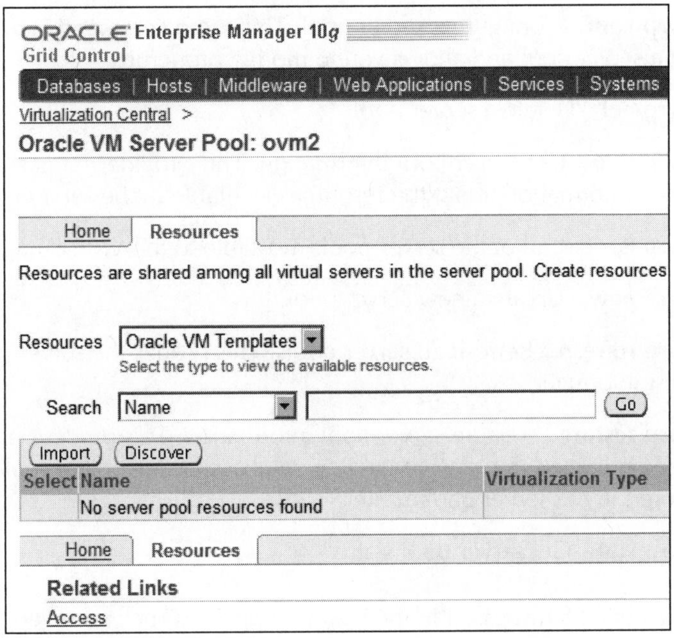

FIGURE 12-8. *The Server Pool Resources screen*

The Clear Operational Error option allows you to clear any errors that might have occurred from the OEM Server Pools screen. Selecting this option is useful for errors that have been addressed but not cleared from the console. Select the errors to clear using the radio buttons and click Go to clear the errors.

The final method of managing Server Pools is via the Oracle VM CLI. The Command-Line Interface (CLI) is used when browser connectivity is not available and/or if scripting is desired.

Using the Oracle VM CLI to Create and Manage Server Pools and Servers

The Oracle VM CLI is an add-on utility available for download from the Unbreakable Linux Network. The CLI does not require browser support but does require a working Oracle VM Manager. Installing the Oracle VM CLI was presented earlier in Chapter 9 and is fairly straightforward. The ovmcli is invoked using the **ovm** command with additional qualifiers.

Creating Server Pools with the Oracle VM CLI

The OVM CLI offers several commands for configuring and managing the server pool. Server pool commands available within the OVM CLI are

- **ovm svrp conf**   Configure a server pool. This same command is used for editing a server pool and allows you to modify properties.

- **ovm svrp del**   Delete a server pool.

- **ovm svrp info**   Get server pool information. This provides interesting, important information about the resources available in the server pool.

- **ovm svrp ls**   List all of the server pools available to the VM Manager.

- **ovm svrp new**   Create a new server pool.

- **ovm svrp refresh**   Refresh all server pools. This probes the server pools for the latest information.

- **ovm svrp restore**   Restore server pool information. This process takes the information in the Oracle VM Manager database and uses it to replace the data stored in the server pool master.

- **ovm svrp stat**   Get server pool status.

These commands will be discussed in the next section. This section covers how to create a server pool from the Oracle VM.

Creating the server pool is done via the **ovm svrp new** command. This command takes a number of qualifiers. These qualifiers are listed in Table 12-1.

Use the **–u** or **–username=** qualifier to pass the VM Manager username. Use the **–p** or **–password** qualifier to pass the password qualifier. List the current server pools using the **svrp ls** command:

```
[root@ptccontrol ~]# ovm -u admin svrp ls.
Password:
Server_Pool_Name Status HA
ptc1-pool        Active Disabled
ptc2-pool        Active Disabled
pe710-pool       Active Disabled
```

Option	Description
-h, --help	Display the help message.
-H hostname, --hostname=hostname	(Required) The server hostname or IP address.
-s server_pool, --server_pool_name=server_pool	(Required) The name of the new server pool.
-a, -ha_enabled	If provided, enables high availability.
-A agent_password, --agent_password=agent_password	The password of the Oracle VM Agent.
-U utility_username, --utility_username=utility_username	(Required) The user for the utility server—can be root or another valid account.
-P utility_password, --utility_password=utility_password	(Required) The utility server user's password (associated with the previous option).
-u user_list, --user_list=user_list	List of non-admin users.
-n server_name, --server_name=server_name	The name of the server being added.
-L server_location, --server_location=server_location	The location comment.
-D description, --description=description	The description of the server pool.

TABLE 12-1. *ovm svrp* Options

Create the server pool using the **svrp new** command and the following syntax:

```
[root@ptccontrol ~]# ovm -u admin svrp new -H ptc3 -s ptc3-pool -A
<agent pwd> -U root -P <svr pwd> -n ptc3 -L "Remote Lab" -D "This
server is used for testing and training"
Password:
Created server pool "ptc3-pool".
```

Verify the pool with the previous command:

```
[root@ptccontrol ~]# ovm -u admin svrp ls
Password:
Server_Pool_Name Status HA
ptc1-pool        Active Disabled
ptc2-pool        Active Disabled
pe710-pool       Active Disabled
ptc3-pool        Active Disabled
```

You manage the server pool via the **ovm svrp** command. You can add servers using the **ovm svr** command, as shown in the next section.

Managing Server Pools and Servers with the Oracle VM CLI

The OVM CLI has a wide range of commands available for monitoring and managing the server pool and servers. The **ovm svrp** and **ovm svr** commands and the options available to these commands are covered in this section. You manage the server pool via the **ovm svrp** command and the servers via the **ovm svr** command.

Managing the Server Pool

ovm svrp has a number of options that were discussed in the last section, including **conf**, **del**, **info**, **ls**, **new**, **refresh**, **restore** and **stat**. The **new** option was covered in the last section; the additional commands are covered here.

Use the **ovm svrp conf** command to configure a server pool and to change the High Availability option, the pool name, and the server pool virtual IP address. The options for **ovm svrp conf** are listed in Table 12-2.

Following is an example of retrieving server pool information:

```
[root@ptccontrol ~]# ovm -u admin -p <password> svrp info -s ptc3-pool
                    ID: 190
      Server Pool Name: ptc3-pool
   Server Pool Virtual IP:
                Status: Active
      High Availability: Disabled
   Total Number of CPUs: 8
   Total CPU Speed(MHZ): 1993
```

Option	Description
-h, --help	Display the help message.
-s server_pool, --serverpool_name=serverpool_name	(Required) Designate the name of the server pool to be configured.
-e, --enable_ha	Enable High Availability in the server pool.
-d, --disable_ha	Disable High Availability in the server pool.
-n new_pool, --new_poolname=new_pool	Rename the server pool to new_pool.
-i VIP, --vip=VIP	Change the virtual IP address to VIP.

TABLE 12-2. *ovm svrp conf* Options

```
          Total Number of Chips: 8
              Allocated VCPUs: 0
            Total Memory(MB): 7679
             Free Memory(MB): 7037
         Free Disk Space(MB): 6566
[root@ptccontrol ~]# ovm -u admin -p <password> svrp conf -s ptc3-pool -n ptc3-new
Server pool updated.
[root@ptccontrol ~]# ovm -u admin -p <password> svrp info -s ptc3-pool
Server pool "ptc3-pool" does not exist.
[root@ptccontrol ~]# ovm -u admin -p <password> svrp info -s ptc3-new
                          ID: 190
            Server Pool Name: ptc3-new
      Server Pool Virtual IP:
                      Status: Active
           High Availability: Disabled
         Total Number of CPUs: 8
         Total CPU Speed(MHZ): 1993
        Total Number of Chips: 8
             Allocated VCPUs: 0
            Total Memory(MB): 7679
             Free Memory(MB): 7037
         Free Disk Space(MB): 6566
```

Use the **ovm svrp del** command to delete a server pool. The **ovm svrp del** command takes the options listed in Table 12-3.

An example of using the **ovm svrp del** command is shown here:

```
[root@ptccontrol ~]# ovm -u admin -p <password> svrp del -s ptc3-pool -d -f
Server pool "ptc3-pool" deleted, with working directories removed.
```

Option	Description
-h, --help	Display the help message.
-s server_pool, --serverpool_name=serverpool_name	(Required) Specify the name of the server pool to be deleted.
-d, --isdelworkingdirectory	If specified, will remove all of the working directories on the server pool.
-f, --force	Will force the server pool delete.

TABLE 12-3. *ovm svrp del* Options

The **ovm svrp ls** command lists the server pools available to the VM Manager and takes no options, as shown here:

```
[root@ptccontrol ~]# ovm -u admin -p <password> svrp ls
Server_Pool_Name Status HA
ptc1-pool        Active Disabled
ptc2-pool        Active Disabled
pe710-pool       Active Disabled
ptc3-pool        Active Disabled
```

The **ovm svrp refresh** command refreshes information available in the VM Manager and VM CLI by querying the VM Servers. The **ovm svrp refresh** command takes no options either.

```
[root@ptccontrol ~]# ovm -u admin -p <password> svrp refresh
Refresh server pool data.
```

The **ovm svrp restore** command restores server pool information. This process takes the information in the Oracle VM Manager database and uses it to replace the data stored in the server pool master. This command takes only the server pool name parameter with either the **–s** or **–serverpool_name=name** option, as shown here:

```
[root@ptccontrol ~]# ovm -u admin -p <password> svrp restore -s ptc3-pool
Restoring server pool data from Oracle VM Manager.
Server pool data restored successfully.
```

The **ovm svrp stat** command provides the server pool status. This command takes only the server pool name parameter with either the **–s** or **–serverpool_name=name** option.

```
[root@ptccontrol ~]# ovm -u admin -p <password> svrp stat -s ptc3-pool
Active
```

Using these commands, you can administer and monitor the server pool via scripts or via a remote console without the benefit of a browser. Other operations such as adding a server to the server pool are done via the **ovm svr** commands, as shown in the next section.

Managing the Servers

Managing servers is also done via the **ovm** commands; however, you use the **ovm svr** commands. The **ovm svr** commands consist of the following:

- **ovm svr add**   Add a server to a server pool.

- **ovm svr agent**   Return the agent version.

- **ovm svr conf**   Configure the server.

- **ovm svr del**   Delete the server from the server pool.

- **ovm svr info**   Get server information. This command provides interesting, important information about the server's resources.

- **ovm svr ls**   List all of the servers available in the server pool.

- **ovm svr mode**   Set the server mode.

- **ovm svr poweroff**   Power off a server.

- **ovm svr pwd**   Reset the utility server or agent password.

- **ovm svr restart**   Restart (reboot) a server.

- **ovm svr stat**   Get server status.

The **ovm svr add** command adds a new server to a server pool. This command takes a number of options that are listed in Table 12-4.

The following is an example of using **ovm svr add** to add a server to a server pool:

```
[root@manager ~]# ovm -u admin -p <password> svr add -s ovm-pool -H ovm2
-n ovm2 -A <agent pwd> -o -L "Remote Lab"
-D "This server is used for demo and training only"
Added server "ovm2" to the server pool.
```

You can query the Agent version on a server by using the **ovm svr agent** command. This command takes the server pool name with the **–s <pool>** or **–serverpool_name=<pool>** option and the **–n <server>** or **–server_name=<server>** option, as shown here:

```
[root@manager ~]# ovm -u admin -p <password> svr agent -s ovm-pool -n ovm1
Agent version: 2.3-38
```

Option	Description
-h, --help	Display the help message.
-s server_pool, --server_pool_name=server_pool	(Required) The name of the server pool that the server is going to be added to.
-H hostname, --hostname=hostname	(Required) The name or IP address of the host that is going to be added to the above-mentioned server pool.
-n server, --server_name=server	The name of the server being added to the server pool.
-A agent_password, --agent_password=agent_password	The password of the Oracle VM Agent on the server being added.
-U utility_username, --utility_username=utility_username	The user for the utility server (if applicable)—can be root or another valid account.
-P utility_password, --utility_password=utility_password	The utility user's password (associated with the previous option).
-o, --vm_only	Designation to add the server as a virtual machine server only.
-u, --uitlity_only	Designation to add the server as a utility server only.
-L server_location, --server_location=server_location	The location comment.
-D description, --description=description	The description of the server pool.

TABLE 12-4. *ovm svr add* Options

Use the **ovm svr conf** command to configure the server. The options available for this command, shown in Table 12-5, are very close to those used for the **ovm svr add** command.

An example of the **ovm svr conf** command is shown here:

```
[root@manager ~]# ovm -u admin -p <password> svr conf -s ovm-pool -n ovm2 -N ovm2-new
Server updated.
```

You can delete a server from the server pool by using the **ovm svr del** command. This command takes the server pool name with the **–s <pool>** or **–serverpool_**

Option	Description
-h, --help	Display the help message.
-s server_pool, --server_pool_name=server_pool	(Required) The name of the server pool that the server is being added to.
-n server, --server_name=server	(Required) The name of the server.
-N new, --new_name=new	The new name of the server.
-A agent_password, --agent_password=agent_password	The password of the Oracle VM Agent on the server being added.
-u utility_username, --username=utility_username	The user for the utility server (if applicable)— can be root or another valid account.
-P utility_password, --utility_password=utility_password	The utility user's password (associated with the previous option).
-t type, --server_type=type	The new server type (comma separated); can be the following: **m** server pool master **v** virtual machine server **u** utility server
-l server_location, --location=server_location	The location comment.
-d description, --description=description	The description of the server pool.
-f, --force	Force a server update.

TABLE 12-5.   *ovm svr conf Options*

name=**<pool>** option and the **–n <server>** or **–server_name=<server>** option. An example is shown here:

```
[root@manager ~]# ovm -u admin -p <password> svr del -s ovm-pool -n ovm2
Removed server "ovm2" from the server pool.
```

You retrieve information about a server using the **ovm svr info** command. This command also takes the server pool name with the **–s <pool>** or **–serverpool_ name=<pool>** option and the **–n <server>** or **–server_name=<server>** option. An example is shown here:

```
[root@manager ~]# ovm -u admin -p <password> svr info -s ovm-pool -n ovm1
            ID: 30
  Server Host/IP: ovm1
    Server Name: ovm1
```

```
      Server Type: Server Pool Master,Utility Server,Virtual Machine Server
           Status: Active
      Server Pool: ovm-pool
   Number of CPUs: 2
  CPU Speed(MHZ): 2265
  Allocated VCPUs: 0
Total Memory(MB): 1023
 Free Memory(MB): 465
         Location: Remote Lab
      Description: This server pool is used for demonstration and training purposes.
```

List the servers known to the VM Manager via the **ovm svr ls** command. This command takes no options and is shown here:

```
[root@manager ~]# ovm -u admin -p <password> svr ls
  Server_Host/IP Server_Name Status Server_Pool
  ovm1           ovm1         Active ovm-pool
  ovm2           ovm2         Active ovm-pool
```

The **ovm svr mode** command takes the server in and out of maintenance mode. In addition to the normal options of server pool name with the **–s <pool>** or **–serverpool_name=<pool>** option and the **–n <server>** or **–server_name=<server>** option, this parameter also takes **–m** or **–maintain** to put the server into maintenance mode and **–N** or **–normal** to take the server out of maintenance mode and back into normal mode, as shown here:

```
[root@manager ~]# ovm -u admin -p <password> svr mode -s ovm-pool -n ovm2 -m
[root@manager ~]# ovm -u admin -p <password> svr stat -s ovm-pool -n ovm2
Maintenance
[root@manager ~]# ovm -u admin -p <password> svr mode -s ovm-pool -n ovm2 -N
[root@manager ~]# ovm -u admin -p <password> svr stat -s ovm-pool -n ovm2
Active
```

Power off a server using the **ovm svr poweroff** command, as shown here. This command takes the typical options of server pool name with the **–s <pool>** or **–serverpool_name=<pool>** option and the **–n <server>** or **–server_name=<server>** option.

```
[root@manager ~]# ovm -u admin -p <password> svr poweroff -s ovm-pool -n ovm2
Shutting down server "ovm2".
```

You can change a utility server or Agent password with the **ovm svr pwd** command. This command takes several options that are shown in Table 12-6. The following is an example of changing the Agent password:

```
[root@manager ~]# ovm -u admin -p pwd123 svr pwd -s ovm -n ovm1 -a -O pwd123
-N 123pwd
Agent password updated.
```

You can restart a server using the **ovm svr restart** command. This command takes the server pool and server options only, as shown here:

```
[root@manager ~]# ovm -u admin -p <password> svr restart -s ovm-pool -n ovm2
Rebooting server "ovm2".
```

Option	Description
-h, --help	Displays the help message.
-s server_pool, --server_pool_name=server_pool	(Required) Specifies the name of the server pool that the server is being added to.
-n server, --server_name=server	(Required) Specifies the name of the server.
-a agent_password, --agent	Specifies the Agent password will be changed.
-u, --utility	Specifies the utility server password will be changed.
-O old_pwd, --old_pwd=old_pwd	Designates the old password.
-N new, --new_pwd=new	Sets the new password.

TABLE 12-6. *ovm svr pwd* Options

Obtain a server's status using the **ovm svr stat** command. The command also takes the server pool and server options, as shown here:

```
[root@manager ~]# ovm -u admin -p <password> svr stat -s ovm-pool -n ovm1
Active
```

Summary

This chapter covered the creation of server pools and how to modify and administer the server pools via three different methods. You have two choices for setting up the management of server pools and servers: the Oracle VM Manager and OEM Grid Control. The Oracle VM CLI is a subset of the VM Manager. For small to medium configurations, the VM Manager is usually the tool of choice. In large Enterprises, OEM Grid Control is often the tool of choice. Either tool will do the job. The CLI is great for scripting and environments where GUI access is not available.

Whatever tool you select, there really isn't much configuration and maintenance needed for the server pools and servers. Most of the work is done in creating and maintaining the virtual machines themselves. How to do this will be covered in a few chapters. The next chapters discuss how to configure server resources, such as templates, images, ISO images, and shared virtual storage.

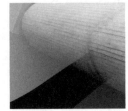

CHAPTER
13

Configuring Server Resources

ne of the major features of Oracle VM that distinguishes it from other virtualization products is the use of templates. Templates are a tool for creating "golden images" of a complete software stack. The Oracle VM Templates are considered one of the server resources. Additional server resources include virtual machine images, ISO images, and shared virtual storage.

This chapter covers managing Oracle VM Server resources. As in the previous chapter, there are three different ways to configure server resources: via the Oracle VM Manager, OEM Grid Control, or the Oracle VM CLI. Each of these methods is covered in this chapter.

Server Resources

The server resources are key features that give Oracle VM its functionality and ease of use. The server resources consist of virtual machine templates, images, and shared virtual disks. Virtual machine templates and images are used to install virtual machines. Shared virtual disks are used in clusters, such as Oracle Real Application Clusters, for shared disk usage. Configuring and administering these server resources are covered in this chapter.

Templates

Virtual machine templates are a core feature of Oracle VM. Virtual machine templates allow you to create virtual machines quickly and efficiently with less chance of making mistakes than if you had to build virtual machines from scratch. Some of the advantages of using VM templates include

- **Ease of use**　By using a template, you can quickly and easily deploy virtual machines. Because templates are preconfigured, you can use them to deploy many consistent copies of the same virtual machine.

- **Consistency**　Because creating a virtual machine from a template does not require extensive configuration changes, the virtual machines are very consistent. If the VM template is configured ready to install the Oracle database, then all virtual machines created from this template will be able to install the Oracle database consistently. If the VM template is configured with the Oracle database preconfigured, then all virtual machines created from this template will include a consistently installed Oracle database ready to go.

- **Provisioning efficiency**　Because templates are preconfigured and can be created or obtained with applications preinstalled, the time it takes to deploy this application can be greatly reduced.

Templates are the preferred method of configuring virtual machines. By using templates, you are guaranteed a consistently configured virtual machine.

VM templates are stored in the /var/ovs/mount/OVS/seed_pool directory. There is a subdirectory for each template and, within that subdirectory, are the virtual disk images and the configuration files—for instance, /var/ovs/mount/<UUID>/OVS/seed_pool/OEL-5.5x64, where an Oracle Enterprise Linux 5.5 template is stored.

Images

Two types of images are available within Oracle VM: the *virtual machine image* that is essentially the virtual machine itself and the *ISO images* that can be used to create a new virtual machine. When a virtual machine is created, a file is created in the server pool to host that virtual machine. To the dom0 domain, this image file is an ordinary file that exists in the domain, but to the virtual domain itself, this file is a hard disk. These files, along with the configuration files, make up the virtual machine image.

An ISO image is a copy of a CD-ROM image that is stored on disk. An ISO image can be used as a virtual CD-ROM within the Oracle VM system. These ISO images are one of the tools that you can use to create and configure virtual machines. When imported into the utility server, the ISO images reside in the iso_pool subdirectory under the OVS directory. These ISO files are stored in subdirectories that keep OS releases together. For example, you might have a directory called /var/ovs/mount/<UUID>/OVS/iso_pool/OEL-5.5x64 that stores all of the OEL 5.5 x64 ISO images.

Shared Virtual Disks

Shared virtual disks are disks that are available to one or more virtual machines. These virtual disks are managed outside of the virtual machine because they are not tied to any specific virtual machine. The shared virtual disks are stored in the /var/ovs/mount/<UUID>/OVS/sharedDisk directory. All of the shared disks are stored in this directory.

The next sections cover configuring and managing server resources using the Oracle VM Manager, OEM Grid Control, and the Oracle VM CLI. Each of these methods is supported. Which one you use depends on your individual configuration and needs.

Configuring Server Resources Using the Oracle VM Manager

The Oracle VM Manager is the most common tool for managing small to medium Oracle VM Server farms. It is easy to install and easy to use. Larger installations that already have Oracle Enterprise Manager (OEM) Grid Control often use this tool to manage the VM Server farm. An add-on to the VM Manager is the Oracle VM CLI. Each of these tools is covered in this chapter.

Managing the server resources via the Oracle VM Manager is done via the Resources tab. From here, you can manage all of the server resources.

Configuring Templates with the Oracle VM Manager

Follow these steps to configure templates with the VM Manager:

1. Creating templates with the VM Manager occurs from the Resources tab, as shown here. From the initial screen, click the Resources tab. From the Resources tab, you can import a template by clicking the Import button.

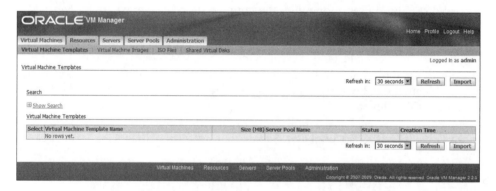

2. Clicking the Import button begins the template import process. On the first screen that appears, you define the source for the template import, as shown next.

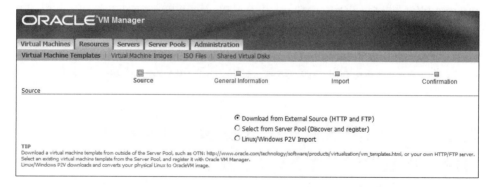

Select the method from the following three options:

- **Download from External Source (HTTP and FTP)**   Download the template from an HHTP or FTP source directly into the Oracle VM system.

- **Select from Server Pool (Discover and Register)**   Discover and register a VM template that has already been downloaded to the utility server.

- **Linux/Windows P2V Import**   The P2V conversion converts a physical server into a virtual server.

3. Once you've selected the import method, the screens that follow will vary, though, for all three options, the screen shown here is similar. You enter the server pool name, enter a name for the template being created (or selected if you chose the discovery option in Step 2), define the OS type, and select valid usernames and passwords. Once you've completed this screen, click the Next button.

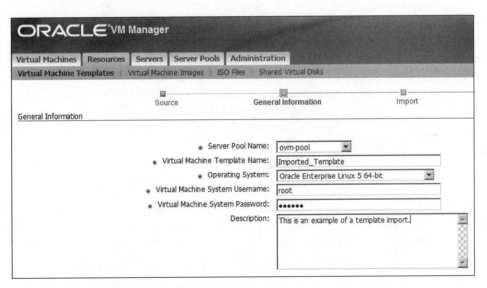

4. The following screen will vary based on your previous selections. If you chose to import from HTTP or FTP in Step 2, you'll see the screen shown next. Enter the URL or address specifying the location of the template. After that, you will see the Confirmation screen.

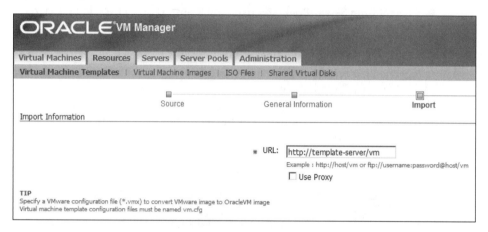

NOTE
If errors occur, you might see a nondescriptive Invalid URL message. You can find more information describing the error in /var/log/ovm-manager/ovm-manager.log on the VM Manager server.

5. If you selected the second option in Step 2—to discover and register—the next screen you'll see is the Confirmation screen. No other input is required except for confirming your choices. On the Confirmation screen, you can add a comment describing the virtual machine template. It is always a great idea to document the template, so you can identify it easily later.

6. In the case of the third option in Step 2—P2V conversion—a screen appears asking you to provide the hostname/IP address of the physical system and then the next screen is the Confirmation screen. In all cases, when you click the Confirm button, the import process begins and control is returned to the Resources tab.

7. Once the template has been successfully imported, you must approve it. The template will remain in the Pending state until you've done this. Approve the template by selecting it and clicking the Approve button. From the Virtual Machine Templates screen, you can delete and edit a template. You can also cancel an import in progress from this screen, and you can reimport a failed import from this screen as well.

Configuring Images with the VM Manager

The VM Manager provides a straightforward and easy way to configure both virtual machine images and ISO images. In this case, the virtual machine images that are referred to are those images that are not part of the virtual machines configured in the server pool, although they are virtual machine images. These images might be copied from another virtual machine or moved from one server pool to another server pool through a copy or move process. They might even be virtual machines that were deleted without checking the Delete Files option.

The images referred to in this section are those that you want to convert into virtual machines from the running pool.

NOTE
It is also important to note that the directory and file structure of a virtual machine image does not change after an import, with the exception of a V2V conversion (from VMware or VHD file formats). Importing the virtual machine image simply updates the database with the appropriate metadata, so the Oracle VM Manager can track and manage the virtual machine. In the case of a V2V, the VMDK or VHD file is converted to an IMG file, and the vm.cfg file is created from the .vmx file.

Virtual Machine Images

Follow these steps to configure virtual machine images from the VM Manager.

1. As with the virtual machine templates, the virtual machine images are configured from the Resources tab. From this tab, click Virtual Machine Images to select its subtab. The Virtual Machine Images tab shows the virtual machine images that are available (if any). In addition, it provides an option to import a virtual machine image by clicking the Import button. Clicking this button displays the Source screen. The Source screen is identical to the Source screen shown in Step 2 in the previous section of this chapter.

2. The Source screen offers several options: Download from External Source, Select from Server Pool, or Linux/Windows P2V Import. Regardless of which option you choose, the General Information screen is the same. The General Information screen collects the same information used to create a virtual machine, as you will see later in this book. This information includes the Server Pool Name, Sharing option, the Virtual Machine Image Name, whether High Availability is to be enabled, followed by Username and

Password information for the virtual machine and console. As always, there is a Description field for entering a comment. The General Information screen is shown here.

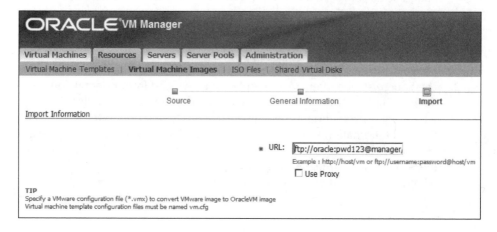

3. If you selected Download from External Source, the next screen you'll see is the Import Information screen, as shown here. Here, you define the HTTP or FTP URL, as you did in Step 4 of the previous section, if you selected to import a template. When using FTP, use this syntax: ftp://<user>:<pwd>@<host>/<directory>.

Take particular note that the path after <host> is relative. For example

 `ftp://oracle:pwd123@host/u01/stage/test2`

will designate a directory under the Oracle login directory of u01/stage/test2 or /home/oracle/u01/stage/test2. If the actual intended path for the virtual machine image is /u01/stage/test2, the following syntax is required:

`ftp://oracle:pwd123@host//u01/stage/test2`

This will designate a path of /u01/stage/test2.

NOTE
If you experience errors, you might get a nondescriptive Invalid URL message. You can find more information describing the error in /var/log/ ovm-manager/ovm-manager.log on the VM Manager server.

4. The final screen is the Confirm Information screen shown here. On this screen, you confirm the settings that you provided earlier. Clicking the Confirm button starts the import process.

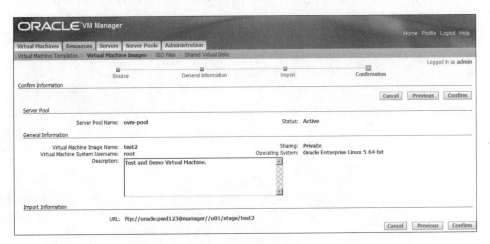

5. As when configuring templates, control is now returned to the Virtual Machine Images screen, where you can track the import's progress, as shown here. When the image has been completely imported, you can then

approve it for use by clicking the Approve button. Upon approval, the newly imported virtual machine is added to the list of available virtual machines.

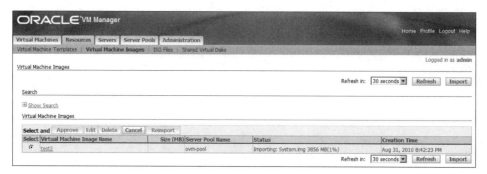

During the import process, clicking the Cancel button will cancel the import. If a failure were to occur, or for some other reason, you can reimport the image by clicking the Reimport button.

6. If you chose Select from Server Pool (Discover and Register) in Step 2, a screen similar to the General Information screen, shown earlier in Step 2, would appear; however, the Virtual Machine Image Name would now be a drop-down list, rather than a field where you type a name. This drop-down list contains the images found in running_pool. Select the virtual machine by selecting the desired image from the list, as shown here.

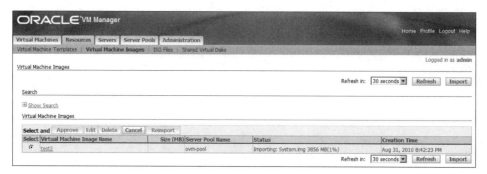

7. This screen is followed by the Confirmation screen, followed by the screen where you can watch the import's progress.

8. If, in Step 2, you selected Linux/Windows P2V Import, you will see an initial General Information screen that is identical to the screen shown earlier in Step 2. Once you've filled in the information, the Import Information screen prompts you for the server's Hostname/IP, as shown here.

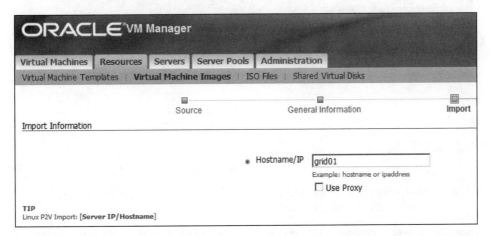

9. This screen is followed by the Confirm Information screen. Click Confirm and you will then see the screen where you track the import. Once you have completed these steps, the import process will finish and the image become available.

ISO Images

The acronym *ISO* stands for *International Standards Organization,* an organization that has put together many technical standards. When the term ISO is used in relation to CD-ROMs, it is actually referring to the ISO 9660 CD-ROM standard. When we speak of an ISO image, a copy of the CD-ROM image is stored on disk. This ISO image file can be mounted by the Oracle VM system to make it appear to the virtual machine as an actual CD-ROM drive.

The ISO images are stored in the /var/ovs/mount/<UUID>/OVS/iso_pool/<group name> directory. A typical ISO image has the suffix .iso on the end of the name. You must import the ISO images into the system for them to be used. There are a number of methods for importing ISO images into the system.

1. As with everything else in this chapter, ISO images are managed from the Resources tab. From the Resources tab, select the ISO Files link to invoke the ISO Files screen. This screen displays the ISO files that are available to

the HVM-enabled VM Server farm. To add an ISO image, click the Import button. The Import button will invoke the Source screen, which is shown next. The Source screen is similar to previous Source screens, but only has two options: Download from External Source (HTTP and FTP) and Select from Server Pool (Discover and Register).

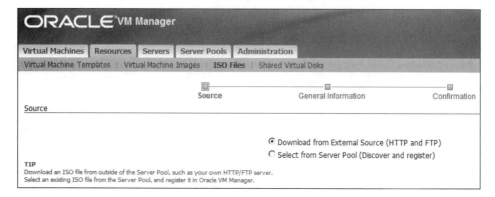

2. If you select Download from External Source, the General Information screen is displayed, as shown here.

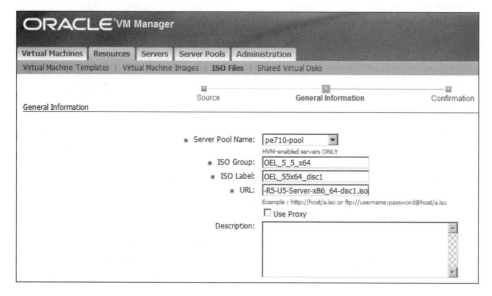

The following information is required:

■ **Server Pool Name**   The server pool that the ISO image will be imported into.

■ **ISO Group**   The high-level product name—something like OEL 5.5 x64 or another description.

- **ISO Label**   The label of the specific CD-ROM.

- **URL**   The source to download from. (This is similar to the URL in Step 3 of the previous section.)

- **Use Proxy**   Check this button and a box will be displayed that allows you to specify a proxy server.

- **Description**   A description of the ISO image.

When you enter the URL option, if you're using FTP, the proper syntax is ftp:<user>:<pwd>@host/<relative path>, where the relative path is from the user's login directory. If you have an absolute path, start with a / in order to specify the root directory. For example, if /u01/stage/OEL is the desired directory, then the FTP syntax is ftp:oracle:<pwd>@host//u01/stage/OEL.

NOTE
If the URL doesn't seem to work, check the log file on the VM Manager system located in /var/log/ ovm-manager. More detailed error messages can be found in the oc4j.log file.

3. Once you've filled out the General Information screen and clicked the Next button, you'll see the Confirmation screen, which is shown here. This is your last chance to confirm everything. This screen will not be visible until some checks (validating the URL, for instance) have been performed.

ORACLE VM Manager

| Virtual Machines | Resources | Servers | Server Pools | Administration |

Virtual Machine Templates | Virtual Machine Images | **ISO Files** | Shared Virtual Disks

Source   General Information   Confirmation

Confirmation

Server Pool

Server Pool Name: **pe710-pool**   Status: **Active**

ISO Information

ISO Group: **OEL_5_5_x64**   ISO Label: **OEL_55x64_disc1**
URL: **ftp://oracle:pwd123@test2//u01/stage/OEL/Enterprise-R5-U5-Server-x86_64-disc1.iso**
Description:

4. Click the Confirm button to begin the import. Control returns to the ISO Images tab. As with templates, you must approve the ISO image for it to be usable. Whether FTP or HTTP is used, the result is the same.

5. If you choose the Select from Server Pool (Discover and Register) option, you will see a different General Information screen. Here, the options consist of drop-down lists for Server Pool Name, ISO Group, and ISO Label. The ISO Group is the name of the directory in the /var/ovs/mount/<UUID>/OVS/iso_ pool directory, and the ISO Label is the name of each individual ISO image. The General Information screen is shown here.

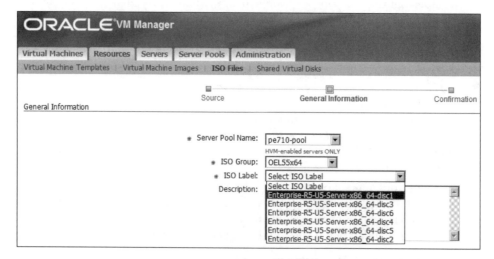

6. Once you've made your selections, the final steps are the same as for the first method of importing ISO images. Complete the confirmation step and then, when the image has finished importing, you approve the ISO image to validate it. Once you've done this step, you can use the image.

Configuring Shared Virtual Disks with the VM Manager

Shared disks are used to support applications that require a disk to be available (read and write simultaneously) from multiple systems. These applications include Oracle Real Application Clusters, Microsoft Cluster Services, and others. Because a shared virtual disk does not belong to any particular virtual system alone, it is part of the server resources. A shared virtual disk is created and then assigned to one or more virtual machines as desired. As with all of the server resources, you can find it on the Shared Virtual Disks tab under the Resources tab. This screen is similar to the other Resources tabs. To create a new shared virtual disk, click either the Create or Import button.

1. Clicking the Create button creates a new virtual machine, whereas clicking the Import button allows you to import an existing shared virtual disk into the server pool. If you click the Create button, the Shared Virtual Disks screen will be displayed and a new shared virtual disk will be created.

2. From the Shared Virtual Disks screen, select the server pool that the shared virtual disk will reside in, the Group Name, and enter the name of the new virtual disk and its size. As always, it is a great idea to include a description for future reference. This screen is shown here.

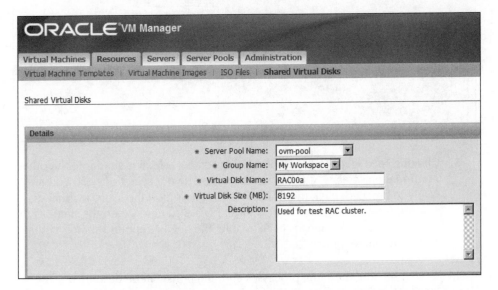

3. Once you've filled out the Shared Virtual Disks information screen and clicked the Next button, you'll see the Confirmation screen. Confirm your choices, and then the shared virtual disk will be created and control returned to the Shared Virtual Disks screen. This screen displays the shared virtual disk and will display that disk as Active once it's been created and is available for use.

4. If you clicked Import option, you'll see different options on the Shared Virtual Disks screen. Here, you select the Server Pool Name, the Group Name, and choose either File-based Disks or Multipath-based Disks, and then make your selection from the Shared Virtual Disk Files drop-down list, as shown next. Finally, in the Description field, describe the shared virtual

disk that will be imported. With the exception of the Description field, all other options are selections rather than fields that you fill in.

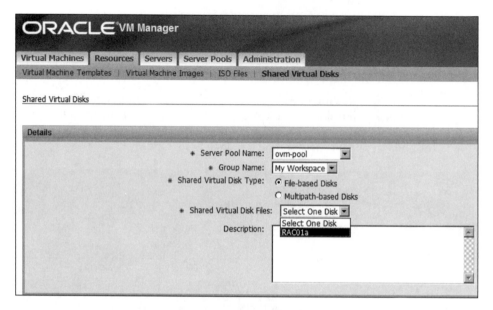

5. Clicking Next leads to the Confirmation screen, which is similar to the other confirmation screens. Once you've confirmed your selections and you are ready to proceed, click the Confirm button to import the shared virtual disk. Control is returned to the Shared Virtual Disks screen. When the status of the shared virtual disk changes to Available, the newly imported shared virtual disk is available for use.

In the next section, the same processes and functions will be described using OEM Grid Control. The end result will be the same; however, the methods and tools are different.

Configuring Shared Physical Devices

In addition to using file-based virtual disks as shared disks for Oracle RAC (or any application that requires a shared disk), Oracle VM allows the virtual machine to use physical devices as well. Physical devices can be shared by all devices in the server pool. Physical devices can be multipath devices, Storage Area Network (SAN) LUNS devices, iSCSI, and so on. When using a physical device, the designation in the vm.cfg file is "phy", rather than "file" as used for a virtual device. Prior to Oracle VM 2.2.0, you could not change multipath devices via the VM Manager. You were required to configure multipath devices in the vm.cfg file as follows:

```
disk = [ 'phy:/dev/mpath/mpath1, hdd,w', ]
```

Follow these steps to set up a multipath device on a virtual machine server:

1. Manually set up the SAN connection and configure the multipath device in Linux on each virtual machine server.

2. Verify that each virtual machine server identifies the same physical device as the same multipath device. For example, the same physical device must be identified as /dev/mapper/*mpath1* on each virtual machine server.

3. Make sure the device is not used for any other purpose than the shared virtual machine device.

4. Create the shared physical device in the VM Server Resources using VM Manager (2.2.0 or later) or in the virtual machine's vm.cfg file (prior to 2.2.0).

5. Allocate the shared disk resource to virtual machines as normal.

Once you've completed these steps, you can use the multipath device as a shared device.

Configuring Server Resources Using OEM Grid Control

OEM Grid Control is often the preferred method of management for not only administering Oracle VM but also for monitoring the virtual machines, applications, and databases that are running within Oracle VM.

Configuring Templates with OEM Grid Control

Follow these steps to configure templates from within OEM Grid Control. Managing server resources is done from the Server Pool Management section of the Virtual Servers tab.

1. From the Virtual Servers main tab, select Virtual Server Pool and Manage Virtual Server Pool from the Action menu, as shown here. Once you've selected these two options, click the Go button.

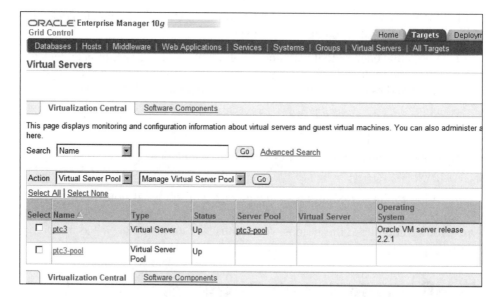

2. The Server Pool Resources screen will be displayed. This screen shows any resources that are already available along with the Import and Discover buttons. Clicking these buttons will invoke more screens that are used to actually import or discover the virtual server template. Click Import to display the Import GVM Template screen.

3. From the Import GVM Template screen, enter the name of the template, a description, and the location of the template. In addition, specify the location as either an HTTP or NFS server along with some information on the OS, such as OS Type, OS Name, and Virtualization Type, as shown here.

4. Unlike the VM Manager, OEM Grid Control also requires server credentials because the Grid Control Agent is used to initiate this request. You can either use preferred credentials or override them and add new credentials. Once you've completed this screen, click Go to continue. This starts the import process and control is returned to the Resources screen. You can track the import's progress.

5. If you click Discover, you will be prompted for a small set of information from drop-down lists. These drop-downs include the following: Undiscovered Template, Virtualization Type, OS Type, and Operating System Details. The Description field is a text box and is optional but recommended. This Discover GVM Template screen is shown here.

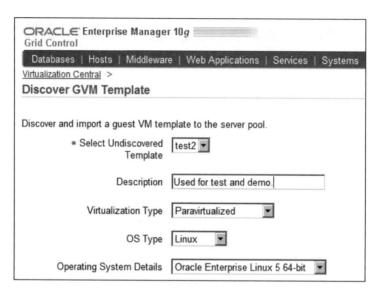

Once the template import process has begun, control returns to the Resources tab and the import's status is displayed. Once the process has completed, the status changes to Ready.

Configuring Images with OEM Grid Control

OEM Grid Control provides a straightforward and easy way to configure both virtual machine images and ISO images. In this case, the virtual machine images that are referred to are those images that are not part of the virtual machines configured in the server pool, although they are virtual machine images. The images referred to in this section are the ones you will convert into virtual machines from the running pool.

Virtual Machine Images

Within OEM Grid Control, importing virtual machine images is referred to a little differently than in the VM Manager.

1. As with the other functions in this section, the process begins from Virtualization Central. The Action drop-down menus are set to Virtual Server Pool and Discover Guest VM. In addition, you must also select the desired server pool. Once you've made your selections, click Go. This will invoke the Discover Guest VM screen. Clicking Discover shows the guests that are available for import. This screen, with the discover task completed, is shown here.

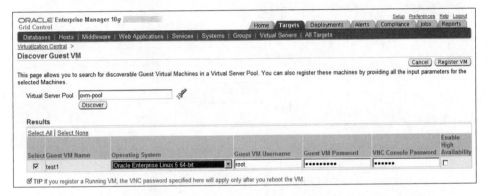

2. Once all of the options have been filled in and the desired guest VM selected, click the Register VM button to import the virtual machine. Once this button has been selected, a job will be created and the virtual machine will be imported. Control is then returned to Virtualization Central, where the new VM will be displayed.

ISO Images

ISO images are imported from the Manage Virtual Server Pool screen.

1. Once again, select Virtual Server Pool and Manage Virtual Server Pool from the drop-down lists and click Go. This time, from the Manage VM Server Pool screen, select ISO Images from the drop-down list. Again there are two buttons: Import and Discover.

2. Clicking the Import button invokes the Import ISO Image screen. From this screen, there are several options. Enter the name of the ISO image, which is required, and a description, which is recommended. The next choice is

whether to upload the ISO images from the OEM Library or to import them from an external location. The Import ISO Image screen is shown here.

3. When specifying an external location, specify either an HTTP or an NFS address in the Location field. Once you've input the URL and clicked the OK button, an OEM Grid Control job will be submitted to perform the import. A screen will be displayed identifying the Grid Control job. Once you have accepted this, control is returned to the Resources screen, where you can track the status of the import. Eventually, the status will change to Ready.

4. If you click Discover, you'll see the Discover GVM Template screen. This screen contains drop-down lists for selecting Undiscovered ISO Images and OS Type, along with a Description of the ISO image text box. Once you've made the selections, the import job will be submitted, and once you've confirmed it, control will be returned to the Resources screen again. Here, the progress of the import is displayed.

5. Once the ISO image has been imported, it is ready to use. You can use the ISO image to create new virtual machines. The final server resource is the shared virtual disk.

Configuring Shared Virtual Disks with OEM Grid Control

Shared disks are used to support applications that require a disk to be available (read and write simultaneously) from multiple systems. These applications include Oracle Real Application Clusters, Microsoft Cluster Services, and others. Because a shared virtual disk does not belong to any particular virtual system alone, it is part of the server resources.

1. Create a shared virtual disk by selecting a server pool and, from the drop-down lists, selecting Virtual Server Pool and Manage Virtual Server Pool.

2. Selecting these options will invoke the Resources screen again. This time select Shared Disks from the Resources drop-down list to see the available shared disks. To create a new shared virtual disk, click the Create button. This will invoke the Create Shared Disk screen.

3. The Create Shared Disk screen has three options: Name, Size(MB), and Description (optional). These options are shown here. Once you've entered these options and clicked the OK button, you will see the job confirmation and the Resources screen.

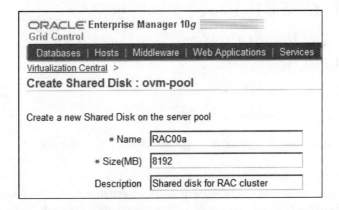

The Resources screen will show the Status as Incomplete as the Shared Virtual Disk is being created. Depending on the speed of the I/O subsystem and the size of the shared virtual disk, it might take a little time to create the shared virtual disk. Once the disk has been created, the status changes to Ready.

Configuring Server Resources Using the Oracle VM CLI

As with the other two methods, you can create the server resources using the VM CLI. The VM CLI has a couple of advantages: you can use scripts, and it uses a single step command. Because it only involves one step rather than multiple screens, using the CLI to configure resources is a much more straightforward process and can be easier and quicker. Depending on your preferences, the CLI is a good choice.

Configuring Templates with the Oracle VM CLI

As with the other options mentioned in this chapter, you have two options for importing templates into the virtual server pool via the OVM CLI. These options are to import from an external source and to discover the template on the virtual server pool. Both options for importing templates use the **ovm tmpl** command. The two options are **ovm tmpl imp** to import from an external source and **ovm tmpl disc** to discover a template from the server pool itself. In addition, several other subcommands are covered in this section. They are

- **tmpl approve**   Approve an imported template.

- **tmpl del**   Delete a template.

- **tmpl disc**   Discover a template.

- **tmpl imp**   Import a template.

- **tmpl ls**   List all available templates.

- **tmpl reg**   Register templates.

- **tmpl stat**   Get the status of a specific template.

As with the other **ovm** commands, the basic options for running the **ovm** command are **–u <username>** or **--username=<username>** and **-p <password>** or **--password=<password>**. If these options are not passed, you will be prompted for these values.

The **ovm tmpl imp** command takes the options listed in Table 13-1.

Option	Description
-h, --help	Displays the help message.
-s server_pool, --server_pool_name=server_pool	(Required) Specifies the name of the server pool that the template is being added to.
-n template, --template_name=template	(Required) Specifies the name of the template being imported.
-u username, --username=username	(Required) Specifies the virtual machine system username.
-p password, --password=password	Specifies the virtual machine system password.
-l URL, --url=URL	(Required) Gives the URL or source location of the virtual machine template.
-X proxy, --proxy=proxy	Specifies the Proxy URL (if applicable).
-o <os type>, --os_type=<os type>	(Required) Specifies the OS type for the virtual machine template.
-D description, --description=description	Describes the template.

TABLE 13-1. *ovm tmpl imp* Options

Here is an example of importing a template using the Oracle VM CLI:

```
# ovm -u admin -p ptc123 tmpl imp -s ovm-pool -n test2 -u root -p pwd123
-l ftp://oracle:pwd123@manager//u01/stage/test2
-o "Oracle Enterprise Linux 5 64-bit" -d "Used for test and demo"
```

To determine the import's status, use the **ovm tmpl stat** command, as shown here:

```
# ovm -u admin -p ptc123 tmpl stat -s ovm-pool -n test2
Importing
```

Once the template has been imported, its status will change from "Importing" to "Pending", as shown here:

```
# ovm -u admin -p ptc123 tmpl stat -s ovm-pool -n test2
Pending
```

As with the VM Manager, you must approve the template using the **ovm tmpl approve** command, as shown here:

```
# ovm -u admin -p ptc123 tmpl approve -s ovm-pool -n test2
Template "test2" approved.
```

If the template has been previously copied to and already exists in the seed_pool directory, use the discover option. Importing a template using the discover method is a two-step process. Step 1 is to discover the template. Step 2 is to register the template.

1. To discover a template, use the **ovm tmpl disc** command. This command takes the server pool name as the only option. The syntax for **ovm tmpl disc** is as follows:

   ```
   ovm tmpl disc -s <server pool> or --serverpool_name=<server pool>
   ```

   The output of this command is a list of templates that have been discovered. A discovered template is one that exists in the seed_pool directory but is not registered with the VM Manager. Here is an example of **ovm tmpl disc**:

   ```
   # ovm -u admin -p ptc123 tmpl disc -s ovm-pool
   Discoverable templates:
   testtmpl
   ```

2. Once the list of templates has been returned and the desired template has been identified, register the template using the **ovm tmpl reg** command. The **ovm tmpl reg** command takes the following options:

Option	Description
-h, --help	Displays the help message.
-s server_pool, --server_pool_name=server_pool	(Required) Specifies the name of the server pool that the template is being added to.
-n template, --template_name=template	(Required) Specifies the name of the template being imported.
-u username, --username=username	(Required) Specifies the virtual machine system username.
-p password, --password=password	Sets the virtual machine system password.

Option	Description
-o <os type>, -- os_type=<os type>	(Required) Specifies the OS type. This is a specific list of OS types and includes the following available operating system types: Oracle Enterprise Linux 4 Oracle Enterprise Linux 4 64-bit Oracle Enterprise Linux 5 Oracle Enterprise Linux 5 64-bit Red Hat Enterprise Linux 3 Red Hat Enterprise Linux 3 64-bit Red Hat Enterprise Linux 4 Red Hat Enterprise Linux 4 64-bit Red Hat Enterprise Linux 5 Red Hat Enterprise Linux 5 64-bit Microsoft Windows Server 2000 Microsoft Windows Server 2003 Edition Microsoft Windows Server 2003 x64 Edition Windows Vista Windows XP Microsoft Windows Server 2008 SP1 Sun Solaris 10 Other
-d description, --description=description	Describes the template.

Register the template as shown in this example:

```
# ovm -u admin -p ptc123 tmpl reg -s ovm-pool -n testtmpl -u root -p pwd123
-o "Red Hat Enterprise Linux 5 64-bit" -d "Used for test and demo"
Registering template. Please check the status.
```

1. Check the template's status using the **ovm tmpl stat** command, as shown here:

```
# ovm -u admin -p ptc123 tmpl stat -s ovm-pool -n testtmpl
Pending
```

2. Once the template is in a pending state, approve it, as shown here:

```
# ovm -u admin -p ptc123 tmpl approve -s ovm-pool -n testtmpl
Template "testtmpl" approved.
# ovm -u admin -p ptc123 tmpl stat -s ovm-pool -n testtmpl
Active
```

Once the template is active, it is available for use. You can easily display the templates that are available for use with the **ovm tmpl ls** command, as in this example:

```
# ovm -u admin -p ptc123 tmpl ls
  Name           Size(MB) Server_Pool Status  Created
  test2template 8001.0    ovm-pool    Active 2010-09-11
  test2          3857.0    ovm-pool    Active 2010-09-11
  testtmpl       3857.0    ovm-pool    Active 2010-09-11
```

The advantage of using the OVM CLI for template operations is that commands are all one-line commands that can easily be scripted.

Configuring Images with the Oracle VM CLI

As with the other management options, there are two types of images: virtual machine images and ISO images. The Oracle VM CLI provides a straightforward and easy way to configure both virtual machine images and ISO images using a simple command. As mentioned previously, virtual machine images are essentially virtual machines; ISO images are copies of CD-ROMs.

Virtual Machine Images

In the Oracle VM CLI, virtual machine images are configured via the **ovm img** command. This command has a number of available subcommands. The subcommands available to **ovm img** are

- **img approve** Approve an imported image.

- **img del** Delete an image.

- **img disc** Discover an image.

- **img imp** Import an image.

- **img ls** List all available images.

- **img reg** Register an image.

- **img stat** Get the status of a specific image.

This command and its subcommands relate only to virtual machine images (essentially a virtual machine copied to the running_pool directory). ISO images are managed with the **ovm iso** command, which is covered in the next section.

Virtual machine images are managed almost identically to virtual machine templates and ISO images. The basic workflow is to import or discover the image and then approve it.

As with the other **ovm** commands, the basic options for running the **ovm** command are **–u <username>** or **--username=<username>** and **-p <password>** or **--password=<password>**. This is the username and password of the VM Manager. If these options are not passed, these values are prompted for.

The **ovm img imp** command takes the options listed in Table 13-2.

Option	Description
-h, --help	Displays the help message.
-s server_pool, --server_pool_name=server_pool	(Required) Specifies the name of the server pool that the virtual machine image is being added to.
-n image, --image_name=image	(Required) Specifies the name of the image being imported.
-H, --enable_ha	Enables High Availability on the virtual machine being imported.
-c <console password>, --console_password=<console password>	Sets the password for the VNC console that will be available for this virtual machine.
-u username, --username=username	(Required) Specifies the virtual machine system username.
-p password, --password=password	Specifies the virtual machine system password.
-l URL, --url=URL	(Required) Specifies the URL or source location of the virtual machine image.
-X proxy, --proxy=proxy	Specifies the Proxy URL (if applicable).
-o <os type>, --os_type=<os type>	(Required) Specifies the OS type of the virtual machine image. A list of the OS types was shown in the previous section, following Step 2.
-g <group>, --group=<group>	Specifies the name of the group that the image will be imported into. The default value (if not specified) is My Workspace.
-D description, --description=description	Describes the virtual machine.

TABLE 13-2. *ovm img imp* Options

Here is an example of importing an image using the Oracle VM CLI:

```
# ovm -u admin -p ptc123 img imp -s ovm-pool -n test123 -c pwd123 -u root
-p pwd123 -l ftp://oracle:pwd123@manager//u01/stage/test2
-o "Oracle Enterprise Linux 5 64-bit" -d "Used for test and demo"
Downloading virtual machine image. Please check the status.
# ovm -u admin -p ptc123 img stat -s ovm-pool -n test123
Importing
```

Eventually the state of the virtual machine image will change from "Importing" to "Pending". At that point, you must approve the image. Once approved, this image will no longer be a server resource but will be a virtual machine and will not be seen in the **ovm img** command anymore. These steps are shown here:

```
# ovm -u admin -p ptc123 img stat -s ovm-pool -n test123
Pending
# ovm -u admin -p ptc123 img approve -s ovm-pool -n test123
Virtual machine image "test123" approved.
# ovm -u admin -p ptc123 img stat -s ovm-pool -n test123
Virtual machine image "test123" does not exist, or an error occurred
while getting the image resource.
# ovm -u admin -p ptc123 img ls
Virtual machine image not found.
```

Because it is now a virtual machine image, you can see it by running **ovm vm ls**:

```
# ovm -u admin -p ptc123 vm ls
Name      Size(MB) Mem VCPUs Status       Server_Pool
test2     3857     450 1     Powered Off ovm-pool
test1     8001     450 1     Powered Off ovm-pool
test123   3857     450 1     Powered Off ovm-pool
```

The virtual machine is now ready to be powered on.

Discovering a virtual image is very similar to the process involved in discovering a template. This is a multistep process that involves discovering the image, registering the image, and then approving the image. The commands are similar to those used to import an image.

1. The first step is to discover a virtual machine image. This is an image that exists in the running_pool but is not registered in the VM Manager. The discovery process is started by running the **ovm img disc** command. That subcommand takes on the server pool name as a parameter. Here is an example:

    ```
    # ovm -u admin -p ptc123 img disc -s ovm-pool
    Discoverable virtual machine images:
    test3
    testabc
    ```

2. Once the desired image has been identified, you can import the image with the **ovm img reg** command. The options for this command are shown here:

Option	Description
-h, --help	Displays the help message.
-s server_pool, --server_pool_name=server_pool	(Required) Specifies the name of the server pool that the virtual machine is being added to.
-n image, --image_name=image	(Required) Specifies the name of the image being imported.
-u username, --username=username	(Required) Specifies the virtual machine system username.
-p password, --password=password	Sets the virtual machine system password.
-c <console password>, --console_password=<console password>	Sets the password for the VNC console that will be available for this virtual machine.
-o <os type>, --os_type=<os type>	(Required) Specifies the OS type. The list of OS types appears in the table following Step 2 in the previous section.
-a, --enable_ha	Enables High Availability on the virtual machine being imported.
-g <group>, --group=<group>	Specifies the name of the group that the image will be imported into. The default value (if not specified) is My Workspace.
-d description, --description=description	Describes the virtual machine.

Register the virtual machine image, as shown here. The discovery process is repeated for completeness.

```
# ovm -u admin -p ptc123 img disc -s ovm-pool
Discoverable virtual machine images:
test3
testabc
# ovm -u admin -p ptc123 img reg -s ovm-pool -n testabc -u root -p pwd123
-c pwd123 -o "Oracle Enterprise Linux 5 64-bit" -d "Used for test and demo"
Registering virtual machine image. Please check the status.
# ovm -u admin -p ptc123 img stat -s ovm-pool -n testabc
Pending
```

3. Unlike the import process, the registery process is very fast. Once the virtual machine status shows "Pending", the final step is to approve it. This approval process is the same that you performed earlier. Here is an example:

```
#  ovm -u admin -p ptc123 img approve -s ovm-pool -n testabc
Virtual machine image "testabc" approved.
#  ovm -u admin -p ptc123 img stat -s ovm-pool -n testabc
Virtual machine image "testabc" does not exist, or an error occurred while
getting the image resource.
#  ovm -u admin -p ptc123 vm ls
Name    Size(MB) Mem VCPUs Status       Server_Pool
test2   3857     450 1     Powered Off ovm-pool
test1   8001     450 1     Powered Off ovm-pool
test123 3857     450 1     Powered Off ovm-pool
testabc 3857     450 1     Powered Off ovm-pool
```

This completes the virtual machine import process.

ISO Images

ISO images are treated in much the same way as the virtual machine images; except, at the conclusion of the process, the ISO images are still server resources. The basic steps are again to either import or discover and register the ISO image and then to approve it, as you will see in this section.

In the Oracle VM CLI virtual machine, you configure images via the **ovm iso** command. A number of subcommands are available for this command. The subcommands available to **ovm iso** are

- **iso approve**   Approve an imported ISO image.

- **iso del**   Delete an ISO image.

- **iso disc**   Discover an ISO image.

- **iso imp**   Import an ISO image.

- **iso ls**   List all available ISO images.

- **iso reg**   Register an ISO image.

- **iso stat**   Get the status of a specific ISO image.

The ISO images within Oracle VM reside in the iso_pool directory on the utility server. The process of managing virtual machine images is almost identical to managing virtual machine templates and virtual server images. The basic workflow is to import or discover the image and then approve it.

As with the other **ovm** commands, the basic options for running the command are **–u <username>** or **--username=<username>** and **-p <password>** or **--password=<password>**. This is the username and password of the VM Manager. If these options are not passed, you will be prompted for these values.

The **ovm iso imp** command takes the options listed in Table 13-3.
Here is an example of importing an ISO image using the Oracle VM CLI:

```
# ovm -u admin -p pwd123 iso imp -s ovm-pool
-g "Enterprise-R5-U5-Server-x86_64"
-l Enterprise-R5-U5-Server-x86_64-disc1.iso -u ftp://oracle:pwd123@
manager//u01/stage/Enterprise-R5-U5-Server-x86_64-disc1.iso
-d "OEL 5.5 Disc 1"
Downloading ISO image. Please check the status.
# ovm -u admin -p pwd123 iso stat -s ovm-pool
-g "Enterprise-R5-U5-Server-x86_64"
-l Enterprise-R5-U5-Server-x86_64-disc1.iso
Importing
```

Once the ISO image has completed the import process, its status will change
from "Importing" to "Pending". At this point, the image is ready to be approved.
This process is shown in the following example:

```
# ovm -u admin -p pwd123 iso approve -s ovm-pool
-g "Enterprise-R5-U5-Server-x86_64"
-l Enterprise-R5-U5-Server-x86_64-disc1.iso
ISO image "Enterprise-R5-U5-Server-x86_64-disc1.iso" approved.
```

Option	Description
-h, --help	Displays the help message.
-s server_pool, --server_pool_name=server_pool	(Required) Specifies the name of the server pool that the ISO image is being added to.
-g <iso group>, --iso_group=<iso group>	(Required) Specifies the name of the ISO image group. This is essentially the name of the OS release of the set of ISO images, such as OEL_5_5_x64.
-l <iso label>, --iso_label=<iso label>	(Required) Specifies the name of the actual ISO image.
-u URL, --url=URL	(Required) Specifies the URL or source location of the virtual machine image.
-X proxy, --proxy=proxy	Specifies the Proxy URL (if applicable).
-d description, --description=description	Describes the ISO image.

TABLE 13-3. *ovm iso imp* Options

You can check the image from the Oracle VM CLI in a couple of ways: using the **ovm iso stat** command or the **ovm iso ls** command. They are both shown here:

```
# ovm -u admin -p pwd123 iso stat -s ovm-pool
-g "Enterprise-R5-U5-Server-x86_64"
-l Enterprise-R5-U5-Server-x86_64-disc1.iso
Active
# ovm -u admin -p pwd123 iso ls
ISO_Label                              ISO_Group                      Status Server_Pool
Enterprise-R5-U5-Server-x86_64-disc1.iso Enterprise-R5-U5-Server-x86_64
Active ovm-pool
```

If the ISO image already exists on the Oracle VM utility server in the iso_pool/<group> directory, you can choose to discover the ISO image. This is useful when ISO images are being downloaded directly to the utility server or they are being copied from one environment to another. The discovery process uses the **ovm iso disc** and **ovm iso reg** commands.

1. To begin the discovery process, use the **ovm iso disc** command, which only takes the server pool as a parameter. The value returned is a list of ISO images, as shown here:

```
# ovm -u admin -p pwd123 iso disc -s ovm-pool
Discoverable ISO images:
ISO_Group  ISO_Label
Enterprise-R5-U5-Server-x86_64 Enterprise-R5-U5-Server-x86_64-disc5
Enterprise-R5-U5-Server-x86_64 Enterprise-R5-U5-Server-x86_64-disc2
Enterprise-R5-U5-Server-x86_64 Enterprise-R5-U5-Server-x86_64-disc4
Enterprise-R5-U5-Server-x86_64 Enterprise-R5-U5-Server-x86_64-disc3
Enterprise-R5-U5-Server-x86_64 Enterprise-R5-U5-Server-x86_64-disc6
```

2. Select the Group and ISO image to be imported and use the **ovm iso reg** command to perform the import. The **ovm iso reg** command takes the following options:

Option	Description
-h, --help	Displays the help message.
-s server_pool, --server_pool_name=server_pool	(Required) Specifies the name of the server pool that the ISO image is being added to.
-g <iso group>, --iso_group=<iso group>	(Required) Specifies the name of the ISO image group. This is essentially the name of the OS release of the set of ISO images, such as OEL_5_5_x64.
-l <iso label>, --iso_label=<iso label>	(Required) Specifies the name of the actual ISO image.
-d description, --description=description	Describes the ISO image.

Register the ISO image using the **ovm iso reg** command, as in the example provided here:

```
# ovm -u admin -p pwd123 iso reg -s ovm-pool
-g Enterprise-R5-U5-Server-x86_64
-l Enterprise-R5-U5-Server-x86_64-disc2 -d "OEL 5.5 x64 disc 2"
ISO image "Enterprise-R5-U5-Server-x86_64-disc2" registered.
```

3. As with image discovery, the process is very fast because no file copy is needed. Once the import has completed, it displays a status of "Pending" as shown here. This indicates the ISO image is ready to be approved.

```
# ovm -u admin -p pwd123 iso stat -s ovm-pool
-g Enterprise-R5-U5-Server-x86_64 -l Enterprise-R5-U5-Server-x86_64-disc2
Pending
```

4. As with previous examples, approve the image via the **ovm iso approve** command, as shown here:

```
# ovm -u admin -p pwd123 iso approve -s ovm-pool
-g Enterprise-R5-U5-Server-x86_64 -l Enterprise-R5-U5-Server-x86_64-disc2
ISO image "Enterprise-R5-U5-Server-x86_64-disc2" approved.
```

You can validate this step with both the **ovm iso stat** command and the **ovm iso ls** command. These commands are shown here:

```
# ovm -u admin -p pwd123 iso stat -s ovm-pool
-g Enterprise-R5-U5-Server-x86_64 -l Enterprise-R5-U5-Server-x86_64-disc2
Active
# ovm -u admin -p pwd123 iso ls

ISO_Label                                ISO_Group                      Status
Server_Pool
Enterprise-R5-U5-Server-x86_64-disc1.iso Enterprise-R5-U5-Server-x86_64 Active
ovm-pool
Enterprise-R5-U5-Server-x86_64-disc2     Enterprise-R5-U5-Server-x86_64 Active
ovm-pool
```

At this point, the ISO images have been successfully imported and are ready to use.

Configuring Shared Virtual Disks with the Oracle VM CLI

Shared disks are used to support applications that require a disk to be available (read and write simultaneously) from multiple systems. These applications include Oracle Real Application Clusters, Microsoft Cluster Services, and others. Because a shared virtual disk does not belong to any particular virtual system alone, it is part of the server resources.

Shared disks are created in the Oracle VM CLI using the **ovm sd** command. This command has a number of different options. These options are

- **sd del**   Delete a shared virtual disk.

- **sd disc**   Discover a shared virtual disk.

- **sd new**   Create a new shared virtual disk.

- **sd ls**   List all available shared virtual disks.

- **sd reg**   Register a shared virtual disk.

- **sd stat**   Get the status of a specific shared virtual disk.

The shared disks within Oracle VM reside in the shareDisk directory on the utility server. Unlike with templates and ISO images, no approval is needed for shared virtual disks. The process is to either create a new disk or discover and register an existing shared disk.

To create a new shared virtual disk, use the **ovm sd new** command. This command creates a new shared virtual disk in a single command.

The **ovm sd new** command takes the options listed in Table 13-4.

Option	Description
-h, --help	Displays the help message.
-s server_pool, --server_pool_name=server_pool	(Required) Specifies the name of the server pool that the shared virtual disk is being added to.
-n name, --disk_name=name	(Required) Specifies the name of the shared virtual disk being created.
-d size, --disk_size=size	Specifies the size in megabytes of the shared virtual disk being created.
-g <group>, --group=<group>	Specifies the name of the group that the disk will be created in. The default value (if not specified) is My Workspace.
-c comments, --comments=comments	Describes or includes comments about the shared virtual disk.

TABLE 13-4.   *ovm sd new* Options

The **ovm sd new** command is shown in this example:

```
# ovm -u admin -p pwd123 sd new -s ovm-pool -n RAC0a -d 4092
Shared virtual disk "RAC0a" is being created. Please check the status.
```

Once the process has begun, you can check the status using the **ovm sd stat** command. When the new shared virtual disk is "Active", it is ready to use.

```
# ovm -u admin -p pwd123 sd stat -s ovm-pool -n RAC0a
Active
```

If the shared virtual disk already exists in the sharedDisk directory, you can discover and register it. This occurs when the shared disk is a copy of an existing shared disk, it was restored from a backup, or it was copied from another environment. The discovery is a two-step process: first, the disk is found using **ovm sd disc** and then it is registered using **ovm sd reg**.

The **ovm sd disc** command takes only the server pool name as an option, as shown here:

```
# ovm -u admin -p pwd123 sd disc -s ovm-pool
Virtual_Disk_Name Virtual_Disk_Type
RAC1a             File-based
```

Once the name of the available discovered shared disk has been established, you can register it using the **ovm sd reg** command. This command takes the options listed in Table 13-5.

Option	Description
-h, --help	Displays the help message.
-s server_pool, --server_pool_name=server_pool	(Required) Specifies the name of the server pool that the shared virtual disk is being added to.
-n name, --disk_name=name	(Required) Specifies the name of the shared virtual disk being created.
-m, --multipath	If set, registers a multipath-based disk.
-g <group>, --group=<group>	Specifies the name of the group that the disk will be created in. The default value (if not specified) is My Workspace.
-c comments, --comments=comments	Describes or gives comments about the shared virtual disk.

TABLE 13-5. *ovm sd reg* Options

An example of using **ovm sd reg** is shown here:

```
# ovm -u admin -p pwd123 sd reg -s ovm-pool -n RAC1a -c "Used for RAC1 cluster"
Shared virtual disk "RAC1a" registered.
# ovm -u admin -p pwd123 sd stat -s ovm-pool -n RAC1a
Active
```

Once the disk has been registered, it is active and ready to be used. No further actions are necessary.

Summary

This chapter covered server resources and how to administer them via three different options available to the Oracle VM administrator: the Oracle VM Manager, OEM Grid Control, and the Oracle VM CLI. Each tool has advantages and its own specific way of working. Which tool you use depends on your environment and your specific needs.

The VM Manager is easy to install and easy to use, as is the VM CLI. These tools work together because the VM CLI requires and uses the VM Manager. This OVM CLI tool is readily downloadable from Oracle and can be quickly installed and configured.

OEM Grid Control is a very powerful and highly configurable tool that is very flexible but more difficult to install and maintain. This tool is typically used in larger environments. The big advantage of OEM Grid Control is the ability to monitor and manage the actual operating systems running in the VM environment as well as the applications and databases that those operating systems are using.

All of these tools work well and essentially accomplish the same thing. Which tool you use is up to you and depends on what works well in your environment. As you have seen from this chapter, the server resources—templates, images, and shared virtual disks—can all be configured with each tool. You will learn more about each of these resources later in the book as they are used to create and manage virtual machines.

In the next chapter you will learn how to monitor and tune the Oracle VM Server. A poorly tuned or overloaded server will lead to virtual machine performance issues. By monitoring the load on the VM Servers you can often head off problems before they occur.

CHAPTER
14

Monitoring and Tuning the Virtual Machine Server

nce the virtual machine environment has been configured and deployed, it must be continually monitored and managed to provide an efficient and well-performing system. An overloaded virtual machine server and I/O subsystem results in a poorly performing virtual environment and unhappy customers and users. There are two parts to tuning and monitoring the virtual environment: monitoring and tuning the VM Server and monitoring and tuning the virtual machines themselves. Monitoring and tuning the virtual machines will be covered later in Chapter 19; this chapter covers monitoring and tuning the VM Server itself.

Performance Monitoring

Performance monitoring can be done via several tools that are available within the VM Server system. Remember, the domain-0 (dom0) system is not a normal virtual machine, though it has some of the properties of a virtual machine. For example, running top, sar, or vmstat (Linux monitoring utilities) in dom0 only provides statistics for dom0 itself. To determine what is happening on the entire VM Server, you must use other utilities. Let's look at a couple of examples.

Running top (Display Top Linux Tasks) in dom0 gives you information on the dom0 system only. You can see this in Figure 14-1. In Figure 14-1, top shows a

```
root@ovm1:/OVS                                                            _ □ ×
top - 07:15:03 up 40 min,  1 user,  load average: 0.03, 0.01, 0.02
Tasks: 103 total,    1 running, 101 sleeping,   0 stopped,   1 zombie
Cpu(s):  0.0%us,  0.0%sy,  0.0%ni, 99.7%id,  0.2%wa,  0.0%hi,  0.0%si,  0.2%st
Mem:    557056k total,   185992k used,   371064k free,    40284k buffers
Swap:  1052216k total,        0k used,  1052216k free,    59388k cached

  PID USER      PR  NI  VIRT  RES  SHR S %CPU %MEM   TIME+  COMMAND
    8 root      10  -5     0    0    0 S  0.3  0.0  0:01.29 events/0
 9610 root      15   0  2212 1068  840 R  0.3  0.2  0:00.21 top
    1 root      15   0  2080  712  612 S  0.0  0.1  0:00.74 init
    2 root      RT  -5     0    0    0 S  0.0  0.0  0:00.22 migration/0
    3 root      34  19     0    0    0 S  0.0  0.0  0:00.00 ksoftirqd/0
    4 root      RT  -5     0    0    0 S  0.0  0.0  0:00.00 watchdog/0
    5 root      RT  -5     0    0    0 S  0.0  0.0  0:00.12 migration/1
    6 root      34  19     0    0    0 S  0.0  0.0  0:00.00 ksoftirqd/1
    7 root      RT  -5     0    0    0 S  0.0  0.0  0:00.00 watchdog/1
    9 root      10  -5     0    0    0 S  0.0  0.0  0:00.01 events/1
   10 root      10  -5     0    0    0 S  0.0  0.0  0:00.00 khelper
   11 root      11  -5     0    0    0 S  0.0  0.0  0:00.00 kthread
   13 root      10  -5     0    0    0 S  0.0  0.0  0:00.00 xenwatch
   14 root      10  -5     0    0    0 S  0.0  0.0  0:00.07 xenbus
   17 root      10  -5     0    0    0 S  0.0  0.0  0:00.33 kblockd/0
   18 root      10  -5     0    0    0 S  0.0  0.0  0:00.31 kblockd/1
```

FIGURE 14-1. *Example of top run in dom0*

system with 1 CPU and 557056k of total system memory. The VM Server used in this example actually has 1GB of RAM and 2 CPUs. What Figure 14-1 reveals is the performance and resources that have been allocated to dom0.

By using **xm top**, a Xen command, you can gather information from the hypervisor and display it within dom0. The information from **xm top** in Figure 14-2 shows two domains: dom0 and a virtual machine named 50_test1. In addition, the summary information at the top of the display gives configuration information for the entire VM Server with 1GB of RAM and two CPUs. The **xm top** command is one of several **xm** commands that provide performance and configuration information.

You can use most of the **xm** commands to manage the VM Server, but there are several that you can use to monitor the VM Server, including

■ **xm list**   Lists the virtual machines.

■ **xm top**   Displays performance usage of virtual machines.

■ **xm uptime**   Displays the uptime of all of the virtual machines on the VM Server.

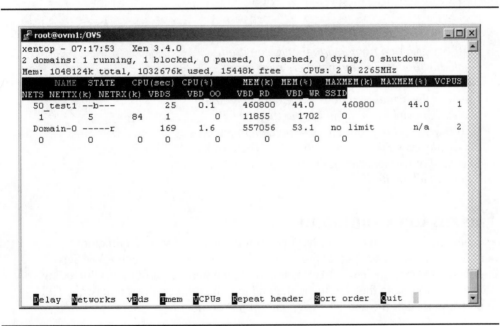

FIGURE 14-2.   *Running the **xm top** command in dom0*

In addition to the **xm** commands used for monitoring, a number of **xm** commands provide specific information about devices and resources. These include

- **xm vcpu-list**   Lists the VCPUs for domains.

- **xm info**   Provides information on the VM Server system (not dom0). This command provides information about the resources available to dom0 and the hypervisor. **xm info** output is shown later in this section.

- **xm log**   Prints the Xen error log.

- **xm block-list**   Lists the block devices for the virtual machines.

- **xm network-list**   Lists the virtual machine networks and their MAC addresses.

Examples from some of the commands are provided in the upcoming sections. These commands are useful for monitoring the VM Server and the virtual machines. In addition to these commands, you can also monitor from within the virtual environment, but monitoring within the virtual machine only gives you performance and resource utilization from the perspective of the virtual machine itself and does not provide information on the entire environment.

CAUTION
Statistics gathered from a virtual machine itself (including dom0) are, by their very nature, not accurate because a virtual machine is only allocating a part of the actual resources. For example, within the virtual machine it might appear that the CPU is 100 percent busy, but that 100 percent might be physically only 50 percent of the CPU. Therefore, be skeptical of any statistics gathered from within the virtual machine itself.

The xm top Command

As mentioned earlier in this chapter, the **xm top** command shows a different perspective. In the upper part of the screen, the resources for the entire VM Server are listed, as shown in Figure 14-2. You can see the number of domains (including dom0) and what state they are in, as shown here. In addition, the memory and CPU information reflects the entire VM Server, not just dom0.

```
xentop - 10:15:08   Xen 3.4.0
3 domains: 1 running, 2 blocked, 0 paused, 0 crashed, 0 dying, 0 shutdown
Mem: 2096700k total, 1503868k used, 592832k free    CPUs: 2 @ 2265MHz
```

Below the information about the VM Server, you'll see information on each of the virtual machines, including information on how much activity is happening in that particular domain. Note that this information includes dom0 as one of the domains.

```
NAME   STATE  CPU(sec) .CPU(%)  MEM(k) .MEM(%)  MAXMEM(k)  MAXMEM(%)  VCPUS
NETS   NETTX(k)  NETRX(k)  VBDS  VBD_OO  VBD_RD  VBD_WR  SSID
50_test1  --b---    315    0.0   460800   22.0   460800    22.0     1
2   17   383     1     0    47109   54262    0
Domain-0  -----r    945   99.3   557056   26.6  no limit    n/a     2
0    0    0     0     0     0     0     0
test3     --b---    311    0.0   460800   22.0   460800    22.0     1
1    2   175     1     0    47044   54607    0
```

The **xm top** command is very useful for finding out which domains are the busiest and contributing the most to the VM Server's load.

The xm list Command

The **xm list** command lists the virtual machines that are currently running, how much memory they are allocated to use, the number of virtual CPUs, the state, and the time that they have been running. This output is shown here:

```
[root@ovm1 ~]# xm list
Name                      ID   Mem VCPUs     State   Time(s)
50_test1                   4   450     1     -b----     74.6
Domain-0                   0   544     2     r-----    712.9
test3                      5   450     1     -b----     63.9
```

The **xm list** command does not show significant information about system performance, but it does provide a quick way to determine which virtual machines are running and how many resources have been allocated to each.

The xm uptime Command

The **xm uptime** command does not provide significant information and is redundant with **xm list**, but with less information. The **xm uptime** command basically lists how long each virtual machine has been running, as shown here:

```
Name                      ID Uptime
50_test1                   4  2:27:09
Domain-0                   0  2:46:46
test3                      5  2:25:48
```

As you can see, this command only provides minimal information.

The xm info Command

The **xm info** command provides a great deal of information about the VM Server:

```
host                   : ptc5
release                : 2.6.18-128.2.1.4.25.el5xen
version                : #1 SMP Tue Mar 23 12:43:27 EDT 2010
machine                : i686
nr_cpus                : 16
nr_nodes               : 1
cores_per_socket       : 4
threads_per_core       : 2
cpu_mhz                : 2261
hw_caps                : bfebfbff:28100800:00000000:00000340:009ce3bd:00000000:00000
001:00000000
virt_caps              : hvm
total_memory           : 73718
free_memory            : 72367
node_to_cpu            : node0:0-15
node_to_memory         : node0:72367
xen_major              : 3
xen_minor              : 4
xen_extra              : .0
xen_caps               : xen-3.0-x86_64 xen-3.0-x86_32p hvm-3.0-x86_32
hvm-3.0-x86_32p hvm-3.0-x86_64
xen_scheduler          : credit
xen_pagesize           : 4096
platform_params        : virt_start=0xfb400000
xen_changeset          : unavailable
cc_compiler            : gcc version 4.1.2 20080704 (Red Hat 4.1.2-44)
cc_compile_by          : mockbuild
cc_compile_domain      : (none)
cc_compile_date        : Wed Mar 24 16:00:43 EDT 2010
xend_config_format     : 4
```

This command does not provide specific performance information, but it can be used to provide significant information about the resources used by the system as well as about the system's configuration.

The xm vcpu-list Command

The **xm vcpu-list** command provides information about CPU allocation and affinity, which can be useful in determining which physical CPUs a virtual CPU is running on. This command will be shown in further detail later in this chapter in the section "Tuning Virtual Machines." The **xm vcpu-list** command is shown here:

```
[root@ovm1 ~]# xm vcpu-list
Name                              ID  VCPU   CPU State   Time(s) CPU Affinity
50_test1                          4    0      1   -b-     325.6 any cpu
Domain-0                          0    0      0   r--     638.0 any cpu
Domain-0                          0    1      1   -b-     443.4 any cpu
test3                             5    0      1   -b-     318.8 any cpu
```

This command also gives the CPU time accumulated by the virtual machine, not the clock time that the virtual machine has been running.

The xm log Command

The **xm log** command is simply a shortcut to the VM Server log. Running this command prints the Xend log (/var/log/xen/xend.log) to the screen. Beware: The log can be quite long.

The xm block-list Command

The **xm block-list** command lists the virtual block devices that have been allocated to a domain. The **xm block-list** command requires a domain name to be passed to it, as shown here:

```
[root@ovm1 ~]# xm block-list test3
 Vdev  BE handle state evt-ch ring-ref BE-path
 51712  0    0    4     8      8      /local/domain/0/backend/vbd/5/51712
```

Passing a domain number is usually easier than passing a domain name. Find the domain number using **xm list**, and then run **xm block-list 1**, for example. Domain names can get long and confusing in Oracle VM because the Oracle VM Manager prepends a unique number to the name of the domain, like 542_test3.

```
[root@ovm1 running_pool]# xm list
 Name                                  ID   Mem VCPUs     State   Time(s)
 330_test2                              1   512    1     -b----     13.6
 Domain-0                               0   543    2     r-----    389.8
 [root@ovm1 running_pool]# xm block-list 1
 Vdev  BE handle state evt-ch ring-ref BE-path
 51712  0    0    4     8      8      /local/domain/0/backend/vbd/1/51712
 51728  0    0    4     9      9      /local/domain/0/backend/vbd/1/51728
```

The xm network-list Command

The **xm network-list** command lists the virtual network devices that have been allocated to a virtual machine, including the MAC address of the virtual adapter, as shown next. This command can be very useful for troubleshooting network problems or configuring DHCP and so on.

```
[root@ovm1 ~]# xm network-list test3
 Idx BE     MAC Addr.      handle state evt-ch tx-/rx-ring-ref BE-path
 0   0  00:16:3E:54:E7:1E     0     4     9      768  /769     /local/
 domain/0/backend/vif/5/0
```

Most of these commands provide information only and not performance data; however, some of this information can be useful when tuning the system. This will become evident in the next sections.

Tuning the Oracle VM Server System

There really isn't a lot that you have to tune in the VM Server system. In fact, as you will see, tuning the VM Server system actually involves monitoring and adjusting the resources, rather than tweaking parameters and settings. The VM Server system is based on Xen, with Oracle enhancements, and as such is set up and ready to go when installed. dom0 is based on a stripped-down version of Linux. The next few sections provide tips on tuning the OS, network, and I/O subsystem. In this case, OS tuning includes not only software (Linux and Oracle VM tuning) but also hardware tuning as well.

Tuning the OS and CPUs

From a software perspective, there really aren't any OS tuning changes that can be made. Hardware tuning at the OS layer consists of CPU and memory. As shown earlier in this chapter, you can monitor memory and CPU utilization via several Xen commands such as **xm top**. If additional memory and/or CPUs are needed, you can add them (depending on your current hardware configuration).

You can do a few things at the virtual machine level to tune the CPUs. Virtual CPUs can run on one or more physical CPUs. The physical CPUs are the actual hardware that is running on the VM Server, where the virtual CPUs are the CPUs that are seen by the virtual machine. The virtual machine's virtual CPUs can run on one or more physical CPUs. Oracle VM allows virtual CPUs to be pinned to physical CPUs. This gives you a lot of control over how the system resources are used.

There are two ways to allocate CPU resources: by using the **xm vcpu** command or by configuring the **vm.cfg** file. Each of these methods is described here.

Pinning CPUs Using xm vcpu Commands

Three commands are used to configure CPU affinity on a live system. These commands are **xm vcpu-list**, **xm vcpu-pin**, and **xm vcpu-set**. Each command serves a slightly different purpose.

NOTE
*Any changes made using the **xm vcpu** commands are lost when the virtual machine is restarted.*

The **xm vcpu-list** command lists the virtual machines (domains) and their current CPU settings. This command takes the domain as an optional qualifier. If the domain or set of domains is not provided, all of the domains on the system will be displayed, as shown here:

```
[root@ptc5 4590_pvtest2]# xm vcpu-list
Name                               ID  VCPU    CPU State    Time(s) CPU Affinity
4572_pvtest1                       92     0     10  -b-       14.8 any cpu
4590_pvtest2                       96     0     15  -b-        2.6 any cpu
4590_pvtest2                       96     1      8  -b-        2.2 any cpu
4590_pvtest2                       96     2     11  -b-        1.1 any cpu
4590_pvtest2                       96     3     10  -b-        1.2 any cpu
Domain-0                            0     0      4  r--    55036.3 any cpu
Domain-0                            0     1     14  -b-    10755.1 any cpu
Domain-0                            0     2      5  -b-     4142.5 any cpu
Domain-0                            0     3      2  -b-     3142.6 any cpu
Domain-0                            0     4      8  -b-     3409.5 any cpu
Domain-0                            0     5     14  -b-     2752.8 any cpu
Domain-0                            0     6      0  -b-     2769.7 any cpu
Domain-0                            0     7      6  -b-     7399.5 any cpu
Domain-0                            0     8     14  -b-     2883.2 any cpu
Domain-0                            0     9      1  -b-     2543.7 any cpu
Domain-0                            0    10     14  -b-     7722.4 any cpu
Domain-0                            0    11      3  -b-     3462.9 any cpu
Domain-0                            0    12      3  -b-     2846.4 any cpu
Domain-0                            0    13     12  -b-     3633.2 any cpu
Domain-0                            0    14      6  -b-     7968.6 any cpu
Domain-0                            0    15      5  -b-     2530.6 any cpu
```

Optionally, you can provide a domain as a qualifier. In this case, the **xm vcpu-list** command provides only CPU information about the requested domain:

```
[root@ptc5 4590_pvtest2]# xm vcpu-list 4590_pvtest2
Name                               ID  VCPU    CPU State    Time(s) CPU Affinity
4590_pvtest2                       96     0     15  -b-        2.6 any cpu
4590_pvtest2                       96     1      8  -b-        2.2 any cpu
4590_pvtest2                       96     2     11  -b-        1.1 any cpu
4590_pvtest2                       96     3     10  -b-        1.3 any cpu
```

Notice in this example that the four virtual CPUs allocated to the domain named 4590_pvtest2 are configured to run on any of the physical CPUs in the system. To pin a virtual CPU to a physical CPU, use the **xm vcpu-pin** command. The syntax is as follows:

```
xm vcpu-pin <domain> <VCPU> <CPU>
```

For example, to pin the four virtual CPUs just shown on physical CPUs 2, 4, 6, and 8, use the following commands:

```
[root@ptc5 ~]# xm vcpu-pin 4590_pvtest2 0 2
[root@ptc5 ~]# xm vcpu-pin 4590_pvtest2 1 4
[root@ptc5 ~]# xm vcpu-pin 4590_pvtest2 2 6
[root@ptc5 ~]# xm vcpu-pin 4590_pvtest2 3 8
[root@ptc5 ~]# xm vcpu-list 4590_pvtest2
```

```
Name                              ID  VCPU   CPU State   Time(s) CPU Affinity
4590_pvtest2                      96    0     2   -b-     38.4 2
4590_pvtest2                      96    1     4   -b-     31.8 4
4590_pvtest2                      96    2     6   -b-     28.4 6
4590_pvtest2                      96    3     8   -b-     29.9 8
```

Use the **xm vcpu-set** command to limit (set) the number of virtual CPUs that a domain can see. The number of VCPUs can be decreased from the limit that they were originally set to, but not increased above that number. In this example, some of the virtual CPUs can be paused by setting the number of CPUs lower than the currently running number of CPUs:

```
[root@ptc5 ~]# xm vcpu-list 4590_pvtest2
Name                              ID  VCPU   CPU State   Time(s) CPU Affinity
4590_pvtest2                      96    0     2   -b-     38.5 2
4590_pvtest2                      96    1     4   -b-     31.9 4
4590_pvtest2                      96    2     6   -b-     28.4 6
4590_pvtest2                      96    3     8   -b-     29.9 8
The CPUs can be set to 2 by using the xm vcpu-set command as shown here:
[root@ptc5 ~]# xm vcpu-set 4590_pvtest2 2
[root@ptc5 ~]# xm vcpu-list 4590_pvtest2
Name                              ID  VCPU   CPU State   Time(s) CPU Affinity
4590_pvtest2                      96    0     2   -b-     38.5 2
4590_pvtest2                      96    1     4   -b-     31.9 4
4590_pvtest2                      96    2     -   --p     28.4 6
4590_pvtest2                      96    3     -   --p     29.9 8
```

You can then re-enable them by using the **xm vcpu-set** command again, this time with the number of CPUs set to 4:

```
[root@ptc5 ~]# xm vcpu-set 4590_pvtest2 4
[root@ptc5 ~]# xm vcpu-list 4590_pvtest2
Name                              ID  VCPU   CPU State   Time(s) CPU Affinity
4590_pvtest2                      96    0     2   -b-     38.6 2
4590_pvtest2                      96    1     4   -b-     31.9 4
4590_pvtest2                      96    2     6   -b-     28.4 6
4590_pvtest2                      96    3     8   -b-     30.0 8
```

Using CPU affinity can be a good way to prioritize specific virtual machines. Please note that it is possible and likely to have two virtual CPUs sharing the same physical CPU. In fact, with **xm vcpu-pin**, you can set all of the VCPUs to the same physical CPU.

NOTE
The state field in **xm vcpu-list** *can have several values. These values are*
r   *running*
b   *blocked*
p   *paused*
s   *shutdown*
c   *crashed*
d   *dying*
The virtual CPUs must exist in one of those states.

In addition to the **xm** commands, CPUs can be configured in the vm.cfg file as well.

Pinning CPUs Using the vm.cfg File

In addition to using the **xm** commands, you can configure the number of CPUs and their affinity within the vm.cfg file. The vm.cfg file has two pertinent parameters. The vcpus parameter specifies the number of CPUs used by the VM. In addition, an optional cpu parameter can be added, specifying the physical CPUs that the virtual CPUs can run on. This parameter takes single quotes, as shown here:

```
vcpus = 4
cpu = '2,4,6,8'
```

A vm.cfg file generated by the VM Manager only has the vcpus parameter specified. Setting the cpu parameter, as shown here, locks the virtual CPUs to physical CPUs 2, 4, 6, and 8. If you want to set a specific order, put it in the cpu variable, as shown here:

```
cpu = '6,4,2,8'
```

The resulting configuration locks the CPUs, as shown here:

```
[root@ptc5 4590_pvtest2]# xm vcpu-list 4590_pvtest2
Name                    ID  VCPU   CPU State   Time(s) CPU Affinity
4590_pvtest2             4    0     4   -b-       1.6 2,4,6,8
4590_pvtest2             4    1     2   -b-       2.9 2,4,6,8
4590_pvtest2             4    2     6   -b-       0.5 2,4,6,8
4590_pvtest2             4    3     8   -b-       0.4 2,4,6,8
```

As mentioned earlier, you can also lock one or more virtual CPUs to the same physical CPUs. The cpu variable will take either a specific set of CPUs that are comma separated or a set of CPUs with a range. The result differs based on the configuration, for example:

- Specifying a range of CPUs as in "cpu = '1-2'" locks the four virtual CPUs to physical CPUs 1 and 2; however, they will be able to move between those CPUs.

- Specifying a single CPU as in "cpu = '1'" locks all four virtual CPUs to the same physical CPU.

- Specifying a specific list of CPUs that has the same number of CPUs as specified in the vcpus parameter locks each virtual CPU to a physical CPU, as shown previously.

CPU affinity is presented in this chapter because it is not just a tool for tuning the virtual machine; it is also a tool for tuning the VM Server as well by specifying the load on the VM Server's CPUs.

Tuning the Network

As with the OS, from a software standpoint, there really isn't much to tune in the Oracle VM Server. The network is tuned via what I like to refer to as *hardware tuning*. Hardware tuning involves properly allocating the hardware resources to take advantage of these resources and to not overload them. Because the network devices are physically limited to a specific speed (i.e., gigabit, etc.) the only way to improve network performance is to add more network interfaces. Fortunately, Oracle VM is perfectly suited for that.

You can monitor network utilization via the **sar** command. The **sar –n DEV** command presents information on the utilization of each network device. The **sar** command takes two parameters that specify the time interval and count of results. For example, **sar –n DEV 10 100** displays results every 10 seconds, 100 times. This is shown here:

```
[root@ptc5 ~]# sar -n DEV 10 100
Linux 2.6.18-128.2.1.4.25.el5xen (ptc5)          10/08/2010

04:50:49 PM  IFACE  rxpck/s  txpck/s  rxbyt/s  txbyt/s  rxcmp/s  txcmp/s  rxmcst/s
04:50:59 PM     lo     0.00     0.00     0.00     0.00     0.00     0.00      0.00
04:50:59 PM   eth0    37.46    37.46  3634.07  4804.50     0.00     0.00      0.00
04:50:59 PM   eth1     2.30     0.00   151.05     0.00     0.00     0.00      0.00
04:50:59 PM   eth2     2.30     0.00   151.05     0.00     0.00     0.00      0.00
04:50:59 PM   eth3     2.30     0.00   151.05     0.00     0.00     0.00      0.00
04:50:59 PM xenbr0     3.40     2.40   355.24   305.29     0.00     0.00      1.80
04:50:59 PM xenbr1     1.80     0.00    86.71     0.00     0.00     0.00      1.80
04:50:59 PM xenbr2     1.80     0.00    86.71     0.00     0.00     0.00      1.80
04:50:59 PM xenbr3     1.80     0.00    86.71     0.00     0.00     0.00      1.80
04:50:59 PM  IFACE  rxpck/s  txpck/s  rxbyt/s  txbyt/s  rxcmp/s  txcmp/s  rxmcst/s
04:51:09 PM     lo     0.00     0.00     0.00     0.00     0.00     0.00      0.00
04:51:09 PM   eth0    36.80    38.00  3642.10  4954.70     0.00     0.00      0.00
04:51:09 PM   eth1     1.60     0.00   131.10     0.00     0.00     0.00      0.00
04:51:09 PM   eth2     1.50     0.00   100.00     0.00     0.00     0.00      0.00
04:51:09 PM   eth3     1.60     0.00   131.10     0.00     0.00     0.00      0.00
04:51:09 PM xenbr0     3.30     3.00   415.70   476.80     0.00     0.00      1.10
04:51:09 PM xenbr1     1.10     0.00    79.30     0.00     0.00     0.00      1.10
04:51:09 PM xenbr2     1.10     0.00    79.30     0.00     0.00     0.00      1.10
04:51:09 PM xenbr3     1.10     0.00    79.30     0.00     0.00     0.00      1.10
```

This information is very useful for determining if a specific network adapter is saturated. If it is, some of the load (some of the virtual machines on that adapter) should be shifted to another adapter.

Bits and Bytes

Unfortunately, most of the performance monitors display results in bytes or bytes/sec, whereas the throughput of a network device is in bits. Thus, a gigabit network interface has a theoretical maximum performance of 125 megabytes (MB) per second because there are 8 bits in a byte.

I/O Performance

I/O performance is limited by the performance of the disk drive itself. In disk arrays, more disk drives mean more I/O performance because the performance of the array is the sum of the performance of the individual disk drives. When purchasing an I/O subsystem, make sure you have a sufficient number of disk drives, a large cache, and a high-performing bus. A slow I/O subsystem slows down I/O performance and subsequently the performance of the virtual machines.

Tuning the I/O Subsystem

As with the other components mentioned in this chapter, the I/O subsystem cannot be tuned per se. Rather, you tune it by spreading out the load or by using "out-of-the-box" solutions for solving this problem. I/O performance is probably the most common performance problem associated with virtual machines. The most common solution to this problem is to create the system with sufficient I/O performance to handle the load of multiple virtual machines. In existing systems, you might need to add more I/O storage to improve I/O performance to an acceptable level.

In addition to the more traditional storage systems, newer technologies can be used to vastly improve the I/O performance of virtual machines. These include solid-state disks (SSDs) and other more powerful solutions such as the IODrive by FusionIO. These memory-based solutions provide much higher throughput and response time. Since I/O is such a critical resource in a virtualized environment, it is well worth the investment.

Tuning Virtual Machines

Within the virtual machine, you tune the OS like any other Linux or Windows system. You can modify the parameters and configure the system as necessary to support the application being run on that server. As mentioned earlier in this chapter, you can manage the number of VCPUs and their placement on physical CPUs at the VM Server. In addition, you can configure the priority of the virtual CPUs as well. This will be covered later in Chapter 19.

In general, there is not much to tune at the OS level. Most of the tuning efforts are geared toward proper sizing and planning of the system. Most of the tuning changes that must be made to the OS are to support applications, such as Oracle, so that large amounts of shared memory can be allocated, or to support large numbers of semaphores, etc. Other configuration changes in the OS are to support the addition of new hardware.

Summary

This chapter covered the steps and tools necessary to monitor the VM Server itself. Because the VM Server OS that is visible from a user's prospective is actually dom0, traditional methods of monitoring such as sar, top, and vmstat don't work. This chapter covered some of the utilities that can be used to monitor the hypervisor and VM Server as a whole, such as the xm tools. Tuning the actual I/O subsystem and network involves what I refer to as hardware tuning, which involves allocating the right resources to the right need.

In the next chapter, the focus changes from the VM Server system to the virtual machines themselves. Chapter 15 starts by showing the process of creating templates that can then be used to create virtual machines.

PART
IV

Installing and Configuring
the Guest OS

CHAPTER
15

Creating Templates

ne of the primary advantages of Oracle VM is the Template Library. From the Oracle website, you can download many preconfigured and working Oracle VM templates. These templates range from OS-only templates to entire E-Business Suite environments. The virtual machine templates allow efficient and quick deployment of virtualized environments in a repeatable, reliable manner. This chapter covers the two primary ways of creating a template: creating a template manually and creating a template using the Template Builder.

Creating Templates Manually

Creating a template manually is a very straightforward operation. In order to create a template manually, you simply save an existing virtual machine as a template. You copy the virtual machine, which must be in a stopped state, from the running_pool to the seed pool. You copy the files that make up the virtual machine—the system image, the vm.cfg file, and any other image files—to the seed_pool/<template> directory. These files are almost identical to the files found in the running_pool/<virtual machine> directory that they were created from, with the exception of the data found in the vm.cfg file. The paths of the references in this file have been changed to reflect the template's location. In addition, the MAC address of each network adapter has been changed in the vm.cfg file as well. These changes are done automatically by the Oracle VM Manager when the template is created.

To create a template manually using the VM Manager, select the virtual machine to be used as the target of the template. Using the More Actions drop-down menu, select Save As Template as shown here, and then click the Go button.

Virtual Machines

Select and

| Power On | Console | Power Off | Configure | More Actions: | Save As Template ▾ | Go |

Select	Details	Virtual Machine Name	Memory Size (MB)	Status	Owner	Group Name	Server Name	Server Pool Name
⦿	⊞ Show Demo1		1,024	■ Powered Off	admin	My Workspace	N/A	ovm
○	⊞ Show Manager		1,024	■ Powered Off	admin	My Workspace	N/A	ovm
○	⊞ Show tmpl1		1,024	■ Powered Off	admin	My Workspace	N/A	ovm

Refresh in: 30 seconds ▾ | Refresh | Create Virtual Machine |

After clicking the Go button, the Create Virtual Machine Template screen appears, as shown next. Here, you both name the virtual machine template and validate the size and status of the virtual machine that you are using as the source of the template. Remember, the virtual machine must be in the stopped state in order to create a template from it.

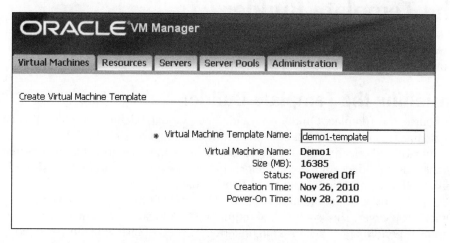

The template will be created in the seed_pool directory, as pointed out earlier. The template must exist in this directory in order to use it to create new virtual machines; however, you can archive it to another disk if necessary. When it is time to use this template, simply copy it back to the seed_pool directory. Sometimes symbolic links are also used to archive templates to other storage; if you are using symbolic links, however, make sure all the nodes in the cluster can resolve the symbolic link.

Once you've created the template, you can use it to create a new virtual machine. This method is the basic way to take an existing virtual machine and save it as a template for further use. In order to create templates more efficiently, however, Oracle has provided the Template Builder—a utility that you can use to create more advanced templates.

Template vs. Image

There really isn't a big difference between copying a virtual machine image and creating a new virtual machine in terms of mechanics. Both methods involve copying the data files, modifying the vm.cfg file, and updating the repository. However, creating a virtual machine from a template automates this process, and in addition to copying the image, a unique IP address for each vNIC's mac address is created. Creating the virtual machine by copying another image and importing it requires manual intervention. In addition, using the Template Builder further automates the process during the initial startup to configure the virtual machine. Using templates is the preferred method of creating virtual machines.

Creating Templates Using the Template Builder

The Template Builder is an Oracle tool that assists with the creation and deployment of virtual machine templates. This chapter shows you how to install and use the Oracle VM Template Builder.

Installing the Template Builder

Of course, the Template Builder is provided as a virtual machine template. You can locate the Template Builder on the Oracle website by browsing the Oracle downloads and selecting the Template Builder from the selection of templates that Oracle has provided. And, if you prefer, you can download and install the Template Builder RPM on an existing Linux server or virtual machine.

The Template Builder requires 1GB of RAM and 60GB of disk space on an Oracle VM Server. This is a minimal requirement. Allocating more RAM typically improves performance. Because the preferred method of installing the Template Builder is via the VM Template Builder template, that method is covered here.

NOTE
If multiple users are utilizing the Template Builder at the same time, memory requirements can be quite high—especially if you are building multiple virtual machines at the same time. Make sure the Template Builder virtual machine has sufficient resources to perform properly or limit it to creating one template at a time.

The Template Builder is downloaded as a zip file called Template Builder x64.zip. Unzip this file using the unzip utility as follows:

```
[root@ovm1 u01]# unzip Template\ Builder\ x64.zip
  Archive:  Template Builder x64.zip
    inflating: OVM_EL5U2_X86_64_TMPLBUILDER_PVM.tgz
```

After unzipping the Template Builder zip file, you'll have a tgz (Tar GNU Zipped) file. This file contains the template itself. Extract the contents of the tgz file using the tar program and the xfz options (x for extract, f for file, and z for compressed). Extracting the contents of the tgz file is shown here:

```
[root@ovm1 u01]# tar xvfz OVM_EL5U2_X86_64_TMPLBUILDER_PVM.tgz
OVM_EL5U2_X86_64_TMPLBUILDER_PVM/
OVM_EL5U2_X86_64_TMPLBUILDER_PVM/README
```

```
OVM_EL5U2_X86_64_TMPLBUILDER_PVM/System.img
OVM_EL5U2_X86_64_TMPLBUILDER_PVM/data.img
OVM_EL5U2_X86_64_TMPLBUILDER_PVM/vm.cfg
```

Included in the zipped tar file are virtual machine files (.img files and a vm.cfg file) and a README file. The contents of the vm.cfg file are very basic and are shown here:

```
bootloader = '/usr/bin/pygrub'
disk = ['file:/OVS/seed_pool/OVM_EL5U2_X86_64_TMPLBUILDER_PVM/System.img,xvda,w',
        'file:/OVS/seed_pool/OVM_EL5U2_X86_64_TMPLBUILDER_PVM/data.img,xvdb,w']
memory = '1024'
name = 'OVM_EL5U2_X86_64_TMPLBUILDER_PVM'
vcpus = 1
on_crash = 'restart'
on_reboot = 'restart'
vfb = ['type=vnc,vncunused=1,vnclisten=0.0.0.0']
vif = ['type=netfront']
```

Once you've placed the template files in the ../seed_pool directory, import the template and then create the Template Builder virtual machine.

Once the template has been created, start the virtual machine, using either the VM Manager or the command line utilities. Once the Template Builder virtual machine has started, you can launch the VNC viewer on that virtual machine's console. During the boot process, you will be prompted as to whether to configure the Template Builder virtual machine to use DHCP or static IP addressing for the network. If you would like to use static networking, press N, as shown here.

```
Configuring network interface.
  Network device: eth0
  Hardware address: 00:16:3E:39:7F:74

Do you want to enable dynamic IP configuration (DHCP) (Y|n)? n

Enter static IP address: 192.168.10.25
Enter netmask: [255.255.255.0]
Enter gateway: 192.168.10.1
Enter DNS server: 192.168.10.1
```

If you choose not to use dynamic IP addressing, enter the IP address, netmask, and gateway. When you are finished, the boot process will continue. When the network card starts, you are prompted for the hostname. Enter the hostname, press ENTER, and the boot process will continue until the configuration is complete, as shown here.

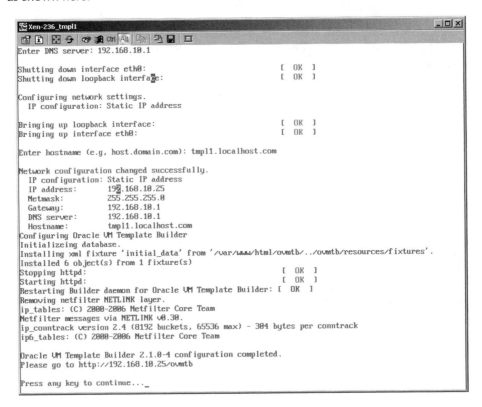

Once the Template Builder virtual machine configuration has completed its task, and the Template Builder virtual machine has fully booted and the applications have started, you can access the Template Builder console.

Accessing the Template Builder Console

The Template Builder console is a web-based application. The console is available from http://<system name>/ovmtb. This will bring up the login screen, as shown next.

Initially, there are no login accounts, so you must create one. Follow these steps to create an account:

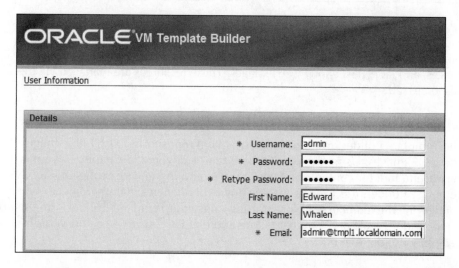

1. Click the Register link to create a login. The User Information screen requires a username, password, first and last name, and an email address to proceed, as shown next. Once this information has been added, click Next to proceed to the confirmation screen.

2. The Confirmation screen allows you to check the configuration and decide if you want to proceed. Click the Confirm button to proceed with creating the account.

3. When the account has been created, the browser returns to the login screen where you can input the newly created credentials. Once you log in to the Template Builder, the Template Projects screen appears, as shown here.

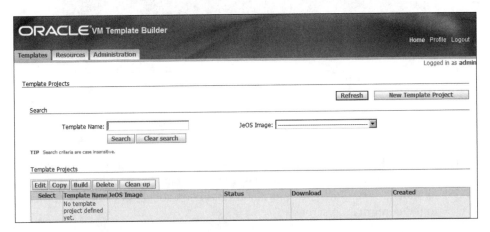

Before you can start creating templates, you need to perform a few setup steps and configure the resources that will be used by the Template Builder during the template creation process. These resources consist of yum repositories, DVD ISO images, and JeOS (Just enough OS) images. These resources are managed via the Resources tab.

Managing Template Builder Resources

The Template Builder resources consist of yum repositories, DVD ISO images, and JeOS images. Using the yum repository was covered in Chapter 9. yum is a very useful tool for configuring OS packages, and in the case of the Oracle VM Template Builder, it is used to resolve any dependencies that might occur when configuring the templates. Before starting to use the Template Builder some setup is required. At least one yum repository and one ISO image is required for the Template Builder to work.

NOTE
The images included in the Template Builder template are not up to date. You must go to edelivery.oracle.com/linux to get the latest JeOS images.

Managing Yum Repositories

Managing yum repositories is very straightforward.

1. From the main menu, select the Resources tab. The first screen (default) is the Yum Repositories screen. This screen should be configured for the Yum repositories that are required for your environment. The Yum Repositories screen is shown here.

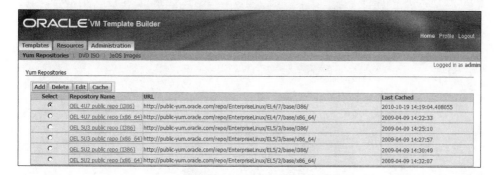

2. Removing any repositories that you don't need is recommended, as is adding any additional yum repositories that you require.

   ■ To remove a yum repository, select it by clicking the radio button and click the Delete button to remove the repository.

   ■ In order to add a yum repository, click the Add button and fill in the Add Yum Repository screen, as shown here:

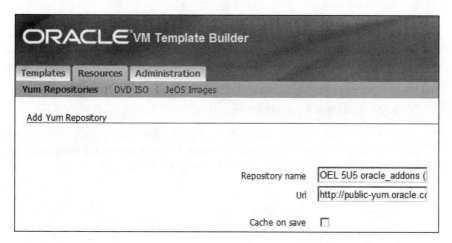

As the yum repository is added, the URL will be checked for validity. Once the repository has been added, the Yum Repositories screen reappears. In addition to adding the yum repositories, the metadata about the yum repositories can be cached, which allows for faster resolving of dependencies and packages, although the package still has to be downloaded from the actual repository. The Yum Repositories screen with additional cached packages is shown here.

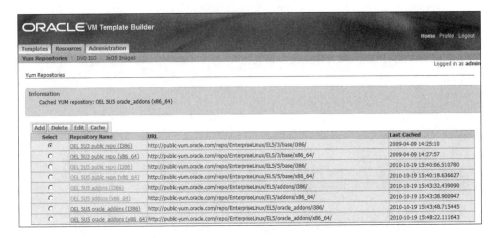

When the yum repositories have been configured, they will automatically be used as needed.

Managing ISO Images

In addition to the yum repositories, at least one DVD ISO image must be configured. As with the yum repositories, you can do this easily via the Resources tab.

1. From the Resources tab, select the DVD ISO subtab. As with the yum repositories, you'll see options to Add, Delete, Edit, and Cache the DVD ISO images.

2. Click the Add button to invoke the Add DVD ISO Location screen.

3. Fill in the DVD ISO name, the Path to the ISO files (not the ISO image), and select whether to cache on save. The path that is specified is not a path to the ISO image itself, but to the files within the ISO image.

   You can create the directory that is needed for the ISO image files in several ways: The DVD itself can be mounted and that path used, the files can be copied from the DVD to the filesystem, or the DVD can be mounted via the loop option. The loop option allows you to mount a DVD (or CD-ROM) image on the filesystem. The syntax used to mount with loop is shown here:

```
mount -o loop /u01/Enterprise-R5-U5-Server-x86_64-dvd.iso /u01/
OEL-5U5-x86_64
```

Either of these mentioned methods works. Once the DVD ISO image has been added, you should cache it in the same way you did the yum repositories. The completed operation is shown here:

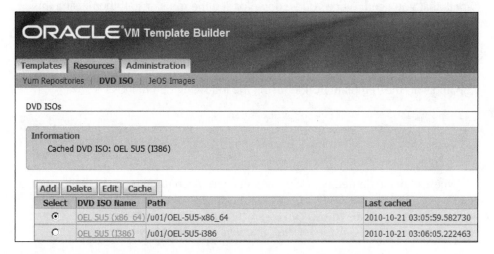

Once the yum repositories and DVD ISOs have been configured, you can begin the template creation process.

Managing JeOS Images

On the Resources tab, you'll also see a subtab for the JeOS Images, which are the core of the template building process. These JeOS images can be viewed, edited, and deleted, as shown here:

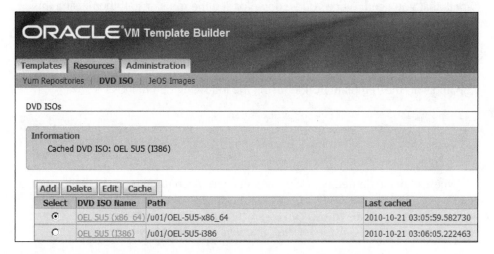

This list is the available images that you can use to create virtual machine templates. You can download additional JeOS templates from edelivery.oracle.com/linux. From the Linux downloads, select the JeOS rpms, choosing the version of Oracle that you need. Once you've downloaded the rpms, install them using this command:

```
$ rpm -ivh <rpm name>
```

The Template Builder must then be restarted for them to be available for use. Stop and start the Template Builder using the following commands:

```
[root@tmpl1 JeOS]# service ovmtb stop
Stopping Builder daemon for Oracle VM Template Builder: [  OK  ]
[root@tmpl1 JeOS]# service ovmtb start
Starting Builder daemon for Oracle VM Template Builder: [  OK  ]
```

When all of the desired operating systems have been installed in all three resource areas—yum repositories, DVD ISO, and JeOS images—then all of the prerequisites have been put into place so you can begin creating templates. Note that these three components must be available for the same version of the OS you're using.

Creating Templates with the Template Builder

Creating templates is done from the Template Projects screen. This screen has options such as Edit, Copy, Build, Delete, and Clean Up for existing templates and New Template Project for creating a new template. Follow these steps to create a new template:

1. Click the New Template Project button. This screen is used to describe the template. Fields that you must fill in are

   - **Template Name**   This is a name that you make up to give the template.

   - **Template Version**   This is a number that you define to keep track of the version of the template.

   - **Vendor**   This is the software (OS and/or application) vendor, such as Oracle Corporation.

   - **JeOS Image**   This is an image chosen from the drop-down list.

   - **Description**   This is a description of the template. This field is useful when you don't remember what you created.

   - **End User License Agreement**   This is the End User License Agreement.

The completed Description screen is shown next. When you have completed this step, click Next to continue. This will take you to the Virtual Machine Hardware screen.

2. The Virtual Machine Hardware screen is where you define the hardware and disk allocation that you will use for the virtual machine. The selection includes VCPUs, Memory, System Disk Size, and Swap Space, as shown here. The System Disk Size specified in this screen is not the total amount of disk space; it is the amount of free space to be left after the OS has been installed. Click Next to continue or click Add to add more disks.

3. If you click Add, the Virtual Machine Hardware – Add Disk Image screen will appear, as shown next. The options that you enter here are Size, Mount Point, and the Disk Image File name. Complete these options and click Save to save this disk definition and continue. You'll be returned to the Virtual Machine Hardware screen. Click Next to continue.

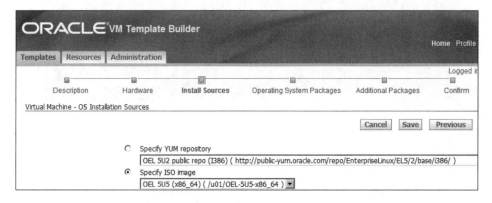

4. The next screen is the Virtual Machine – OS Installation Sources screen, which is shown next. Here is where you define either a yum repository or an ISO image to use as the installation source. Select which option you want by clicking the appropriate radio buttons, and then choose the specific OS using the drop-down menus. Once you have made your selections, click Next.

5. From the Virtual Machines – Operating System Packages screen, select all of the package groups and packages that are needed for your application and purpose. The Oracle documentation contains information on which packages are needed based on the Oracle product that you are installing. The Virtual Machines – Operating System Packages screen is shown here. Click Next when you have made your selections.

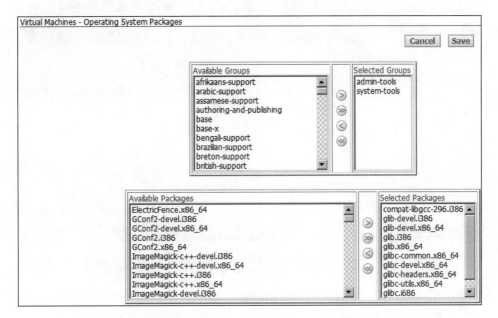

6. The Additional Software Packages screen, shown next, is where you specify external packages. These can be any packages that are available on the Template Builder system and are used to make sure the desired applications can be installed and that any additional applications you might need are installed. This is also your opportunity to provide scripts to include as part

of the template for both configuration and cleanup. Once you have added additional packages and scripts, click Next to continue.

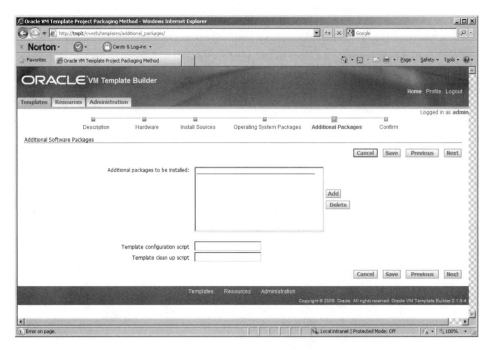

7. The final step in defining the template is the Confirm Information screen, which you can see here. This is your last chance to review all of your changes and either go back and make additional changes, or click Save and Build to build the template.

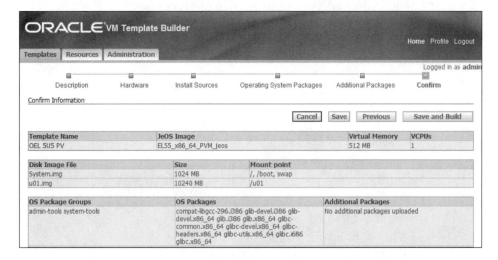

8. Clicking Save and Build brings up the Template Log screen. This screen doesn't contain much information initially, but it is refreshed at a regular interval and you will begin to see information about the build process, as is shown here.

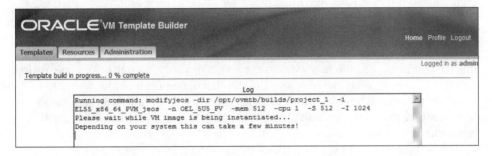

9. The template build process may take awhile to complete. When the process is 100 percent complete, the message Template Build Completed will be displayed. Click Return to Template Projects Screen to return to the main screen. Here, you will see the template that you have just created.

At this point, you can now download and use the templates. Specifics on how to do this are presented in the next section.

Accessing the Templates

Once you've created the template, it is available for you to download and use. The compressed tarball of the project is available via your browser from the Template Builder system at http://<tmpl builder>/ovmtb/data/tarballs. Browse to this URL and you will see a list of tgz files. Click one of the files and you will be prompted to open or download the file.

Browsing from the VM Server

One question that will immediately arise when downloading templates is how do you get them from the Template Builder to the VM Server. Installing X-Windows on the VM Server is not recommended, nor do you typically want to download the file twice—once to your PC and then to the VM Server. The answer is *Elinks*. The Elinks program is a character-based browser that is already installed on the VM Server system. Using elinks, you can browse the Template Builder URL and download the template.

Elinks is a fairly simple-to-use browser; however, it is character based. This is a big benefit of Elinks because no additional software needs to be added to the system. This benefit far outweighs the drawbacks.

In addition, the images and vm.cfg file are available directly from http://<tmpl builder>/ovmtb/builds/<project name>. From this URL, you can download the files by clicking them and choosing save.

Once you've downloaded the template, you can import the virtual machine template and finally create the virtual machine from the template.

Summary

This chapter presented the two ways to create a template: manually from an existing virtual machine or using the Template Builder. Each method provides a way to create preconfigured templates that you can easily use to reliably and repeatedly deploy virtual machines. By using templates much of the guesswork is removed from virtual machine creation.

The Template Builder is a useful tool for creating a JeOS version of Linux to be used to deploy systems quickly and easily. For many people, however, the most common way to create a custom template is to download a template from Oracle, create a virtual machine from that template, and modify it to suit their environment: security, networking, etc. They then run the template cleanup script, shut down, and save that as their new golden image. This process is a very effective way of creating and using templates. Creating virtual machines from templates is the most reliable and most recommended method of creating virtual machines. The next chapter covers just that—how to create virtual machines using templates.

CHAPTER
16

Using Templates to Create Virtual Machines and Configuring Resources

he previous chapter covered how to create templates, both using an existing virtual machine as the source of the template or using the Template Builder. Templates are probably the best way to create a virtual machine because they are based on an actual functioning system. You can create a template from any virtual machine that is currently running in your environment, and as you will see in Chapter 18, you can even take a VMware virtual machine or a physical machine and convert it into a virtual machine and subsequently save that as a template.

The collection of templates are stored in the seed_pool directory and are accessed from the utility server when a virtual machine is created. When the template creates a new virtual machine, it does so in the running_pool directory. Once the virtual machine has been created using a template, you can modify as necessary. This chapter covers creating a virtual machine from a template, configuring the virtual machine, and adding and/or modifying virtual resources on that virtual machine.

Creating the Virtual Machine Using a Template

Several tools are available to manage the Oracle VM environment. As with earlier chapters, all three methods for creating virtual machines using templates are covered: the VM Manager, OEM Grid Control, and the Oracle VM CLI. Regardless of the method chosen, the end result will be the same—a virtual machine created from a template.

Creating Virtual Machines Using the VM Manager

One of the most common methods of creating virtual machines is with the VM Manager. The VM Manager is included with Oracle VM and is easy to install and use. Throughout this book, you have seen numerous examples of the VM Manager.

To create a virtual machine from a template using the VM Manager, follow these steps:

1. From the VM Manager Virtual Machines screen, click the Create Virtual Machine button. This will invoke the process to create a new virtual machine.

2. The first screen is the Creation Method screen. Here, you create a virtual machine using one of three different methods:

    ■   Create Virtual Machine Based On A Virtual Machine Template. In this chapter, this option is what we are interested in.

- Create From Installation Media. With HVM systems, you can create a virtual machine using virtual CD-ROM or DVD-ROM images.

- Create From A Network Bootable Virtual Machine (pxeboot). This method allows you to create a system by performing a network boot and installing from a network system using PXE boot.

  All of these methods work well, but the second and third methods involve installing an OS from scratch, whereas, when using a template, the OS is already configured and ready to go. Select Create Virtual Machine Based on A Virtual Machine Template.

3. From the Server Pool screen, select the server pool in which to create the virtual machine. If there are multiple server pools, select the desired one by clicking the radio button next to it. Once you have made your selection, click Next.

4. The Source screen contains a list of virtual machine templates that can be used as the source of the virtual machine. In addition to the list of virtual machines, you can get a little more information about the virtual machine by clicking the + Show button in the details column of the display. This expands the information about that particular virtual machine, as shown here.

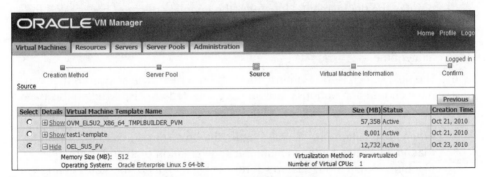

5. The Virtual Machine Information screen is where you get to make some choices about the particular virtual machine being configured. First, give it a name and a console password. The name should be something descriptive. Once you have a number of virtual machines, it can be difficult to tell them apart or to remember which one is which. A descriptive name helps.

This screen is also where you can delete a virtual network interface. If available in your configuration, this is also where you enable High Availability. The Virtual Machine Information screen is shown here. Click Next to continue.

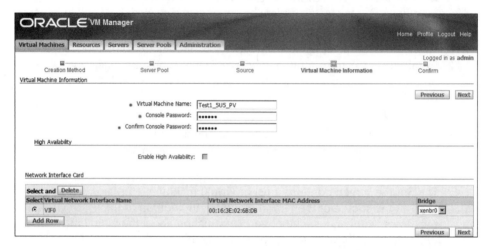

It is unlikely that you will need to add or delete network interfaces at this point of the deployment. Hopefully, the template designer has created the template with the needed number of network interfaces for the desired application; however, if you do need a network interface, you can add it at a later time.

6. The next screen is the Confirm Information screen. The selections that you have chosen and options that you have selected are displayed on this page. Once you have verified that all of the selections are correct, click Confirm.

7. When the creation process has begun, the browser returns to the Virtual Machines screen. Here, you can track the creation of the new virtual machine. When the virtual machine has been created, the status changes to Powered Off.

This completes the steps necessary to create a virtual machine from a template using the VM Manager. As you can see, it is a very straightforward process. Now that the virtual machine has been created, you can modify it as necessary.

Creating Virtual Machines Using OEM Grid Control

Creating a virtual machine from a template using OEM Grid Control is a very straightforward process. Follow these steps to create a virtual machine from a template using OEM Grid Control:

1. From the Targets tab of OEM Grid Control, select the Virtual Servers tab, as shown here. From the Action drop-down menus, select Guest VM and Create Guest VM and then click Go.

2. This invokes the Create Guest Virtual Machines: Server Pool screen, which is shown here. Fill in the number of virtual machines to be created and the name of the server pool. By clicking the flashlight icon, you can select the server pool from a pop-up. Click Next to continue.

3. From the Create Guest Virtual Machines: Source screen, shown next, select the method for creating the virtual machine—Oracle VM Template, ISO Image, or PXE boot—and the type—Imported Resources, External Location, or Software Components. Click the radio button next to the template you want to use to create the virtual machine.

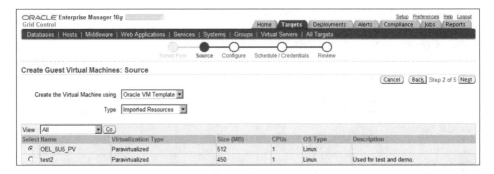

4. In the Create Guest Virtual Machines: Configure screen, you enter information about the new virtual machine, as shown here. This information includes the following:

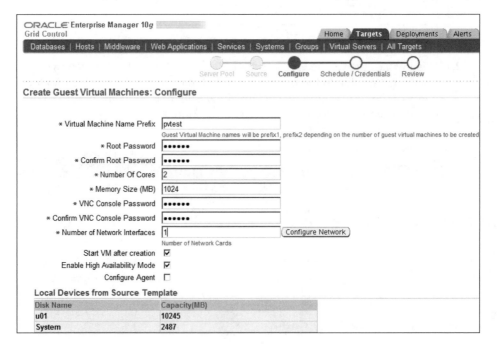

■ **Virtual Machine Name Prefix**   Enter the name that will be used to create the actual virtual machine name.

■ **Root Password (with confirmation)**   Enter the root password of the virtual machine.

■ **Number of Cores**   Enter the number of cores that will be assigned to the virtual machine.

■ **Memory Size (MB)**   Decide how much memory will be assigned to the virtual machine.

■ **VNC Console Password (with confirmation)**   Enter the password that will be used for VNC console access.

■ **Number of Network Interfaces**   Define the number of virtual NICs that the virtual machine will have. Click the Configure Network button to configure the networks.

In addition, several check boxes allow you to define the virtual machine's properties:

■ **Start VM After Creation**   Automatically starts the virtual machine after the creation process has completed.

■ **Enable High Availability Mode**   Configure the newly created virtual machine in High Availability mode.

■ **Configure Agent**   Configure the OEM Grid Control agent on the newly created virtual machine.

In addition to these options, the local device sizes are shown along with an option to create additional disk devices and shared disks. When you have entered the information, click Next to continue.

5. The next screen is the Create Guest Virtual Machines: Schedule/Credentials Screen. This screen is where you set Grid Control scheduling and the credentials for creating the virtual machine. Options are available for scheduling creation of the virtual machine and entering both the monitoring server and virtual server host credentials.

6. The final screen is the Create Guest Virtual Machines: Review screen where you can review all of the settings that you have specified. Once you have reviewed everything, click Finish to launch the virtual machine creation process.

7. Control returns to the Virtual Servers screen. You will then see the new virtual machine with a status of Creating. When the creation process is finished, the status will change to Halted, and if you selected to start the virtual machine after creation, the status will eventually change to Running.

As you can see, regardless of which process you use, using a template to create a virtual machine is very straightforward and easy to do. In the next few chapters, you will learn the other methods to create virtual machines.

Creating Virtual Machines with the VM Manager CLI

Creating a virtual machine using the VM Manager CLI is also a very straightforward process. Creating a new virtual machine is done using the CLI command **ovm vm new**. As with most Oracle VM CLI commands, a number of options are available.

As with the other **ovm** commands covered earlier in this book, the basic options for running the **ovm** command are **–u <username>** or **--username=<username>** and **-p <password>** or **--password=<password>**. These represent the username and password of the VM Manager. If these options are not passed, you will be prompted for these values.

The **ovm vm new** command takes the options described in Table 16-1.

An example of importing an image using the Oracle VM CLI is shown here (note that you can use **ovm tmpl ls** to list the templates):

```
[root@manager ~]# ovm -u admin -p pwd123 vm new -m template -s ovm
-t OEL_5U5_PV -n test2 -c pwd123
Virtual machine "test2" is being created. Please check the status.
```

Once the process has started, please check the status occasionally to see if it has completed. Eventually the status will change, as shown here:

```
[root@manager ~]# ovm -u admin -p pwd123 vm stat -s ovm -n test2
Creating
[root@manager ~]# ovm -u admin -p pwd123 vm stat -s ovm -n test2
Powered Off
```

At this point, the virtual machine has been created and is in a powered off state. It is now ready to be started.

Option	Description
-h, --help	Displays the help message.
-s server_pool, --server_pool_name=server_pool	(Required) Specifies the name of the server pool that the virtual machine image is being added to.
-m method, --method=method	(Required) Specifies the virtual machine method type. Options are template, ISO, or PXE.
-n vm_name, --vm_name=vm_name	(Required) Specifies the virtual machine name.
-c <console password>, --console_password=<console password>	Sets the password for the VNC console that will be available for this virtual machine.
-a, --ha_enabled	Enables High Availability.
-x, --hvm	Creates a hardware virtualized guest.
-g iso_group, --iso_group=iso_group	Specifies the ISO image group.
-l iso_label, --iso_label=iso_label	Specifies the ISO image label.
-L location, --location=location	Sets the paravirtualized guest installation source. This is something like http://host/path or ftp://host/path or nfs:host:/path.
-o OS, --os=OS	Specifies the OS type.
-V vcpus, --vcpus=vcpus	Sets the number of VCPUs.
-y memory, --memory=memory	Specifies the memory size in megabytes.
-d disksize, --disksize=disksize	Specifies the virtual disk size in megabytes.
-p preferred_server, --preferred_server=preferred_server	Specifies the preferred server (comma separated).

TABLE 16-1.   *ovm vm new* Options

Configuring Resources on the Virtual Machine

Once the virtual machine has been configured, you might need to add more resources to the system, such as additional disk drives, additional network controllers, and so on. You can do this using the familiar three methods: the VM Manager, OEL Grid Control, or the Oracle VM CLI. Each is covered in this section.

Configuring Resources with the VM Manager

From the VM Manager Virtual Machines tab, select the desired virtual machine by clicking the radio button beside it and then clicking the Configure button. The main Virtual Machines screen is shown in Figure 16-1.

A number of independent configuration screens are available within the Virtual Machine Configure module. These different configuration tabs are General, Network, Storage, Policies, and Profiles. The General Screen is where you configure the virtual machine and group as well as set the maximum and current memory size. Simply fill in the new values as shown in Figure 16-2 and click Save. Here, you can also add a description if desired.

NOTE
The maximum memory cannot be exceeded and can only be changed while the virtual machine is not running. The memory size setting is the initial memory allocated and can be changed dynamically, as long as it is less than or equal to the maximum memory setting.

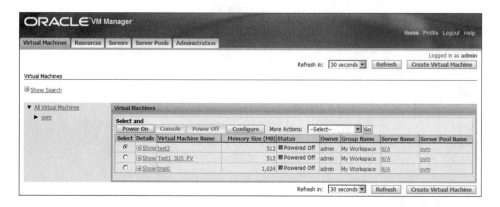

FIGURE 16-1. *The Oracle VM Manager Virtual Machines screen*

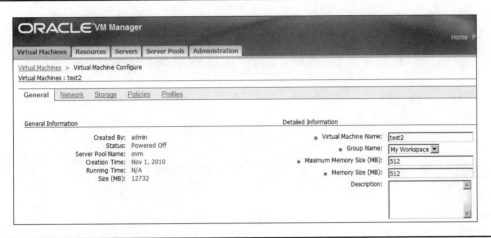

FIGURE 16-2. *The Virtual Machine Configure General tab*

From the Network tab, you can modify, add, or delete a virtual network adapter as well as change the Xen bridge that the adapter utilizes. Select the desired network adapter and click Edit to make changes, as shown in Figure 16-3. Click the Add or Delete button to add or remove network adapters.

From the Storage tab, you can add, remove, or modify virtual disks as shown in Figure 16-4. Here, you can also delete or edit virtual disks as well as create a new virtual disk or attach a shared virtual disk. Each button invokes another screen that performs these functions. When adding a new virtual disk, you are prompted for the disk name, the disk size, and the disk type. The disk type can be SCSI, IDE, or XVD. In addition, you set QoS and Priority here.

In addition to disk drives, the Boot Source/CDROM tab is where you set the boot source. The boot source can be HDD or PXE (for Paravirtualized systems) or HDD, PXE, or CDROM (for HVM systems). With HVM systems, choose the CDROM from the set of ISO images defined on that server pool.

On the Policies tabs, you'll find two tabs. The High Availability tab, shown in Figure 16-5, is where you configure the Number of Virtual CPUs, Scheduling Priority, and Scheduling Cap, as well as whether to enable High Availability. The Placement Policy tab is where you configure the placement on servers in the server pool. The automatic placement policy is the recommended policy, but manual is allowed.

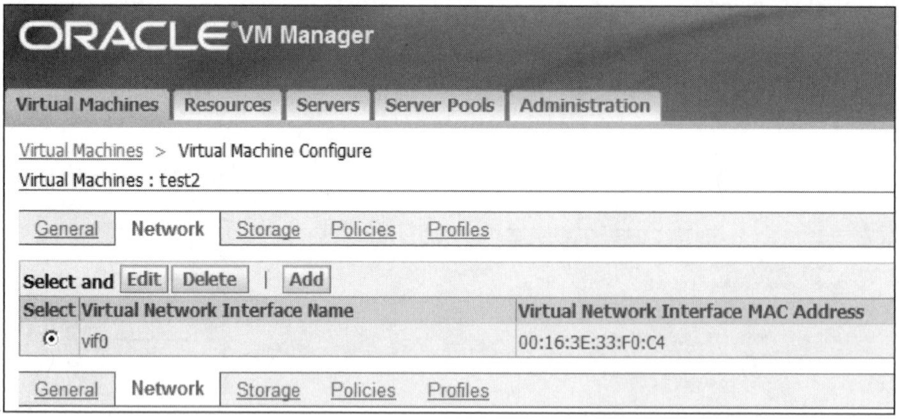

FIGURE 16-3. *The Virtual Machine Configure Network tab*

The Profiles tab, shown in Figure 16-6, is where you set the login and password values for the virtual machine. This is also where you set the console password. In addition, the Operating System tab is where you define the OS and keyboard layout.

As you can see, you can make a number of additional configuration changes and additions after the virtual machine has been created. The VM Manager provides a straightforward way to make these changes. None of these changes are complicated or confusing.

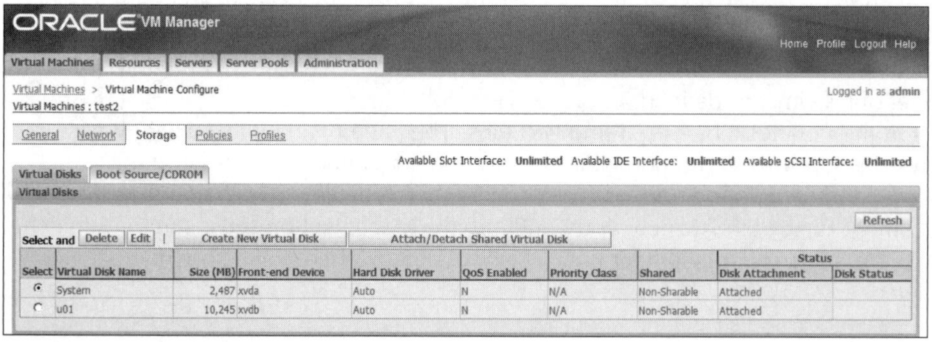

FIGURE 16-4. *The Virtual Machine Configure Storage tab*

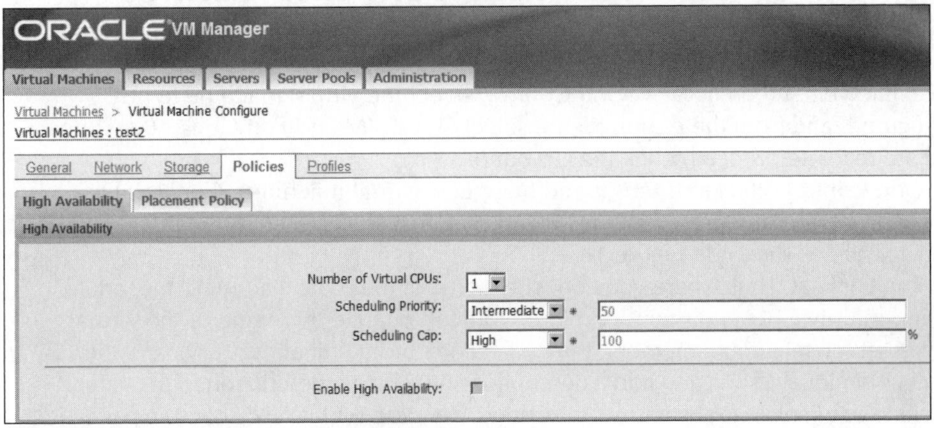

FIGURE 16-5.   *The Virtual Machine Configure Policies tab*

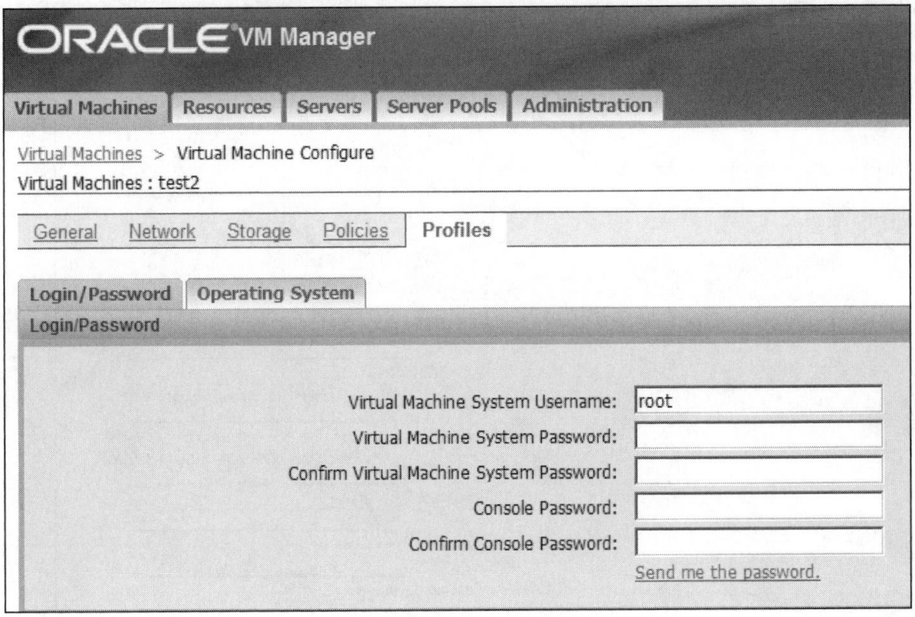

FIGURE 16-6.   *The Virtual Machine Configure Profiles tab*

Configuring Resources with OEM Grid Control

Configuring virtual machines with OEM Grid Control is also very straightforward. The OEM Grid Control interface for Oracle VM is very easy to use. From the main Virtual Servers screen in OEM Grid Control, select the virtual machine to be configured, and from the Action menu, select Guest VM and Edit Guest VM. When you are ready to proceed, click the Go button.

Grid Control offers four tabs for editing guest virtual machines: General, Disk Storage, Network Interface, and Advanced. The first screen that you will see is the General tab, as shown in Figure 16-7.

The General tab is where you configure some of the basic features of the virtual server, mainly CPU and memory. Here, you can change the name of the virtual server; set the maximum memory, the dynamic memory (initial memory), and the number of virtual CPUs; and add a description. Attaching a description to the virtual machine or template is always recommended. You also set the VNC console password

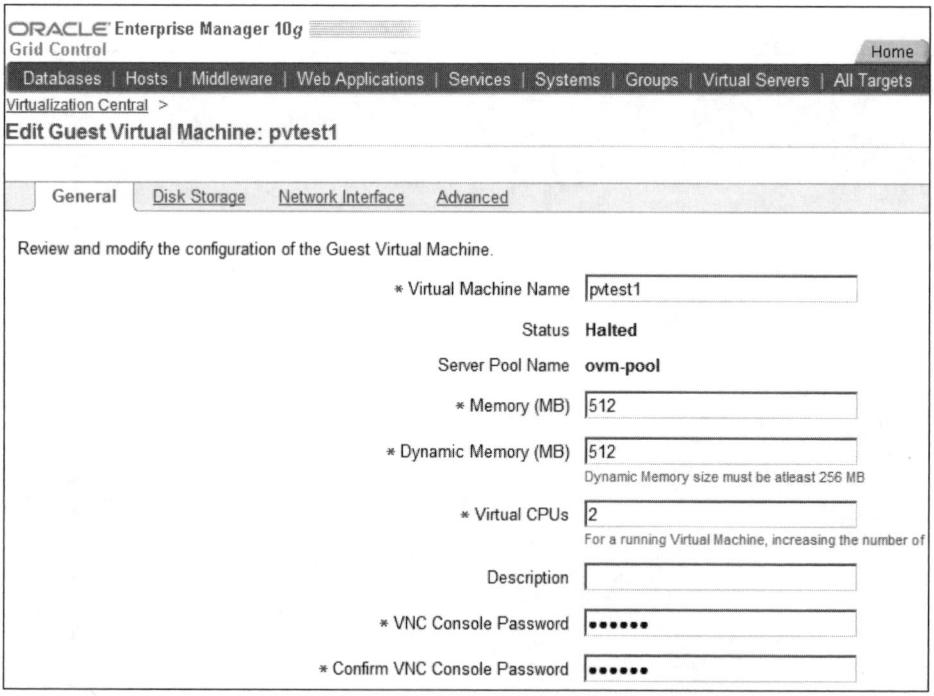

ORACLE Enterprise Manager 10g
Grid Control

Home

Databases | Hosts | Middleware | Web Applications | Services | Systems | Groups | Virtual Servers | All Targets

Virtualization Central >

Edit Guest Virtual Machine: pvtest1

General | Disk Storage | Network Interface | Advanced

Review and modify the configuration of the Guest Virtual Machine.

* Virtual Machine Name	pvtest1
Status	**Halted**
Server Pool Name	**ovm-pool**
* Memory (MB)	512
* Dynamic Memory (MB)	512
	Dynamic Memory size must be atleast 256 MB
* Virtual CPUs	2
	For a running Virtual Machine, increasing the number of
Description	
* VNC Console Password	••••••
* Confirm VNC Console Password	••••••

FIGURE 16-7. *Edit Guest Virtual Machine General tab*

on this screen. When you have entered all of the information, click the Continue button or another tab to finish the virtual machine editing process.

Use the Disk Storage tab, shown in Figure 16-8, to configure system storage. Here, you can add or delete virtual disks or attach shared disks. There is no option to edit a disk after it has been attached. If you want to change the disk, you must remove it and add a new one.

You can modify the virtual network interfaces on the Network Interface tab, as shown in Figure 16-9. This tab is where you can add, delete, or edit network interfaces. The edit process only allows for changing the Xen bridge. You cannot change the MAC address from the GUI tools. It can only be changed by editing the vm.cfg file.

The Advanced tab only allows you to change the boot order from Disk to Network. Once you made the change (if any), click the Continue button.

Clicking the Continue button at any stage brings you back to the Virtual Servers main screen. From here, you can perform any number of other tasks. As you have seen, the process of editing virtual machines from OEM Grid Control is very straightforward.

Configuring Resources with the VM CLI

As you have seen in previous chapters, the Oracle VM CLI is the most direct way of making configuration changes, since the changes are all done in one step.

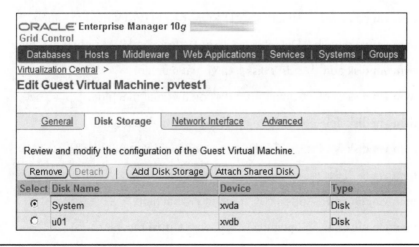

FIGURE 16-8.   *Edit Guest Virtual Machine Disk Storage tab*

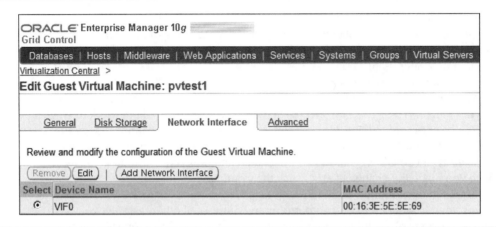

FIGURE 16-9. *Edit Guest Virtual Machine Network Interface tab*

Many options are available for the **ovm vm** command that you can use to configure/reconfigure the virtual machine. These commands include the following:

- **ovm vm bootdev**   Sets the boot device type as either HDD, PXE, or CDROM.

- **ovm vm cd attach**   Attaches a CD-ROM to an HVM virtual machine.

- **ovm vm cd detach**   Detaches a CD-ROM from an HVM virtual machine.

- **ovm vm disk add**   Adds a disk to a virtual machine.

- **ovm vm disk conf**   Configures a disk on a virtual machine.

- **ovm vm disk del**   Removes a disk from a virtual machine.

- **ovm vm disk ls**   Lists the disks associated with a virtual machine.

- **ovm vm ls**   Lists the virtual machines known to the VM Manager.

- **ovm vm nic add**   Adds a NIC to a virtual machine.

- **ovm vm nic conf**   Configures a NIC on a virtual machine.

- **ovm vm nic del**   Deletes a NIC from a virtual machine.

- **ovm vm nic ls**   Lists the NICs that are assigned to a virtual machine.

- **ovm vm sd attach** Attaches a shared virtual disk to a virtual machine.
- **ovm vm sd detach** Detaches a shared virtual disk from a virtual machine.
- **ovm vm vncpwd** Sets the VNC console password for a virtual machine.

Rather than go through all of the parameters for each of the above-mentioned commands, examples will be provided. The syntax of each specific command can be obtained by using the **help** qualifier as shown here:

```
[root@manager ~]# ovm vm bootdev -h
usage: ovm vm bootdev [options]
Set primary boot device

options:
  -h, --help              Display this help message
  -s SERVERPOOL_NAME, --serverpool_name=SERVERPOOL_NAME
                          (Required) Server pool name
  -n VM_NAME, --vm_name=VM_NAME
                          (Required) Virtual machine name
  -b BOOT_DEVICE, --boot_device=BOOT_DEVICE
                          (Required) Boot device types: CDROM, HDD, PXE
```

The following are examples of how to use each of the previously mentioned commands in order to edit and configure the system using the Oracle VM CLI.

ovm vm bootdev:

```
[root@manager ~]# ovm -u admin -p pwd123 vm bootdev -s ovm -n test2 -b HDD
Boot device set to HDD.
```

ovm vm cd attach:

```
[root@manager ~]# ovm -u admin -p pwd123 vm cd attach -s ovm -n test2
-g OEL-5.5-x86_64 -l Enterprise-R5-U5-Server-x86_64-disc1
Attached CD-ROM to the virtual machine.
```

ovm vm cd detach:

```
[root@manager ~]# ovm -u admin -p pwd123 vm cd detach -s ovm -n test2
Detached CD-ROM from the virtual machine.
```

ovm vm disk add:

```
[root@manager ~]# ovm -u admin -p pwd123 vm disk add -s ovm -n test2 -d u02
-S 10240 -t auto
Adding virtual disk. Please check the status.
[root@manager ~]# ovm -u admin -p pwd123 vm disk ls -s ovm -n test2
Disk_Name Size(MB) Hard_Disk_Driver Shared      QoS Attachment Status
u02       10240    AUTO             Non-Sharable N:0 Attached   Active
System    2487     AUTO             Non-Sharable N:0 Attached
u01       10245    AUTO             Non-Sharable N:0 Attached
```

ovm vm disk conf:

This command to configure the virtual disks has these additional options:

-t <type>, --drive_type=<type>	Hard drive type (auto/hd/sd/xvd)
-p <priority class>, --priority_class=<priority class>	Priority class (0–7) – requires QoS
-q, --enable_qos	Enable QoS
-D, --disable_qos	Disable QoS

Here is an example:

```
[root@manager ~]# ovm -u admin -p pwd123 vm disk conf -s ovm -n test2 -d u02
-t sd -p 3 -q
Virtual disk updated.
```

ovm vm disk del:

```
[root@manager ~]# ovm -u admin -p pwd123 vm disk del -s ovm -n test2 -d u02
Removed virtual disk from the virtual machine.
```

ovm vm disk ls:

```
[root@manager ~]# ovm -u admin -p pwd123 vm ls
Name           Size(MB) Mem  VCPUs Status       Server_Pool
tmpl1          77599    1024 2     Powered Off  ovm
test2          12732    512  1     Powered Off  ovm
Test1_5U5_PV   12732    512  1     Powered Off  ovm
```

ovm vm ls:

```
[root@manager ~]# ovm -u admin -p pwd123 vm ls
Name          Size(MB)  Mem   VCPUs       Status   Server_Pool
srac00a       18433     3072  2     Powered Off    ovm2-pool
srac00b       18433     3072  2     Powered Off    ovm2-pool
ebiz12_db     1         4096  2         Running    ovm2-pool
3580_rac08b   28385     3072  1     Powered Off    ovm2-pool
3575_rac08a   28385     3072  1         Running    ovm2-pool
OEL56PV64     28673     4096  1     Powered Off    ovm2-pool
```

ovm vm nic add:

```
[root@manager ~]# ovm -u admin -p pwd123 vm nic add -s ovm -n test2 -N vif1
-b xenbr1
NIC has been added to the virtual machine.
```

ovm vm nic conf:

The **vm nic conf** command takes the following parameters:

-N <name>, --nic_name=<name>	(Required) NIC name
-i <new name>, --new_nic_name=<new name>	New NIC name
-b <bridge>, --bridge=<bridge>	Network bridge
-r <rate limit>, --rate_limit=<rate limit>	Rate limit in megabits
-e, --enable_qos	Enable rate limit
-d, --disable_qos	Disable rate limit

```
[root@manager ~]# ovm -u admin -p pwd123 vm nic conf -s ovm -n test2 -N vif1
-i vif2 -b xenbr2
NIC updated.
```

ovm vm nic del:

```
[root@manager ~]# ovm -u admin -p pwd123 vm nic del -s ovm -n test2 -N vif2
NIC has been deleted from the virtual machine.
```

ovm vm nic ls:

```
[root@manager ~]# ovm -u admin -p pwd123 vm nic ls -s ovm -n test2
NIC_Name MAC_Adress          Bridge Status Interface Rate_Limit
vif0     00:16:3E:33:F0:C4 xenbr0 Active netfront  False:0.0
```

ovm vm sd attach:

```
[root@manager ~]# ovm -u admin -p pwd123 vm sd attach -s ovm -n test2
-d shared01
Attached shared virtual disk to the virtual machine.
```

ovm vm sd detach:

```
[root@manager ~]# ovm -u admin -p pwd123 vm sd detach -s ovm -n test2
-d shared01
Detached shared virtual disk from the virtual machine.
```

ovm vm vncpwd:

```
[root@manager ~]# ovm -u admin -p pwd123 vm vncpwd -s ovm -n test2 -c pwd123
Updated VNC console password.
```

There is nothing overly complex about configuring the virtual machines via the Oracle VM CLI. The VM CLI is very convenient when you need to perform many operations and you want to do so without much manual intervention.

Summary

This chapter covered some very straightforward, but crucial topics: how to create a new virtual machine from a template and how to modify a virtual machine. As you have noticed throughout this book, preparation is really most of the work. Once the VM Servers and support systems, such as templates, ISO images, and so on, are set up, creating the virtual machine is not very difficult.

Though installing virtual machines using templates is usually the preferred method, in order to create a machine from scratch, you will install the virtual machine using installation media manually. This is covered in the next chapter.

CHAPTER
17

Creating Virtual
Machines Manually

reating a virtual machine manually involves installing the OS from scratch. This method is more time consuming than creating a virtual machine from a template but gives you more control over what and how the OS is installed. Depending on the type of virtual machine server hardware, there are different possibilities for installing a new virtual machine.

The three main options for creating a virtual machine are templates, installation media, and PXE boot. The previous chapter covered installing a virtual machine using a template. This chapter will cover installing a virtual machine using installation media and PXE boot. Once the installation begins, using these methods, the procedure itself is no different than installing the OS on hardware.

Creating a Virtual Machine Using ISO Images and Installation Media

Creating a virtual machine manually using installation media is done by making the virtual machine installation believe that it is installing from a CD-ROM, when in fact it's actually installing from a virtual image. In either case, whether CD-ROM or ISO image, the process is the same.

If a VM Server supports hardware virtualization, ISO images can be imported into the server, which gives you the ability to use those ISO images as the source of the installation. For VM Servers that don't support HVM, the installation process can only be done using the installation media on NFS or using PXE boot, which will covered later in the chapter.

Creating a Virtual Machine Using the VM Manager

From the VM Manager's Virtual Machines screen, select Create Virtual Machine to begin the virtual machine creation process. The first screen you'll see is the Creation Method screen. On this screen, you are presented with three options:

- Create Virtual Machine Based on a Virtual Machine Template

- Create from Installation Media

- Create a Network Bootable Virtual Machine (pxeboot)

The Create from a Template option was covered in the last chapter and Create a Network Bootable Virtual Machine (pxeboot) will be covered later in this chapter. Because the methods of installing a fully virtualized virtual machine from ISO images and a paravirtualized virtual machine from installation media differ, they are covered separately.

NOTE
Oracle does not recommend creating virtual machines from scratch as described in this chapter. They have put significant effort into the template process and the Template Builder. Creating virtual machines via that method is preferred.

Creating a Fully Virtualized Virtual Machine from ISO Images

Follow these steps to create a fully virtualized VM from ISO images:

1. Select Create Virtual Machine.

2. For this example, select Create from Installation Media.

3. Select the server pool from the list of virtual machines, as shown next. For the example provided here, the VM Server pools ptc1-pool and ptc2-pool do not support HVM, whereas pe710-pool does support HVM. Select the server pool name and click the Next button.

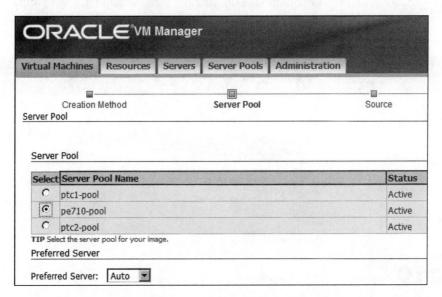

4. If the server pool supports HVM and ISO images are available via the server pool resources, select Fully Virtualized from the Virtualization Method drop-down list, as shown here. If HVM is not available on the server pool, only paravirtualized guests can be created from installation media. If a fully

virtualized guest is desired on a non-HVM enabled server, you must install it using a template or PXE boot. Click Next after you've made your selection.

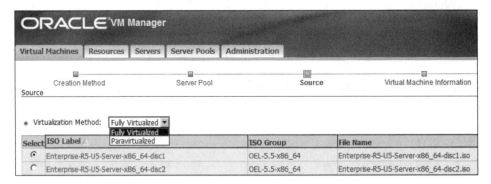

5. The Virtual Machine Information screen, shown next, is where you specify information about the virtual machine. The information consists of the Virtual Machine Name (try to be descriptive), Operating System, Number of Virtual CPUs, Keyboard Layout, Memory Size, Virtual Disk Size, and the Console Password. Here you can also choose to modify or add virtual network interfaces.

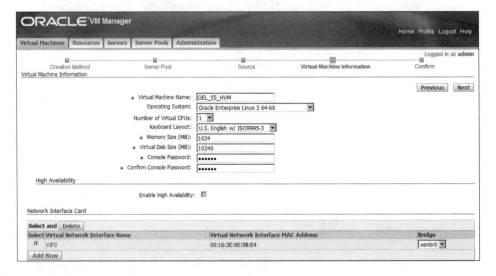

NOTE
If you intend to use DHCP for networking, this is a good time to grab the MAC address, as this is when the MAC address is defined.

6. The final screen is the Confirm Information screen, which is shown next. Review all of the information that you provided, and when you are satisfied, click Confirm.

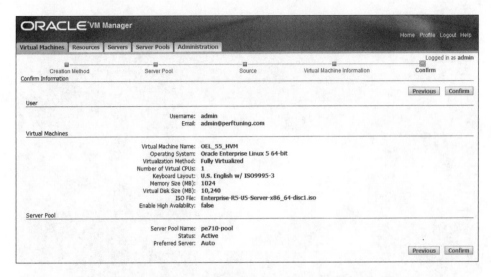

7. Once the virtual machine creation process begins, control returns to the Virtual Machines tab. The virtual machine status will show as Creating and then as Running. Expand the virtual machine details in the VM Manager and make note of the VNC console number, as shown here.

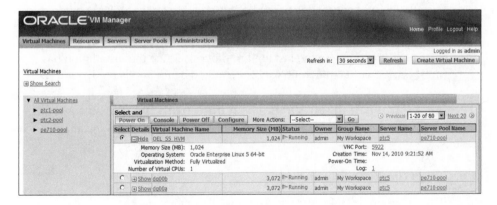

8. Using a VNC client program, open the VNC console by using the address <VM Server>:<VNC port>. The VNC console is where you perform the OS installation; the first screen is shown here.

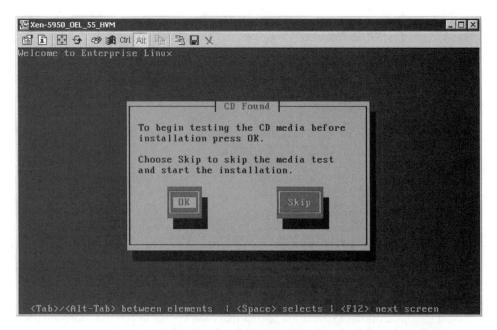

9. At this point, the OS installation will proceed as normal. During the installation procedure, you might be prompted to change CDs. You do this by editing the virtual machine and selecting a new CD-ROM source. The first time the virtual machine is rebooted, you must reconnect to the console with VNC to complete the installation process. Once the installation has finished, the virtual machine can be rebooted again and is ready for use.

Creating a Paravirtualized Virtual Machine from Installation Media

Follow these steps to create a paravirtualized virtual machine from installation media:

1. Select Create Virtual Machine.

2. For this example, select Create from Installation Media.

3. Select the server pool from the list of virtual machines (this is the same screen shown in Step 3 of the previous section). For the example provided here, the VM Server pool does not support HVM. Select the server pool name and click the Next button.

4. If the server pool supports HVM and ISO images are available via the server pool resources, you can select Fully Virtualized from the Virtualization Method drop-down list. If HVM is not available on the server pool, only paravirtualized guests can be created from installation media. If a fully virtualized guest is desired on a non-HVM enabled server, you must install it using a template or PXE boot. If you selected Fully Virtualized and clicked Next, the error "Invalid Resource" will appear. Select Paravirtualized as shown in the next screen. The source of the installation media is the full NFS path shown here:

```
nfs:<server>/<mount point>
```

For example:

```
nfs:manager/u01/stage/
```

Once you have defined the resource location, click Next to proceed.

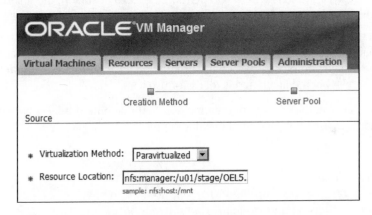

5. You will proceed to the Virtual Machine Information screen. The Virtual Machine Information screen is where you specify information about the virtual machine. The information consists of the Virtual Machine Name (try to be descriptive), Operating System, Number of Virtual CPUs, Keyboard Type, Memory Size, and Virtual Disk Size, and the Console Password. Here, you can also choose to modify or add virtual network interfaces. (This screen is shown in Step 5 of the previous section.)

NOTE
If you intend to use DHCP for networking, this is a good time to grab the MAC address, as this is when the MAC address is defined.

6. The final screen is the Confirm Information screen, which is the same screen shown in Step 6 of the previous section. Review all of the information that you provided, and when you are satisfied, click Confirm.

7. The virtual machine creation process begins. Once the process has begun, control returns to the Virtual Machines tab. The virtual machine status will show as Creating and then as Running. At this point, you need to connect to the virtual machine console using VNC. You can do this in one of two ways: by selecting the virtual machine to be connected to and clicking the Console button or by determining the VNC console and connecting via an external VNC program.

   To use an external VNC program, expand the virtual machine details in the VM Manager and make note of the VNC console number. Using a VNC client program, open the VNC console using the address <VM Server>:<VNC port>. The VNC console is where you perform the OS installation, the first screen of which is shown in Step 7 of the previous section.

8. At this point, the OS installation proceeds as normal. The first time the virtual machine reboots, you must reconnect to the console with VNC to complete the installation process. Once the installation has finished, the virtual machine can be rebooted again and is ready for use.

As you can see, the process of creating a virtual machine differs between using ISO images and using an prestaged installation media.

NOTE
In addition to using an NFS server other than the VM Server, you can also set up the VM Server itself as an NFS server. Once you've done this, simply mount the files from the localhost itself.

Creating a Virtual Machine Using OEM Grid Control

OEM Grid Control is another great tool for creating and managing virtual machines. With OEM Grid Control, you can not only manage the virtual machines but also the applications and databases as well. From the main OEM Grid Control screen, select the Targets tab and then select Virtual Machines. This will invoke the Virtual Servers screen, as shown here.

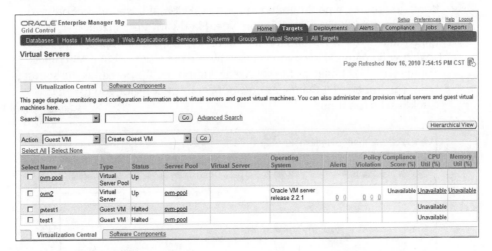

From the Virtual Servers screen, you can then create a new virtual machine from scratch by following these steps.

1. From the Action drop-down lists, select Guest VM and Create Guest VM. Click Go.

2. The Create Guest Virtual Machines: Server Pool screen will appear, as shown next. Here, you will input the number of virtual machines you want to create and select which server pool to create them in. You can click the flashlight icon to choose the server pool from a list. Click Next to continue.

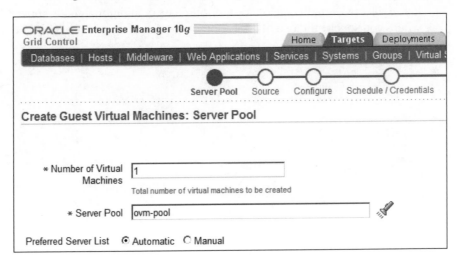

3. The next screen is the Create Guest Virtual Machines: Source screen. Select the source of the virtual machine (Template, ISO Image, or PXE boot), the source type (Imported Resources, External Location, or Software Components) and the virtualization type (Hardware Virtualization or Paravirtualized). Depending on the source type, the other options on this screen will change. Here, you can see the Create Guest Virtual Machines: Source with ISO Image as the source and Imported Resources as the source type. The imported ISO images now appear as options for you to select. Click Next to continue.

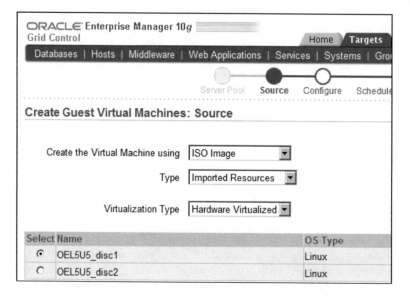

If you select External Location for the source type, additional fields appear where you specify the external location of the ISO image. This allows you to take the image from another system, as shown in this screen. Click Next to continue.

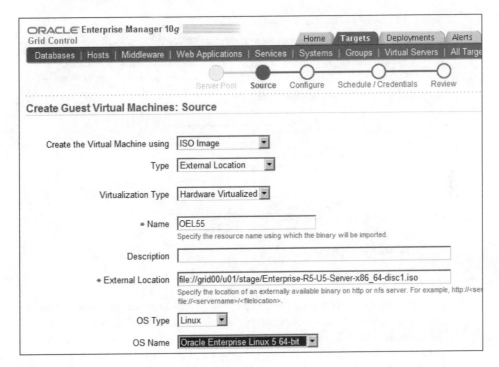

4. Regardless of the method you chose, the Create Guest Machines: Configure screen is next. This screen is where you specify the Virtual Machine Name Prefix, Number of Cores, Memory Size (RAM), Primary

Disk Name, Primary Disk Size, and VNC Console Password. The options are shown here. Click Next to continue.

5. As with other OEM Grid Control tasks, the actual creation process is done as a scheduled job. The scheduled job is defined in the Create Guest Machines: Schedule / Credentials screen, which is shown next. This is where you schedule the job to run immediately or at a later time and modify the credentials used for running the job (if necessary). Click Next to continue.

6. The final screen is the Create Guest Virtual Machines: Review screen, which you can see here. As with other review screens, once you have reviewed the settings and are satisfied, click the Finish button.

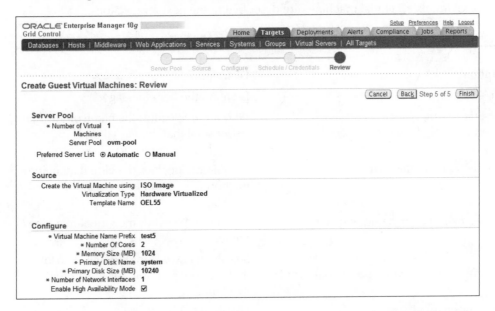

7. Once you have completed this operation, control returns to the Virtual Servers screen. You can track the progress of the new virtual machine as it is being created; it will be displayed along with any other virtual machines that might already exist. Once the virtual machine has been created, its status will change.

The process to create a virtual machine with OEM Grid Control is not quite as easy as with the VM Manager, but for many people, this method is preferred.

Creating a Virtual Machine Using the Oracle VM CLI

Creating a virtual machine using the VM Manager CLI is also a very straightforward process. Creating a new virtual machine is done using the CLI command **ovm vm new**, as shown in the previous chapter. As with most Oracle VM CLI commands, this command has several available options.

As with the other **ovm** commands covered earlier in this book, the basic options for running the **ovm** command are **–u <username>** or **--username=<username>** and **-p <password>** or **--password=<password>**. These options specify the username and password of the VM Manager. If these options are not passed, you will be prompted for these values.

The **ovm vm new** command takes the options described in Table 17-1.

Unlike the previous chapter, when creating an image from installation media a few more options are required. The basic options needed for fully virtualized and paravirtualized virtual machines are described in the next few sections.

Option	Description
-h, --help	Displays the help message.
-s server_pool, --server_pool_name=server_pool	(Required) Specifies the name of the server pool that the virtual machine image is being added to.
-m method, --method=method	(Required) Specifies the virtual machine method type. Options are template, iso, or pxe.
-n vm_name, --vm_name=vm_name	(Required) Specifies the virtual machine name.
-c <console password>, --console_password=<console password>	Sets the password for the VNC console that will be available for this virtual machine.
-a, --ha_enabled	Enables High Availability.
-x, --hvm	Creates a hardware virtualized guest.
-g iso_group, --iso_group=iso_group	Specifies the ISO image group.
-l iso_label, --iso_label=iso_label	Specifies the ISO image label.
-L location, --location=location	Specifies the paravirtualized guest installation source, which is something like http://host/path or ftp://host/path or nfs:host:/path.
-o OS, --os=OS	Specifies the OS type.
-V vcpus, --vcpus=vcpus	Sets the number of VCPUs.
-y memory, --memory=memory	Specifies the memory size in megabytes.
-d disksize, --disksize=disksize	Specifies the virtual disk size in megabytes.
-p preferred_server, --preferred_server=preferred_server	Sets the preferred server (or server list, which is comma separated).

TABLE 17-1. *ovm vm new* Options

Creating a Fully Virtualized Virtual Machine from ISO Images

The following options are required for creating a fully virtualized virtual machine from ISO images:

- -m iso
- -s <server pool>
- -n <vm name>
- -c <console pwd>
- -x
- -g <ISO Group>
- -l <ISO Label>
- -o OS
- -y <memory size>
- -d <disk size>

Other options are not required, but can be used if desired. The following is an example of creating a virtual machine using these options:

```
[root@manager ~]# ovm -u admin -p pwd123 vm new -m iso -s ovm -n test2
-c pwd123 -x -g OEL-5.5-x86_64 -l Enterprise-R5-U5-Server-x86_64-disc1
-o "Oracle Enterprise Linux 5 64-bit" -y 1024 -d 10240
Virtual machine "test23" is being created. Please check the status.
```

Once the process has started, please check the status occasionally to see if it has finished running. Eventually the status will change.

```
[root@manager ~]# ovm -u admin -p pwd123 vm stat -s ovm -n test2
Creating
[root@manager ~]# ovm -u admin -p pwd123 vm stat -s ovm -n test2
Running
```

At this point, you have created the virtual machine and it is in a powered-off state but ready to be started. Once you have started the machine, connect to the console using VNC. To find the VNC console port, use the Xen command **xm list** on the VM Server. The ID listed for each virtual machine is equivalent to the VNC port number. An example of **xm list** is shown here:

```
[root@ovm1 ~]# xm list
Name                           ID   Mem VCPUs      State   Time(s)
255_tmpl1                       1  1024     2     -b----     341.5
392_OEL55_HVM                   2  1024     1     -b----      16.8
Domain-0                        0   543     2     r-----    3301.9
```

Another way to determine the VNC port is to use the command **xm list –l**. This command produces a large amount of data. Look for location. The location value will show the VNC port.

You can now connect to the virtual machine console and install the OS as you would install any stand-alone Linux server. If more than one ISO image is required, the CD-ROM image can be changed using the **ovm vm cd attach**, **ovm vm cd detach**, and **ovm vm ls** commands. Using these commands is shown here:

```
[root@manager ~]# ovm -u admin -p pwd123 vm cd attach -s ovm -n OEL55_HVM
-g OEL55x64 -l Enterprise-R5-U5-Server-x86_64-disc1.iso

[root@manager ~]# ovm -u admin -p pwd123 vm cd detach -s ovm -n OEL55_HVM

[root@manager ~]# ovm -u admin -p pwd123 vm cd ls -s ovm -n OEL55_HVM
```

CD-ROM operations are only available for hardware virtualized guests.

Once the virtual machine installation process has completed, you will most likely need to reboot it again using the VNC console to the complete post-installation steps.

Creating a Paravirtualized Virtual Machine from Installation Media

The options required for creating a fully virtualized virtual machine from ISO images are the following:

- -m iso
- -s <server pool>
- -n <vm name>
- -c <console pwd>
- -L <location>
- -o OS
- -y <memory size>
- -d <disk size>

Other options are not required, but can be used if desired. The following is an example of creating a virtual machine using these options:

```
[root@manager ovm-manager]# ovm -u admin -p pwd123 vm new -m iso -s ovm
-n test3 -c pwd123 -L nfs:manager:/u01/stage/OEL5.5x64
-o "Oracle Enterprise Linux 5 64-bit" -y 1024 -d 10240
Virtual machine "test3" is being created. Please check the status.
```

Once the process has started, please check the status occasionally to see if it has changed:

```
[root@manager ovm-manager]# ovm -u admin -p pwd123 vm stat -s ovm -n test3
Creating
```

Eventually the status will change to running, as shown here. At this point, you should connect to the VNC console in order to complete the installation.

```
[root@manager ovm-manager]# ovm -u admin -p pwd123 vm stat -s ovm -n test3
Running
```

As with the previous example, to find the VNC console port, use the Xen command **xm list** on the VM Server. The ID listed for each virtual machine is equivalent to the VNC port number.

Once the virtual machine installation process has completed, you will most likely need to reboot it again using the VNC console to complete the post-installation steps.

Creating a Virtual Machine Using PXE Boot

The Preboot Execution Environment (PXE) is a protocol designed to assist with booting an OS without the use of a local disk drive. With PXE, the OS can boot via a network device. The PXE boot environment allows you to configure the system to boot into an environment automatically where it will not only boot an OS, but also install it as well. As with the other configuration options, configuring a virtual machine using PXE boot can be done via the Oracle VM Manager, OEM Grid Control, and the Oracle VM CLI.

Creating a Virtual Machine Using PXE Boot and the VM Manager

Follow these steps to create a virtual machine using PXE boot and the VM Manager:

1. As with the earlier example, the Create Virtual Machine process begins with clicking the Create Virtual Machine button.

2. From the Creation Method screen, select Create a Network Bootable Virtual Machine (pxeboot). Click Next to proceed.

3. From the Server Pool screen, select the server pool where you want to create the new virtual machine by clicking the radio button next to the desired server pool. Click Next to continue.

4. On the Virtual Machine Information screen, fill in the Virtual Machine Name, select the Virtualization Method (Fully Virtualized or Paravirtualized) and the Operating System, fill in the Number of Virtual CPUs, Memory Size, and Virtual Disk Size, and enter and confirm the Console Password. In addition, at the bottom of the screen, you can modify and obtain the MAC address. PXE boot requires DHCP to configure the network address, so make note of this MAC address. Click Next to continue.

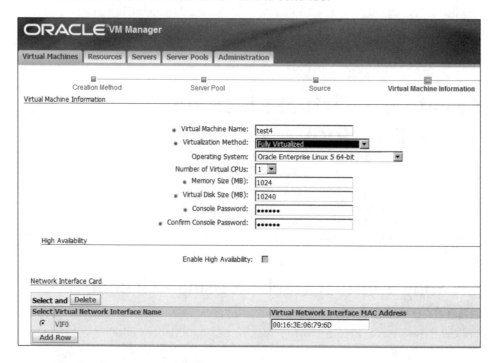

5. The final screen is the Confirm Information screen. Once you have confirmed your choices, the virtual machine will be created. As with the other methods, you must connect in with the VNC console to perform the installation unless an automated kickstart process is initiated. PXE boot with kickstart is detailed in Appendix A.

Creating a Virtual Machine Using PXE Boot and OEM Grid Control

Creating a virtual machine with OEM Grid Control using PXE boot is essentially the same process as described previously; however, you select PXE Boot from the Create the Virtual Machine drop-down list. In addition to Virtualization Type, the MAC address can be automatically or manually generated, as shown here.

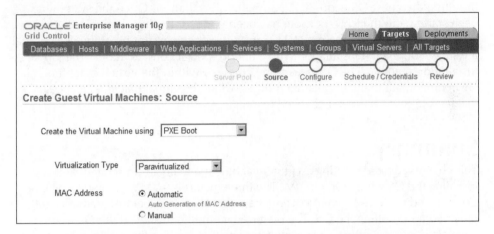

The rest of the process is identical to the process described earlier in this chapter. As with the all PXE boot installations, you must find the MAC address and set up DHCP, PXE boot, and, optionally, kickstart.

Creating a Virtual Machine Using PXE Boot and the Oracle VM CLI

Creating a virtual machine using the Oracle VM CLI with PXE boot is very straightforward. You use the **ovm vm new** command, as shown earlier in this chapter, but with just a few different parameters. Use the **–m pxe** parameter to designate PXE boot for the source of the boot media. Once the VM has been created, you must determine the MAC address as mentioned earlier. The process is shown here:

```
[root@manager ~]# ovm -u admin -p pwd123 vm new -m pxe -s ovm -n test4
-c pwd123 -o "Oracle Enterprise Linux 5 64-bit" -V 1 -y 1024 -d 10240
Virtual machine "test4" is being created. Please check the status.
[root@manager ~]# ovm -u admin -p pwd123 vm stat -s ovm -n test4
Powered Off
```

Once the virtual machine has been created, you can proceed with installing the operating system. Start up the virtual machine and then connect to the virtual machine console using VNC and proceed with the OS installation, as described in the next section.

Installing the Guest OS

Installing the guest OS is done like any other installation. Once the system has been started and the VNC console has been opened, the installation process is indistinguishable from a bare metal OS install, with the exception of the devices that are shown during the installation. There are no special considerations. The virtual installation media (CD-ROM) has to be changed within the virtual machine environment, but to the installation process within the virtual machine, it appears that the CD-ROM has been changed manually.

Summary

This chapter covered creating a virtual machine manually (from scratch) and installing the OS within Oracle VM. The three methods—VM Manager, OEM Grid Control, and OVM CLI—were covered here, however, manual installation is not preferred for installing the OS. The preferred method of installing the OS is to create a template, or install from an existing template that you modify and then create new templates from. Templates are one of the key features of Oracle VM and are easy to use and very powerful.

Now that you have seen how to create new virtual machines, you will next be introduced to the process of converting existing virtual machines (from a different product) into Oracle VM virtual machines. Chapter 18 discusses how to convert VMware images, Hyper-V images, and physical machines into Oracle VM virtual machines.

CHAPTER
18

Converting Other Virtual
Images to Oracle VM

s you have seen in many of the previous chapters, there is an emphasis on reuse of work and leveraging existing configurations in order to provide a stable, reliable, and faster-to-deploy virtual environment. In addition to using templates as a source of virtual machine images, you can also take virtual machine images that were created in a different product's system and convert them to Oracle VM virtual machines. This chapter shows you how to do just that.

In addition, you will learn how to take a physical server and turn it into an Oracle VM virtual machine. This process allows any Linux server to be converted into a virtual machine image.

Converting External Virtual Images to Oracle VM

The ability to convert an external virtual image to an Oracle VM image is an important feature of Oracle VM. Utilities are provided with Oracle VM to convert these virtual images from other virtualization software programs to Oracle VM. This chapter covers how to convert VMware, Microsoft Hyper-V, and Virtual Iron images to Oracle VM, how to test them, and how to modify them (if applicable). Once you have converted the image to Oracle VM, you can modify the image and make a template, which is now an Oracle VM native template.

Several virtualization products are available today, including Xen, VMware, and Microsoft Hyper-V. Because Oracle VM is based on Xen, no conversion is necessary for a Xen image file. You simply import a Xen image into Oracle VM. VMware and Hyper-V images need to be converted, however. The next few sections detail how to convert these images.

VMware

VMware was really the first virtualization product to make it mainstream. VMware was founded in 1998 and made significant progress in providing virtualization solutions to the general public. VMware was acquired by EMC in 2004. VMware provides both a type 1 and type 2 hypervisor. Although VMware is the most popular and recognizable name in virtualization, it is seeing significant competition from Oracle VM.

Converting VMware Images to Oracle VM

Converting a VMware virtual machine to an Oracle VM virtual machine is actually done automatically as part of the import process. However, once the import process has completed this conversion, a few more things need to be done to verify that the virtual machine has been converted correctly. You do this via the VM Manager.

Optionally, you can import the VMware virtual machine via OEM Grid Control or the OVM CLI. The steps to convert the VMware virtual machine into an Oracle VM virtual machine are detailed here:

1. Copy or move the VMware virtual machine to the running_pool directory on a VM Server system.

2. From the VM Manager, select the Resources tab and then the Virtual Machine Images tab. Click the Import button to begin the import process.

3. From the Source screen, choose Select from Server Pool (Discover and Register) and click Next.

4. On the General Information screen, select the Server Pool Name and Sharing (Private). Once you've done this, you should see the recently copied virtual machine name in the Virtual Machine Image Name drop-down list. Select it. Other required options you must provide are the Operating System (from a drop-down list), the Virtual Machine System Username (root) and Password as well as the Console Password. Adding a description is always a good idea as well. The completed screen is shown here. Click Next to continue.

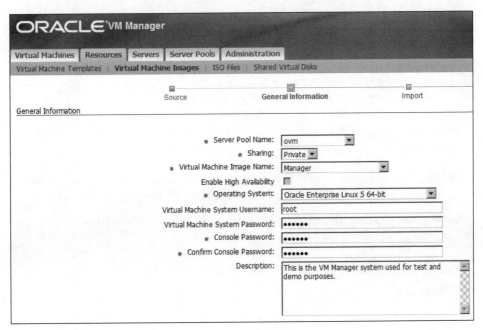

5. On the Confirm Information screen, shown next, there is one option: Delete V2V Source Image Files. This box is unchecked by default, but checked in this example, where the import process has been instructed to delete the VMware image files after they have been converted to Oracle VM. It is your choice whether to do this or not. Once you have verified all of the information, click Confirm to continue.

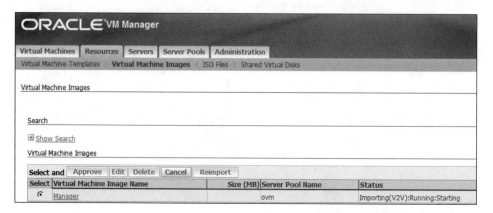

CAUTION
VMware image conversions are not always successful, even if the import says they are. Using the delete option is not recommended—ever. It is always a good policy to be careful and to test before deleting.

6. The VM Manager returns to the Resources–Virtual Machine Images screen where you will see the virtual machine image importing, as shown here.

7. As soon as the import process has completed, the image will be shown in the Resources: Virtual Machine Images tab with a Pending status. Approve the image and it will be moved to the Virtual Machines tab with the other virtual machines.

Once the virtual machine has been imported, it is important to verify a few things that might need to be modified before putting this virtual machine into production. The next section covers how to test and configure the newly converted VMware image, which, at this time, is now an Oracle VM image.

NOTE
If there is a problem during the conversion, the first step in debugging the problem is to look at the log files. The log files are located in /var/log/ovs-agent. During the conversion process, you can use the **tail –f** *command to see what is going on by looking at the ovs_operation.log file.*

Testing and Configuring the Image

Once the virtual machine has been converted, there are a few things that you should check and potentially change before continuing on to either save this virtual machine as a template or use it. Some of these items are external to the virtual machine and some are within the virtual machine. They include the following:

- **VCPUs**   Depending on the VMware settings, you might want to increase or decrease the number of VCPUs that are allocated to the virtual machine. You can change this with either the VM Manager, OEM Grid Control, or the Oracle VM CLI.

- **Memory**   You might want to adjust the amount of memory that is allocated to the virtual machine. You can change this with either the VM Manager, OEM Grid Control, or the Oracle VM CLI.

- **Network**   If the network is configured as static within the VM, you must either modify it to use DHCP and give it a unique MAC address, or modify it within the /etc/sysconfig/network-scripts/ifcfg-eth*n* files to be allocated a unique IP address.

■ **MAC address** The MAC address should be unique. The import process itself assigns a unique MAC address. However, if necessary you can change this in the vm.cfg file. It must begin with 00:16:3e. Oracle has provided a tool to generate a new random MAC address. Run it as shown here:

```
[root@ovm1 ~]# export PYTHONPATH=/opt/ovs-agent-2.3
[root@ovm1 ~]# python -c "from OVSCommons import randomMAC; print randomMAC()"
00:16:3e:3b:4d:83
[root@ovm1 ~]# python -c "from OVSCommons import randomMAC; print randomMAC()"
00:16:3e:7e:78:fd
```

Once you have the new MAC address, edit the vm.cfg file and change the line that has mac=00:16:3E:xx:xx:xx to use the new MAC address.

■ **Files** The virtual machine that has been converted from VMware will still have both the .img (Oracle VM) and .vmdk (VMware) disk files in the running_pool directory, unless you checked the Delete V2V Source Image Files box in the Confirm Information screen. In order to save space, delete the .vmdk files.

In addition to making these changes, test the virtual machine before putting it into production. Templates can be created along the way, or you can wait until you are fully satisfied with the testing before saving the virtual machine as a template.

Microsoft Hyper-V

Microsoft Hyper-V is the latest entry into the world of virtualization. Microsoft introduced it as a beta product with Windows 2008 and it was later updated to the production version in June 2008. There are two versions of Microsoft Hyper-V: a stand-alone "virtualization server," and a part of Microsoft Windows Server 2008 R2. Microsoft Hyper-V only runs on x86_64 hardware.

Converting Microsoft Hyper-V Images to Oracle VM

A few steps are involved in converting a Hyper-V disk to Oracle VM. The first is to copy the .vhd file to the running_pool on the Oracle VM Server. Because Hyper-V does not use a vm.cfg file, you must create one. When you are finished, there should be at least two files in the running_pool/<virtual machine> directory: a vm.cfg file and at least one .vhd file, as shown here:

```
[root@ovm1 hyperv]# ls
hyperv.vhd  vm.cfg
```

> **Virtual Iron**
> Virtual Iron is a proprietary virtualization product that does both virtualization and virtual machine management. In 2009, Oracle purchased Virtual Iron and has integrated it into Oracle VM. Since the Virtual Iron virtual machine uses a .vhd file like Hyper-V, the conversion process is identical. Follow the procedures outlined in the "Microsoft Hyper-V" section to convert a Virtual Iron virtual machine.

The minimal contents of a vm.cfg file are as follows:

```
acpi = 1
apic = 1
builder = 'hvm'
device_model = '/usr/lib/xen/bin/qemu-dm'
disk = ['file:/OVS/running_pool/hyperv/hyperv.vhd,sda,w',]
kernel = '/usr/lib/xen/boot/hvmloader'
keymap = 'en-us'
memory = '1024'
on_crash = 'restart'
on_reboot = 'restart'
pae = 1
timer_mode = 1
vcpus = 2
```

Once the files are in place, perform the same import via the Resources – Virtual Machine Images screen as was shown previously in the "VMware" section. Optionally, you can perform this import via OEM Grid Control or the OVM CLI.

As with the VMware conversion, once the .vhd file has been converted and the vm.cfg file has been properly configured, the virtual machine can be booted and run as any other virtual machine.

Physical Machines

Part of the conversion software that Oracle has provided as part of Oracle VM includes the ability to convert a physical machine to a virtual machine. This process involves booting the Oracle VM installation CD-ROM and performing steps to convert the system from a physical machine to a virtual machine. The basic steps for creating a virtual machine image from a physical machine are as follows:

1. Boot the Oracle VM Server CD-ROM to the P2V utility.

2. Configure the network of the booted image.

3. Configure settings for the new virtual machine.

4. Run the P2V utility from the VM Manager to import the virtual machine.

This process works very well to convert a physical machine to a virtual machine. When the process is completed, you should test and verify the virtual machine.

Converting a Physical Machine to Oracle VM

The steps to convert a physical machine to Oracle VM are presented in this section. The process is not very hard, but should be done with care.

1. The first step occurs on the physical machine itself. On the physical machine, boot the Oracle VM Server CD-ROM. When the CD-ROM is at the boot prompt, type linux p2v and press ENTER, as shown here.

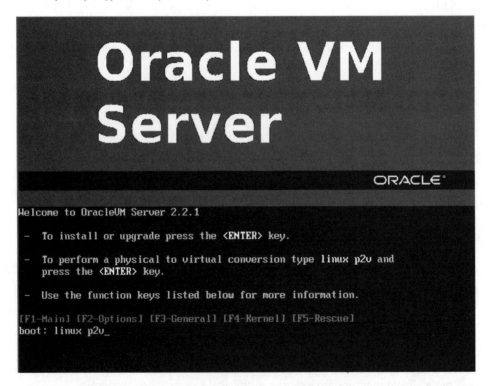

2. Once you have booted P2V, the first screen that you will see is the test media screen. I typically skip the media test unless I've had CD-ROM problems on this system or the system that I created the CD-ROM on. Click Skip to continue.

3. The next screen, shown here, allows you to configure the network of the system that you just booted. Fill in the IP Address, Netmask, Gateway, Domain, and Nameserver for your network. It is not necessary to use the IP address of the current physical system unless your network configuration mandates this. Once you have completed this operation, click OK.

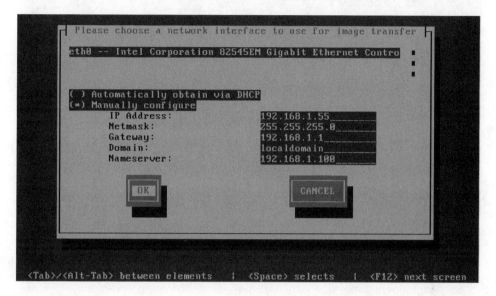

4. Next select all of the disks that you want converted to Oracle VM virtual disks. Select them by tabbing to the desired disk and pressing the SPACEBAR. Tab to the OK button, as shown in the next screen, and press ENTER to continue.

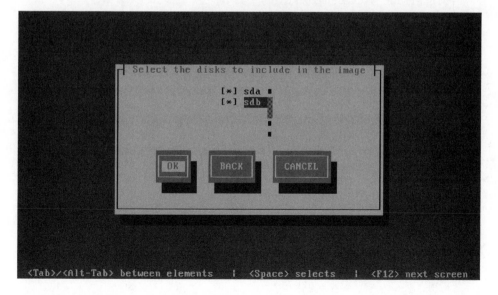

5. Next define the attributes of the new virtual machine you are creating. The requested parameters are the VM Name, VM Memory, Virtual CPUs, and the Console Password. Enter these values and tab to the OK button and press ENTER, as shown here.

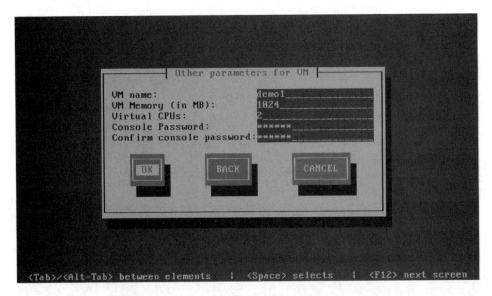

6. The following message is then displayed on the system console:

```
Starting web server
HTTPS web server is running on <IP Address> Port 443...
Interrupt with control-C
```

At this point, you switch to the VM Manager. From the VM Manager Resources – Virtual Machine Images screen, select Import. On the Sources screen, select Linux/Windows P2V Import, as shown here. This starts the import process from the P2V service directly into Oracle VM. Click Next to continue.

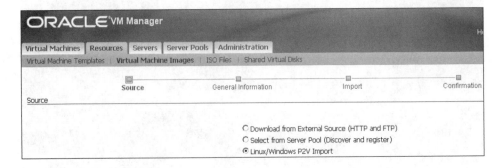

7. The General Information screen looks somewhat familiar but with one important difference. Fill in the Server Pool Name, Sharing, and in the Virtual Machine Image Name field, fill in the name of the new virtual machine. For other import operations, you selected the name from a drop-down list. Now you must define it. In addition, enable High Availability (if desired and available), select the Operating System, and assign the Virtual Machine System Username and Password, and enter the Console Password. As always, I recommend filling in the Description field. You can see the completed screen here.

8. In the Import Information screen, type in the IP address or hostname of the system being converted. This IP address is the one that you set in Step 3. If you are using a proxy, check the Use Proxy checkbox and fill in the additional information, as shown here.

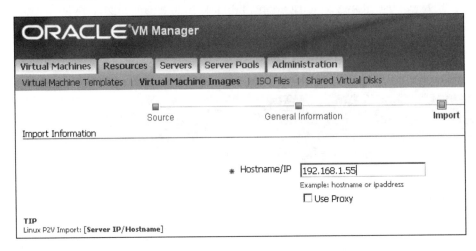

9. Next is the Confirm Information screen. Check the information that you have provided and click Confirm to start the import process.

10. Once you have clicked Confirm, control is returned to the Resources – Virtual Machine Images screen where you can watch the progress of the virtual machine import process. In addition, you can use the **tail –f** command on the VM Server to watch the progress of the import. The log file to monitor is /var/log/ovs-agent/ovs_operation.log.

11. Once the import has completed, the image will be in a pending state. When you are satisfied with the image, approve it, and it will be moved to the virtual machine images and can be booted.

This process is very straightforward, and as with other tasks, the second part of the import can be done via OEM Grid Control or Oracle VM CLI.

Testing and Configuring the Image

As with the other conversion processes, some clean-up might be necessary. The MAC address will automatically be converted to an Oracle VM MAC address, but you might need to boot the virtual machine and configure the network configuration by hand.

Image Conversion Best Practices

Regardless of the type of system you are converting from, following a few guidelines and best practices will help make the conversion more efficient and, in some cases, will help to save space. Remember, when converting an image, your system will have a copy of both the original image and the new image; therefore, you need twice the size of the virtual machine for the conversion. If you have a 100GB VMDK, you will need an additional 100GB of space for the conversion. Only after the image is converted and *tested* should the VMDK be deleted. Here are a few tips for converting an external image to an Oracle VM image:

- Remove all unnecessary programs before the conversions. There is no use in converting programs that won't be used. They take time to convert and use space, and these programs will have to be removed later.

- Remove VMware's Guest Additions before doing the conversion. The Guest Additions will not provide any benefit and will need to be removed after the conversion if not done before.

- Remove any unnecessary disk drives. If there are drives and devices that aren't being used, they should not be converted.

These are just a few tips on improving the conversion process in order to make the process more efficient.

Summary

This chapter covered several ways that existing systems can be converted to Oracle VM virtual machines. This allows you to preserve and reuse a system that is set up and configured optimally for your environment without having to start from scratch. Oracle VM is focused on reuse of work and leveraging existing configurations to provide a stable, reliable, and faster-to-deploy virtual environment. In this chapter, you learned how to convert virtual machine images and physical machines into Oracle VM virtual machines.

Chapter 19 will present examples of day-to-day administration tasks that are done by the Oracle VM administrator in order to keep the VM Server farm in optimal condition.

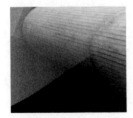

CHAPTER
19

Managing the VM
Environment and
Virtual Machines

hroughout this book, you have seen how to configure the VM Server farm and virtual machines. This chapter focuses on some of the day-to-day operations that the VM administrator will perform. This includes state management and configuring options that might change regularly, such as memory, the network, and disks. As with most operations, you have several ways to perform these tasks: the VM Manager, OEM Grid Control, Oracle VM CLI, and Xen **xm** commands.

Managing the State of the Virtual Machines

As you learned in Chapter 4, the virtual machine can exist in many states. The current state of the virtual machine determines what states the virtual machine can transition into. In this section, you will learn or review the available state transition commands. Some of these were covered in earlier chapters, but are provided here for completeness.

Starting Virtual Machines

The most basic of the virtual machine commands is to start the virtual machine. How to perform this function is detailed in the following table:

Management Application	Description
VM Manager	Select the virtual machine by clicking its radio button and click the Power On button. The status of the virtual machine will change to Running.
OEM Grid Control	Select the virtual machine by selecting its checkbox. From the Action menu, select Guest VM and Start Guest VM, and click Go to start the virtual machine.
Oracle VM CLI	Use the command **ovm vm poweron –s <server pool> -n <virtual machine>** to start the desired virtual machine.
Xen Tools	Using the Xen **xm** command, start a virtual machine from the VM Server with the following syntax: **xm create <path to vm.cfg file>** (e.g., xm create /OVS/running_pool/test2/vm.cfg).

You can determine the status of the virtual machine in a number of ways, including **xm list** (on the VM Server), **ovm vm ls**, and, of course, using the GUI tools.

Stopping Virtual Machines

Stopping the virtual machine is also a very important command. How to perform this function is detailed in the following table:

Management Application	Description
VM Manager	Select the virtual machine by clicking its radio button and click the Power On button. The status of the virtual machine will change to Running.
OEM Grid Control	Select the virtual machine by selecting its checkbox. From the Action menu, select Guest VM and Stop Guest VM, and click Go to stop the virtual machine.
Oracle VM CLI	Use the command **ovm vm poweroff –s <server pool> -n <virtual machine>** to migrate the desired virtual machine.
Xen Tools	Using the Xen **xm** command start a virtual machine from the VM Server with the following syntax: **xm shutdown <virtual machine name>** (e.g., xm shutdown test2).

NOTE
In an emergency use **xm destroy**. *The* **xm destroy** *command powers off the guest immediately. The* **xm shutdown** *command performs an orderly shutdown.*

You can determine the status of the virtual machine in a number of ways, including **xm list** (on the VM server), **ovm vm ls**, and, of course, using the GUI tools.

Pausing/Unpausing Virtual Machines

Pausing a virtual machine causes the virtual machine to stop executing; however, it still remains in memory. If the VM Server is rebooted, the virtual machine state is lost. A paused virtual machine can be unpaused in order to restart execution. How to perform this function is explained in the following table:

Management Application	Description
VM Manager	Select the virtual machine by clicking its radio button, select either Pause or Unpause from the More Actions drop-down list, and click the Go button. This will pause or unpause the virtual machine.
OEM Grid Control	Select the virtual machine by selecting its checkbox. From the Action menu, select Guest VM and Pause Guest VM or Resume Guest VM, and then click Go to pause or unpause the virtual machine.

Management Application	Description
Oracle VM CLI	Use the command **ovm vm pause –s <server pool> -n <virtual machine>** to pause the desired virtual machine and **ovm vm unpause –s <server pool> -n <virtual machine>** to unpause it.
Xen Tools	Using the Xen **xm** command, pause or unpause a virtual machine from the VM Server with the following syntax: **xm pause <Domain>** or **xm unpause <Domain>**.

The paused virtual machine remains in memory and can be unpaused very quickly. If the VM Server reboots, however, the paused virtual machine's state will be lost.

Suspending/Resuming Virtual Machines

Suspending a virtual machine causes the virtual machine to stop executing and the state is written out to disk and removed from memory. If the VM Server is rebooted, the virtual machine is still available. A suspended virtual machine can be resumed to restart execution. How to perform this function is explained in the following table:

Management Application	Description
VM Manager	Select the virtual machine by clicking its radio button and select either Suspend or Resume from the More Actions drop-down list and click the Go button. This will suspend or resume the virtual machine.
OEM Grid Control	Select the virtual machine by selecting its checkbox. From the Action menu, select Guest VM and Suspend Guest VM or Resume Guest VM, and click Go to suspend or resume the virtual machine.
Oracle VM CLI	Use the command **ovm vm suspend –s <server pool> -n <virtual machine>** to suspend the desired virtual machine and **ovm vm resume –s <server pool> -n <virtual machine>** to resume it.
Xen Tools	Using the Xen **xm** command, suspend or resume a virtual machine from the VM Server with the following syntax: **xm suspend <Domain>** or **xm resume <Domain>**.

The suspended virtual machine is written to disk and its state removed from memory. If the VM Server reboots, the suspended virtual machine can still be restored.

Migrating Virtual Machines

Migrating virtual machines can be performed via several different methods, including the GUI tools as well as the command line tools detailed in the following table:

Management Application	Description
VM Manager	Select the virtual machine by clicking its radio button and click the Live Migration button.
OEM Grid Control	Select the virtual machine by selecting its checkbox. From the Action menu, select Guest VM and Live Migrate Guest VM, and click Go to migrate the virtual machine to another VM Server.
Oracle VM CLI	Migrate the virtual machine to another VM Server by using the **ovm vm mig** command. Migrate all virtual machines on a VM Server to another VM Server using the **ovm vm mig all** command: **ovm vm mig –s \<Server Pool> -n \<name> -t \<Target Server>** **ovm vm mig all –s \<Server Pool> -n \<Source Server> -t \<Target Server>**
Xen Tools	Utilize the Xen tools to migrate a virtual machine using the **xm migrate** command: **xm migrate \<Domain> \<Host>**.

Migrating a virtual machine can be done live, with only a very small interruption in service. This interruption in service is rarely noticed by users.

Changing the Configuration of the Virtual Machines

From time to time, it is necessary to make changes to both the environment and the virtual machines themselves. Oracle VM is very adaptable and can be configured as needed. You can add hardware and make changes to storage and the network as necessary. Changes fall into two categories: changes to the virtual machines and changes to the VM Servers.

NOTE
Making changes to the VM Servers is covered in Chapters 10 and 11 and throughout the early chapters of this book.

Modifying Virtual Machines

On occasion you must modify a virtual machine. A number of different commands can be used to change the configuration and/or attributes of the virtual machines, as detailed in the following table:

Management Application	Description
VM Manager	Select the virtual machine by clicking its radio button and click the Configure button.
OEM Grid Control	Select the virtual machine by selecting its checkbox. From the Action menu, select Guest VM and Edit Guest VM, and click Go to start the virtual machine.
Oracle VM CLI	The Oracle VM CLI has a number of specific commands to change specific attributes. They include **ovm vm disk [add, conf, del]**, **ovm vm nic [add, conf, del]**, and **ovm sd [attach, detach]**.
Xen Tools	There are no xm tools for configuring the virtual machines per se. The virtual machines are configured by editing the vm.cfg file for each virtual machine. Some dynamic changes such as pinning VCPUs can be performed using **xm** commands; however, dynamic changes will not survive a reboot or migration, thus pinning VCPUs using **xm** commands does not meet Oracle's definition of "pinned CPUs."

Modifying the virtual machines should be done with care because changing the configuration might also require changes within the virtual machines themselves.

Configuring Virtual Machine Networks

Virtual machines networks are easy to modify. They can be configured graphically via the VM Manager or OEM Grid Control. The network can also be modified via the Oracle VM CLI. Once you have added the virtual network adapter to the virtual machine, you will need to configure the adapter in the virtual machine itself. The first step is to add the network adapter to the virtual machine. The second step is to reboot the virtual machine and configure the network during the startup process as normal. Configuring the network was covered in more detail back in Chapter 10.

Configuring Storage on the VMs

Multiple methods are available for configuring storage on the virtual machine. Several methods can be used to add storage to a virtual machine. The primary storage method is a virtual disk, which is created by Oracle VM and assigned to the virtual machine, but other methods exist as well. Storage was covered in more detail back in Chapter 11.

Using Virtual Storage

The primary method of adding storage to an Oracle VM virtual machine is as a virtual disk. You can easily add a virtual disk to a virtual machine via the Oracle VM Manager, OEM Grid Control, or the Oracle VM CLI. Depending on the underlying operating system, a reboot of the virtual machine may or may not be required.

Using iSCSI Storage

Because the virtual machine has a network, any network storage that is supported on the guest OS is supported on the virtual machine. If the guest OS supports iSCSI, then this is a good choice for network storage. No additional configuration steps are needed just because it is a virtual machine. You simply follow the normal iSCSI setup steps.

Using NFS Storage

Just as with iSCSI, because the virtual machine has a network, any network storage that is supported on the guest OS is supported on the virtual machine. NFS is a good choice for network storage because of its ease of use and built-in support. As with iSCSI, no additional configuration steps are needed just because it is a virtual machine.

NOTE
The network on a paravirtualized guest is much faster than the network on a HVM guest. If the intent is to use network storage, keep this in mind. The HVM accelerations speed up memory access, so it is a tradeoff among I/O and network (paravirtualized) and memory (HVM).

Mapping a PCI Controller

A third option is to map a PCI controller from the VM Server directly into the virtual machine. You do this by inserting the address of the PCI bus device into the vm.cfg file or by using the **xm pci-attach** command. This works with some devices that are assignable. To find assignable devices, run **xm pci-list-assignable-devices**.

TIP
xm commands are dynamic in nature and, as such, are not persistent. Changes made with xm commands will not survive a reboot or migration. Therefore, using the vm.cfg file for making these type of changes is recommended.

Deploying and Cloning Virtual Machines

Deploying and cloning virtual machines gives you the ability to copy virtual machines from one server pool to another server pool. *Deploying* a virtual machine allows you to copy a single copy of the virtual machine between or within a server pool. *Cloning* a virtual machine allows you to copy multiple copies of a virtual machine to another server pool. Deploying and cloning are very similar, and, in fact, cloning has really made the deploying process obsolete; for instance, OEM Grid Control only supports the cloning process.

Deploying Virtual Machines

Deploying virtual machines allows you to copy a virtual machine from one server pool to another server pool. You can deploy the virtual machine using the VM Manager, OEM Grid Control, or the Oracle VM CLI.

Deploying Virtual Machines with the VM Manager

Using the Oracle VM Manager, you deploy a virtual machine by first selecting the virtual machine by clicking its radio button and then selecting Deploy from the More Actions menu. Once you've done that, click Go to invoke the Virtual Machine Information screen, as shown here.

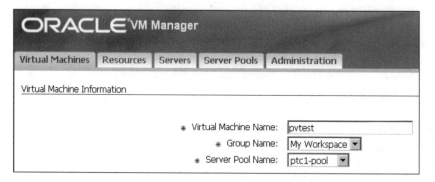

Input the Virtual Machine Name and select the Group Name and Server Pool Name from the drop-down lists. Once you are satisfied with your selections, click Next to continue to the Confirm Information screen, shown next.

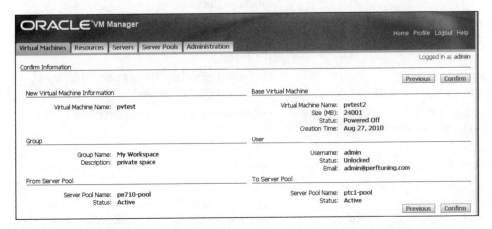

If you are satisfied with the configuration, click the Confirm button to deploy the virtual machine. When the virtual machine has been deployed, it will appear in the main Virtual Machines screen.

NOTE
OEM Grid Control does not support deploying, only cloning, virtual machines.

Deploying Virtual Machines with the Oracle VM CLI

To deploy a virtual machine from within the Oracle VM CLI, use the **ovm vm deploy** command. The **ovm vm deploy** command takes options detailed in Table 19-1.

An example of deploying a virtual machine with the Oracle VM CLI is shown here. Use **ovm vm stat** to check the status of the deployment.

```
[root@ptccontrol ~]# ovm -u admin -p ptc123 vm deploy -s pe710-pool
-n pvtest2 -N newpvtest2 -t ptc1-pool -g "My Workspace"
Deploying.
[root@ptccontrol ~]# ovm -u admin -p ptc123 vm stat -n newpvtest2 -s ptc1-pool
Creating
[root@ptccontrol ~]# ovm -u admin -p ptc123 vm stat -n newpvtest2 -s ptc1-pool
Powered Off
```

Once the deployment process has completed, the virtual machine will be in the Powered Off state.

Option	Description
-h, --help	Displays the help message.
-s server_pool, --serverpool_name=server_pool	(Required) Specifies the name of the server pool that the virtual machine image is being deployed from.
-n source_vm, --source_vm_name=source_vm	(Required) Specifies the name of the virtual machine being deployed.
-N target_vm, --target_vm_name=target_vm	(Required) Specifies the name of the target machine being deployed.
-t target_pool, --target_serverpool_name=target_pool	(Required) Specifies the name of the server pool that the virtual machine image is being deployed to.
-g target_group, --target_group=target_group	(Required) Specifies the group that the virtual machine image is being deployed into.

TABLE 19-1.   *ovm vm deploy Options*

Cloning Virtual Machines

The cloning process is only slightly different from the deployment process. Cloning allows you to create several copies of the same virtual machine. These copies are then copied to the same or a different server pool.

Cloning Virtual Machines with the VM Manager

With the VM Manager, cloning begins with selecting the virtual machine to be cloned by clicking its radio button and then selecting Clone from the More Actions menu. When you've made your selections, click Go to invoke the Clone Virtual Machine screen, as shown here.

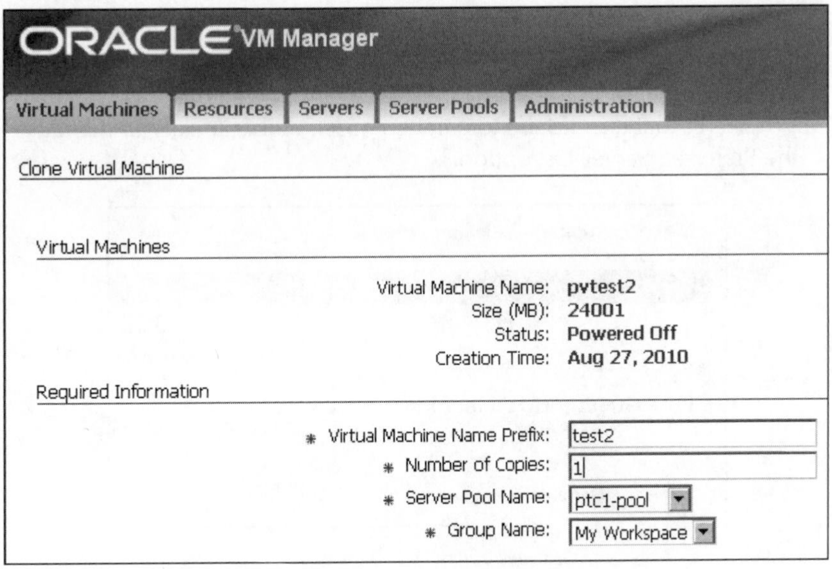

Input the Virtual Machine Name Prefix and Number of Copies, and select the Server Pool Name and Group Name from the drop-down lists. Once you are satisfied with your selections, click Continue to start the cloning process. There is no confirmation screen for this task. Once you have clicked Confirm, cloning begins and control returns to the Virtual Machines screen where you can watch the progress of the cloning process.

Cloning Virtual Machines with OEM Grid Control

With OEM Grid Control, select the virtual machine by checking the box next to the source virtual machine and selecting Guest VM and Clone Guest VM from the Action menus and clicking Go. This will activate the Clone Guest Virtual Machines utility. Follow these steps to clone a virtual machine:

1. Invoke the Clone Guest Virtual Machines utility as just described. The Clone Guest Virtual Machines: Server Pool screen will appear, as shown here. Fill in the Number of Virtual Machines you want to create and click Next. The VM Server that it is cloned to can be chosen automatically or manually with the Preferred Server List option.

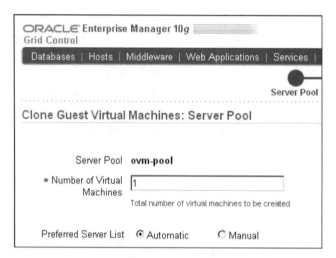

2. From the Clone Guest Virtual Machines: Configure screen, which is shown next, fill in the Virtual Machine Name Prefix for the new virtual machine and both the Root Password and VNC Console Password. Other options include Number of Network Interfaces, Enable High Availability Mode, and Configure Agent. There is also an option to Start VM After Creation. On this screen you also have the opportunity to add more disks and to attach

virtual disks. Many of these options can be set after the virtual machine has
been created, however. Click Next to continue.

ORACLE Enterprise Manager 10*g*
Grid Control   Home

Databases | Hosts | Middleware | Web Applications | Services | Systems | Groups | Virtual

Server Pool   **Configure**   Schedule / Cred

Clone Guest Virtual Machines: Configure

* Virtual Machine Name Prefix	test3
	Guest Virtual Machine names will be prefix1, prefix2 depending on the
* Root Password	••••••
* Confirm Root Password	••••••
* VNC Console Password	••••••
* Confirm VNC Console Password	••••••
* Number of Network Interfaces	1 [Configure Network]
	Number of Network Cards
Start VM after creation	☑
Enable High Availability Mode	☑
Configure Agent	☐

Local Devices from Source VM

Disk Name	Capacity(MB)
System	3857

Additional Disks

[Add]

Select	Disk Name	Capacity(MB)
	No Additional Disks	

3. After you have set up all of the parameters, you will see the Clone Guest
    Virtual Machines: Schedule / Credentials screen where you can set up the
    cloning schedule and select which credentials to use for the cloning process.
    You have seen this same screen several times before. Click Next to continue.

4. The final screen is the Clone Guest Virtual Machines: Review screen, which is shown next. This screen is your last chance to confirm that everything is correct and ready to go. When you are satisfied, click Finish to schedule the cloning process.

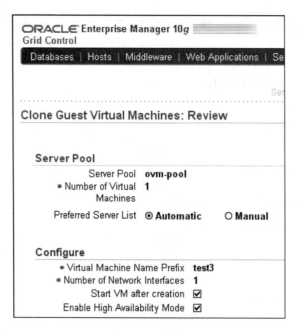

Once the cloning process has been submitted, it will run as a regular OEM Grid Control job, which can be monitored. Once the process is complete, it will show up on the OEM Grid Control Virtual Machines screen, showing a status of either Running or Stopped, depending on the setting you chose.

Cloning Virtual Machines with the Oracle VM CLI

To clone a virtual machine from within the Oracle VM CLI, use the **ovm vm clone** command. The **ovm vm clone** command takes the options listed in Table 19-2.

An example of cloning a virtual machine with the Oracle VM CLI is shown here. Use **ovm vm clone** to check the status of the cloning process.

```
[root@ptccontrol ~]# ovm -u admin -p ptc123 vm clone -s pe710-pool
-n pvtest2 -p pvtest2 -t ptc1-pool -g "My Workspace" -c 1
Cloning.
[root@ptccontrol ~]# ovm -u admin -p ptc123 vm stat -n pvtest2 -s pe710-pool
Cloning
[root@ptccontrol ~]# ovm -u admin -p ptc123 vm stat -n pvtest2 -s ptc1-pool
Creating
```

Option	Description
-h, --help	Displays the help message.
-s server_pool, --serverpool_name=server_pool	(Required) Specifies the name of the server pool where the virtual machine image being cloned resides.
-n source_vm, --source_vm_name=source_vm	(Required) Specifies the name of the virtual machine being cloned.
-p target_prefix, --target_vm_prefix=target_prefix	(Required) Sets the prefix of the target machine that being cloned. The OVM CLI will make this name unique for all virtual machines being created.
-t target_pool, --target_serverpool_name=target_pool	The name of the server pool that the cloned virtual machine image is going to be copied to. The default is the current server pool.
-g target_group, --target_group=target_group	The group that the cloned virtual machine image will be copied into. The default is My Workspace.
-c copies, --num_of_copy=copies	The number of copies to make of the clone. The default is 1.

TABLE 19-2.   *ovm vm clone* Options

To see the status of the entire cloning process, use the following command:

```
[root@ptccontrol ~]# ovm -u admin -p ptc123 vm ls | grep pvtest2
pvtest2          24001      3000 8      Creating     ptc1-pool
pvtest2          24001      3000 8      Cloning      pe710-pool
```

Once the cloning process has completed, the new systems are ready for use, as shown here:

```
[root@ptccontrol ~]# ovm -u admin -p ptc123 vm stat -n pvtest2 -s pe710-pool
Powered Off
[root@ptccontrol ~]# ovm -u admin -p ptc123 vm stat -n pvtest2 -s ptc1-pool
Powered Off
```

The cloning process copies the virtual machine exactly, so be sure to check the MAC address and change it as necessary.

CAUTION
Having duplicate MAC addresses can cause network problems. When cloning or deploying, it is always a good idea to check the MAC address and change it as necessary.

Summary

This chapter covered some of the different options for managing the state of Oracle VM virtual machines including the starting and stopping, pausing and unpausing, and suspending and resuming of virtual machines, as well as the older deployment process, and the cloning process. Managing the state of the virtual machines is really the most important task that the administrator has to take on, in addition to making sure everything is properly backed up.

The final chapter covers some virtualization best practices.

CHAPTER
20

Virtualization Summary
and Best Practices

irtualization is changing the face of computing at a dramatic rate. The concept of cloud computing and public and private clouds is now being commonly discussed in both commercial and government boardrooms. Oracle has committed themselves to supporting virtualization not only through the efforts they have put into Oracle VM, as you have learned from this book, but also through the efforts they are undertaking with Sun Solaris virtualization. In the next few years, virtualization will become the cornerstone for many new technologies and applications, and you will see that we are only now at the beginning. This chapter touches on a few of the future visions of virtualization as well as best practices and techniques.

The Future of Virtualization

Predicting the future is always difficult. A less difficult exercise, however, is to examine trends and see where they are going. From this perspective, we can follow the massive acceptance of virtualization technologies and the virtualization vendors' race to get their share of the market. Virtualization is still a young technology, but it is growing at a very fast pace. In the next few years, we will continue to see growing acceptance of virtualization and new technologies, but, as with most things, as the technology matures and becomes more mainstream, the pace of change will slow and shift from functionality features to manageability and performance features.

Based on research, I will make the following predictions about the future of virtualization and virtualization technologies. One thing is certain: The technology will continue to evolve, driven by business needs and competition. The following sections contain a list of predictions for the future of virtualization, in no particular order or priority of importance.

Virtualization Will Move into the Hardware

If the past few years are any indication, more and more virtualization functions, such as memory access, I/O, and network operations, will move to the hardware, rather than requiring software processing. In fact, some predict that the entire hypervisor might move into hardware. Throughout the history of computing, anything that can be done in hardware significantly outperforms anything that runs in software. Running in hardware has several advantages. First, code doesn't have to be loaded in for hardware operations because the instructions are already in the hardware. Second, hardware operations usually require much fewer instructions. This results in much faster operations.

Currently hardware accelerations have focused on improving memory access from within the virtual machine. This has improved performance significantly but has some drawbacks since this technology requires HVM virtual machines. Because paravirtualized machines offer better network and I/O performance, a decision must be made. I predict future technologies will enable hardware acceleration within paravirtualized guests.

Both Intel and AMD continue to improve their virtualization acceleration hardware. Features such as memory lookup tables, use of RING 2 for privileged operations, and so on, have been moved to hardware in the latest releases. In the future, the focus will turn from the memory and CPU to the I/O subsystem. For future chips, efforts are being made to implement hardware-based driver emulation and direct access to I/O, bypassing the hypervisor. Improvements are being made on a regular basis.

Cloud Computing as a Way of Doing Business

Cloud computing has already become a standard way of doing business, and this will continue to increase. There are two main types of clouds: the public cloud and the private cloud. The type of cloud that is right for you depends on your business requirements and budget.

Public Cloud

The *public cloud* is a term used to describe a cloud computing (virtualized) environment that is shared among many businesses and individuals. A virtual machine in a public cloud is mixed into a server pool with many other virtual machines. The public cloud servers are configured so they are able to meet a specific service level. Typically, public clouds are very large server farms that are constantly load balancing in order to meet service levels. Public cloud virtual machines are typically rented based on number of VCPUs, amount of memory, and amount of disk space. Many public cloud service providers also include managed services, wherein the provider offers not only the virtual machine, but also applications such as file and print services as well as email and collaboration. The public cloud can be quite cost effective in many cases.

TIP
Be sure to read all of the fine print when signing up for a public cloud. In addition to fixed costs related to the number of VCPUs and memory, there are often additional costs for the amount of network bandwidth used as well as the amount of I/O used. Depending on your application, these costs can add up.

Private Cloud

A *private cloud* is a virtualized environment entirely owned and controlled by a single business or entity. For larger environments, where a business requires many systems, it becomes more cost effective for the business or individuals themselves to own and manage the cloud. In addition, private clouds are typically found in environments where security is an issue. The federal government is a large consumer of virtual machines; most of these are private cloud systems, as a public cloud might not be considered secure enough. The private cloud still offers all of the benefits of the cloud computing environment, but with additional security and control.

Cloud Bursting

In addition to public and private clouds, another common practice employed to save on additional capital expenditures, administration, and management costs for seasonal processing need increases is to use *cloud bursting*. With cloud bursting, a company runs a private cloud for day-to-day business and a public cloud infrastructure when seasonal increases in workload require additional resources for a short period of time. By preparing ahead of time, companies can seamlessly move processing from private to public clouds on demand. Some see this as the future of virtualization.

Best Practices

A *best practice* is a technique that is considered the industry standard best and most efficient way of performing a particular task. In computer terms, a best practice is generally used to describe the best configuration or best method of performing specific computer tasks. This section contains a number of Oracle VM best practices, in no particular order of priority or importance.

Properly Size the VM Server Farm

Sizing is a very important part of setting up the virtualized environment. An undersized VM Server farm can cause many problems that are difficult to solve without either sacrificing performance or purchasing more hardware. When configuring the VM Server farm, perform a thorough sizing, keeping in mind the growth of systems that will be experienced in the next three to five years. A properly sized system helps avoid a number of problems later on.

Perform Regular Capacity Planning Projects

In conjunction with the sizing project just mentioned, capacity planning should be done on an annual or semiannual basis. The focus of the capacity planning project is to determine if and/or when the VM Server farm will not have sufficient capacity to run the required workload at the required service level. Capacity planning differs from sizing in that sizing involves determining the equipment needed for a new workload, whereas capacity planning involves determining when the existing hardware and software will no longer be sufficient to maintain the workload at the required service level.

Tracking capacity-related data in a long-term manner is necessary for performing capacity planning. This information should include items such as CPU utilization and memory utilization as well as information such as the amount of space added to the system. This information can be used to predict additional space that might be needed in the future. In addition, you should track events related to storage as well, for example, when you move files from the /u01 virtual disk to the /u02 virtual disk. This information will explain why space utilization changed in the past.

Perform Regular Monitoring

Perform regular performance monitoring. Performance problems must be found and addressed before customers complain. Proactive performance monitoring and alerting is crucial in a large VM Server farm. With many virtual machines, constantly knowing what is happening in the environment in order to maintain the required service level is important.

It is much better to monitor the systems and determine proactively that you have a performance problem, rather than learn of performance problems from the user community. Remember to use the proper tools to monitor virtual machine performance. If necessary, tune the memory and VCPUs of the virtual machines.

Monitor Oracle VM Logs

In addition to monitoring performance, constantly monitor the Oracle VM logs for errors. Oracle VM uses multiple log files in order to determine immediately if a problem has occurred or is about to occur. The log files are the first place to look for errors. The goal is to find and fix errors before users complain. The virtual machine logs are described in Appendix B.

Allocate Memory Generously

A system with insufficient memory uses more I/Os than are necessary. Because I/O is usually one of the biggest performance problems in a system, not having a sufficient amount of memory will cause more problems. In the past few years, the cost of memory has come down dramatically, making it economically viable to allocate the memory needed for the required workload. Depending on the workload being driven by the virtual machine, the amount of memory allocated to the virtual machine varies.

Allocate Sufficient I/O

In addition to memory, I/O is also a critical system resource. The amount of I/Os per second (IOPS) per disk that can be sustained is finite. Requesting more IOPS than the disk device can support increases the response time of the disk (latency). Higher latencies mean worse performance. A typical disk drive can do 150 IOPS per disk at a reasonable latency of 20ms or less. More IOPS cause the latencies to rise, sometimes dramatically. High latencies translate into poor performance.

Because a single disk drive can do 150 IOPS, a RAID array can handle as many I/Os as the number of drives in the array. The performance improvement from the increase in the number of disks will scale near-linearly when serving data. For example, an array of 10 disks can handle 1,500 IOPS. In addition, RAID arrays support redundancy, where the failure of a single disk drive will not incur any loss.

Allocate Sufficient Network Resources

A virtual machine can often consume significant network resources. To support these needs sufficiently, configuring several (if not many) network devices in the VM Server system is often necessary. This task is not difficult, and many of the newer servers that are designed for virtualization come standard with four or more network cards. If necessary, order the server with additional network cards. These additional network resources can be used both for more performance as well as for redundancy.

Network adapter cards are one of the less expensive hardware options available today. Most network adapters support gigabit speeds, but newer 10 gigabit cards are now available on the market as well as Infiniband and IP over Infiniband. As part of the sizing project for the VM Server farm, network adapter cards are an important component.

NOTE
Current Oracle VM versions do not support Infiniband, but support is planned for future versions.

Carefully Choose the Type of Virtual Machine

A virtual machine can be created as either an HVM or paravirtualized machine. Because HVM virtualized machines take advantage of hardware accelerations, they typically perform memory operations much faster than paravirtualized machines. Paravirtualized machines perform network and disk operations better than HVM machines. Based on the type of workload that will be run on the guest, either HVM or paravirtualization will perform better. Make this decision during the planning phase for the virtual machine. The Oracle VM Server supports both types of systems simultaneously; thus you can mix virtual machine types in the Oracle VM environment. Choose which type is right for each virtual machine individually and configure appropriately.

Configure High Availability

Oracle VM supports a robust highly available configuration. Take advantage of Oracle VM's High Availability. The High Availability feature uses minimal resources unless it is needed to take over for a failed system. During normal operations, the feature does not take significant resources. In order to take advantage of High Availability, you need a shared disk resource. Then, in the event of a VM Server failing, a remaining server will take over.

Only Use as Much OS as Needed

The reason that Oracle recommends the JeOS model is that any unnecessary processes or daemons that run on the system consume resources that they don't need. By reducing extra overhead in a template that might be used multiple times, the benefit of reducing that waste is multiplied. Each additional service or process takes not only CPU resources but also memory and I/O as well.

Configure Flexibility

If you think you might need more memory in the future, configure the maximum memory size larger than the memory size. This allows for dynamic memory adjustment (if the guest OS supports it).

Summary

This chapter covered both some predictions for the future of virtualization as well as some miscellaneous best practices that you can use to configure and maintain an optimal VM Server farm. Oracle VM is very stable and high performing, but any improperly configured or undersized system will perform poorly.

This book has covered many different topics related to configuring and administering Oracle VM. Oracle has made a commitment to Oracle VM and will continue to support industry-standard high-performance virtualization. With the recent acquisition of Sun Microsystems, Oracle has also now endorsed Sun virtualization in addition to Xen technologies. For Oracle, the future of virtualization will now include a combination of all of its products and technologies.

PART V

Appendixes and Glossary

APPENDIX

A

Configuring Linux Support Functions

ppendix A includes several miscellaneous support functions, such as the process for staging installation images, setting up an NFS server, and configuring PXE boot. This appendix is provided for reference in order to assist with some of these basic Linux tasks.

Staging Images

Regardless of which installation method you use, you must stage the installation media by placing all of the media in a single directory. You can mount the image files (or CD-ROMs) and copy the files to a single directory. You can mount ISO images on a server using the loop option as follows:

```
[root@manager ~]# mount -o loop /u01/stage/OEL5-x86_64-disc1.iso /media/cdrom
```

Once you've mounted the media, copy the entire contents of the CD-ROM to the installation directory. An example is shown here:

```
[root@manager ~]# cp -R /media/cdrom /u01/stage/OEL5-5-x64
```

Repeat this process for each of the CD-ROM images in the installation set: mount each CD-ROM, copy the files, and then unmount the CD-ROM. Once you've copied all of the images, you can use the directory.

Configuring the NFS Server

Configuring NFS consists of two parts: setting directory permissions and enabling NFS. Configuring permissions is done in the /etc/exports file. The /etc/exports file consists of two fields: the directory and the permissions. The directory field contains the top-level directory being exported. The second field consists of a username (or *) and the permissions:

```
<directory> <user>(<permissions>)
```

An example is shown here. The root_squash permission prohibits root access; no_ root_squash allows root access. Here is an example of an /etc/exports file:

```
/u01/stage  *(rw,no_root_squash)
/u01/apps   oracle(rw)
```

In addition to /etc/exports, the NFS service must be enabled. To enable it by default, use **chkconfig**:

```
# chkconfig nfs on
```

To start NFS, use the **service** command:

```
# service nfs start
```

If you experience errors connecting, you might need to modify and/or disable the Linux firewall. You can disable it entirely by using **service iptables stop**. You can stop it permanently with **chkconfig iptables off**.

Once the NFS server is running, you can use the filesystem for installation. In order to test the NFS mount point, mount it using the **mount** command, as shown here:

```
[root@manager ~]#  mount -t nfs <server>:<NFS filesystem> <mount point>
```

An example is shown here:

```
[root@ovm1 ~]# mount -t nfs manager:/u01/stage/OEL5.5x64 /media/nfs
```

Once the filesystem has been mounted, use the **ls** command to run a listing to validate that it has been mounted and the needed files are there.

Configuring PXE Boot

Creating a reproducible and reliable method for installing Linux in an efficient manner is desirable. The installation is unattended and automatic, requiring minimal intervention during the boot process when you select PXE boot. You only need to make minor modifications to a few files on the Linux tftpboot/NFS server to customize the installation for each target system.

The solution is set to up PXE boot with a tftp server and then use NFS to install or upgrade the Linux system to OEL. Several documents were available via a Google search, but none seemed to work completely. This appendix documents the solution that ultimately did work.

The basic steps are as follows:

1.   Set up a DHCP server.

2.   Set up tftp/PXE boot.

3.   Configure media files via NFS.

4.   Boot to PXE.

Details of how this is done are covered in the next sections.

Required Linux Packages

The following Linux packages are required for the Linux PXE server:

- tftp-server

- dhcp

- syslinux

1. Set Up a DHCP Server

For PXE to work, you must set up a Linux DHCP server. This system can be the same as the PXE/NFS server or a different server. To configure a Linux DHCP server, first install the DHCP RPM. Once you have installed the DHCP RPM, modifying the /etc/dhcpd.conf file, as shown in later in this section, is necessary. For the hosts being installed, add the following lines:

```
host ptc3 {
}
hardware ethernet 00:0D:56:B8:B3:12;
fixed-address 192.168.50.105;
option host-name "ptc3";
filename "linux-install-x86/pxelinux.0";
next-server 192.168.50.103;
```

For this example, the system being installed/upgraded is named ptc3 with a MAC address of 00:0D:56:B8:B3:12 and an IP address of 192.168.50.105. Because it is a 32-bit server, the install directory is called linux-install-x86. The next-server argument specifies the tftp server. The name is not very descriptive, but this line is crucial for the target to boot.

/etc/dhcpd.conf

```
#
# DHCP Server Configuration file.
#   see /usr/share/doc/dhcp*/dhcpd.conf.sample
#

ddns-update-style interim;
subnet 192.168.50.0 netmask 255.255.255.0 {
range 192.168.50.107 192.168.50.110;
default-lease-time 3600;
max-lease-time 4800;
option routers 192.168.50.1;
option domain-name-servers 192.168.50.101, 192.168.50.102;
```

```
option subnet-mask 255.255.255.0;
option domain-name "perftuning.com";
option time-offset -8;
}

host ptc3 {
hardware ethernet 00:0D:56:B8:B3:12;
fixed-address 192.168.50.105;
option host-name "ptc3";
filename "linux-install-x86/pxelinux.0";
next-server 192.168.50.103;
}

host ptc4 {
hardware ethernet 00:06:5B:F4:F2:BF;
fixed-address 192.168.50.106;
option host-name "ptc4";
filename "linux-install-x86/pxelinux.0";
next-server 192.168.50.103;
}
```

2. Set Up tftp/PXE Boot

If necessary, install the tftp-server RPM. Then enable tftpd in Linux. The tftpd server is enabled in the file /etc/xinetd.d/tftpd. The line **disabled = yes** should be changed to **disabled=no**. This is shown next.

/etc/xinetd.d/tftp

```
# default: off
# description: The tftp server serves files using the trivial file transfer \
#       protocol.  The tftp protocol is often used to boot diskless \
#       workstations, download configuration files to network-aware printers, \
#       and to start the installation process for some operating systems.
service tftp
{
        socket_type             = dgram
        protocol                = udp
        wait                    = yes
        user                    = root
        server                  = /usr/sbin/in.tftpd
        server_args             = -s /tftpboot
        disable                 = no
        per_source              = 11
        cps                     = 100 2
        flags                   = IPv4
}
```

Once you've enabled tftpd, restart xinetd as shown here:

```
# service xinetd restart
Stopping xinetd:                                [  OK  ]
Starting xinetd:                                [  OK  ]
```

Verify with **chkconfig**.

```
# chkconfig --list | grep tftp
        tftp:              on
```

The tftp server allows clients to access files in the /tftpboot directory. If there is a possibility of booting more than one architecture, then create multiple subdirectories that designate the architecture. These directories are called linux-install-x86_64 and linux-install-x86. The 32-bit files are kept in linux-install-x86 and the 64-bit files in linux-install-x86_64.

Copy the boot kernel and image files into the /tftpboot/linux-install-x86 directory. These files are vmlinuz and initrd.img, and they can be copied from the first CD of the Linux distribution in the /images/pxeboot directory. In addition, you must copy the pxelinux.0 file from the /usr/lib/syslinux directly on the Oracle VM server into the /tftpboot/linux-install-x86 directory.

Next, create a subdirectory /tftpboot/linux-install-x86/pxelinux.cfg. This directory will contain a number of files coded to the server MAC address and IP address. The first file is the MAC address with 01 pre-pended; 01 designates an Ethernet adapter. Use lowercase for the hex letters in the MAC address. This file contains the information needed to boot the server.

Upon PXE booting, the boot process will look for a file based on the MAC address of the server, followed by a progressively more general hex representation of the IP address. In this example, the MAC address is 00:06:5B:F4:F2:BF and the IP address is 192.168.50.106, which is equivalent to:

```
192=C0
168=A8
50=32
106=6A
192.168.50.106=C0A8326A
```

Create the following files in the /tftpboot/pxelinux.cfg directory:

```
01-00-06-5b-f4-f2-bf   (boot contents)
C0A8326A (empty)
C0A8326 (empty)
C0A832 (empty)
C0A83 (empty)
C0A8 (empty)
C0A (empty)
C0 (empty)
C (empty)
default (either boot contents or empty)
```

During the boot, the PXE boot process searches through the files in that order until it finds the information that it needs. If all servers are the same, then you can use the lowest common denominator. If each server is different, use the MAC address.

/tftpboot/linux-install-x86/pxelinux.cfg/default
/tftpboot/linux-install-x86/pxelinux.cfg/01-00-0d-56-b8-b3-12

```
prompt 1
default linux
timeout 10

label linux
kernel vmlinuz
append initrd=initrd.img ramdisk_size=9216 ksdevice=eth4 noipv6
ks=nfs:192.168.50.103:/stage/Linux-5.2-x86/ks-ptc3.c
```

Directory Structure Summary

Figure A-1 is a representation of the necessary disk structure for the /tftpboot directory tree.

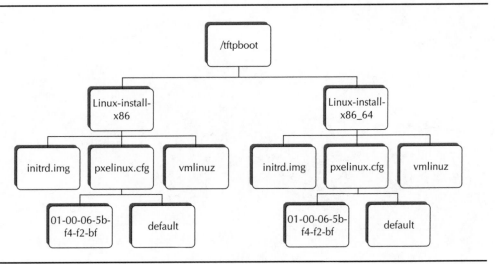

FIGURE A-1. *The tftpboot directory structure*

3. Configure Media Files Via NFS

NFS must be running on the NFS server and the directory specified in the boot configuration file must be available via NFS. This directory for our installation is nfs:192.168.50.103:/stage. This directory must contain the disk images. The disk images must be readable.

Directories available to NFS are in the /etc/exports file, as shown here:

```
/sto   *(rw,no_root_squash)
```

4. Boot to PXE

Using the VNC console, select PXE boot. If all is set up correctly, the system should boot and you will be able to run the installer from the VNC console.

APPENDIX

B

Oracle VM Log Files

number of log files are relevant to Oracle VM. Their location and contents are described in this appendix.

VM Server Log Files

The VM Server log files are stored in the /var/log/xen directory on each VM Server:

- **domain-builder-ng.log**   Logs the creation of domains (virtual machines).

- **xend.log**   Logs all of the Oracle VM Server deamon actions. This log is very detailed and contains a lot of information. This same information can be retrieved via the **xm log** command.

- **xend-debug.log**   Logs some limited debug and trace information related to the Xen server daemon.

- **xen-hotplug.log**   Contains a log of hotplug events. A *hotplug event* occurs when a device or network script either does not start up or state changes.

- **qemu-dm.*pid*.log**   Contains a log for each hardware virtualized guest. These logs are created by the qemu-dm process. The *pid* is the process identifier of the qemu-dm process.

VM Agent Log Files

The Oracle VM Agent log files are stored in the /var/log/ovs-agent directory on each Oracle VM Server:

- **ovs_autorun.log**   Logs the automatic startup of the Agent whenever the VM Server boots. This is where you will find the OCFS startup information as well as the Agent startup information.

- **ovs_guard.log**   Logs cluster information used in an Oracle VM High Availability (HA) environment.

- **ovs_operation.log**   Logs Oracle VM Agent operations.

- **ovs_performance.log**   Logs the collection of VM Server performance information and includes some performance data.

- **ovs_query.log**   Logs queries to the VM Agent. These queries are related to the state of the VM Server and include virtual machines as well as utility server status.

- ◼ **ovs_remaster.log**   Logs remaster information.

- ◼ **ovs_root.log**   Logs operations run as root, such as starting up the VM Agent.

- ◼ **ovs_upgrade.log**   Logs upgrades of the Oracle VM Agent.

VM Manager Log Files

The Oracle VM Manager log files are found in the directory /var/log/ovm-manager on the Oracle VM Manager server:

- ◼ **ovm-manager.log**   Contains the Oracle VM Manager installation log.

- ◼ **db.log**   Contains the Oracle Database log. This log is only used when the Oracle VM Manager has been installed on an existing database.

- ◼ **oc4j.log**   Contains the Oracle Containers for J2EE (OC4J) log. This important log can be used to debug Oracle VM Manager issues. This log is rotated whenever it exceeds 10MB. When the log exceeds 10MB, a new log is created and the old log is renamed to oc4j.log.1 and older logs are then renumbered.

- ◼ **upgrade_*old_new*_log.log**   Logs an upgrade of the Oracle VM Manager from *old* version to *new* version.

General Log Files

The general Linux server log files are found in the directory /var/log. The most important of these logs are described here:

- ◼ **cron**   Contains the crontab log. Scheduled jobs are logged here when crontab runs scheduled jobs.

- ◼ **messages**   Contains the general Linux alert log. Both startup and event (errors) information are stored in this log.

- ◼ **rpmpkgs**   Lists the packages installed on this system.

- ◼ **secure**   Contains the security log. Logs connections to the server.

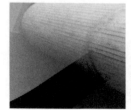

Glossary

AMD   Advanced Micro Devices is a semiconductor company. AMD, a competitor to Intel, makes the Opteron chip. AMD processors are compatible with the Intel x86 and x86_64 line of processors.

AMD-V technology   The virtualization technology that has been added to the AMD processor line to accelerate virtualization functions. The AMD-V technology works by intercepting system calls that would normally be processed in software and processing them in hardware. Currently, more of the hardware virtualization focuses around memory access.

backend drivers   The part of the device driver that runs in dom0. The front-end driver runs in the virtual machine; the back-end driver runs in dom0 and in the hypervisor.

bridged network   The default bridged network type allows the virtual machine network to reside on the same network as the Xen bridge.

browser   An application that is used to access the Internet's World Wide Web. A browser is typically a graphical application. Examples of browsers are Mozilla Firefox and Microsoft Internet Explorer.

capacity planning   Capacity planning is the act of determining the amount of additional hardware that you need to add to an existing system in order to meet future workloads.

CLI   Command line interface. The nongraphical character-based interface that is available in many applications.

cloud computing   A generic term for the use of virtualization to provide on-demand system (virtual) resources.

cluster root   The main storage system used by a server pool. This can be thought of as the first disk drive. /OVS is a link to the cluster root.

core   A core is a CPU within a CPU. As integrated circuit density has increased, the ability to add more compute power to the CPU by essentially creating multiple CPUs within the CPU chip has been developed. The local terminology for the CPU chip is a *socket* whereas the individual compute engines within the chip are referred to as the *cores*.

CPU   The central processing unit, or CPU, is the brains of the computer system. The computer processing is done in the CPU.

data center   The facility used to house computer systems and their supporting network. This is also referred to as a server farm.

DHCP   A protocol whereas a systems network address is assigned to it by a DHCP server, rather than being statically defined within the server itself.

dom0   Included with the Oracle VM Server, dom0 is a small Linux OS that assists with the management of the hypervisor and virtual machines. This special Linux system is called domain 0 or dom0.

domain   The terms *domain, guest, virtual machine,* and *VM guest* are sometimes used interchangeably, but there are a few differences among them. The *domain* is the set of resources in which the virtual machine runs. These resources were defined when the domain was created and include CPU, memory, disk, etc. The term *guest* or *VM guest* defines the virtual machine that is running inside of the domain. A *guest* can be Linux, Solaris, or Windows and can be fully virtualized or paravirtualized. A *virtual machine* is the OS and application software that runs within the guest.

Dynamic Host Configuration Protocol   *See* DHCP.

E-Business Suite   Oracle E-Business Suite is a suite of business and financial applications developed and sold by Oracle Corporation.

elinks   A character-based browsing tool.

enterprise metrics   The set of metrics (data points) that is used to define the current state of the enterprise. The metrics can be performance metrics, uptime metrics, etc.

EULA   End User License Agreement. This is the license agreement that is agreed to in order to use software.

FCoE   Fibre Channel over Ethernet. This is the encapsulation of Fibre Channel Frames over Ethernet. It is used to allow for Fibre Channel networking to use 10 Gigabit Ethernet hardware while preserving the Fibre Channel protocol.

Fibre Channel   Fibre Channel, or FC, is a multigigabit-speed network technology primarily used for storage networking. Although the name implies the use of fiber optics, that is only one transport method. Fibre Channel can also use copper wire as well.

firewall   A computer appliance or software designed to shield a network from unwanted access.

full software virtualization   *See* software virtualization.

guest   The terms *domain, guest, virtual machine,* and *VM guest* are sometimes used interchangeably, but there are a few differences among them. The *domain* is the set of resources in which the virtual machine runs. These resources were defined when the domain was created and include CPU, memory, disk, etc. The term *guest* or *VM guest* defines the virtual machine that is running inside of the domain. A guest can be Linux, Solaris, or Windows and can be fully virtualized or paravirtualized. A *virtual machine* is the OS and application software that runs within the guest.

HA   *See* High Availability.

hardware-assisted software virtualization   Hardware-assisted software virtualization is software virtualization with hardware acceleration. This technology takes advantage of new hardware technology that intercepts certain system calls and performs those functions in hardware. Performing operations in hardware is much more efficient and faster than running in software.

hardware virtualization   Hardware virtualization is where the abstraction of the hardware is done completely at the hardware level. This hardware is specifically designed to be virtualized.

HBA   Host Bus Adapter. The Host Bus Adapter is the hardware component that communicates to SAN storage.

High Availability   A system configuration that is capable of surviving a single point of failure. High Availability systems are configured for critical applications in order to achieve maximum uptime.

Host Bus Adapter   See HBA.

HTTP   Hypertext Transport Protocol (HTTP) is a networking protocol for delivering graphical web pages.

HTTPS   Secure Hypertext Transport Protocol (HTTP) is a secure networking protocol for delivering graphical web pages.

HVM   Hardware virtual machine describes the hardware-assisted virtual machines.

hyperthreading   Also known as *hyperthreaded CPU,* a CPU technology for taking advantage of wasted CPU cycles. To the PC, the hyperthreaded CPU appears as an additional CPU, but in reality, it is a method of taking advantage of CPU instruction cycles that might otherwise be wasted. Even though the OS thinks that the hyperthreaded CPU is an additional CPU, in reality it only provides an additional 30 to 50 percent more performance.

Hyper-V   A virtualization product from Microsoft.

hypervisor   The hypervisor is the software that provides the abstraction between the hardware and guest operating systems. There are several types of hypervisors. The hypervisor is also known as the virtual machine manager.

IDE   Integrated Drive Electronics, or IDE, is a basic way of connecting peripherals such as disk drives, CD-ROM drives, and tape drives to your system. IDE is really not the technical name of the interface standard, however. The interface standard is called *AT Attachment* or *ATA.*

image   In the context of this book, an image is a disk file that is either the virtual machine disk file or a disk copy of a CD-ROM.

Intel   Intel is the world's largest and most famous semiconductor company. Intel pioneered the x86 and x86_64 architecture.

Intel VT-x technology   The virtualization technology that has been added into the Intel processor line to accelerate virtualization functions. The Intel VT-x technology works by intercepting system calls that would normally be processed in software and processing them in hardware. Currently, more of the hardware virtualization focuses around memory access.

Intelligent Agent   The Intelligent Agent is the heart of the OEM system. The Agent resides on each system that is being monitored and managed and performs the duties of collecting data and uploading that data to the OMS server, which, in turn, inserts that data into the database repository. The Agent is also responsible for running scheduled tasks as well as performing corrective action that might be required.

inventory   A repository that is used to store Oracle installation configuration information.

iSCSI   Internet Small Computer System Interface. Small Computer System Interface, or SCSI, is a standard protocol used for storage devices. iSCSI encapsulates SCSI commands over IP networks, allowing SCSI devices to operate remotely. *See also* SCSI.

ISO image   An image copy of an ISO format CD-ROM or DVD-ROM. *See also* image.

iso_pool   The directory in the storage repository that is used to hold ISO images.

JeOS   Just enough OS, or Just enough Operating System. An operating system that has just enough of the software components or packages that it needs for the purpose it is designed for. For example, a database server does not need packages used to manage DHCP or web server applications.

lifecycle management   Lifecycle management describes the change in the state of the virtual machine from creation to destruction and every state in between.

Linux   A family of Unix-like computer operating systems based on the Linux kernel.

Live Migration   Live Migration allows a virtual machine to be moved from one VM Server to another with only a very short interruption in service.

MAC address   Machine Access Control address. A unique identifier assigned to each network hardware component. MAC addresses are used for numerous network technologies.

memory over-commit   Memory over-commit is where more memory is allocated to virtual machines than is available in the VM Server. If more memory than is actually available is used, that memory is paged out, as in a normal virtual memory system. With Oracle VM, physical memory is allocated for each virtual machine when the virtual machine is created. Oracle VM does not over-commit memory.

multipath   A device or software that utilizes multiple paths from the system to the peripheral device for redundancy. If a single path were to fail, connectivity to the peripheral device would not be lost.

NAS   Network Attached Storage. This type of storage is an appliance that is accessible via the system's network. It can be an appliance or software added to a system, such as Network File System (NFS) or Common Internet File System (CIFS). Essentially, any storage that can be accessed over the network can be loosely considered NAS.

NAT network   Network Address Translation networks take the IP address of the VM Server. This allows multiple virtual machines to appear to themselves and to other virtual machines as if they have their own IP address, but to the outside world, it appears as if there is only one IP address—that of the VM Server.

network bonding   A feature of Linux (or Windows) where two network adapters can be configured to act as one. This is done for both redundancy and performance, depending on how the adapters are configured.

NIC   Network Interface Card. This is the hardware that is used in the computer to connect the system to the network. The NIC can be Ethernet (10 Gigabit, 100 Gigabit, 1000 Gigabit, or 10000 Gigabit) or another network protocol.

NUMA   Non-Uniform Memory Architecture (NUMA) systems use multiple memory controllers that are each assigned to a CPU or set of CPUs. This is different from a Symmetric MultiProcessor (SMP) system, where all CPUs share the same memory controller. NUMA allows more CPUs to be added to the system with better performance. Because a memory controller is a finite component, in an SMP environment, the number of CPUs supported can be limited by the memory controller.

OCFS and OCFS2   Oracle Cluster File System. OCFS is a filesystem developed by and provided by Oracle. OCFS was replaced by OCFS2. This filesystem, which Oracle made open source, is clusterable. OCFS2 (version 2) was integrated into version 2.6.16 of the Linux kernel. OCFS2 uses a distributed lock manager that resembles the OpenVMS DLM but is much simpler.

OEL   Oracle Enterprise Linux (OEL) is a popular Linux distribution provided by Oracle Corporation.

OEM   Oracle Enterprise Manager. A generic term used to describe the Oracle management tools. OEM DB Control and OEM Grid Control are both OEM tools. *See also* Oracle Enterprise Manager.

OMS   Oracle Management Service is a component of OEM Grid Control. The OMS consists of the programs that are used to process the connections from the Agents, process the scheduled tasks, and provide web services for the management console.

OPatch   The Oracle patch utility. An Oracle-supplied utility that assists with the process of applying interim patches to Oracle's software and rolling back interim patches from Oracle's software.

Oracle   *See* Oracle Corporation.

Oracle AS   Oracle Applications Server is a web and application server sold by Oracle Corporation. Oracle Applications Server is going through extensive changes since Oracle Corporation acquired BEA Systems in 2008.

Oracle Corporation   A computer corporation that manufactures, markets, and sells software and hardware. Oracle Corporation was founded as Software Development Laboratories (SDL) in 1977 by Larry Ellison, Bob Miner, and Ed Oates. SDL was eventually renamed Oracle Corporation and is one of the largest corporations in existence.

Oracle Enterprise Manager   Oracle Enterprise Manager (OEM) is an enterprise management tool. OEM is a web-based tool designed to manage and monitor thousands of Oracle databases, servers, and operating systems as well as applications.

Oracle VM   Oracle's virtualization product.

Oracle VM Manager   *See* VM Manager.

OUI   Oracle Universal Installer. A graphical tool used to install Oracle software.

over-allocating   The act of allocating more resources than are actually physically present. An example would be allocating 10 vCPUs to virtual machines on a host that has 8 physical CPUs.

OVM   *See* Oracle VM.

OVM Agent   The OVM Agent is what makes Oracle VM work. The OVM Agent resides on each Oracle VM Server and makes a Linux server into an OVM server pool master, OVM utility server, or OVM virtual machine server.

OVM CLI   The Oracle VM Manager Command Line Interface. A command-line tool that performs the same functions as the Oracle VM Manager.

OVM Manager   Oracle VM Manager. *See* VM Manager.

P2V   A translation of physical to virtual. In this book, it refers to converting a physical server to a virtual server.

paravirtualization   In a paravirtualized system, the guest operating system is aware that it is virtualized and has a kernel and device drivers that can take advantage of this fact. In a paravirtualized system, some operations, such as I/O and networking, are faster than in a software virtualized system.

peak load   The performance load on a system at its maximum.

Perl   Perl is a high-level, general-purpose, interpreted, and dynamic programming language.

plug-in   An add-on component that can be dynamically added.

provisioning   The process of creating a new virtual or physical server including installation of OS and configuration.

publish_pool   The area of the storage repository that holds publicly published virtual machines.

PV   Paravirtualized. A virtual system that has been created using paravirtualization. *See also* paravirtualization.

PXE   Preboot Execution Environment. An environment to bootstrap computers using a network interface card.

PXE Boot   A method where a system is configured to boot from network boot media using the PXE protocol.

Python   Python is an interpreted computer language. It is used extensively for installation and configuration applications.

RAC   *See* Real Application Clusters.

RAID   Redundant Array of Inexpensive Disks. A standard for creating redundant storage.

Real Application Clusters   The Oracle Real Application Clusters (RAC) is a true database cluster where multiple Oracle instances residing on separate physical servers access the same Oracle database.

Red Hat   Red Hat is a company that distributes an open source Linux called Red Hat Linux. Red Hat was founded in 1993 and is a major source of Linux software.

Red Hat Linux   Red Hat Linux is the name of the Linux distribution sold by Red Hat.

redundant storage   Storage that is highly available. Storage is made redundant via hardware or software mirroring or parity.

repository   The storage used to hold Oracle VM's virtual machines, ISO images, shared disks, etc.

routed network   With routed networking, traffic is routed through the dom0 (VM Server) system to a private subnet that is accessible by one or more virtual machines.

RPM   Red Hat Package Manager. The RPM utility is used to add, modify, and delete packages on a Linux system. Software that is configured for RPM is called an *RPM package*.

running_pool   The area of the storage repository that holds active virtual machine images.

SAN   Storage Area Network. A network that is specifically designed and only provides network services for storage. Whereas the typical general-purpose network uses Ethernet, the SAN typically uses Fibre Channel as its transport layer.

SAS   Serial Attached SCSI. A new type of storage protocol that uses the SCSI command set but transmits data serially rather than in parallel.

SATA   Serial ATA or Serial Advanced Technology Attachment. A computer bus interface used to connect the system's memory bus to peripherals.

SCSI   Small Computer System Interface is a set of standards for physically transferring data between computers and peripheral devices. The SCSI standard is well established and used extensively in the computer industry. *See also* iSCSI.

Secure Shell   Secure Shell is a secure network protocol. Secure Shell has several utilities for remote system connectivity as well as for remote file copy. Utilities include ssh (Secure Shell), sftp (Secure FTP), and scp (Secure Copy).

seed_pool   The area of the storage repository that is used to hold templates.

server farm   A server farm is another word for a data center. The server farm is a collection of systems that are used to serve an enterprise when the use of one system will not provide sufficient capacity to support the enterprise. Thus, the enterprise VM Server farm is the collection of systems used to support the virtualization needs of the enterprise. The enterprise VM Server farm can be made up of one or more VM server pools, which are made up of one or more VM Servers.

server pool   A server pool is a group of Oracle VM Servers made up of one server pool master and one or more virtual machine servers and utility servers. Oracle VM virtual machines run in server pools.

server pool master   A server pool master is the component of the Oracle VM Agent that is used as the contact point between the VM Server and the VM Manager. There is only one VM Server in a server pool.

sharedDisk   The area of the storage repository that holds the shared disk images that are used for clusters (virtualized clusters).

shared server pool   A server pool that is spread across two or more VM Servers and uses shared storage for redundancy. It is also known as a *cluster* or *shared server pool cluster*. Used for HA. *See also* High Availability.

shared storage   Storage that can be accessed by multiple systems. Shared storage is typically SAN or NAS storage.

sizing   Sizing is the act of determining the amount of hardware needed for an anticipated workload.

SMP   A Symmetric MultiProcessor (SMP) system is a multiprocessor computer system where all CPUs share the same memory controller. Because a memory controller is a finite component, in an SMP environment, the number of CPUs supported can be limited by the memory controller.

SMTP   Simple Mail Transport Protocol. A standard used for sending and processing e-mail.

socket   This term is often used to describe a physical CPU chip. A system with 2 CPUs and 4 cores might be described as a 2 socket system with 4 cores.

software virtualization   Software virtualization is where the entire hardware is simulated by a software program. Software virtualization performance can be improved with hardware-assisted software virtualization.

ssh   *See* Secure Shell.

storage repository   The disk storage for the virtual environment.

storage virtualization   A storage system where the actual physical disks are abstracted from the logical disks that are allocated to a system. This might be a SAN or NAS storage.

template   In terms of Oracle VM, a template is a saved copy of a fully functional virtual machine that can easily, repeatedly, and quickly be used to create a new fully functional virtual machine.

type 1 hypervisor   The type 1 (or embedded) hypervisor runs directly on the hardware and interfaces with the CPU, memory, and devices. Oracle VM and VMWare ESX Server use type 1 hypervisors.

type 2 hypervisor   The type 2 hypervisor is a program that runs in the OS and provides virtualization services.

ULN   Oracle's Unbreakable Linux Network. A website and application used to download Oracle Enterprise Linux software and updates.

URL   Uniform Resource Locator. An identifier that specifies where an identified resource is available and the mechanism for retrieving it. The best-known example of a URL is the *address* of a web page on the World Wide Web.

utility server   The utility server is the part of the Agent responsible for performing I/O intensive operations such as copying, moving, and renaming files in operations such as cloning, etc. The utility server performs operations such as creating new virtual servers, removing virtual servers, and cloning.

V2V   Virtual to virtual. This refers to converting a virtual machine (such as VMWare) to another virtual machine (such as Oracle VM).

VCPU   Virtual CPU. A Virtual CPU appears to be a CPU to the virtual system but is, in reality, an entire CPU or a portion of a CPU that has been allocated to that virtual machine.

virtual disk   A file or files on the host system that appear to the guest system as a disk drive.

virtual machine   The terms *domain, guest, virtual machine,* and *VM guest* are sometimes used interchangeably, but there are a few differences among them. The *domain* is the set of resources in which the virtual machine runs. These resources were defined when the domain was created and include CPU, memory, disk, etc. The term *guest* or *VM guest* defines the virtual machine that is running inside of the domain. A guest can be Linux, Solaris, or Windows and can be fully virtualized or paravirtualized. A *virtual machine* is the OS and application software that runs within the guest.

virtual machine image   The files that make up the essence of the virtual machine. This usually describes a non-running virtual machine.

virtual machine manager (VMM)   *See* hypervisor.

virtual machine server   The virtual machine server is part of the server pool and is the component that runs virtual machines.

virtualization   Virtualization is the abstraction of computer hardware resources. Virtualization can be done either in hardware or software. The most common virtualization products use a hypervisor to provide a layer between the virtual machine and the hardware. There are many different types of virtualization.

VM Manager   The Oracle VM Manager is an enhancement that provides a web-based graphical user interface (GUI) that allows for configuration and management of Oracle VM Servers and virtual machines. The Oracle VM Manager is a standalone application that can be installed on a Linux system.

VM Server   A hardware system that is used to host Oracle VM. The VM Server is the host for the guest virtual machines.

VM Server farm   *See* server farm.

VMware   A company and a product. A company founded in 1998 that is a leader in virtualization software. VMware is owned by EMC. VMware is also the name of their virtualization software.

VNC   Virtual Network Computing (VNC) is a graphical desktop sharing system. It consists of both a server component (vncserver) and a client component. TightVNC is an example of a popular VNC client program.

WWN   The Fibre Channel World Wide Name is a unique identifier for every Fibre Channel component.

Xen   Xen virtualization products were developed around the same time as VMware. Xen technology is used by Oracle VM and Citrix and is open source.

Xen bridge   The Xen bridge is the interface between the virtual world (virtual machines) and the physical world (your company network).

xm commands The xm commands are Xen commands used to monitor and manage the Xen virtualization environment. You can use Xen commands to manage Oracle VM. Other supported methods are the Oracle VM Manager, OEM Grid Control, and OVM CLI.

yum Yellowdog Updater Modifier. Yum is a repository-based tool used to update Linux packages and to add new Linux packages easily and quickly. Yum determines dependencies and installs dependent objects automatically.

Index

GET YOUR FREE SUBSCRIPTION
TO *ORACLE MAGAZINE*

Oracle Magazine is essential gear for today's information technology professionals. Stay informed and increase your productivity with every issue of *Oracle Magazine*. Inside each free bimonthly issue you'll get:

- Up-to-date information on Oracle Database, Oracle Application Server, Web development, enterprise grid computing, database technology, and business trends
- Third-party news and announcements
- Technical articles on Oracle and partner products, technologies, and operating environments
- Development and administration tips
- Real-world customer stories

If there are other Oracle users at your location who would like to receive their own subscription to *Oracle Magazine*, please photo-copy this form and pass it along.

Three easy ways to subscribe:

① **Web**
Visit our Web site at **oracle.com/oraclemagazine**
You'll find a subscription form there, plus much more

② **Fax**
Complete the questionnaire on the back of this card
and fax the questionnaire side only to **+1.847.763.9638**

③ **Mail**
Complete the questionnaire on the back of this card
and mail it to **P.O. Box 1263, Skokie, IL 60076-8263**

ORACLE®

Want your own FREE subscription?

To receive a free subscription to *Oracle Magazine*, you must fill out the entire card, sign it, and date it (incomplete cards cannot be processed or acknowledged). You can also fax your application to +1.847.763.9638. **Or subscribe at our Web site at oracle.com/oraclemagazine**

○ **Yes, please send me a FREE subscription** *Oracle Magazine*.　　○ No.

○ From time to time, Oracle Publishing allows our partners exclusive access to our e-mail addresses for special promotions and announcements. To be included in this program, please check this circle. If you do not wish to be included, you will only receive notices about your subscription via e-mail.

○ Oracle Publishing allows sharing of our postal mailing list with selected third parties. If you prefer your mailing address not to be included in this program, please check this circle.

If at any time you would like to be removed from either mailing list, please contact Customer Service at +1.847.763.9635 or send an e-mail to oracle@halldata.com. If you opt in to the sharing of information, Oracle may also provide you with e-mail related to Oracle products, services, and events. If you want to completely unsubscribe from any e-mail communication from Oracle, please send an e-mail to: unsubscribe@oracle-mail.com with the following in the subject line: REMOVE [your e-mail address]. For complete information on Oracle Publishing's privacy practices, please visit oracle.com/html/privacy.html

X

signature (required)　　　　　　　　　　date

name　　　　　　　　　　　　　　title

company　　　　　　　　　　　　　e-mail address

street/p.o. box

city/state/zip or postal code　　　　telephone

country　　　　　　　　　　　　　fax

Would you like to receive your free subscription in digital format instead of print if it becomes available? ○ Yes ○ No

---

YOU MUST ANSWER ALL 10 QUESTIONS BELOW.

① WHAT IS THE PRIMARY BUSINESS ACTIVITY OF YOUR FIRM AT THIS LOCATION? (check one only)

- ☐ 01 Aerospace and Defense Manufacturing
- ☐ 02 Application Service Provider
- ☐ 03 Automotive Manufacturing
- ☐ 04 Chemicals
- ☐ 05 Media and Entertainment
- ☐ 06 Construction/Engineering
- ☐ 07 Consumer Sector/Consumer Packaged Goods
- ☐ 08 Education
- ☐ 09 Financial Services/Insurance
- ☐ 10 Health Care
- ☐ 11 High Technology Manufacturing, OEM
- ☐ 12 Industrial Manufacturing
- ☐ 13 Independent Software Vendor
- ☐ 14 Life Sciences (biotech, pharmaceuticals)
- ☐ 15 Natural Resources
- ☐ 16 Oil and Gas
- ☐ 17 Professional Services
- ☐ 18 Public Sector (government)
- ☐ 19 Research
- ☐ 20 Retail/Wholesale/Distribution
- ☐ 21 Systems Integrator, VAR/VAD
- ☐ 22 Telecommunications
- ☐ 23 Travel and Transportation
- ☐ 24 Utilities (electric, gas, sanitation, water)
- ☐ 98 Other Business and Services _____

② WHICH OF THE FOLLOWING BEST DESCRIBES YOUR PRIMARY JOB FUNCTION? (check one only)

CORPORATE MANAGEMENT/STAFF
- ☐ 01 Executive Management (President, Chair, CEO, CFO, Owner, Partner, Principal)
- ☐ 02 Finance/Administrative Management (VP/Director/ Manager/Controller, Purchasing, Administration)
- ☐ 03 Sales/Marketing Management (VP/Director/Manager)
- ☐ 04 Computer Systems/Operations Management (CIO/VP/Director/Manager MIS/IS/IT, Ops)

IS/IT STAFF
- ☐ 05 Application Development/Programming Management
- ☐ 06 Application Development/Programming Staff
- ☐ 07 Consulting
- ☐ 08 DBA/Systems Administrator
- ☐ 09 Education/Training
- ☐ 10 Technical Support Director/Manager
- ☐ 11 Other Technical Management/Staff
- ☐ 98 Other

③ WHAT IS YOUR CURRENT PRIMARY OPERATING PLATFORM (check all that apply)

- ☐ 01 Digital Equipment Corp UNIX/VAX/VMS
- ☐ 02 HP UNIX
- ☐ 03 IBM AIX
- ☐ 04 IBM UNIX
- ☐ 05 Linux (Red Hat)
- ☐ 06 Linux (SUSE)
- ☐ 07 Linux (Oracle Enterprise)
- ☐ 08 Linux (other)
- ☐ 09 Macintosh
- ☐ 10 MVS
- ☐ 11 Netware
- ☐ 12 Network Computing
- ☐ 13 SCO UNIX
- ☐ 14 Sun Solaris/SunOS
- ☐ 15 Windows
- ☐ 16 Other UNIX
- ☐ 98 Other
- 99 ☐ None of the Above

④ DO YOU EVALUATE, SPECIFY, RECOMMEND, OR AUTHORIZE THE PURCHASE OF ANY OF THE FOLLOWING? (check all that apply)

- ☐ 01 Hardware
- ☐ 02 Business Applications (ERP, CRM, etc.)
- ☐ 03 Application Development Tools
- ☐ 04 Database Products
- ☐ 05 Internet or Intranet Products
- ☐ 06 Other Software
- ☐ 07 Middleware Products
- 99 ☐ None of the Above

⑤ IN YOUR JOB, DO YOU USE OR PLAN TO PURCHASE ANY OF THE FOLLOWING PRODUCTS? (check all that apply)

SOFTWARE
- ☐ 01 CAD/CAE/CAM
- ☐ 02 Collaboration Software
- ☐ 03 Communications
- ☐ 04 Database Management
- ☐ 05 File Management
- ☐ 06 Finance
- ☐ 07 Java
- ☐ 08 Multimedia Authoring
- ☐ 09 Networking
- ☐ 10 Programming
- ☐ 11 Project Management
- ☐ 12 Scientific and Engineering
- ☐ 13 Systems Management
- ☐ 14 Workflow

HARDWARE
- ☐ 15 Macintosh
- ☐ 16 Mainframe
- ☐ 17 Massively Parallel Processing

- ☐ 18 Minicomputer
- ☐ 19 Intel x86(32)
- ☐ 20 Intel x86(64)
- ☐ 21 Network Computer
- ☐ 22 Symmetric Multiprocessing
- ☐ 23 Workstation Services

SERVICES
- ☐ 24 Consulting
- ☐ 25 Education/Training
- ☐ 26 Maintenance
- ☐ 27 Online Database
- ☐ 28 Support
- ☐ 29 Technology-Based Training
- ☐ 30 Other
- 99 ☐ None of the Above

⑥ WHAT IS YOUR COMPANY'S SIZE? (check one only)

- ☐ 01 More than 25,000 Employees
- ☐ 02 10,001 to 25,000 Employees
- ☐ 03 5,001 to 10,000 Employees
- ☐ 04 1,001 to 5,000 Employees
- ☐ 05 101 to 1,000 Employees
- ☐ 06 Fewer than 100 Employees

⑦ DURING THE NEXT 12 MONTHS, HOW MUCH DO YOU ANTICIPATE YOUR ORGANIZATION WILL SPEND ON COMPUTER HARDWARE, SOFTWARE, PERIPHERALS, AND SERVICES FOR YOUR LOCATION? (check one only)

- ☐ 01 Less than $10,000
- ☐ 02 $10,000 to $49,999
- ☐ 03 $50,000 to $99,999
- ☐ 04 $100,000 to $499,999
- ☐ 05 $500,000 to $999,999
- ☐ 06 $1,000,000 and Over

⑧ WHAT IS YOUR COMPANY'S YEARLY SALES REVENUE? (check one only)

- ☐ 01 $500, 000, 000 and above
- ☐ 02 $100, 000, 000 to $500, 000, 000
- ☐ 03 $50, 000, 000 to $100, 000, 000
- ☐ 04 $5, 000, 000 to $50, 000, 000
- ☐ 05 $1, 000, 000 to $5, 000, 000

⑨ WHAT LANGUAGES AND FRAMEWORKS DO YOU USE? (check all that apply)

- ☐ 01 Ajax
- ☐ 02 C
- ☐ 03 C++
- ☐ 04 C#
- ☐ 13 Python
- ☐ 14 Ruby/Rails
- ☐ 15 Spring
- ☐ 16 Struts
- ☐ 05 Hibernate
- ☐ 06 J++/J#
- ☐ 07 Java
- ☐ 08 JSP
- ☐ 09 .NET
- ☐ 10 Perl
- ☐ 11 PHP
- ☐ 12 PL/SQL
- ☐ 17 SQL
- ☐ 18 Visual Basic
- ☐ 98 Other

⑩ WHAT ORACLE PRODUCTS ARE IN USE AT YOUR SITE? (check all that apply)

ORACLE DATABASE
- ☐ 01 Oracle Database 11*g*
- ☐ 02 Oracle Database 10*g*
- ☐ 03 Oracle9*i* Database
- ☐ 04 Oracle Embedded Database (Oracle Lite, Times Ten, Berkeley DB)
- ☐ 05 Other Oracle Database Release

ORACLE FUSION MIDDLEWARE
- ☐ 06 Oracle Application Server
- ☐ 07 Oracle Portal
- ☐ 08 Oracle Enterprise Manager
- ☐ 09 Oracle BPEL Process Manager
- ☐ 10 Oracle Identity Management
- ☐ 11 Oracle SOA Suite
- ☐ 12 Oracle Data Hubs

ORACLE DEVELOPMENT TOOLS
- ☐ 13 Oracle JDeveloper
- ☐ 14 Oracle Forms
- ☐ 15 Oracle Reports
- ☐ 16 Oracle Designer
- ☐ 17 Oracle Discoverer
- ☐ 18 Oracle BI Beans
- ☐ 19 Oracle Warehouse Builder
- ☐ 20 Oracle WebCenter
- ☐ 21 Oracle Application Express

ORACLE APPLICATIONS
- ☐ 22 Oracle E-Business Suite
- ☐ 23 PeopleSoft Enterprise
- ☐ 24 JD Edwards EnterpriseOne
- ☐ 25 JD Edwards World
- ☐ 26 Oracle Fusion
- ☐ 27 Hyperion
- ☐ 28 Siebel CRM

ORACLE SERVICES
- ☐ 28 Oracle E-Business Suite On Demand
- ☐ 29 Oracle Technology On Demand
- ☐ 30 Siebel CRM On Demand
- ☐ 31 Oracle Consulting
- ☐ 32 Oracle Education
- ☐ 33 Oracle Support
- ☐ 98 Other
- 99 ☐ None of the Above

08014Q04